Siege Warfare

Christopher Duffy

Siege Warfare

The Fortress in the Early Modern World 1494–1660

Routledge & Kegan Paul
London and Henley

First published in 1979
by Routledge & Kegan Paul Ltd
39 Store Street,
London WC1E 7DD and
Broadway House,
Newtown Road,
Henley-on-Thames,
Oxon RG9 1EN
Set in Monophoto Ehrhardt
and printed in Great Britain by
BAS Printers Limited, Over Wallop, Hampshire
© Christopher Duffy 1979

British Library Cataloguing in Publication Data

Duffy, Christopher

Siege Warfare.
1. Attack and defence (Military science)   2. Sieges
I. Title
355.4'4'09031   UG444   78-41274

ISBN 0 7100 8871 X

Contents

Illustrations

Maps

Preface

Many solemn ventures of mankind are impelled by impulses which are more trivial than the voyagers would care to admit – the rationalisations are often left until later. It so happens that the present work, for all the pomposity of its title, was inspired by nothing more exalted than the sight of a traffic-island of turf and stone in my native Blackheath.

Fortunately it was not difficult to find ample justification for writing a book about the fascinating and still very little known subject of artillery fortification. Fifteen years ago, when I first began work, the darkness was complete. Most people who were interested in the history of war or architecture would have agreed with the man who said that 'nothing is more conspicuously lacking in the field of military studies than a well-illustrated history of the arts of fortification and siegecraft' (Guerlac, 1944). There was certainly a plethora of studies on 'Crusader Castles' and the like, but when we inquired about fortresses of the artillery age the authorities took us on a gentle guided tour of sixteenth-century Italy and seventeenth-century France, and ushered us out again with the inevitable reference to Sterne's Uncle Toby.

In recent years things have changed for the better. Not only have we had good technical overviews of fortification from Quentin Hughes and Ian Hogg, but the military history of the early modern period has 'come alive' in a remarkable fashion, as you can see from our bibliography.

However, there is still a need for a reasonably concise and readable commentary on the far-reaching ways in which fortress warfare has influenced statecraft, strategy, architecture and ordinary human affairs. A study of this kind ought to range beyond Western Europe and tell us something of how the Scandinavians, Russians and Asians went about their business. In span of time we should be allowed to travel over the centuries from the date of the appearance of the first truly mobile siege artillery, in the later fifteenth century, and go on to see (in further studies) how fortification has been transformed by seventeenth-century absolutism, and the advent of the 'heavy' Industrial Revolution of the nineteenth century and the 'light' Industrial Revolution of the twentieth.

Most important of all we should bear in mind that the phenomenon of fortress warfare is not explicable in purely technical terms. Fortresses rose on particular sites because of certain strategic or economic considerations; they were defended and attacked by living engineers and armies; they were usually peopled by civilian urban communities; their successful resistance or fall could well determine the preponderance of one state over another. An examination of walls and trenches would be a valuable exercise, to be sure, but by itself it would be as deficient as a history of religion which drew its evidence exclusively from ecclesiastical architecture.

These considerations have determined the form of the present work. We shall hear more about policies, strategies and the lives of soldiers than about the technicalities of the thousands of 'systems' of fortification, of which only a few were ever borne in mind by the serious engineer, and which even then were carried out in a radically simplified shape.

I could not have entertained the thought of writing this book without the help of the London Library and the Army Department Library of the Ministry of Defence. I also owe a great deal to Lt.-Col. Alan Shepperd MBE, who has built the Library of the RMA Sandhurst into one of the finest collections of its kind in the country.

Quite recently I expressed some very gloomy sentiments about the historical and physical neglect of some of the architectural gems of fortification (*Fire and Stone*, 1975, p. 198). I would not write in the same unreservedly pessimistic tone today. In Britain my friends Quentin Hughes and Anthony Kemp of the Fortress Study Group have helped to create an atmosphere in which it is possible to enthuse about artillery fortification without being thought a complete lunatic. Valiant work is also being done on the Continent by the French Inspection du Génie, and organisations like the Stichting Menno van Coehoorn (Holland) and the Stichting Simon Stevin (Belgium). The beneficial results of their concern are already evident. On the far side of the Atlantic the membership of the Council for Abandoned Military Posts is numbered in the thousands, and many impressive works of restoration have been carried out by the national parks services of Canada and the United States.

Prologue   The Earliest Artillery Fortification

A small dog, chased by a larger one, will sometimes take refuge beneath a nearby thicket, so forcing his enemy to fight at a disadvantage or go away. For centuries military engineers have sought to attain the same end as our canine tactician: that is, to arrange obstacles that will enable a weaker power to withstand the attacks of a stronger one.

In medieval times the architects came close to achieving their aim, for as long as muscle-power and gravity offered the only propulsive force for missiles, the soaring walls of castle and city were capable of keeping out any enemy who was not prepared to devote weeks or perhaps months to the work of reducing them.

Historians argue about the origins of gunpowder. Some claim that it came from China, others that it was concocted nearer to home in Arabic North Africa or in Europe itself. There are those who would agree with Marshal de Tavannes when he wrote that, along with Lutheranism and other evil inventions, it was the sort of thing which naturally originated among the Germans, for 'the coldness of the climate keeps them shut up seven months on end in their chambers, where they have ample leisure to dream up these fantasies' (Tavannes, 1850, 97).

The cannon first appears in European iconography as an urn-like object which is represented in an English manuscript of 1326. In the fifteenth century gunpowder artillery came to play a regular, but (outside France) only occasionally decisive, part in fortress warfare. If cannon cracked open Harfleur in 1415, Constantinople in 1453, and Krems in 1477, there was still not much evidence to show that artillery favoured the attack very much more than the defence.

In an age when pieces were judged more by their intended malice than by their proven efficacy, a sovereign of any standing felt himself bound to have in his arsenal at least a quantity of monster cannon ranging in calibre from twelve to thirty-two inches or even more.

The 'great gonnes' held a special fascination for late-medieval and Renaissance sovereigns, who were almost the only people who could afford the vast expense of artillery. Monarchs like John II of Portugal, Charles VIII of France, Henry VIII of England, and the emperors Maximilian and Charles V, were all renowned as enthusiastic cultivators of ordnance and gunners. These costly habits inevitably drew them into collaboration with the great towns of Europe, with their resources of finance, bell-founders, smiths, carriage workers and hired gunners. Well into the sixteenth century the emperor still looked to the cities of Austria and Germany for help in making up the siege train for his Italian and French wars. A nineteenth-century gunner historian was driven to the 'inescapable conclusion that city walls were the cradle of artillery and that the citizens were its solicitous foster-parents. Artillery remains even today a weapon proper to the middle classes' (Dolleczek, 1887, 53).

The independent, faction-ridden nobility was unable to keep up in the technical race. Already in the early fifteenth century Elector Frederick I of

Brandenburg was able to consolidate the power of the house of Hohenzollern by bringing up his cannon against the castles of the Quitzow clan, battering them down one by one. Thus the development of artillery contributed powerfully to the consolidation of state power in the early modern period. Also the new style in fortifications – low and sprawling – demanded garrisons of a size which only states, cities and towns could provide. It had been easier in the old days, when many a castle had been held effectively by a handful of men.

Independent bourgeois military power too was ultimately doomed, though 'it is quite clear that at least until the middle of the seventeenth century subjects were still capable of successfully resisting their princes and, if necessary, overthrowing them by armed force. Neither artillery nor the new fortifications, whatever their cost, worked unequivocally to the prince's advantage' (I. A. Thompson, 1976, 2).

With the help of hindsight, we may put forward a number of basic requirements for fortifications which were fitted to withstand, as well as employ, muzzle-loading smooth-bore artillery:

1 A rampart that was spacious and low-lying enough to provide a stable platform for artillery, and to evade or resist the blows of the enemy shot.

2 A ditch and a wall that were sufficiently formidable to deter escalade.

3 A trace (ground plan) so arranged as to leave no dead ground by which an enemy might reach the rampart unscathed.

To satisfy more than one of these requirements was not an easy task for the medieval architect. Small wonder is it that serious attempts to meet all three were postponed until after the full power of a mobile, state-owned artillery was first revealed to military men in 1494. The earlier, partial solutions may be summed up in the term the 'reinforced castle'.

Until at least the end of the sixteenth century, the majority of strongholds which came under siege dated from the times before gunpowder. Fortifications of this kind could be trimmed, expanded, razed or bolstered up by engineers in a variety of more or less drastic ways. The passive resistance of a tower could be readily enhanced if you removed the

pointed cap or roof, cut down the masonry to a height little more than that of the adjacent curtain, and filled the resulting stump with earth. Even with this heroic treatment, the cramped ground plan of a medieval tower seldom allowed you to install more than two or three cannon inside.

The main business of the active defence was accordingly transferred to the curtain wall, the gangway of which could be transformed into an effective platform if you heaped up a wide bank of earth behind, a process called 'rampiring'. Unfortunately for the defenders, the new earthen rampart exerted a heavy pressure against the masonry wall in front. That was why Duke Philip of Cleves complained at the end of the fifteenth century that 'whenever the guns batter the wall, the earth tumbles down with the masonry, which makes it all the easier for the enemy to climb the breach' (Louis-Napoléon Bonaparte, 1851, II, 104).

The fact that a rampired wall tended to collapse outwards was particularly unwelcome to the bowmen and gun-crews who were defending any work which you might have improvised in the space between the foot of the wall and the edge of the ditch. The most fashionable fortification of this kind was the fausse-braye: a low outer wall of masonry, timber or sods, packed up behind with rammed earth, which served to defend the ditch which could now scarcely be seen, let alone commanded, from the thickened curtains and truncated towers.

All of these were essentially improvised expedients. When it came to building a new reinforced castle from the ground upwards, the military architects abandoned angular towers in favour of tub-like cylindrical constructions, which offered a glancing surface to cannon shot. In some castles the towers were built flush with the curtain walls, so as to facilitate the movement of men and guns. The base of the towers and curtains usually flared outwards, again in the interests of presenting an inclined surface, and the crenellations along the top were replaced by curved or bevelled parapets. The walls as a whole were thickened up, and furnished with embrasures and vaulted casemates for cannon. These developments were most evident in fifteenth-century France, and were to be seen in varying degrees in works like the Bastille, and the towers or

1   Late medieval fortification in picturesque decay (Sarzanello, *c.* 1377)

castles at Tarascon, Coucy, Langres, Toulon, Nantes and Saint-Malo. The results were impressive enough to look at, but they remained mere adaptations of medieval motifs.

Other nations were still less adventurous. The English were content to pierce their city and castle walls with little gun ports, while as late as 1450 the Italians could run up a construction like the lofty Sforza Castle at Milan, furnished with towers that were more useful for the views they commanded over the neighbourhood than for the mounting of artillery. This is not to deny that as late as 1601 the sheer bulk of the place had the power to impress an authority like Busca. Only in the second half of the century do we find architects of Tuscany and the

Papal States exploring the style of the reinforced castle with assurance (Volterra *c.* 1472, the rocca of Senigallia 1480, Sarzana 1487, etc.), producing works that are of real beauty, and (to our eyes at least) full of a sense of impending change. However, the Italians clung on surprisingly long to devices like machicolations, and the coastal fortresses as a whole were decidedly old-fashioned. Such was the stronghold of Civitavecchia, designed by Antonio da Sangallo the Younger, or his uncle Giuliano's triangular castle at Ostia. These works have high bare curtain walls, tub-like towers, and an inner *maestio* or keep.

Altogether in Europe up to the later 1480s we see no convincing evidence that military architects appreciated that artillery had the power to transform the active defence of fortresses, from the principle of merely dropping things on people, to the one of hitting them hard and low with missiles impelled by gunpowder.

The story of the reinforced castle comes to a fitting end in the discussion by Albrecht Dürer (1471–1528) in his *Etliche Underricht zur Befestigung der Stett Schloss und Flecken*, which was printed in Nuremberg in 1527. In the *Etliche Underricht*, as elsewhere in his artistic work, much of the fascination of Dürer's achievement derives from his blend of Gothic and Renaissance motifs. He is known to have travelled to Italy in 1494 and 1505, but he was denied contact with the most advanced military engineering of his time because he failed to venture as far as Florence or Rome. Hence his military architecture remains an isolated, North European attempt to meet the challenge of problems that were already finding more convincing solutions in Italy.

The most interesting and original sections of Dürer's book relate to a projected town fortification, where the walls are dominated by massive and squat semi-circular 'roundels', or towers. In the first of Dürer's manners, the casemated roundels rise to a height of seventy feet above the ditch, and twenty-nine feet above the level of the surrounding country. Dürer certainly provides us with a stable gun-platform, but the sprawling obesity of his dimensions only serves to render the problem of close-range defence more difficult than ever. In particular the curve of the ground plan of the roundel is so gentle that no gun is capable of directing a flanking fire along the ditch, which leaves the besieger free to plant his ladders and begin his mines in dead ground at the salient of the adjacent roundel.

Dürer's work was ignored in his native Nuremberg, and we may gauge his influence only through the handful of North European fortresses which appear to reflect his notions: the roundels at the Kronenburger and Roseneck Gates at Strasbourg, perhaps, or the vast and stately Munot tower which rose at Schaffhausen between 1563 and 1582. Oddly enough it was England, almost the least advanced of European states in artillery fortification, which chose to build not just a single fortress but a whole

system of national defence which closely parallel Dürer's ideas.

The impulse for the English fortress-building was given by the anti-heretical alliance of Francis I of France and the Emperor in 1538. The English king Henry VIII was something of an engineer in his own right, but he stood in urgent need of advice on the programme of coastal defence he was setting in train, and thus he came under German influence through the channel of the Bohemian architect Stevan v. Haschenperg, who is known to have worked on Sandgate Castle and the Citadel of Carlisle. Certainly the cockles of Dürer's heart would have warmed at the sight of the forts which sprang up along the south coast of England in the following years, and which found their most elaborate expression at Deal and St Mawes. The Henrician fort is on a much more modest scale than Dürer's designs, but it skilfully adapts some of his motifs to the circumstances of a small self-contained coastal work. The whole has an air at once sturdy and festive, rather like a squashed wedding cake.

Dürer's designs look mostly to the past, and their influence on actual construction is limited and indirect. All the same, the *Etliche Underricht* is of unique significance because it was the first printed work on the subject of permanent fortification.

Books of this kind held a tremendous appeal. Practical soldiers were eager for information on specialities like engineering and gunnery, where knowledge of the most advanced techniques was difficult to obtain by personal experience. Civilians in their turn came to see fortification as one of the elements of a gentleman's education, along with architecture and mathematics; and the study-bound scholar derived much satisfaction from devising elegant and seemingly faultless solutions to military problems by means of pen, ruler and compasses.

The *Etliche Underricht* therefore had hundreds if not thousands of successors. Not all of these works were of equal value. Indeed Dürer himself must be held partly responsible for having infected the literature of fortification with some of its most persistent diseases. Rather than content himself with postulating some basic principles which could have been applied, with appropriate modifications, to any site, he preferred to set up four separate manners or

2 Exterior view of one of Dürer's roundels

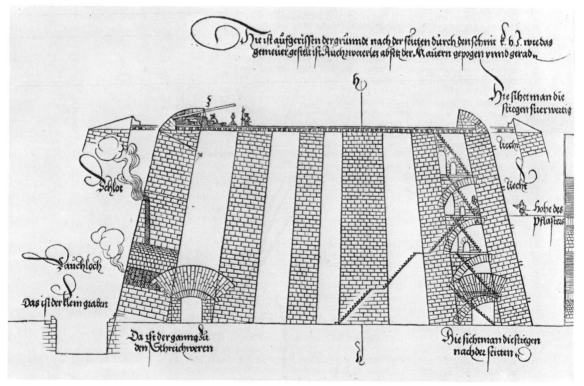

3 Section of one of Dürer's roundels

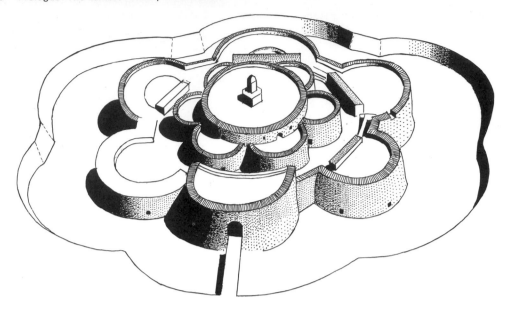

4   Deal Castle. In the event of a siege, the parapets would have been crowned with baskets packed with earth (gabions). The walls are massive, but the roof is very thin, and therefore vulnerable to mortar fire

systems, a number which was inflated a few decades later by a sensible person like Marchi to no less than 161.

Then again, Dürer and his successors pay little heed to the cost of their plans, though he at least tries to justify such an enormous investment: 'If people say that all of this work will cost a great deal of money, they should remember that we are expending very little compared with the great sums that the Pharaoh of Egypt devoted to the Pyramids, which were a useless expense, whereas our money is very usefully invested' – not, perhaps, the most happy of illustrations.

For all its internal turmoil, the Germany of Dürer's century was free from major foreign invasion. To find truly significant developments in fortress warfare we have to turn to Italy, where decades of peace had just come to an end.

One   Fortress Warfare in Renaissance Italy

The offensive on the rampage 1494–1503

Charles VIII and the advent of mobile siege artillery
In military affairs, the events of 1494 did much to bring the Middle Ages to an end. In that year King Charles VIII of France led his army across the Mont-Genèvre Pass into Italy, and marched across the Lombard plain and the Apennines to the port of La Spezia, where he picked up the forty or so siege guns with which he intended to make good his claim to the Kingdom of Naples.

These guns were the lineal descendants of the state-owned artillery which had enabled the French to burst open the English strongholds in Normandy and Guyenne in the middle of the century. Craftsmen and bell-founders worked tirelessly to improve the weapon, and by the 1490s they had evolved a cannon that was recognisably the same creature that was going to decide battles and sieges for nearly four hundred years to come.

The medieval bombard was a massive pipe of wrought-iron rods or bronze, designed specifically to throw a large but relatively light ball of stone. The weapon was by no means without its virtues. In relation to muzzle velocity, the stone ball required only one-half the weight of powder as an iron shot of the same calibre, and it exercised a considerable smashing effect on targets like walls, siege towers, ships and trenches full of men. At the same time the bombard and its ammunition were undeniably bulky. The gun was usually fired from a solid block of wood, which rested directly on the earth; it put up a valiant fight against any gunners who threatened to disturb its repose. For transport, the bombard had to be lifted bodily onto an ox waggon running on disc-like wheels which, whenever the cart was canted over to one side, threatened to collapse and deposit the whole load gently back to earth again.

Another disadvantage concerned the manufacture of the missiles. Whereas the casting or forging of an iron cannon ball was a hot but satisfying business, skilled stonemasons had to be paid highly if they were to address themselves to the laborious and frustrating work of carving a stone ball that was just going to be fired from a gun.

In the train of Charles VIII, however, the bombard had been largely supplanted by cannon with homogeneous bronze barrels no more than eight feet long. These pieces could be transported and loaded with ease, and they discharged wrought-iron balls which could compete in range and accuracy with stone-firing bombards of at least three times their calibre. The barrel of the French cannon was readily elevated or depressed around the fulcrum formed by two trunnions (prongs). These were cast into the barrel just forward of the centre of gravity, and rested almost over the axle of the two-wheeled gun carriage beneath. For traversing, the trail of the carriage was lifted from the ground and swung to right or left.

The numerous and well-trained French gunners knew how to take advantage of their new weapon, and an Italian contemporary (Guicciardini, 1562, Bk I) wrote that the cannon were

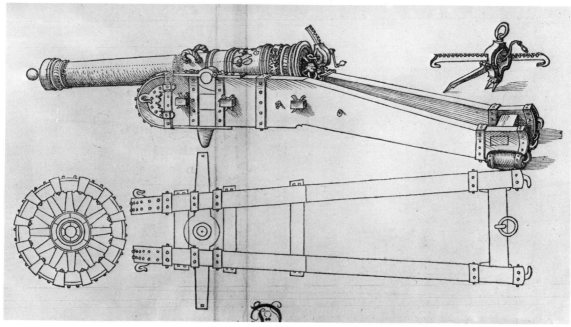

5 Renaissance cannon (Dürer, 1527)

planted against the walls of a town with such speed, the space between the shots was so brief, and the balls flew so speedily, and were driven with such force, that as much execution was inflicted in a few hours as used to be done in Italy over the same number of days.

The enhanced mobility of the French guns was, if possible, still more important than their fire-power. Over long distances the heavier of the barrels still had to be loaded onto separate waggons, as before, but gun carriages and waggons alike were now drawn by strong and trained horses, and travelled on 'dished' wheels which stood up stoutly to the strains imposed upon them by fifteenth-century roads.

By all reasonable calculations Charles should have been stopped short by one of the Florentine or papal fortresses long before he could reach his goal of Naples. Unfortunately for Italy, the French and their artillery were not reasonable opponents. Charles directed his march down the western side of the Apennines against the northern frontier of the state of Florence, the first obstacle in his path. Florence was on the verge of one of its bouts of

puritanical, patriotic republicanism, and the poor Duke Piero de' Medici, already insecure at home, threw himself on the mercy of Charles as soon as he learnt that the little fortress of Fivizzano had fallen to the French. Sarzana, Sarzanello, Pietra Santa and the citadels of Pisa and Leghorn, all were delivered up without resistance, and on 17 November the pale little French king made his triumphal entry into Florence, lance balanced on thigh. The terrified Pope Alexander VI followed Piero's example, and hastened to place his strongholds at the disposal of the French.

There was nothing to stand between Charles and the kingdom of Naples. The small Neapolitan citadel of Monte Fortino capitulated as soon as the cannon were planted against it; and the French took a mere eight hours for the business of breaching the important frontier stronghold of Monte San Giovanni and massacring its garrison. The place had once withstood a siege of seven years. With horrifying consistency the French later used the same cruelty at Capua in 1501, Pavia in 1527, and Melfi in 1528.

In the short term the impact of the new French methods was devastating, and on 22 February 1495

Italy in the early sixteenth century: political

Charles was able to ride into the city of Naples in the same style as he had entered Florence.

The French successes had conjured up a hostile league of Venice, the Pope, Milan and Spain. Charles accordingly retraced his steps and smashed open his communications back to France. The king thereafter lost interest in his new conquests, and over the course of 1496 his negligence and cowardice permitted the Spanish to starve into submission all the strongholds in Naples – an episode which indicated that it was nowadays far easier to conquer a kingdom than to hold it.

The Spanish counter-attack and the gunpowder mine
Objections may be made to the choice of the year 1494 to mark the beginning of early modern fortress warfare. Italian military technology had not been entirely static and, as we shall see, the all-important device of the angle bastion was invented seven years before Charles VIII burst into Italy. Then again, the occasions on which the French needed to plant their cannon were surprisingly few, because fortresses tended to surrender at the very wind of their coming. However, Macchiavelli, Guicciardini and almost all the people who have written since about Renaissance warfare are surely right to stress the revolutionary impact of the French and their new artillery. What the authorities are talking about was essentially a *Blitzkrieg*, which depended as much for its effect upon speed, energy and the potential for destruction, as the actual scale of physical damage. Warfare was prosecuted with a new urgency and tempo, and, no less importantly, big-power politics intruded on Italian affairs.

The newly-revealed power of the offensive fired the ambition of all the hungry southern princes, and upset the equilibrium which had reigned among the major Italian states since the middle of the fifteenth century. In 1502 the French and Spaniards came to blows over the possession of Naples. Acting with admirable energy, the Spanish defeated the French field army twice over, then proceeded to mop up the isolated enemy garrisons all over Naples.

Out of all the doomed strongholds, the Castle of Uovo (by the city of Naples) was certainly the one that was taken in the most spectacular fashion.

Cannon alone were powerless to reduce the place, situated as it was on a narrow peninsula separated from the mainland by a deep ditch. The Spaniards, however, had in their ranks one Pedro Navarro, 'a thin little man', who had perfected the gunpowder mine, the one weapon capable of blasting the French from their rocky retreat.

Gunpowder mines had figured in the treatises of Taccola, Mariano of Siena, and Francesco di Giorgio Martini, but it seems that they were first used in actual warfare in 1439, when the Italian-educated John Vrano used a countermine in his defence of Belgrade against Sultan Amurath. Under the direction of Martini, the Genoese used gunpowder below ground in their attack on the Florentine-held fortress of Sarzanello in 1487. The effect on this occasion was small, for the gallery had not been driven far enough under the foundations. Pedro Navarro, who is said to have witnessed the experiment as a private soldier, went on to remedy this effect at the siege of the Turkish fortress of San Giorgio on the island of Cephalonia in 1500. On that occasion Navarro tunnelled out long galleries beneath the citadel rock, stuffed them with gunpowder 'to excite the flames', and produced a devastating flare-up.

The wording of the descriptions of these early mines leaves open the possibility that the powder charges were not primarily explosive in character, but rather intended to hasten the burning of the props which supported the undermined masonry. No such doubt attaches to Navarro's device at the Castle of Uovo in 1503. He piled his men and tools into covered boats, brought them unknown to the French to the side of the cliff facing Pizzafalcone, and laboured for three weeks to drive a gallery through the rock. On 26 June the Spanish touched off the charge, and part of the rock sprang into the air. The governor and his council were at debate in the chapel above, and despite their misuse of these sacred precincts they were propelled heavenwards with greater force than all the saints of Christianity. Thus Navarro 'gained great credit at this siege, and struck a terror into everybody' (Guicciardini, 1562, Bk I).

For a time the older and newer methods of mining co-existed. As late as 1537 the Spaniards attacked

Saint-Pol by cutting a gash in the salient of a tower, supporting the masonry by timber, and then burning away the props. In the main, however, besiegers avidly seized on the possibility of wrecking a wall by an explosion, rather than effecting its tame subsidence by the 'burnt-prop' method. The explosive mine furthered the work of the cannon in wiping from the strategic map the hosts of small medieval castles which had disrupted and bedevilled so many offensive campaigns in the past. Only a good wet ditch, or a deep and well-flanked dry one was capable of deterring the enemy from 'attaching the miner' to the scarp.

The political and strategic consequences

The Italian theatre of war

The events of 1494 and the following years shook the colourful patchwork of Italian politics into a disorganised kaleidoscope, in which the main states – Milan, Venice, Florence, the Papal States and Naples – were slow to arrange themselves into any recognisable pattern. Militarily, the Italian scene was dominated for a few months each year by whatever power could first raise a field army. All the same, the ascendancy of the offensive was such that any conquests made in that period could seldom be maintained long into the next year: allies were unreliable, and still less reliable were your own indisciplined and improvident garrisons. The city of Milan, the prize of so many campaigns, was notoriously taken and lost with equal ease, for the walls were weak in themselves, and the suburbs crowded close in front.

Hardly anywhere do we find people observing 'modern' strategic principles. Victories were left unexploited, mountain barriers undefended, and a fat conquest like the Netherlands disregarded in favour of exhausting campaigns in the remote and rocky Abruzzi. Above the turmoil of immediate events, however, we can already make out the lineaments of future centuries of warfare in Italy.

In the early sixteenth century, just as in later times, the plain of Lombardy was virtually indefensible. An individual fortress, however strong (and some in the sixteenth century were not particularly strong), could be by-passed easily enough. Also, the wide, slow-marching Po offered the aggressor a natural carriageway for his heavy siege trains. The rivers that ran into the Po were treacherous friends for the defender, for they were liable to fall in level without warning, and at all times they could be readily forced by anyone who was ready to go to the trouble of making an outflanking movement, whether on the south bank as by the Austrian general Browne in 1746, or along the Alpine foothills as by Suvorov in 1799.

As far as France and Austria were concerned, they needed to have a foothold beyond the Alps in order to be able to take the field in Lombardy in the first place. The French had two modes of entry into Italy: they could either make agreements with north Italian rulers (the Duke of Milan in 1494, and the Duke of Savoy until 1536 and in various later periods), or they could cling on to one or more fortresses beyond the watershed (among other places, Asti and Turin in the sixteenth century; Casale, Pinerolo and Exilles in the seventeenth century, and Alessandria in Napoleonic times). In this the French had the advantage over the Austrians, whose access to the plain was impeded by the hostility or neutrality of the Venetians. In the eighteenth century the fortress of Mantua offered the Austrians a single and inadequate toehold beyond the Brenner, and only after they had taken over Napoleon's creation of the Quadrilateral did they have an adequate footing in the plain.

Once a power had won the upper hand in Lombardy, it was faced with the problem of how to exploit its success. None of the alternatives was really profitable. In 1524, 1536, 1707 and 1746–7 the Imperialists pursued the alluring prospect of invading France by way of Provence, but on every occasion they were chasing a mirage. The theatre was too remote from the vulnerable heart of France, the country was too barren, supply by sea was too uncertain, and the tracks running along the coastline were too long and difficult.

Both the French (1494, 1525, 1527–8, 1552–3, 1557 and 1799) and the Austrians (1527, 1708 and 1744) were tempted south into misguided ventures in central Italy or Naples, only to withdraw again when frustrated by the inconstancy of the people or an unfavourable turn of events in Lombardy. The Spanish could get to Naples more easily than either of these two powers, as long as the sea was free from hostile squadrons.

The cannon of Charles VIII had therefore won for the French generations of direct involvement in the concerns of Italy, a state of affairs which people like Branthôme and Tavannes began to regret when they looked back over the course of the sixteenth century (Branthôme, 1858–78, book I, part 2; Tavannes, 1850, 7). Tavannes suggested that France would have been better advised to have set up a series of powerful city republics which would favour French interests in Italy. The same notion – that of arranging the politics of independent Italian states to the advantage of France – was revived in the eighteenth century by the statesman d'Argenson.

The Austrian and Spanish potential

All of this was small comfort to states less fitted than France to come to terms with the changes wrought by gunpowder. As we shall see, there was singularly little in the conduct of Emperor Maximilian of Germany to show that he regarded himself as the standard-bearer of any crusade of Habsburg against Valois. This development had to wait until the royal line of Spain died out, and Austria and Spain were united in the common Imperial inheritance of Charles V in 1519.

Maximilian's means of waging fortress warfare or any other kind of warfare were severely limited. He was never able to catch up with the half-century of artillery development which had been undertaken in France, and as a result the Imperial artillery of the early sixteenth century became an extraordinary mixture of ancient bombards, modern pieces after the French model, and trunnionless cannon fixed rigidly to two-wheeled 'block' carriages. Another failing was the lack of draught animals; that was why the transport of the park of 136 pieces against Padua in 1509 had to be arranged in two instalments. Maximilian's gunners were, however, a match for the French, and when a French observer watched the Imperial and French artillery working side by side at a siege in 1510 he had to admit 'that the Emperor's guns kept up a heavier fire than those of

the king of France' (Fleurange, 1850, 20).

The heavy calibre and rapid fire of the Imperial cannon were capable of making extensive breaches in two days, as happened at Mézières in 1521 and Péronne in 1536, but the low velocity of the shot and the frequent employment of stone balls tended to bring down the masonry in large fragments, which were more difficult to scale than the débris produced by the smaller-calibre iron shot.

The Emperor's Venetian campaigns were unpopular in Germany, on account of the disruption which his wars caused to trade. Since he was consequently forced to maintain his adventures from the resources of Austria alone, the Imperial expeditions were short-winded and liable to end in an ignominious scuttle back across the Alps, as in 1496, 1509 and 1516.

When the Emperor attempted to create a reliable native infantry, in the shape of the mercenary landsknechts, he merely added a new element of calamitous unpredictability to fortress warfare. Other sovereigns could have told him how useless they were. Their indisciplined champing and guzzling ran through the provisions of Thérouanne (1513) and Yvoy (1552), and threatened to do the same at Naples in 1528, 'so that', wrote the Abbé Branthôme, 'I have heard great captains affirm that it is not a good idea to shut up landsknechts in a fortress – they are ill-disciplined and think only of their bellies' (Branthôme, 1858–78, book I, part 1). At Siena in 1554 Montluc deliberately let his landsknechts go in the middle of the defence.

Germans as a whole came to be despised as incapable of exercising intelligence or self-restraint. Marshal de Vieilleville was agreeably surprised in 1552 to discover a German who managed to bring him back a detailed and accurate report of the enemy fortifications at Thionville; he had not thought the nation up to such a task. The Swiss were likewise considered to be 'people who were not at all suitable for holding a fortress, for they were naturally inclined to fight in the open field' (Bellay, 1569, 25). They at least were honest enough to recognise their shortcomings, and there was a touching simplicity in the way they left open the gates of Novara in 1513 and invited the French to come in and fight.

Fortunately for the Habsburgs, the union with

Spain in 1519 gave them the services of the Spanish infantry, the finest in Europe: hardy, versatile and enterprising, both in attack and defence, and led by a hungry military aristocracy of the kind that was going to make Prussia so formidable in the eighteenth century. Guicciardini (1562, Bk XI) notes that as early as 1512 the Spaniards were 'of ancient renown ... for their agility and dexterity in besieging and storming towns'. Moreover, Spanish governors were notably severe in keeping their garrisons under control.

The potential of the Italian states

Few of the Italian powers could more than approximate to France and Spain in ferocity and efficiency. Two of the weaklings succumbed early in the century: Naples was gobbled up by the Spanish in 1503, while Milan underwent intermittent periods of French overlordship until the Spanish installed the last of the Sforzas as puppet, and finally established their own Prince Philip as open ruler in 1546.

The Venetians, being better-organised, managed to hang on to the mainland territories they had filched over the course of the last century. The Signoria summoned an effective mixed army of levies and well-paid condottieri, and employed talented and devoted native engineers like the Sanmichelis. The artillery too was taken in hand, and in 1526 the Venetians established a higher artillery school which became a model for the rest of Europe. Their guns were short and light, and less encrusted with ornament than was the fashion at the time.

Just as the past misdeeds of Venice cast that Republic in the role of a defender in the early sixteenth century, so the weakness of the papacy in earlier times inevitably made Alexander VI, Julius II and their successors appear in the light of aggressors when they tried to re-establish the old papal suzerainty over Bologna, Ferrara and other cities on the northern fringes of their dominions.

Papal commanders were on the whole competent and enterprising, and the architects and engineers the most skilled that money could hire. Some of the Popes themselves took a direct part in siege warfare, an interest which reached indecent proportions in the case of Julius II, and which was pursued with scarcely less avidity by Clement VII in his siege of Florence in 1529. Where the papacy fell short was not so much in the building as in the defence of its fortresses. Guicciardini (1562, Bk XI) remarks concerning the citadel of Bologna in 1511 that it was 'spacious and strong, but provided as badly as the fortresses of the Church usually are – the garrison consisted of just a few infantry, who had scanty victuals and hardly any ammunition'.

Nobody doubted the capacity of the Dukes of Ferrara to look after themselves, sandwiched though they were between Venice and the Papal States. Ercole, then (from 1505) Alfonso, improvised fortifications of immense strength, and built up an artillery which was fully equal to the French, and superior to any other in Europe. Duke Alfonso in particular attracted the notice of Bayard and other contemporaries, Fleurange (1850, 25) describing him as 'a gentle prince, and a warrior who was bold and of ready understanding. He devoted all his time to casting artillery, and strengthening and building fortresses'. Alfonso looked to France to help him to maintain his independence, and in return he offered his Gallic friends an avenue into eastern central Italy, and the loan of whatever great guns they chose to pick.

In contrast to Ferrara, the state of Florence displayed the political and military vices of Renaissance Italy to the point of exaggeration. Internally it was riven by feuds between the republican and Medici factions, while its main achievement in the military field was to withdraw on two occasions from the wider theatre of Italian events in order to pursue muddled (if finally successful) campaigns against Pisa at the beginning of the century, and against the Republic of Siena fifty years later. Florence's uniquely talented engineers did some of their best work for other masters, but the state's record of siege warfare on its own account is marked by feebleness and incompetence.

Altogether the survival of Florence presents something of a mystery. It owned desirable seaports like Leghorn, and lay between Lombardy and the Papal States athwart the path of conquest down the western side of the Apennines. Perhaps the answer lies in its very state of internal division, for an enemy always had one Florentine faction or another at his command, and he found it easier to install a native protégé rather than to attempt an outright annexation.

Provisional artillery fortification and the return to equilibrium 1503–30

The sieges of Pisa and Padua

The stories of the development of fortress warfare and permanent fortification had begun to diverge by 1500, and they were not going to join up again for the best part of a hundred years. Just as happened again in the nineteenth century, men were confronted by a sudden advance in the power of artillery, an advance which shattered all conceptions of the shape of permanent works and compelled the defenders to resort to various kinds of field fortification.

Thus the qualities of leadership and improvisation came to the fore. The great exponents of fortress warfare in the sixteenth century are field commanders like Pitigliano or Guise, who have significantly less in common with 'classical' engineers of the stamp of Vauban than they have with those nineteenth-century soldier-sappers Totleben and Osman Pasha, who also had to adapt their ways to a time of revolutionary technical change.

There were two episodes in the first decade of the sixteenth century which established the new pattern of fortress warfare, and went far towards swinging the balance back in favour of the defensive. These were the sieges of Pisa in 1500 and of Padua in 1509.

The city of Pisa had taken advantage of the excitements of 1494 in order to break away from the heavy-handed rule of Florence. The Florentines were slow and clumsy in their attempts to subdue the rebel city, and in 1500 they had to call on the French for help.

The French proceeded to batter the walls on behalf of their friends, and on 30 June they surged forward for the assault. The assailants got over the wall, but they were halted at a ditch and a free-standing rampart which the Pisans had made behind. The morale of the French was shattered, and shortly afterwards the allies gave up the siege.

The Pisans had at once thwarted the Franco-Florentine campaign of 1500, and arrived at a means to stay the course of the offensive in warfare which had raged unchecked since 1494. Their device was simple enough, but the important fact was that the improvised interior rampart did not press directly against the masonry wall, like the medieval 'rampire', but was separated from it by a wide ditch. Thus, when the wall was breached, it gradually subsided into a heap of jagged stones, unmixed with earth, and served as an outer barrier to the interior ditch and the intact earthen rampart behind.

This *retirata*, or 'double Pisan rampart', as we may term it, was itself going to be surpassed by the more systematic and extensive works which the Venetians built at Padua in 1509. Macchiavelli explains that the Pisans built their interior ditches and ramparts at the last moment and only where danger threatened, 'since their walls were good enough to resist for some time, and the earth was solid and suitable for raising into ramparts. Without these advantages they would have been lost' (Macchiavelli, 1520, book VII). Still, the 'double Pisan rampart' remained the foundation for some of the most famous defences of the century, not just at Padua, but also at Brescia in 1515, Parma in 1521, Marseilles in 1524, Metz in 1552, Siena in 1552–3, Saint-Quentin in 1557, Poitiers in 1569, and Haarlem and La Rochelle in 1573.

The Florentines made another unsuccessful siege of Pisa in 1505. They therefore resorted to blockade and by this unheroic means they finally compelled the city to submit in 1509.

If the tiny state of Pisa, using the double rampart, was able to hold out for so long, it was small wonder that the wealthy and unified republic of Venice, employing the same means, was able to defy the best part of Europe.

Venice was compelled to take to arms in 1508, when Maximilian tried to force his way through Venetian territory in order to get at the French forces in Milan. This brought about a general scramble of the powers to dismember Venice. Louis XII of France conveniently forgot about the original cause of the upset, and allied himself with Maximilian against the Venetians.

The Republic, in its turn, poured men and

resources into Padua, its most important foothold on the mainland. The Captain General Pitigliano was accordingly able to make an interior rampart of great solidity, which ran behind the whole perimeter of the walls except where he knew that the enemy could not bring their guns to bear.

In the second half of September 1509 an allied army of 35,000 troops raged impotently against the defences. Repeated assaults were thrown back, and following a particularly spectacular repulse on 29 September Maximilian was forced to ask the armoured French and German nobility to join in one final storm.

The three-mile circuit of the allied camp was buzzing with rumours of the impending assault when La Palice, the commander of the French knights, read out Maximilian's letter to the nobles.

When they had heard what he had to say, they all looked around grinning, to see who would be the first to speak up. 'Monseigneur', said the Seigneur d'Ymbercourt, 'we are brooding altogether too much. Tell the Emperor that we are all ready. I am tired of living in the fields – the nights are getting cold, and we are running out of decent wine' (Mailles, n.d., 118).

To tease his companions La Palice for a time remained silent and picked his teeth, but he finally reported to Maximilian the sense of the meeting, namely that the French nobility were prepared to join in the assault on foot, if the Germans did the same.

Maximilian's request met with a very different reception among the nobles of Germany and the Netherlands:

When the Emperor had finished talking, there arose amongst the Germans a most extraordinary noise, which lasted half an hour before it died down. Then one of the nobles, who had been instructed to reply on everyone's behalf, announced that it was below their dignity to dismount or storm a breach, and that their true calling was to fight like gentlemen, on horseback (ibid., 120).

The assault and with it the whole siege was abandoned, and by the evening of 3 October Padua was free of the enemy.

Already in the following month the Venetians began work on fortifying Treviso, as a further base from which they could reconquer the mainland. The work was entrusted to a man of God, Fra Giocondo, who energetically razed all the buildings which obstructed the field of fire, and built a low-lying enceinte of curtain walls and semi-circular artillery platforms, with ample space left behind for the construction of *retirate*.

The Holy Alliance and its wars

The further survival of Venice was due partly to the way in which the hostile alliance broke up. The warlike Pope Julius II severed himself from the French in 1510, and in the following year he took a personal hand in the reduction of Mirandola, one of the outer bulwarks of Ferrara, 'regardless of the fact that it was unseemly and unworthy of the dignity of his high office, for a Roman pontiff to lead armies in person against Christian towns' (Guicciardini, 1562, Bk IX).

After this success, Julius brought the Spanish over to his side, and early in 1512 the joint Hispano-papal host of 19,400 men turned against the French garrison in Bologna. Pedro Navarro accompanied the allied army, and he 'attached' a mine near the Castiglione Gate in the hope of repeating his success against the Castle of Uovo in 1503. But this time the defenders knew what was in store for them: having established the precise whereabouts of the tunnellers by placing rattles and bells along the walls, the French sank a shaft into the mine chamber with the object of dissipating the force of the explosion. Thus, when Navarro sprang his mine, the wall was severely shaken but remained intact. The garrison continued to resist until a French army broke through to their relief, leaving the allies with no alternative but to raise the siege.

The success of the countermine at Bologna in 1512 showed that defenders were now capable of resisting the attack in every dimension. The offensive mine had now met its match, in the same way as the siege artillery had been frustrated at Padua three years before.

The Pope won the Imperialists over to his side in

6   Defence of a breach at Siena, showing a *retirata* (Viollet-le-Duc)

1512, which added marvellously to the efficacy, if not the sanctity of the Holy Alliance. The French were therefore compelled to pull out of Italy, but in 1515 they returned in force under the command of the ambitious young king Francis I. Francis reduced the Castle of Milan with the help of Pedro Navarro (who had abandoned his former masters), and in the following year the French gained a peace which confirmed them in undisputed possession of the Duchy of Milan.

War broke out again in 1521. This time Francis was not faced by one of the usual shifting coalitions of Italian princes, but by a constant and deadly enemy in the form of the youthful emperor Charles V, who had received Spain and the Netherlands from the extinct house of Spain, and combined them with his Austrian patrimony to form an immense power-block.

Charles regarded the expulsion of the French from Italy as just the first step towards uniting Europe under the House of Habsburg. What was more, he had the means of putting his intentions into effect. He had inherited fifty calibres of artillery from the Spanish and Austrian arsenals (as opposed to the seventeen which had been bequeathed to Francis), which impelled him to combine all the artillery of the Habsburg lands under a single *General-Zeugmeister*, and hire Netherlandish and Italian experts to simplify and modernise the whole range of guns.

Although the regulations of 1552 still specified fourteen varieties of cannon, from the 98-pounder double cannon down to the one-pounder miniature falconet, Charles's favourite piece was probably the 48-pounder single cannon (Nuremberg weight), a gun which could fire the captured shot of the French 42-pounder cannon (Paris weight), and therefore did not need to be replenished constantly from the distant Imperial arsenals.

The Imperialists eagerly joined in a revived Holy League, and in 1521 the allied army set about besieging Parma, which was the first fortress on the eastern frontier of the Duchy of Milan. The allies, however, proceeded to make a number of mis-calculations, and rather than continue their muddled siege any longer they decided to call off the operation and face the French in the open country. Finding

himself the sole object of attention, the French commander Lautrec scattered his troops among a multitude of fortresses, and sedulously kept out of the way of the allies. Thereafter until the peace of 1529, the hold of the Imperialists on North Italy was going to be disturbed only by a series of isolated French incursions, each more disastrous than the last.

Utterly unmemorable at first sight, the campaign of 1521 has an important place in military history, for it saw the first employment of the musket, a six-foot-long hand-gun of one-inch bore, which was levelled on a forked rest for firing, an altogether more formidable weapon than the relatively light arquebus which had preceded it. Although on this occasion the musket was first employed by the Spaniards in the opening stages of their siege of Milan, from now onwards the increasing efficiency of hand-guns in general caused them to be numbered among the most valuable weapons of the defensive. Both the musket and arquebus were equipped with the new inventions of the priming pan and the serpentine match-holder, which meant that the infantryman could devote rather more attention to his aim than to making sure that his gun went off in the first place.

Hand-gunners acquitted themselves very well in defending the breaches at Cremona in 1523 and Marseilles in 1524, and besiegers came to hate and fear the well-aimed musket shot. Thus in 1537 the Imperial commander Del Vasto determined to exact vengeance from the garrison of Carmagnola for the death of the Marquis of Saluzzo, who had been drilled by a sniper during the siege:

When the defenders came out, Marquis Del Vasto praised them for having fulfilled their duty so well, and asked to be shown the soldier who had fired to such good effect from a certain window over the castle gate. The soldier in question, who did not know the identity of the personage he had shot down, declared that he was the one who had been firing from there. On hearing this, the Marquis disregarded his promises, and had the man seized and strung up from the self same window (Bellay, 1569, 456).

Early in 1522 Lautrec descended into the plain to

do something to help his isolated Italian fortresses. The allied commander Prospero Colonna should now have followed established custom, and abandoned his siege of the Castle of Milan rather than undergo the danger of being attacked in the rear by the relieving army. Instead he stood his ground, heaping up mock ramparts of snow to divert the garrison's attention, and casting up an outer perimeter of lines and strong points facing Lautrec and the open country. Colonna hereby revived a medieval siege procedure which was going to become routine over the next centuries, when the earthworks confronting the fortress went under the name of the 'lines of countervallation', and the ones facing outwards as the 'lines of circumvallation'.

In order to avert an imminent mutiny among his Swiss troops, Lautrec on 27 April launched an assault against one of Colonna's strongpoints, the fortified park of Bicocca about four miles north of Milan. Over one thousand Swiss were cut down by the Imperial artillery before the troops so much as reached the ditch. The bellicose independent spirit of the Swiss was broken for ever, and Lautrec had to lead the French away to shelter among their Venetian allies.

The Swiss heretic Zwingli had been a horrified witness of the slaughter of his countrymen, which only served to intensify his spiritual crisis. It so happened that this was the very time when a certain Spanish nobleman, Ignatius of Loyola, was moved to turn his thoughts to religion while he was nursing a leg which had been shattered at the defence of Pamplona. Such was the contribution of fortress warfare to the respective histories of the Reformation and Counter-Reformation.

There was no saving the French garrisons in Lombardy, after the reverse at Bicocca. The Imperialists proceeded to eliminate the isolated strongholds one by one, and in the summer of 1524 they carried the war into France, advancing through Provence until they were checked at Marseilles.

King Francis believed that the opportunity had come for some dramatic counter-blow. He was weary of the commanders who had led successive armies to their defeat in Italy, but instead of drawing the natural lesson – which was to stay out of that country altogether – he once more led an army across the Alps in person. He was still besieging the fortress of Pavia when the Imperialists combined their forces and bore down on him. Taken between the fortress and the hostile army, Francis was finally routed on 23–24 February 1525.

His army killed or captured, Francis was carried off to Spain as a prisoner. He gave his word – for what little it was worth – never to revive his claims on Italy. This calamity served to confirm military men in their growing belief that truly professional warfare was an affair of cautiously-conducted sieges. As late as the 1550s an able commander like the Marshal de Brissac was prepared to spin out campaign after campaign making minor sieges, and justified himself by recalling the terrible battle of Pavia and the disasters which were liable to overtake people who hazarded everything on a field action.

The Imperialists conducted themselves after the victory of Pavia with a callous arrogance which Europe had already begun to recognise as typically Spanish. The Italian powers accordingly gathered together in a revived Holy League which was directed against the Imperialists, and not, as before, against the French. The French were in no fit state to re-enter Italy, and so for nearly two years the Imperialists were free to exact their vengeance on the individual Italian members of the League. They cleared the Duchy of Milan of the troops of Ludovico Sforza and his allies in 1526, and early in the next year Charles v sent the renegade Constable of Bourbon south with an army to settle accounts with the Pope.

Bourbon's plunder-bent army struck down the central spine of the Apennines, and came before Rome early in May 1527. He split his force into three columns, in order to launch an open escalade of the walls, a kind of attack which had fallen out of fashion since siege artillery had been perfected. He really had no alternative, for his guns were hundreds of miles away by rocky roads.

The assault went in early on the foggy morning of 6 May. Bourbon was killed at the outset of the attack, but his infuriated troops fought their way over the walls and into the city to a chant of '*Carne! Carne! Sangre! Sangre! Cierra! Cierra! Bourbon! Bourbon!*' The Pope and over four thousand of his troops and clergy fled into the Castel Sant'Angelo and raised the drawbridge in all haste. Those that were left outside had to be pulled up to safety in a basket – St Pauls in reverse. Pope Clement finally capitulated on 6 June, on condition that he ordered all the other papal fortresses to surrender.

Meanwhile, undeterred by the disaster at Pavia, Francis returned from Spanish captivity and made ready to dispatch yet another army into Italy. The French invasion force penetrated as far as the walls of the city of Naples in the spring of 1528, only to be destroyed by the plague and the gathering Imperialists. Out of the original thirty thousand men of the army, scarcely five thousand survivors of this sixteenth-century Stalingrad found their way back to France.

The Neapolitan disaster, taken with some French reverses in northern Italy, sufficed to damp the ebullience even of King Francis. At Cambrai in August 1529 he renewed his renunciation of all the French conquests in Italy.

The allies of France were left to make what terms they could. The Pope eventually went so far as to lend a contingent of troops to the Imperialists, but the Florentine Republic was determined to continue the struggle, with the result that on 24 October the city of Florence found the Prince of Orange with an Imperial army on its doorstep.

The siege of Florence lasted from October 1529 until August 1530. It made no political stir outside Tuscany, and its feeble motions are of only the slightest military significance. At the same time it had a fascination of its own: it concerned the most culturally fertile city of the Renaissance, and it presented Michelangelo with an opportunity of demonstrating just how far he matched the ideal of the Renaissance superman.

Florence had been in a state of excitement ever since the city had expelled the ruling Medici family and restored the republican constitution in May 1527. Michelangelo, as the most accomplished draftsman in the place, was appointed Commissary General of Fortifications, and over the next two years he furnished Florence with a comprehensive system of works. Amongst other enterprises he canalised the Mugnone stream to act as an outer defence, and threw up earthen bastions to protect the gates. He devoted his chief cares, however, to the

work of defending the dominating hill of San Miniato outside the city, 'for if it fell to the enemy, the city was lost' (Vasari, 1550, part III). He spent six months surrounding the hill with bastions of earth and fascines, which he supported by timber frameworks and courses of roughly-made bricks of tow and dung.

Michelangelo certainly took his duties as a patriot very seriously, but he never allowed them to interfere with his higher obligations to his art. Thus he travelled to Ferrara with the nominal purpose of inspecting the famous fortifications, and ended up by being persuaded by the duke to paint a magnificent Leda in tempera. All the time he was celebrating the memory of the enemies of the Republic by working in secret on the Medici tomb, with its figures of Dawn and Night and the Dukes Lorenzo and Giuliano.

Considering the labour devoted by great minds to the preparations for the siege, the actual event comes as something of an anti–climax. After making a futile cannonade of a new campanile on the San Miniato hill, the Imperialists settled down into a blockade which lasted the best part of a year until, on 2 August 1530, the lack of provisions persuaded the Florentine commander to capitulate. Michelangelo himself had slipped unheroically away during the investment, but he had been overcome by twinges of conscience and returned while the siege was still in progress.

The Medici were restored to Florence in the person of Duke Alessandro. As one of the most deeply-implicated rebels, Michelangelo prudently stayed in hiding until his former patron Pope Clement VII sought him out and promised that no more would be said of the matter. Michelangelo accompanied the Pope to Rome, and could never quite bring himself to trust the sincerity of Duke Alessandro de' Medici, who invited him in vain to return to his native Florence and help him to choose a site for a new citadel.

Provisional fortification

Over the course of thirty years the defensive had adapted itself with considerable success to withstand the new weapons of the attack. At the beginning all the good customs and admirable methods of war of the Ancients had died out almost everywhere, but in Italy they had disappeared altogether. Whatever was of any value, we learnt it from the French strangers from over the Alps. You have probably heard of the extraordinary weakness of the fortresses in our country before Charles VIII came here in 1494. At that period we made our parapets one foot thick; our cannon and archery embrasures were narrow on the outside and wide within, and were subject to a thousand defects which I shall not enumerate for fear of boring you.

Princes still had not learnt that there was more to their trade than writing elegant correspondence, adorning themselves with jewels, and passing their time in gallantry. So writes Macchiavelli (1520, book VII).

Guicciardini pursues the argument further. The peoples, terrified at the easy loss of their towns,

bent all their ingenuity and skill to devise methods of defence, and they have succeeded so well that they have fortified even their smallest towns with ramparts, ditches, flanks, outworks and bastions. And so, being crammed with artillery (which does more damage in the defence than in the attack of towns), the places have been rendered secure, for it is exceedingly hard to take a town fortified in such a manner (Guicciardini, 1562, Bk XV).

With reasonable confidence we may point to the second decade of the sixteenth century as the period when military opinion came to appreciate that a suitably-prepared fortress had a good chance of withstanding an attack. In 1521 the Spanish had at first hesitated to attack Parma, because some of the generals feared 'that the reduction of towns, on account of the changes that have been made in the methods of warfare over a short period, and in the art of defending fortresses, has become notoriously more difficult' (ibid., Bk XIV). Similarly, Macchiavelli was ready to expound the merits of the 'double Pisan rampart' in his *Arte della Guerra*, whereas seven years earlier in one of his *Discorsi* he had declared that fortresses were superfluous if their prince owned a good field army, and indefensible if

he lacked one (Macchiavelli, 1519, book II, chapter 24).

The same decisive period is referred to by Fourquevaux in his *Instructions sur le Faict de la Guerre* of 1548, in which he talks about the change that was effected by the new fortress designs introduced about thirty years before. The earlier strongholds, he wrote, could not be called genuinely strong by any stretch of the imagination. But it was a very different story with the fortresses adapted since, which

with good reason may be regarded as very difficult to conquer, and likely to cost the besieger more than he will gain. Just as there are plenty of fortresses of this kind in Italy and France, so other lands have some already, and in a short time they will have still more, because everybody is building them (Fourquevaux, 1548, book III, 85).

The fortresses these authorities had in mind were works of essentially improvised construction, probably consisting of thick ramparts and small round or angular towers like the ones described by Giambattista della Valle di Venafro in *Vallo. Libro Contenente Appartenentie ad Capitanii, Retenere et Fortificare una Città*, a work which ran through about a dozen editions after it was first published in 1521. Similar ideas were advanced by G. B. Bellucci (1545), Giacomo Lanteri (1559), and others.

Such fortresses were usually of earth, revetted with fascines or timber, and transversed with beams for extra strength, like Michelangelo's bastions on the hill of San Miniato. These materials were of cheaper and more rapid construction than masonry, and averted the splinters which often caused more casualties than the actual enemy cannon shot. A semi-permanent fortress of this nature was Ferrara, the reconstruction of which was begun in 1496, and by 1511 had earned it the title of the 'finest fortified town in the whole of Christendom' (Fleurange, 1850, 23). Duke Alfonso undertook a further rebuilding of the place in 1512, immediately after the Battle of Ravenna. The works of Santhià in Piedmont were of similar construction: in three successive days of siege in 1555 a bastion and a nearby curtain absorbed 3,500, 1,600 and 1,200 Spanish roundshot, and emerged as strong as ever.

Many towns, nevertheless, were still fortified in haste and only when a siege threatened. Tavannes (1850, 132) claimed that the process need not take more than three weeks.

Little or nothing remains of such works on the ground today, but it is possible that they exercised an important influence on the principles of the permanent fortification which gradually supplanted them all over Italy.

Fortress warfare had for the first time assumed the character of an equal duel. The mobile cannon and the explosive mine had certainly destroyed the medieval sense of impregnability, but it was equally true that the besieger would be badly knocked about if he just wheeled his cannon into the open field in front of the ramparts.

Hardly a decade of the early sixteenth century passed without some addition being made to the basic vocabulary of fortress warfare. As early as 1498 Philip of Cleves writes in unimpeachable terms of the need of defilading the siege attacks, 'which must be conducted with caution and sagacity. You have to watch out for the towers, bulwarks and batteries of the town, and you must direct your trenches in such a way that none of the guns can get at you inside.' Sap attacks on an extensive scale were employed by the Imperialists against Padua in 1513, and by the French against the Castle of Milan in 1515 and Pavia in 1524. Batteries varied in size from three to thirty pieces, and were planted in some sieges at a range of four hundred paces from the walls, and in others, as at Casale in 1554, in the fortress ditch itself.

The nobility of Europe accommodated themselves slowly to the muddy yet perilous work of fortress warfare, where personal prowess often went for nothing. Branthôme writes (1858–78, book I, part I) that in the earlier decades of the century it was almost unknown for a young courtier to go off to serve in a siege, and we have seen already how unwilling were the German nobles to get off their horses and serve on foot at Padua in 1509. Bayard too, the epitome of French chivalry, did not like the idea of fighting alongside 'cobblers, farriers, bakers, mechanics and the like, who do not hold their honour in the same high regard as gentlemen' (Mailles, n.d., 119). But in the end it was Bayard and the French knights who saw that they must fight on foot, and the Germans who refused.

Three years later Bayard himself was the first to propose that the armoured nobility should dismount and stiffen the infantry in the assault on Brescia. As the century wore on there are signs that people were ready to look on the defence or attack of a fortress as an affair just as glorious as (and far more important than) a cavalry encounter in the open field. Kings of France made a point of awarding the Order of Saint-Michel to officers who had distinguished themselves in the command of a besieged fortress; Bayard was so honoured for his defence of Mézières in 1521, de Lude for his dogged resistance at Fuenterrabia in 1522, and Montluc for his help to the Sienese in 1554–5. From the middle of the century onwards, we find that commanders like Guise and Coligny no longer stood aloof from the routine and danger of siege warfare, but eagerly sought out and listened to any veteran who had experience of this trade. Parma, for one, never undertook a siege without constantly referring to a centenarian private soldier who had trailed a pike for Spain since as long ago as the Middle Ages.

Two Later Italian Wars and the Origins of Permanent Artillery Fortification 1530–1600

War in a fortified theatre

The Italian wars of the 1530s, 1540s and 1550s were fought under conditions radically different from those of earlier decades. Politically and strategically the scene was simplified by the fact that the House of Habsburg never released its grip on the Duchy of Milan and the Kingdom of Naples, lands which in earlier wars used to change hands several times in a single year. As for the Pope and the Florentines and Venetians, they stood aloof for most of the time from the quarrels of the French and Imperialists, and, having affirmed their neutrality by studding their states with fortresses, they managed to push the theatre of war away from themselves and north-eastwards to the Lombard plain and the Alpine foothills of Piedmont.

Frontiers were congealing and solidifying fast. Bourbon's expedition to Rome in 1527 may be counted the last of the old-style unrestrained rampages which had been devastating Italy since 1494. Antonio da Sangallo the Younger and Michele di Sanmicheli were already at work on strengthening the fortresses of the Pope's northern dominions, and when, thirty years later, the Duke of Guise came south to attack Naples, the French no longer traversed central Italy by right of their cannon, but by invitation of the Pope, who needed help against the Imperialists. While the negotiations were still in progress, Guise wrote to his brother to ask whether His Holiness was aware of the quantity of artillery needed to make up a modern siege train:

You know that when you want to take a fortress of any strength, you have to think of taking along twenty-four heavy cannon to form two batteries, and six or seven powerful culverins to fire at the (upper) defences. You must also have at hand eight or ten thousand shot and 200,000 pounds of powder (Guise, 1850, 251).

The techniques of siege warfare had been worked out and proven during the turmoils of the first three decades of the century. The problems which remained were those of execution rather than invention. Here lay the difficulty: major new theatres of war had opened on the Emperor's frontiers with Turkey and on the northern borders of France, and neither the Imperialists nor the French could spare resources for Italy, where campaigning was consequently feeble and short-winded.

While the Imperialists were fortunate enough to be established in the Duchy of Milan, the entry of the French to Italy still hung upon the goodwill of the Duke of Savoy. This uncertain foundation collapsed altogether when hostilities threatened in 1536, and Duke Charles III refused his uncle Francis I the requested passage across Piedmont.

The French overran the offending territory in a lightning campaign, but the resistance of the fortress of Vercelli destroyed any prospect of their continuing the advance into Lombardy. Now that the French had lost the initiative, Emperor Charles V

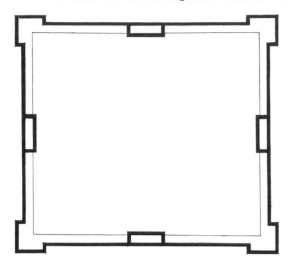

7   The citadel of Turin

gathered together fifty thousand men and dodged around the southern flank of the Maritime Alps into Provence. Here the Imperialists were checked by a retrenched camp at Avignon, and, as was usual in such cases, the invading army was decimated by disease and forced to retreat.

Over the following years the French consolidated their Piedmontese foothold across the Alps. They strengthened Moncalieri, Savigliano and Centallo with the help of Italian engineers, and transformed Turin into the citadel of French power in Italy. The new fort at Turin consisted of a great square which was flanked by four large right-angle bastions. Halfway along the six-hundred-yard length of each of the curtains rose a cavalier or artillery platform, which commanded the curtain and swept the open space lying between the new outer enceinte and the old medieval castle which was preserved within. In the sixth book of his *Quesiti e Inventioni* of 1556 the artillery writer Tartaglia takes the Prior of Barletta to task for claiming that 'as far as the art of fortification is concerned, the human intellect has reached the highest attainable summit'. The Prior produced as evidence a plan of the new fort at Turin, a work 'which all men of understanding regard as impregnable'. Tartaglia riposted that he could find 'no trace of particularly great understanding in that construction', but he was vague as to what he would have preferred to put in its place (Tartaglia, 1556, part 6).

The Imperialists were never able to evict the French from their Piedmontese enclave. A dangerous offensive which began in 1543 was blunted by the French victory at Ceresole on 14 April of the next year. Hostilities broke out again in 1551, but the Marshal de Cossé-Brissac was able to preserve most of the disputed territory by means of bold marches and a well-calculated use of interior lines.

In 1555 the Imperial general Alva came to Italy with an army of some thirty thousand men, together with a 'large number of pioneers who were to follow the practice of the Turks by digging great quantities of earth and filling up ditches with wood and fascines' (Branthôme, 1858–78, book I, part 1). All the Spanish might proved of no avail against the earth-and-log fortress of Santhià, which successfully withstood a three-week siege in August.

By such means the French held on in Piedmont until the Imperialists were compelled to come to terms by a series of reverses in northern Europe. The Peace of Câteau-Cambrésis of 1559 was favourable to the French (apart from compelling them to abandon Turin), and secured them the foothold in Italy for which King Francis had first gone to war in 1536. They owned a secure communication back to France by way of Pinerolo, and they had defensible outposts at Chivasso, Chieri and Villanova d'Asti, which usefully hemmed in Turin.

What truly lay beyond redemption was the former

French influence in central Italy. In a last outburst of the republican spirit of medieval Italy the city of Siena had cast out its Spanish garrison in 1552, and appealed to France for help. The Imperialists closed in from all sides, and although successive French reinforcements under Piero Strozzi and Blaise de Montluc managed to prolong the resistance of the Sienese, the city itself capitulated from hunger on 21 April 1555. With the fall of the last stronghold, Montalcino, in 1559, the republic was swallowed up altogether in the Grand Duchy of Tuscany.

The development of permanent artillery fortification

The need for permanent fortification
The history of *active* fortress warfare in sixteenth-century Italy may be adequately recounted without a single reference to permanent artillery fortification. A cat would just as soon swim a tub of citrus juice as a sixteenth-century engineer would have set about the siege of some of the new strongholds that were springing up all over Italy. Moreover, some of the most enlightened patrons of the new fortification were careful to keep out of the quarrels of their powerful neighbours. Thus Verona was repeatedly besieged early in the century, yet after it was rebuilt in the 1530s it never saw a determined enemy until 1797; thus Rome in 1527 was as thoroughly sacked as a city can be, and did not undergo a further siege until 1849.

If the permanent fortification of the Italian Renaissance was of purely deterrent and negative value in its own time, the brilliance and originality of its designs nevertheless determined the shape of strongholds until the middle of the nineteenth century.

The strong provisional works of the early sixteenth century were gradually replaced by fortresses in masonry. These were costly, but always available for use. Whereas provisional fortresses like Santhià were cheap to build and offered almost inexhaustible passive resistance, they proved to be difficult to keep up in time of peace. In the course of time the earthen banks subsided and the palisades decayed – which was dangerous in the case of a frontier fortress, and fatal if the stronghold was intended to hold down restless people like the citizens of Pisa, Florence, Siena or Antwerp.

The permanent fortress also had the advantage of appealing to a certain aspect of human nature. Fortress-building gave a cowardly sovereign something literally and metaphorically concrete to do, in time of deepest peace, which could directly influence the course of a future war. Whereas the finest field regiments were at the mercy of accidents or poor leadership, a well-built fortress could intervene in wars which were waged years or generations hence, long after the writs of other legacies had run their course.

The bastion system: its nature, origins and development
The new fortresses were traced according to a revolutionary principle. The younger generation of Italian military architects rejected the circular towers of medieval times in favour of a four-sided angular construction called the 'bastion', which consisted of two sideways-facing 'flanks', and two outward-facing 'faces'. Three far-reaching consequences were inherent in the new shape:
1   The provision of a distinct and wide flank enabled the defender to bring a heavy cross-fire to bear along the ditch.
2   The meeting of the two faces of the bastion in an angular salient effectively eliminated the patch of dead ground which had existed in front of the circular medieval tower, and opened clear fields of fire for the flanks of the neighbouring bastions. No longer did an individual tower have to provide for its own close-range defence.
3   The long, straight parapets of an angular bastion enabled the defender to mount a greater quantity of cannon than was possible in the case of a circular tower of similar dimensions and cost.

Among the supposed forerunners of the bastion system are numbered certain wedge-shaped towers in the designs of Francesco di Giorgio Martini in the 1470s (La Croix, 1963, 265), a triangular spur on the northern tower of Mont Saint-Michel, and the extraordinary outer enceinte of the Castle of Lucera (1269–83) (Langenskiöld, 1938, 265–7). Claims

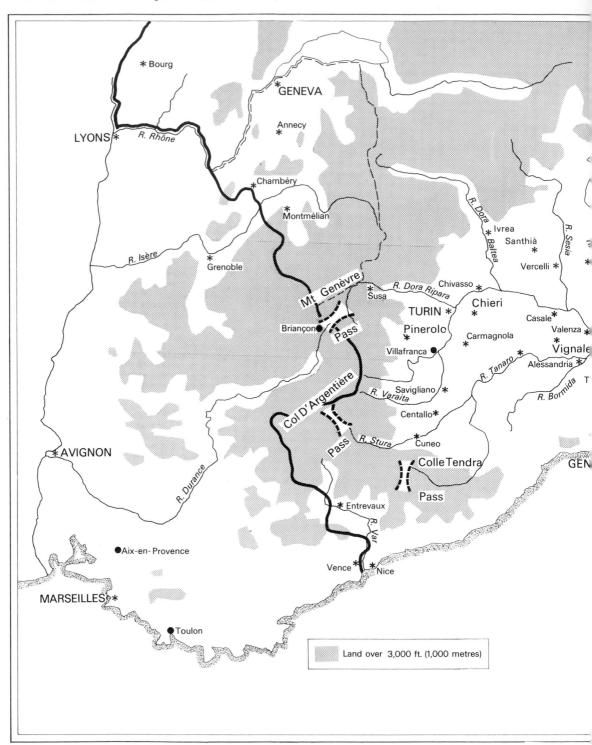

North Italian fortresses in the sixteenth and early seventeenth centuries

VALTELLINE

* Fort Fuentes

* Trent

Bergamo *

Brescia *

* Palmanova

Vicenza *

Lodi * * Crema

Peschiera *

* Verona

Padua *

VENICE
* Lido

Cremona *

MANTUA

Chioggia

PIACENZA

R. Adda

R. Trebbia

R. Po

Mirandola *

R. Adige

R. Po

* PARMA

FERRARA

* BOLOGNA

Ravenna *

| 0 | 25 | 50 |

Miles

Fivizzano *

* La Shpezia

* Sarzanello

* Marradi

Pietrasanta *

* LUCCA

Fucecchio *

FLORENCE

PISA
R. Arno
Coiano *

* LEGHORN

Poggibonsi *

Volterra *

* SIENA

* Montalcino

8   A bastioned fortress under siege, showing a retired flank in action (Viollet-le-Duc)

have been lodged on behalf of the Hussites, the Turks, the Spanish (Un Antiguo Oficial, 1846, 52–3), and, rather tentatively, the Peruvian Indians.

We are on much surer ground when we turn to the work of the Florentine family of Sangallo, which reshaped the sloping walls which had been built in Tuscany since the middle of the fifteenth century into something which is undeniably 'bastioned' in concept. Giuliano di Francesco Giamberti da Sangallo (1445–1516) was almost certainly the architect who in 1487 drew up the designs for the castle and the town enceinte of Poggio Imperiale, which present ten unmistakable bastions. In 1494 his brother, Antonio da Sangallo the Elder (1455 or 1463–1534) began to reconstruct the fort of Civita Castellana for Pope Alexander VI as a small pentagonal fortress incorporating four bastions, a single round tower and an octagonal inner *maestio* or keep.

After taking these first decisive steps, the Sangallos began to employ the angular bastion with increasing freedom and invention. The four bastions of Giuliano's square fort at Nettuno (1501–3) show a significant development, namely the recessing of the greater part of the flank into a 'retired flank', a feature which was to become one of the hallmarks of Italian fortification. The outer part of the flank, where it met the face, followed the line of the earlier straight flanks, so forming an ear-like lobe or 'orillon'. The orillon screened the retired part of the flank from view, and enabled it to proceed undisturbed with its vital work of defending the ditch.

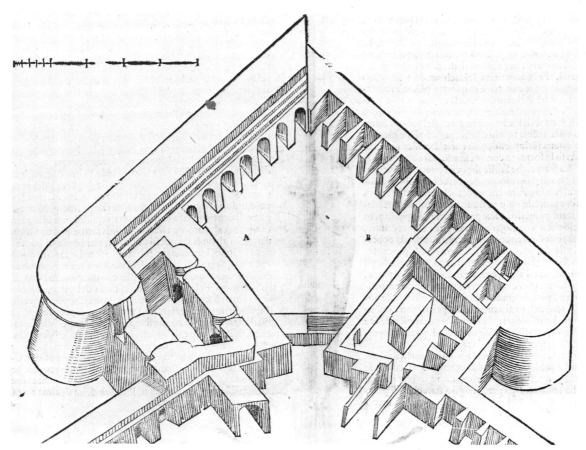

9 View of the masonry of a bastion, showing massive interior buttresses (counterforts), and a double retired flank (on left) (G. Zanchi, 1560)

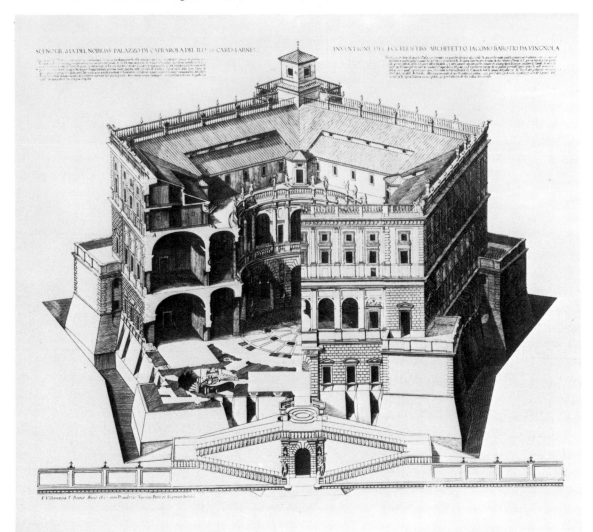

10   Caprarola

Giuliano was a devotee of orillons with rounded corners, whereas Antonio favoured the squared-off variety.

At Caprarola in 1515, Antonio da Sangallo the Younger began to build the fortified basement of the future palace of Cardinal Alessandro Farnese in the form of a regular pentagon, a classic shape of artillery fortification which became very popular in later times for the design of citadels. The actual palace (1559–73) was piled immediately on top of the fortification by Giacomo Barozzi ('il Vignola'). The tradition of the fortress-villa survived well into the seventeenth century in central Italy; the motives were partly symbolic, and partly practical – as a deterrent against restless vassals or Moslem pirates. The most spectacular construction of the kind was Buontalenti's Fort Belvedere (1590) at Florence, which formed a defensible perimeter around a villa which had stood for many years on Monte Magno. This kind of arrangement also held a strong appeal for the nobles of eastern Europe, who were isolated on their plains amid potential enemies, and in the seventeenth century we encounter Polish 'Caprarolas' at Krzyztopor and Podhorce, and an Italo-Moravian counterpart in the palace of the princes Kaunitz at Austerlitz. There are similar buildings at Verdala and Mellieha on the island of Malta.

While the Caprarola fortification was still a-building, the bastioned motif was being applied to the urban enceintes of Civitavecchia, Ferrara, Urbino, Pesaro and Senigallia. The first large-scale and systematic application of the bastion motif to the fortification of a town was, however, the work of the Venetian architect Michele di Sanmicheli (1484–1559).

Sanmicheli had made the acquaintance of the Sangallo family while he was in the Pope's employ, but in the desolate months after the sack of Rome in 1527 he travelled north to the comforts of his native Venetia. There he attracted the suspicion of the authorities by taking an excessive interest in the fortifications at Padua. But this little misunderstanding was soon cleared up, and on 14 April he was given the title of *Ingegner al Servizio dello Stato per le Lagune e Fortificazioni*, an unusually responsible post for a son of Verona.

In 1530 Sanmicheli had already taken over the

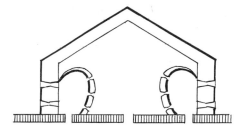

11 The San Bernardino Bastion at Verona

task of reconstructing the works of his home town Verona, which was one of the key fortresses of the Venetian mainland. Verona had been seized and held by the Imperialists earlier in the century, and Sanmicheli and his masters were determined never to let foreigners get possession of such an important position again. The mountains formed a natural barrier to the north of the town, but Sanmicheli had to strengthen the western and southern sectors of the enceinte by remaking long stretches of the curtains, and building in succession the bastions of Trinita, San Bernardino, San Zeno and Spagna.

These Verona bastions were angular, in the Sangallo tradition, but they themselves incorporated some influential novelties. The bastions and curtains alike were low-lying, and their revetments of brick masonry were backed up by counterforts (interior buttresses), a narrow internal arched corridor, and a thick rampart of solid earth. Stout ashlar courses bound the bastions together at the angles. All of this made for a design of great stability and endurance. Sanmicheli elaborated on the Sangallos' simple retired flank by building his retired flanks on two levels: an upper, concave flank on the level of the terreplein of the bastion, and, further to the front, a lower straight flank near the floor of the ditch.

For the Porta Nuova at Verona, Sanmicheli devised a gateway in the form of an ancient triumphal arch. The design of gateways had languished in recent decades, but in the Porta Nuova Sanmicheli built a work which matched his bastions in strength and novelty, and proved to be at once artistically and militarily satisfying. With its severe yet effective architectural decoration, lateral guard-rooms, and arrangements for gates – a large central arch for vehicles, and smaller side arches for pedestrians – the Porta Nuova was going to influence the form of gateways for more than three centuries to come.

To follow the later career of Sanmicheli is to discover in him the qualities which place him as first in the direct line of the great engineers of the sixteenth and seventeenth centuries. He was as liberal-minded and considerate as Vauban, while he bore with Coehoorn all the tribulations of having to work for a republic. In his appearance, at least, he was an original: he owned a hooked nose, a keen eye, and a long curly beard which strangely matched his bald and decidedly pointed head.

Far more than a hired technician, Sanmicheli served the Venetian Republic with complete devotion, concerning himself not just with fortifications, but with public health, civil architecture and engineering, as well as the wider issues of state defence. He travelled as far afield as Crete to build new defences against the Turks, and he secured the mainland possessions of the Republic by strengthening Chiusa, Legnago, Peschiera, Brescia and Bergamo. He was especially proud of the new works at Padua which, he claimed, made that place the strongest fortress in Italy, 'and when I say Italy, I mean all Christendom' (Langenskiöld, 1938, 30).

Sanmicheli designed his fortifications according to the nature of the site, and made no attempt to impose the model of his Verona works as a rigid 'system' that was to be applied in all cases. Thus the main defence of Chioggia, at the southern entrance to the Venetian lagoon, resided in a wide ditch, not in masonry ramparts as at Verona or Padua. A similar freedom is shown in the design of the massive seven-sided casemated fort of Sant' Andrea, on the Lido sandspit guarding the northern channel into

12 Porta San Pietro (Lucca). A characteristic fortress gate, with a central arch and two smaller entrances for pedestrians. The stout masonry is crowned by a pavilion

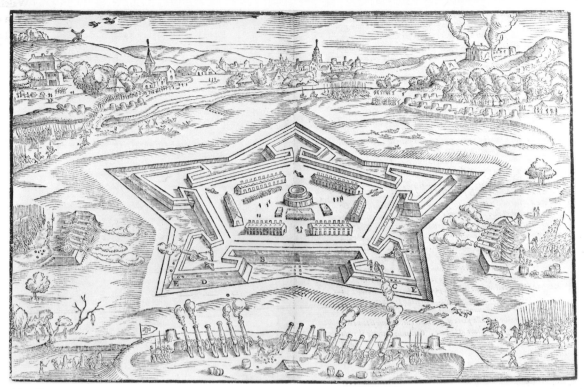

13   Classic pentagonal citadel, of the type made famous by Paciotto

the lagoon. The Senate, taking into account Sanmicheli's achievements in the distant colonies, decided that he deserved the honour of being commissioned to fortify this prominent site, which lay within view of the city of Venice. He began to work in about 1543, by driving a double row of piles into the marshy ground, and assembling a huge labour force which set down the first layer of stones in one go. After allowing the foundations some time to settle, he built up a stout masonry fort on top, and finished off the outside with hard-wearing Istrian stone. Some malignant spirits suggested that this wonderful work would collapse under the concussion of the firing of its own artillery, whereupon the Signoria piled a large number of its heaviest guns into the fort, and discharged them simultaneously without the slightest damage to the fabric.

What Sanmicheli did for the fortified town, the Duke of Savoy's engineer Francesco Paciotto da Urbino (1504–76) did for the design of the military citadel. In 1564 he founded the new citadel of Turin, a work which was universally admired for its regularity and the magnificence of its conception. Gabrio Busca proclaims that Paciotto was

the first engineer to make the curtains and bastions of reasonable size, and arrive at a rational allotment and distribution of the parts of fortification. For this reason we may say that he was the first man to put his profession on firm foundations. I am quite certain that nobody built so many royal fortifications as he did, whether in Flanders, Savoy, Piedmont or elsewhere in Italy. The architects who preceded him used to grope their way forward by guesswork, and they followed no regular manner in the design of their shoulder angles, flanks or curtains (Promis, 1863a, 429–30).

By the end of the sixteenth century all the advances of the earlier decades had been incorporated into a coherent system of fortification called the 'New Italian School' (Tartaglia, 1556; Cataneo, 1554; Maggi and Castriotto, 1564; da Carpi, 1570, 1584; de' Marchi, 1599; Scamozzi, 1615; Sardi, 1639). The hammer-headed bastions had by now become massive and powerful affairs, and they were grouped closely enough together to permit the whole of the intervening ground to be swept by artillery. At Sarzanello in 1497 the Genoese had devised a free-standing triangular outwork, an important new fortification which later became known as the 'ravelin'. The ravelin was placed in front of the curtain, on the same site as the old medieval barbican. Its most immediate function was to cover the gateway in the curtain wall behind. Towards the end of the sixteenth century, however, engineers came to appreciate that a sufficiently large ravelin could protect the curtain as a whole and lay down a cross-fire over the ground in front of the neighbouring bastions. For those reasons ravelins began to appear on ordinary fronts which were devoid of gates.

In the first decades of the new artillery fortification, the musketeers and the cannon had been crowded into the single line of defence which was formed by the bastions and curtains. In 1556 Tartaglia made the excellent suggestion of stationing some of the infantry in a walkway (*via coperta* or *via segreta*) which was to be cut into the top of the outer rim of the ditch. Pietro Cataneo added to the efficiency of this 'covered way' by broadening the salient and re-entrant angles of the work into 'places of arms', where large numbers of infantry could congregate for the purposes of defence or counter-attack. The ground in front of the ditch was heaped up into a bare fire-swept slope called the 'glacis', which acted as a massive parapet to the covered way, and helped to screen the masonry of the ravelins, bastions and curtains from artillery fire.

Taken together, the main rampart, the ravelin and the covered way made up a triple line of works, which formed an effective defence in depth and went far to fulfil the requirements for a true artillery fortification.

It was not altogether surprising that the bastion system should have originated in Italy. On the one hand, the Italians were the people who were the first to encounter the power of the new artillery. On the other, they were well suited by character and circumstances to devise the best counter-measures. A naval historian has discovered an illuminating parallel for the work of the influential warship-designer Cuniberti at the beginning of the twentieth century:

Ever since the Renaissance, the Italian engineering mind has always had a special capacity for viewing a project with a fresh and practical artistry. The Italian talent for stripping down to bare essentials the elements of compromise, which is the heart of all creative design, has never been surpassed (Hough, 1964, 4).

There is every reason to regard bastion fortification as a characteristic product of fifteenth- and sixteenth-century Italy, alongside more 'artistic' manifestations like painting and sculpture. Great civil building projects such as the Duomo at Milan or St Peter's at Rome gave men unrivalled experience in assembling labour and materials on the same scale that was needed for fortress construction, and provided meeting places where engineers could exchange ideas, and find patrons and colleagues who would help them to put their military designs into effect. The clearest example of this process in operation is offered by the construction of the Borgo enceinte at Rome.

Moreover the men of the Renaissance held that fortification obeyed the same laws of organic symmetry as governed all branches of architecture. According to Scamozzi, 'for a powerful and well-designed fortress, you must dispose and arrange the elements in the same way that Nature, the true teacher of all things, has ordered the parts of the human body' (Scamozzi, 1615, 191). Cataneo and Sardi expressed similar sentiments. The organic ideal was expressed in geometrical terms, reflecting contemporary advances in surveying and cartography, and perhaps also a survival of medieval obsessions with mystical symbols and numbers. The pentagon in particular was invested with a magical significance.

Programmes of fortress-building
By the middle of the sixteenth century all the major states of Italy and most of the minor ones had

14 Ravelin at Sarzanello. Probably the earliest example still standing

undertaken schemes of defence which were based on the new fortification.

The doyen of the Venetian architects, Sanmicheli, died in 1559, and his place was eventually taken by Giulio Savorgnano, one of the twenty-three sons of the vigorous old general Girolamo Savorgnano. Giulio worked at Zara, Zante, Candia and on the Cyprus fortifications, and in 1593 he co-operated with Vincenzo Scamozzi to build the important mainland fortress of Palmanova, which stood in the Friuli plain in the path of Austrian and Turkish invasions. The 1600s witnessed a lavish new Venetian expenditure on fortifications, this time prompted by the growing power of the Spanish in Lombardy. The military commentator Federico Ghislieri dal Bosco began to wonder whether all the

effort was worth while, for 'this republic will be incapable of waging offensive war as long as she keeps 15,000 and more "dead" troops locked up in her fortresses' (Promis, 1863b, 620).

If Florentine sieges tended to be feeble and long drawn-out, there was no mistaking the sense of purpose behind the fiercely-indented bastioned works which the Medici dukes were now building to overawe their cities. Significantly, one of the first works undertaken by the Medici after their restoration in 1530 was the Citadel da Basso, which was sited between the Prato and San Gallo gates of the city of Florence. The foundation stone was laid on 15 June 1534, and the building was prosecuted with great speed by Antonio da Sangallo the Younger (1485–1546). The result was a deliberately aggressive-looking polygonal fort, with narrow curtains, and acute bastions which were revetted in ashlar blocks studded with disc and diamond decorations. Only later came the fortification of the city enceinte and the hill of San Miniato, according to the designs of the former wool-merchant Giambattista Bellucci (1506–54). In the same way the subjugation of Siena was celebrated by the construction in about 1560 of the large brick-revetted citadel of Santa Barbara, planned by Baldassare Lanci on the orders of Duke Cosimo I.

The Popes were in no way outdone by the Medici dukes. Once Orvieto had been strengthened as a vital refuge immediately after the sack of Rome, the papacy could afford to look wider afield. In 1536 Antonio da Sangallo the Younger built a citadel crowning a dominating height at Ancona, the main papal port on the Adriatic coast. Nine years later work was begun on Piacenza on the plans of the same architect, so helping to defend the landward approaches to the north-west flank of the Romagna.

Rome itself was dangerously vulnerable, as was shown by episodes like the great sack of 1527, or the appearance of a Turkish fleet off the Tiber in 1534. A series of engineers completed the outer bastioned defences of the Castel Sant' Angelo, and in 1537 Paul III and his *Dieta* of architects set about the task of fortifying the Borgo (Vatican City) with nearly two miles of enceinte, ten large bastions and five main gates. The bursts of activity in the 1530s, and again in 1548, 1563 and 1613 were interspersed with long periods of lassitude brought on by lack of money, lack of interest, and stultifying arguments.

Out of all the Borgo works, none attracted wider attention than Antonio da Sangallo's elaborate and splendidly-proportioned bastion by the Porta Ardeatina, at the southern extremity of the enceinte. It was not too polite for a stranger to inquire after the cost.

Meanwhile in the far north-west corner of Italy, Duke Emanuel Philibert of Savoy (1528–80) was making a skilful job of piecing Savoy and Piedmont together again after the bout of Franco–Spanish wars which came to an end in 1559. He was a student of engineering and artillery, and he had a command of Latin and five modern languages. He therefore conceived very firm ideas on what had to be done for

the defence of his domains, and he exercised a tight personal control over the ring of gifted engineers he summoned to help him at his work: Paciotto, Vitelli, Orologi, Busca and others.

Turin was at last recovered from the French on 12 December 1562. Emanuel Philibert accordingly moved the capital thither from Chambéry, and, since the place was still encircled by French posts, he presided over the building of a powerful citadel, according to the designs of Paciotto, and ringed it with a stupendous system of brick-lined countermines. The Duke of Alva, the famous Spanish commander, was so impressed with what had been done at Turin that he whisked Paciotto off to the Netherlands and asked him to repeat the performance at Antwerp.

On the Alpine flank of his states, Emanuel Philibert set Gabrio Busca to work to strengthen the Savoyard frontier by building the castle of Montmélian, 'a fortress of a most unusual site and construction, being largely cut out of very hard rock' (Promis, 1874, 620). The duke himself designed the companion fortress at Bourg-en-Bresse, which occupied another cramped and difficult site. He completed the triangle of mountain fortresses by constructing the great stronghold of the Annunziata, which helped to overawe the heretical city of Geneva and leant some colour to the Duke's declaration that all his effort was devoted to containing Protestantism. This pious striving did not deter him from planting a fortress on the site of the monastery of Mondovi, and buying up unoffending popish church bells from the Huguenots and having them recast into cannon by Protestant German foundrymen.

All the time Emanuel Philibert was working hard to recover the rest of the alienated territories on the north Italian plain. The Spanish restored Asti and Santhià in 1575, and the Duke was still trying to persuade the French to disgorge the Marquisate of Saluzzo when he died in 1580.

To the south of Piedmont-Savoy, the coastal republic of Genoa cast around in 1536 for the best possible advice in modernising the defences of the capital city. Antonio da Sangallo the Younger proved to be too busy to attend to the work in person, but from Milan the Senate managed to

15 Defence of a bastion. The salient has been lost, but the garrison is resisting behind elaborate retrenchments inside the bastion

The Sangallo 'Family'

Francesco Giamberti (da Sangallo) (1405–80)

Smeralda = Bartolomeo Coriolani

Giuliano di Francesco Giamberti
(1445–1516)
Ostia, Poggio Imperiale, Poggibonsi

|
pupil
|

Antonio da Sangallo the Elder
(1455 or 1463–1534)
*Castel Sant' Angelo, Sarzana,
Poggio Imperiale, Nephi, Marradi,
Civita Castellana, Fucecchio,
Leghorn, Civitavecchia, Nettuno,
Caprarola*

Antonio da Sangallo the Younger
(1485–1546)
Piacenza, Orvieto, Citadel da Basso ––– colleague ·–– *Piacenza, Orvieto, Verona, Padua,
at Florence, Rome, Castro, Ancona,
Monte Fiascone*

Michele Sanmicheli
(1484–1559)
*Piacenza, Orvieto, Verona, Padua,
the Lido, Legnago, Brescia, Bergamo,
Candia, Sebonico, Corfu, Canea, Rettimo*

pupil   pupil

Nanni di Baccio Bigio
*Fano (The rival of
Michelangelo)*

Galeazzo Alghisi
*Mil. engineer. Still living
1570*

nephew

Gian Girolamo Sanmicheli ———— brother-in-law ————
Zara, Famagusta, Corfu, Sebenico

Luigi Brugnoli
Famagusta

The Savorgnano 'Family'

Girolamo Savorgnano (1466–1529)
Venetian commander, 4 wives and 23 sons

Mario Savorgnano
(c. 1513–74)
Rome

Germano Savorgnano
(1514–55)
Lyons?

Giulio Savorgnano
(1516–95)
Zara, Candia, Zante, Palmanova

colleague   colleague

Buonaiuto Lorini
(c. 1540–c. 1611)
Brescia, Palmanova

Vincenzo Scamozzi
(1522–1616)
Palmanova

The Antonelli 'Family'

Girolamo Antonelli

Antonio Antonelli

Caterina Antonelli = Giuseppe Carabelli

Giambattista Antonelli
(1531–88)
Mers-el-Kebir, Gibraltar

Battista Antonelli
(?–1615)
*Peñiscola (Spain), Havana,
San Juan del Puerto Rico*

Cristoforo Antonelli
(1560–1607)

Polidoro Antonelli

Francesco Antonelli
(1563–90)
Various fortifs. in Portugal and Africa

The Peruzzi 'Family'

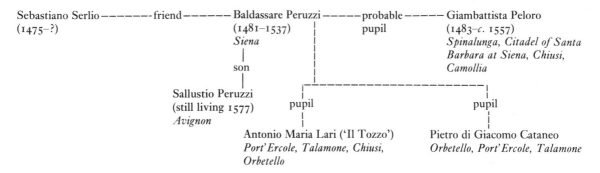

Sebastiano Serlio ------- friend ------ Baldassare Peruzzi ----- probable ----- Giambattista Peloro
(1475–?)   (1481–1537)   pupil   (1483–c. 1557)
                                            Siena   *Spinalunga, Citadel of Santa*
                                                                                                 Barbara at Siena, Chiusi,
                                              son   *Camollia*

                          Sallustio Peruzzi
                          (still living 1577)   pupil   pupil
                          Avignon

                                    Antonio Maria Lari ('Il Tozzo')   Pietro di Giacomo Cataneo
                                    Port' Ercole, Talamone, Chiusi,   *Orbetello, Port' Ercole, Talamone*
                                    Orbetello

The Genga 'Family'

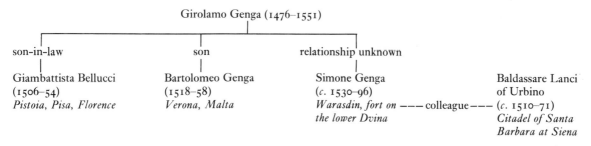

Girolamo Genga (1476–1551)

son-in-law   son   relationship unknown

Giambattista Bellucci   Bartolomeo Genga   Simone Genga   Baldassare Lanci
(1506–54)   (1518–58)   (c. 1530–96)   of Urbino
Pistoia, Pisa, Florence *Verona, Malta*   *Warasdin, fort on* --- colleague --- (c. 1510–71)
                                                 the lower Dvina   *Citadel of Santa*
                                                                               Barbara at Siena

Other 'Families'

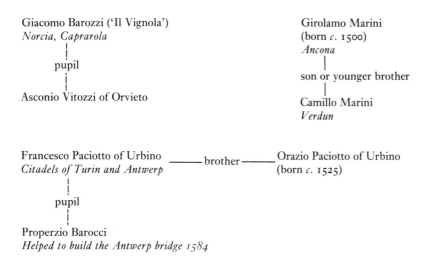

Giacomo Barozzi ('Il Vignola')   Girolamo Marini
Norcia, Caprarola   (born c. 1500)
                                         Ancona
          pupil
                                         son or younger brother

Asconio Vitozzi of Orvieto   Camillo Marini
                                         Verdun

Francesco Paciotto of Urbino ------ brother ------ Orazio Paciotto of Urbino
Citadels of Turin and Antwerp   (born c. 1525)

          pupil

Properzio Barocci
Helped to build the Antwerp bridge 1584

16   'Families' of Italian engineers

obtain the services of Giovanni Maria Oligati, who had the advantage of having been born in Genoa. Oligati planned a bastioned enceinte for the immediate urban area, and the news of an unexpected passage of French troops into Italy gave a new impetus to the work. The citizens made some large voluntary contributions, and the landward defences were completed in essentials in 1538, which was a very short time indeed.

In the seventeenth century the increasing power of artillery, together with the ambitions of Piedmont-Savoy, induced the Genoese to carry the line of defence well inland to the summits of the hills which overlooked the city. Work on the *Nuove Mura* began in 1627, and the vast twelve-mile circuit was mostly finished by 1633.

Only Genoa's relative commercial prosperity enabled the republic to entertain mighty undertakings such as these. A common feature of all the new plans of bastioned defence was their immense cost. Thus the Pope himself found it difficult to cast an enceinte around the Vatican (see p. 36), while even the model Venetian fortress of Palmanova, as built, represented a twenty-five per cent reduction on the scope of the original plan. For a struggling little state like Siena the burden proved to be catastrophic. In the interests of cohesion, the embattled republic made the decision to defend as many as possible of its component towns in the face of the Imperial attack of 1553. The antiquated financial system was quite unequal to the strain. By prodigies of effort a dozen or so strongpoints were put in an adequate state of defence, but as a consequence the republic was left without troops or supplies to face the second and fatal onslaught of 1554–5.

The Renaissance engineer

The Italian military engineer enters our period as the characteristic Renaissance jack-of-all-trades. The tradition of versatility goes back at least as far as Filippo Brunelleschi (1377–1477), one of the leading lights of the early Renaissance, who designed two citadels at Pisa, as well as building the famous dome of Florence cathedral.

The progress from one branch of learning to another was natural and easy. Francesco di Giorgio Martini began his professional life as a sculptor, and then took up bronze-founding after metal statuary came into fashion. This experience equipped him to cast artillery, and thus gave him an insight into the wider field of military affairs. Likewise Michelangelo Buonarotti, who is now remembered chiefly for his titanic struggles with blocks of marble and the ceiling of the Sistine Chapel, was also renowned in his own time as a military engineer. He did not regard his essays in fortification as being in any way inferior to the rest of his *oeuvre*, and in 1545, in the course of an argument with Antonio da Sangallo the Younger, he gave vent to the astonishing statement that

I don't know very much about painting and sculpture, but I have gained a great experience of fortifications, and I have already proved that I know more about them than do you and the whole tribe of the Sangallos (Clauses, 1900–2, II, 351).

The Italian architects of the sixteenth century managed their affairs very well without the support of anything that resembled a modern engineering corps. Their genius for association enabled them to group themselves together in Mafia-like bands which were contained by ties of blood, companionship and patronage. Several such 'families' may be identified, though it is easier to trace their ramifications diagrammatically than in prose. At a lower level we encounter family groups of skilled fortress masons, from Lucca and other places, who hired themselves out through the medium of subcontractors. They were paid by the measure, and not by the day, and in the long run their services proved to be cheaper than those of unskilled low-paid labourers.

Every now and then the building of particularly ambitious fortifications or churches would cause members of several engineer families to associate for a common purpose. Martini, Giuliano da Maiana, Giuliano da Sangallo, Fra Giocondo, Benedetto da Maiana and Antonio Marchesi da Settignano are all known to have worked in Naples some time between 1484 and 1495. Similarly in the next generation the construction of the Borgo fortifications at Rome brought together Michelangelo, Antonio da Sangallo the Younger, Giovanni Mangone, Galeazzo

Alghisi, Jacopo da Ferrara, Bellucci, Castriotto, Laparelli and Marchi.

The concept of loyalty to a particular state or regime seems to have weighed fairly lightly upon most engineers. Pietro Cataneo wrote *I Quattro Primi Libri d'Architettura* (Venice, 1554) as an apparently whole-hearted servant of the Sienese Republic. He later added four more books, and incorporated them with the earlier ones and coolly presented the whole to his new master Francesco de' Medici, as conqueror of Siena and Grand Duke of Tuscany. Leonardo da Vinci nowadays appears as one of the towering figures of the Renaissance, and yet his contemporaries seem to have regarded him as little more than a foot-loose dilettante. His note-books were full of doodlings of old-fashioned catapults and bombards, and he peddled his limited capacity as a practical engineer to the Venetian Republic, the Pope and the king of France. He died in 1519 at the palace of Amboise, where he had earned his keep as a deviser of mechanical entertainments for festivities.

We have already seen that when the Florentine Republic stood in mortal danger in 1529, Michelangelo felt some of the urgings of patriotism which befitted a great man, and not just a great artist. However he could not compare in purity of republican principle with Baldassare Peruzzi, who was sent by Pope Clement to help in the siege, but refused to have anything to do with the unholy work.

In the middle decades of the sixteenth century the Italian architect began to lose something of his splendid versatility:

It was a time when the field of human knowledge had grown to the point at which a single individual was no longer able to master it in all its aspects and when the accumulated knowledge had to be divided into a number of as yet loosely defined segments, each of which became the focus of attention for groups of newly emerging specialists . . . . Sanmicheli and Antonio da Sangallo the Younger were at once the last dual-purpose architects who worked in both civil and military architecture, and the first representatives of the new trend of specialisation (La Croix, 1963, 273–4).

Another significant development was the way the Italian engineers dispersed over all the nations of Europe and some of their most distant colonies. Military skills at that time were still very much a matter of national speciality. Just as the Swiss were famed for their pikemen, or the Spanish for their musketeers, so the Italians were prized by all the warring parties as the masters of the novel science of artillery fortification. We saw a smaller phenomenon after World War II, when the Americans and Russians set their hands on the German missile experts.

Where Italian engineers were not available, or where they were not trusted, native architects did their best to imitate the southern style. Thus all over Europe there sprang up little military Italies, whether works of authentic Italian construction, like the citadel of Antwerp and the fortress of Navarrens in the Pyrenees, or home-grown renderings such as Meister Johann's enceinte at Düsseldorf. Most striking of all, perhaps, is the example of the still well-preserved granite fortification of Berwick-upon-Tweed, which was begun among the links of the Northumbrian coast by Sir Richard Lee.

Even the Spanish, as fellow-Catholics, did not like to overburden the Italians with their confidences. Luis Collado, writing in 1592, argued that Spanish artillery officers ought to make themselves acquainted with engineering matters, for the engineers 'for the most part are foreigners who, on the least excuse, will go over to the enemy camp on the next day' (Vigon, 1947, I, 129).

An Italian historian is at pains to explain that the notorious restlessness of the engineers did not proceed from capricious instability:

We must put ourselves in the position of these men. They were short of money, and yet they were aware of their own talents and regarded themselves as superior beings who moved among folk who were less civilised than the Italians. They were upset by the example of the few men among them who rose to the highest ranks, and they were liable to go off and serve any distant prince who attracted them by tempting promises. And yet they did not end up any better off – their creditors were many, their purses light, and the expense of long journeys made it difficult for them to return to their homeland. They had to put up with the scorn which the soldiers reserved for those among their comrades who tried to combine the theory of war with the weapons of war . . . . The Spanish offered perhaps one exception, for their indolence and their trading connections with Italy helped them to get on rather well with the Italians. At the same time the Spaniards could never forget that they were masters. They were not at all inclined to obey or respect inferior people who did not have Castilian blood flowing in their veins (Promis, 1874, 541).

Three   The Frontiers of France 1513–59

France on the defensive 1513–50

The northern border

Sometimes the late medieval mind defies penetration. In 1494, seized by a fit of strategic madness, Charles VIII delivered vast tracts of the French borderlands to powers which, by any sane reckoning, ought to have been counted the natural enemies of his kingdom. Cerdagne and Roussillon went to the Spaniards, giving them a foothold on the northern side of the Pyrenees. Worse still, Louis ceded Franche-Comté and Artois to Maximilian of Austria. The purpose of all this largesse was to buy a free hand to pursue the Italian wars, those ventures which brought calamity to Italy, and came close to visiting the same on France. These losses represented the rough equivalent of a century of campaigning, and they forced a united population of fifteen million people into decades of disadvantageous defensive.

The borders of France in the early sixteenth century ran at almost every point well within the modern demarcation, and seldom rested on adequate geographical barriers. Along nearly every sector the advantage of the higher ground lay with the enemy, and the thin line of French fortresses touched for only brief stretches on major rivers such as the Saône or Meuse. Indeed the Somme and the Marne were the only water obstacles completely in the command of the French.

Considered as a whole, the northern and eastern frontiers took the shape of a long double curve. The first arm fell back from the Channel coast at Boulogne to the Somme at Abbeville, then slowly bulged forward again to an apex at Sainte-Menehould and Bar-le-Duc, facing the Moselle gap. From there the line fell gradually back by way of Langres to the Côte d'Or at Dijon and Beaune, and terminated at the border of the territory of Bresse, which was the north-eastern outpost of Piedmont-Sardinia.

Now to turn back along the same line, and follow the chain of fortresses in more detail. The south-eastern sector was fairly secure, for the Imperial territory of Franche-Comté was contained by the ninety-mile chain of strongholds which extended north from the Saône at Chalon-sur-Saône and Seurre (which was re-fortified by Francis I) by way of Beaune and Dijon to the plateau of Langres, the great watershed of northern France. The line of fortresses was certainly thin, but in compensation hostile Franche-Comté was wedged against Switzerland and was difficult to support from the Empire. Only once in this period did it form the path for an offensive, when Maximilian paid the Swiss to go out and attack Dijon in 1513.

The real danger lay elsewhere along the frontier, where the upper reaches of the Moselle, Meuse and Scheldt snaked into France, bearing provisions and siege guns from the great cities of Germany and the Netherlands.

Northwards from the plateau of Langres, where we last left off, Champagne and Paris were threatened by a group of neutral or actively hostile lands

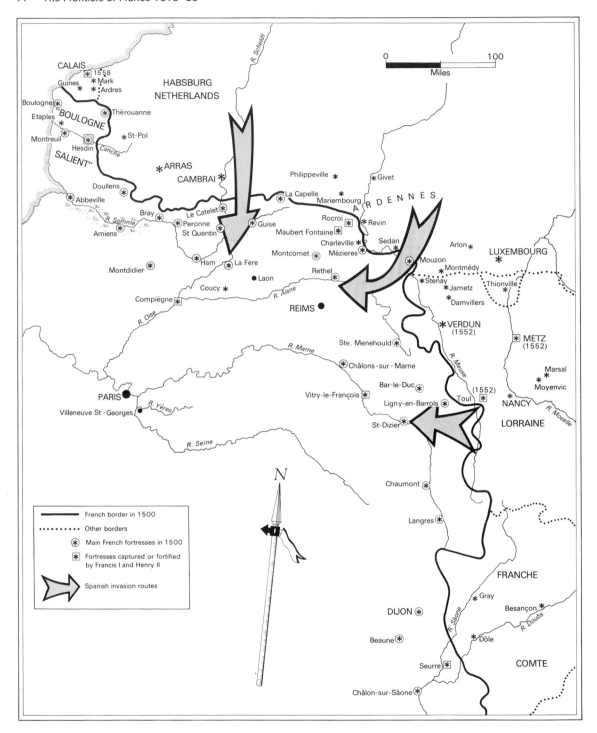

North and north-east France in the sixteenth and early seventeenth centuries

which pressed forward to the Meuse. These were the independent duchy of Lorraine, the three bishoprics of Metz, Toul and Verdun, and the Ardennes regions of Luxembourg and the south-eastern Netherlands. Charles v had the right to call on these territories to afford him passage and assistance as Emperor of Germany and ultimate ruler of the Netherlands.

Along the threatened Champagne frontier the French strongholds assumed the character of a double barrier. The outer perimeter of Ligny-en-Barrois, Bar-le-Duc and Sainte-Menehould ran behind the Argonne hills to where Sedan and Mézières retained a tenuous grip on a short stretch of the Meuse. Along the Marne there extended a rearward chain of fortresses: Chaumont, Saint-Dizier, Vitry-le-François (fortified by Francis I) and Châlons-sur-Marne.

Westwards now, the fortress line reached across Maubert-Fontaine, Montcornet and Guise, all disadvantageously placed on the slopes of the Ardennes, to Saint-Quentin near the source of the Somme. From Saint-Quentin the Somme pushed through the chalk hills of Picardy to the sea as an ever-widening trench, its floor filled with myriad channels, lakes and marshes, and its most important crossings defended by the fortresses or castles at Ham, Péronne, Bray, Amiens and Abbeville.

With the lower Somme as a base line, an important salient ran along the Channel coast to Boulogne, which stood no more than twenty miles from the English possession of Calais, and within sight of the coast of Kent. This salient into the Netherlands was stronger than it seemed. The English could dash out from Calais and isolate Boulogne easily enough, but they were ill-advised to advance any further without clearing Thérouanne, a small but strong fortress which was situated amid marshes and woods on the left bank of the Lys and at the head of the Roman road to Arras. Thérouanne had been mentioned in the commentaries of Julius Caesar, and successive kings of France had fortified it to 'act as a bulwark and frontier against the English and the Flemings, among whose territory it was buried. Over the years it inflicted a great deal of damage upon them, and frustrated several enterprises which were directed against Picardy'

(Rabutin, 1850, 450). With Boulogne and Thérouanne taken, or at least blockaded, there still lay in front of the English the river Canche. The Canche was no great barrier in itself, but it was defended by the fortresses of Montreuil and Hesdin, which could embarrass any offensives aimed at the line of the Somme.

From these details emerges the pattern of the northern French wars of the first half of the sixteenth century: a struggle to hold off English and Imperialist forces which were disposed in an arc never more than 150 miles from Paris.

French military men were alive to the catastrophic effects if the monarchy ever lost the capital. As Marshal de Tavannes commented (1850, 35), 'great empires and powers must be attacked in their hearts and guts'. Henry II was of the same persuasion, and he wisely rejected the advice of the people who wanted him to abandon Paris after the disaster of Saint-Quentin in 1557.

Francis I did everything that lay within his power to bolster up his frontier by artificial means. Since Italian engineering was in fashion, he went to the expense of hiring the ex-papal engineer Girolamo Marini who 'was reckoned to be the greatest man in Italy for besieging fortresses' (Montluc, 1571, I, 129). Girolamo came to France in 1534 in the company of his younger brother (or son) Camillo and five of their countrymen. They were just the vanguard of a host of engineers, and by 1543 no less than one hundred of the Italians were working under the direction of Girolamo on the fortifications of Luxembourg.

France owed a good deal to the tenuous line of her scattered fortresses, but still more to the lack of purpose among her enemies. In the early years of the century grand strategic plans were rare and ill-managed. As long as the German princes remained indifferent, and the Netherlands were committed to neutrality, the Emperor could offer his English and Spanish allies little more than encouraging noises. When the Netherlands came to be directly involved in the wars, during the reign of Charles v, the conditions were much more favourable for a combined offensive. But in the event the allies fumbled and miscalculated in 1552 and again in 1553. Even the ambitious and royal 'Enterprise of

Paris' of 1544 merely demonstrated that the king of England and the emperor of Germany, for all their lofty viewpoints, were just as liable as any of their subordinates to forget what they were about and waste a campaign sitting down before some wretched frontier fortress.

By the time that wars on a large scale broke out on the northern frontiers of France, the military capabilities of Spain, Austria and France had been amply tested in the Italian theatre. England, however, embarked on Continental warfare for the first time in several decades with the Artois campaign of 1513, and her military prowess remained an unknown quantity for long after that date. With the decay of the old magic of 'bow and bill', King Henry VIII was forced to hire foreign pikemen, cavalry and arquebusiers in order to have an army fit to take the field on the Continent. According to Fleurange (1850, 39), the native English were 'good people, who put up a stout fight in broken and naturally strong terrain', but he added that they and their bows were of little avail outside defensive positions.

It was a rather different story with fortress warfare, since the English sieges were the equal of any in display and noise. Henry matched the Marinis and Mellonis of the French with a hired Italian of his own, the failed painter Girolamo Pennacchi ('Girolamo da Trevigli'), and by the middle of the century the English production of artillery compared in quantity and quality with any in Europe, due largely to habits acquired in casting great numbers of guns for the new English navy. Iron cannon were first manufactured on a large scale in England, if not actually invented there, and in 1543 the foreign specialists Peter Baude and Peter of Cologne devised at Greenwich some of the first recorded explosive bombs, 'hollow shot of cast-iron stuffed with fireworks, fitted with screws of iron to receive a match to carry fire kindled, that the fireworks might be set on fire, to break in pieces the same hollow shot, whereof the smallest piece hitting any man did kill or spoil him' (Stowe, quoted in Oman, 1937, 351).

The wars

In 1513 the English opened the campaigns in the northern theatre by setting themselves down before Thérouanne with a host of 31,000 troops. 'This multitude encamped in a mass, and according to the old custom of the English they surrounded their quarters with trenches, waggons and ramparts of timber. Artillery was planted all around the perimeter, and the whole gave the impression of a walled town which enclosed the troops' (Guicciardini, 1562, Bk XII).

Thérouanne was persuaded to submit on 22 August, after an army of relief had been defeated in the Battle of the Spurs, and King Henry razed the offending fortress to the ground.

However, the year 1514 found the English and their Imperialist friends in no fit state to prosecute the war on the northern frontier. Henry therefore came to terms with the French, and restored to them what was left of Thérouanne.

In 1521 the Imperialists for the first time took a direct part in the northern campaigns, setting in train a struggle which was going to last, with intermissions, for the best part of three centuries. In that year an Imperial army under Count Henry of Nassau bore down on perhaps the weakest sector of the frontier, where the Ardennes fronted onto the Meuse, and no more than a thin crust of fortresses – Mouzon, Sedan and Mézières – stood between the invaders and Champagne. Mouzon fell after a feeble resistance, making it all the more urgent for the French to cling onto Mézières, 'for if it fell the province of Champagne would be in a bad way' (Mailles, n.d., 250).

Nassau duly presented himself before Mézières on 21 September 1521, expecting the same easy success as at Mouzon. He prosecuted the siege in the usual Imperialist fashion, bringing up fifty-eight cannon and firing over five thousand rounds in a single period of four days. He soon discovered that he had underestimated the fibre of the French commander, the Chevalier de Bayard, who hastily reinforced the defences, launched damaging sorties, and led the Imperialists astray by allowing false dispatches to fall into their hands. Bayard's resistance gave time for Francis to bring up the field army, which forced the enemy to abandon the siege on 27 September. For years afterwards the priests of the town, at the end of their prayers for the king, used to add the phrase, 'and for Bayard, who saved the kingdom of France' (ibid., 250).

Just as the English in Calais remained supine in 1521, and let their allies fail before Mézières, so in 1522 the Duke of Suffolk spent several weeks in a vain blockade of Hesdin, allegedly the 'weakest fortress along the whole frontier' (Bellay, 1569, 168), and received not the slightest help from the Imperialists. The apparently simple act of working together on the same theatre seemed to be quite beyond the power of the allies.

The later wars on the northern frontier were prosecuted in much the same way, with the allies launching isolated, unsupported offensives which shattered on the resistance of lone French fortresses. In 1536 our old friend Henry of Nassau broke his teeth on Péronne, the guardian fortress of the Somme. The French plucked up courage, and in the following year King Francis launched a successful 'pre-emptive' attack in the Boulogne salient. Now that the allies were cleared from the area, Francis set about fortifying Saint-Pol on the urging of 'an Italian engineer, Antonio da Castello by name, who boasted that within six weeks he would make the town impregnable against the whole world, not to mention the Emperor' (ibid., 441). Trusting in the Italian's assurances, Francis drew back his army towards the Somme, only to give the Imperialists the opportunity to pounce on Saint-Pol in June, wreck the half-completed works with their usual violent cannonades, and sweep in and massacre the garrison. Montreuil fell in its turn, but Thérouanne was still holding out when peace restored all the fortresses of the Boulogne salient to France. No wonder that the French began to speculate whether the Italian engineers were always as competent as they claimed.

In the 1540s all the belligerents began to attach much more importance to the northern theatre than in earlier times. With his gaze at last torn away from Italy, Francis set the pace by going over to the attack with powerful forces in 1542 and 1543. He was rewarded with the capture of Arlon and Luxembourg on the Meuse-Ardennes sector of the frontier. Military opinion was in favour of re-fortifying Arlon

as the eastern bastion of a new French border, but for dynastic reasons the king insisted that Luxembourg must be strengthened instead, 'saying that it was his inheritance, and that if the Emperor was unreasonable enough to hang on to the Duchy of Milan, he, by the same forcible means, and with still more justification, could retain Luxembourg' (ibid., 517). Here Francis showed himself in the same unrealistically optimistic light as in his Italian campaigns of 1515 and 1524–5. He did not appreciate that Arlon would have been a much better choice. Its compact hilltop site was easier to fortify than the straggling rock plateau of Luxembourg, while its situation near the French frontier placed it within convenient reach of support.

The Emperor Charles v had spent the same year in a very profitable manner, by swallowing up the lands of the Duke of Gelders, an old and useful ally of the French. He took Düren and Jülich in August, and he forced the Duke to make his submission.

In 1544 Henry of England and Emperor Charles turned their undivided attention to Francis, who was now ageing like themselves, and undertook their only powerful and well-concerted invasion of his kingdom.

This time the Imperialists came across the frontier further south than ever before, seeking to turn the fortresses which were springing up along the Netherlands frontier. They starved Luxembourg into capitulation on 6 June, which cleared their right flank; and by taking Ligny-en-Barrois later in the month they opened up a good line of communication through Lorraine. Only Saint-Dizier, in the rearward line of French fortresses, still barred their way through Champagne. Here they were stuck fast until 18 August.

Effectively the Emperor had shot his bolt, for the long siege of Saint-Dizier had consumed his provisions, and he shrank from the ordeal of crossing the dusty chalk plains of the Champagne Pouilleuse. At Crépy on 18 September Charles therefore came to terms with the French and restored the frontier to its pre-war state. The English were left in the lurch.

Henry VIII and his men had sat down before Boulogne on 19 July. Their hired Italian engineer, Girolamo Pennacchi, was anxious to do his best, for the king had awarded him a salary of £5,000, and allowed him to build a fine house at the royal expense. After a few days of happy fort-building, however, he was cut in two by a cannon ball and all his good intentions went for nothing. An Englishman unfeelingly described the event as something 'which would save the king five thousand pounds' (Oman, 1937, 344).

After a creditable five-week defence the governor surrendered Boulogne on 13 September. The news of the Emperor's deal with the French arrived only a little later, and the discouraged Henry shipped the greater part of his army back to England. Only four thousand troops were left in France, and from then onwards the operations were confined to artillery duels across the lower Liane and a half-hearted French blockade of Boulogne. In 1550 a peace treaty finally restored the place to the French.

All the campaigning of the Emperor and the rival kings had done singularly little to change the strategic map of France. Charles and Henry had failed in all their more ambitious undertakings, while Francis never advanced his borders beyond the disadvantageous line which had been bequeathed to him.

The one permanent achievement of Francis was to consolidate the existing frontier into the solid base-line which was to be the foundation for the conquests of Henry II, Louis XIII and Louis XIV. Particularly valuable was his work for the Champagne frontier in the 1540s. He strengthened the existing fortresses of Maubert-Fontaine, Mézières and Mouzon, and built an entirely new stronghold on the west bank of the Meuse at Villefranche-sur-

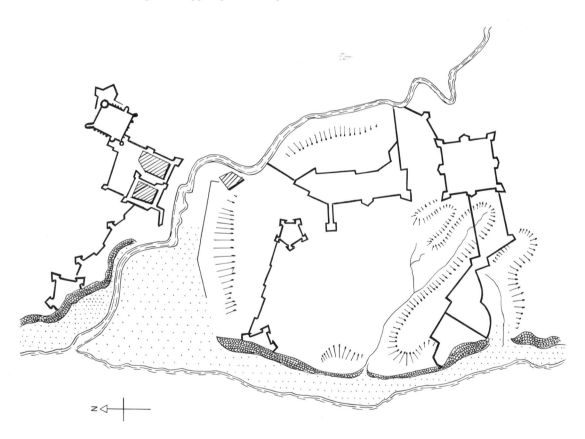

17   Boulogne. A plan of actual and projected works in the period of the English occupation. On the north bank of the Liane the English have reinforced the town by bastioned works (among the first they ever built). South of the Liane can be seen the pentagonal Fort d'Outreau and the other fortifications of the French camp

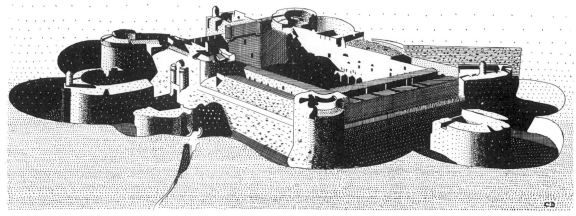

18 Salses. Henri de Campion observed in 1639: 'Salses is built in the flat country of Roussillon, out of cannon shot from the mountains. In any case its ramparts are proof against artillery, for they are thirty-six feet thick, and the parapets sixteen. At the four corners there are four towers of the same thickness, as well as a donjon or redoubt between two of these towers. The whole is countermined. The dry, brick-revetted ditch is extremely wide and deep, and there is an excellent counterscarp. In short, as all-masonry fortresses go, I believe it is the best in Europe.'

Meuse, a site which helped to nullify Stenay, which was in the hands of the Duke of Lorraine. Charles V duly countered by strengthening Damvillers, and by constructing a small fortress much further down river at Revin, due east of Rocroi. Inland, well within the frontier, Francis built the stronghold which still bears his name, Vitry-le-François, which filled the wide gap between Châlons-sur-Marne and Saint-Dizier, and completed a second line of fortresses facing Lorraine.

The Pyrenean frontier

On the southern frontier a curious polarity reduced both the French and the Spanish to defensive campaigning. At the western end of the Pyrenees lay the territory of Navarre, 'a kingdom though of small extent and revenues, yet very commodious in its situation' (Guicciardini, 1562, Bk XI). As long as it lay in the hands of the Albret dynasty, Navarre offered the French a bridge into Spain at Fuenterrabia (where the Pyrenees met the Bay of Biscay) and a potential staging-post on the road to Madrid at Pamplona.

Conversely, on the eastern end of the mountain chain, the misguided generosity of Charles VIII had delivered to the Spanish the lands of Cerdagne and Roussillon, which gave them a deep and wide foothold extending from the peaks of the Pyrenees northwards to the edge of the coastal plain of Languedoc. The fortress of Perpignan acted as the citadel of Spanish power in this part of the world, and it possessed an important outpost further north along the main coastal road at Salses, where Don Ramirez completed a powerful fortress in 'reinforced castle' style in 1503.

Thus the French and Spanish were preoccupied with pinching out the threatening enemy salient, each on his own side of the Pyrenees. More far-reaching offensive opportunities were ignored.

The advantage, if not the glory, of these Pyrenean campaigns lay undoubtedly with the Spaniards. They overran the kingdom of Navarre in 1513, and, although the French again recovered Pamplona in 1521, the Spaniards never entirely lost their initial advantage at this western end of the Pyrenees.

At the far, eastern end of the mountain chain, King Francis launched a determined attempt to push the enemy from Roussillon in 1542.

On 23 August of that year the Dauphin began the siege of Perpignan, 'the main, or rather the only barrier and bulwark of the Spaniards on the southern theatre' (Bellay, 1569, 490). At forty thousand strong the army seemed strong enough for its task, but 'the town was so amply furnished with platforms mounting artillery, that it seemed like a porcupine . . . presenting points in all directions' (ibid., 494). The technical director of the siege works, Girolamo Marini, ignored reliable reconnaissance reports, and chose to attack a particularly strong stretch of the walls. So it was that a month later the works were no farther forward, and the army was still encamped in the sandy plain, now sodden with the rains of autumn. Francis wisely ordered the siege to be raised, and until the next century the Spanish were left in undisturbed possession of their bridgehead beyond the Pyrenees.

France on the offensive 1552–9

Henry II and his band of captains
Francis I died in 1547, and the period of fanciful adventures in French campaigning came to an end. It was replaced by a way of conducting war that was much more purposeful. The new king, Henry II, delighted in siege warfare as much as his predecessor, but in place of mad enterprises like the campaign of Pavia this sombre man set himself the task of pushing the northern frontiers onto more advantageous and tenable ground. His objectives were limited and realistic, and they were pursued by a team of commanders who were unsurpassed in the France of their century. Not even Henry IV had such a talented band at his disposal.

The high commander Francis of Lorraine, Duke of Guise (1519–63) earned the praise of officers who were not always generous in their encomiums. He chatted easily with generals and men in their native dialects, and he set a standard of close involvement in siege operations which was going to be imitated by Henry III (as Duke of Anjou) and by Henry IV.

At the same time Guise imposed an unusually severe measure of restraint on the appetites of his troops. He forbade the men to subject conquered fortresses to sack, even after such a hard siege as at Thionville in 1558, and when he was on the defensive he husbanded their rations and carefully portioned them out. The prolonged resistance at

Metz in 1552, Siena in 1554–5 and Saint-Quentin in 1557 would scarcely have been possible if the French commanders had not learnt to curb the guzzling of their garrisons. Things had once been very different. Branthôme heard old officers say

that in earlier times there was a very bad and stupid custom by which the opening of the enemy battering fire was the signal for everyone inside a besieged town to live as they wished, pillaging, ravaging and taking provisions wherever they were to be found. Food-stocks were eaten up in no time at all, and towns in those days could be taken at the drop of a hat, as the saying goes (Branthôme, 1858–78, book I, part 2).

Strategically, Guise excelled in the practice of moving his army at a great speed from one sector of the northern frontier to another, so that they could take a town before the enemy could intervene.

As for the technical direction of the sieges, a large part was taken by Marshal Piero Strozzi, a blasphemous Florentine atheist who was reckoned to be 'mightily industrious and a very great engineer' (ibid., book I, part 1).

The enterprising spirit of Guise and the engineering expertise of Strozzi were backed up by a generation of guns and gunners created by Jean d'Estrées, the Grand Master and Captain General of the Artillery. This tall commanding veteran, savage in temper, and of frightening aspect in his long beard, had trained up a school of young gunner officers, mostly Protestant like himself, and had cast a new range of cannon which were capable of firing one hundred rounds in rapid succession. 'Before the new manufacture, our guns were of much poorer quality. They were exceedingly fragile and they had to be washed out with vinegar and other liquids, which was a laborious business' (ibid., book I, part 2).

Below ground the French seemed to have looked mostly to renegade English miners. One Englishman called 'Lauxfort' was prominent in the defence of Saint-Quentin in 1557, and several of his compatriots were employed in the next year by Guise against Thionville.

Guise and his generation were in every way qualified to have taken over the role of conquerors

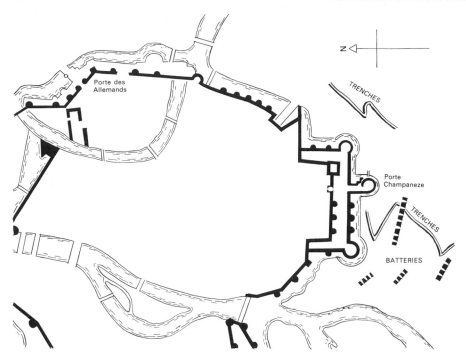

19 The siege of Metz 1552/53, showing the Imperial attack against the multiple defences on the southern sector of the town

which later fell to the generals of Louis XIV. Taking everything into account, Europe was fortunate that the energies of the French were so very soon going to be diverted into civil war.

The last war against the Imperialists and English
Looking at the progress of the Emperor by the middle of the century, and how he had annexed the free towns of Cambrai, Utrecht and Liège to the Netherlands, the Sieur de Vieilleville urged his own King Henry II to take advantage of Charles's troubles with the German Protestants and make some conquests on the upper Moselle. By taking the independent Three Bishoprics of Metz, Toul and Verdun the king would create 'an impregnable rampart for Champagne and Picardy, and open a fine free road along which we could advance to take the Duchy of Luxembourg and all the country as far as Brussels' (Vieilleville, 1850, 123).

Henry accepted Vieilleville's reasoning, and an army of 35,000 French accordingly overran the Three Bishoprics in April 1552. Where Francis would have now rested on his laurels, Henry went on in June to reinforce the left flank of his conquests by reducing the fortresses of Damvillers and Yvoy, 'the two towns which above all others were pernicious and harmful to his poor subjects' (Rabutin, 1850, 424). Damvillers fell to the thunder of thirty cannon, while Yvoy was cracked open by no fewer than fifty-two pieces, of which thirty-four were brought to bear on the main breach. The cannonade of Yvoy represented the first major test of d'Estrées' new artillery, and showed that the French were fully the match of the Imperialists in the gun-power of their siege operations.

Charles patched up his quarrels with the Protestants and moved west to reclaim Metz for the Empire. The scale of his preparations, and the employment of an army of some 45,000 men, made the coming operation the greatest siege since the attack on Padua in 1509. On 19 October 1552 the Duke of Alva with the Imperial advance guard came within sight of the fortress, and Emperor Charles arrived at the scene in person one month later.

The destiny of Metz lay in the hands of the Duke of Guise, who conducted a model defence with the help of Camillo Marini and the French engineer Saint-Rémy, 'men who were very expert and skilled in the matter of fortifications' (Salignac, 1850, 514). Amongst other measures they cast up a 'double Pisan rampart' behind the threatened sector of the enceinte on the right (eastern) bank of the Moselle.

At noon on 28 November, after a severe pounding, the curtain between the old towers of Massieux and Ligniers began to lean outwards, and at two in the afternoon, to the joy of the Imperialists, the whole stretch collapsed onto the fausse-braye. The enemy fell silent again when the air cleared of dust, and there was shown a steep heap of fragments supported by the fausse-braye, and behind it the bank of the new earthen rampart, bristling with planted colours and levelled arquebuses. The ghosts of the old defenders of Pisa must have gibbered with delight.

December came, but still the Emperor clung on tenaciously before Metz. The French wondered at

trenches which were as spacious, broad and deep as any which have been seen for a long time, and at the great quantities of guns and ammunition, and the countless gabions which the Emperor made his pioneers construct and fill without rest. He took no more account of the lives of these wretched people than of brute beasts, and he left them at the mercy of the gunfire from the town (Rabutin, 1850, 441).

The Germans were 'in mud up to their ears' (intercepted letter from Alva, in Vieilleville, 1850, 170), and the trenches were invariably packed with troops. 'This old man is obstinate!' exclaimed the Duke of Guise (Guise, 1850, 137).

The Emperor certainly had the determination to continue the struggle to the end, but he could do little to fight the ill-will of the Protestant contingents, or the bitter frosts which were blackening and killing the ears and toes of the men in the trenches. The Imperialists finally gave up. Charles and the main army marched away at the beginning of January 1553, leaving Margrave Albert of Brandenburg for a few days more to complete the laborious business of dragging away the remaining guns through the mud and slush.

Like most commanders of those days, the Emperor had little feeling for the best moment to call a retreat; an offensive or a siege was usually pressed to the utmost, and if it failed it was immediately succeeded by catastrophe. As in Provence in 1536, so at Metz in 1552–3, the scale of the disaster was in keeping with the size of Charles's forces and the tenacity with which he had kept them at their task. When the French came out to view the wreckage of the Imperial camp

the sight was more reminiscent of the ruin left behind by a beaten army rather than one which had merely raised a siege. There were wretched men on all sides, some half-dead, and some lying ill in their quarters, where we could hear them groaning . . . large burial-grounds were everywhere. The freshly churned-up roads were strewn with dead horses, tents, weapons and other abandoned equipment (Salignac, 1850, 555–6).

In the following years the French consolidated their hold on Metz by strengthening the town walls and building a citadel which

was truly admirable in its perfection. On this model have been built all the other French citadels, whether at Calais, Lyon or on the other frontiers of the kingdom. The citadel dashed the last hopes of the princes of the Empire of ever recovering Metz and the other towns which the Crown of France had snatched from them on this side of the Rhine (Vieilleville, 1850, 348).

In the long term the effects of reducing the Three Bishoprics were immense, for the French had driven a wedge between the Netherlands and Luxembourg on one side, and the Duchy of Lorraine on the other. The apex of the conquests reached to the Moselle, while the base rested solidly on a hundred-mile stretch of the upper Meuse.

By the midsummer of 1554 the French were ready to resume the attack. They made a brief but well-calculated offensive in the western Ardennes, and entrenched themselves in the region by fortifying the village of Rocroi, a 'wonderfully fine, strong and convenient site, well-suited for building a fortress and depôt' (Rabutin, 1850, 536). Originally intended to serve as a link between Maubert-Fontaine and Mariembourg, Rocroi eventually became more important than either of them, for it commanded the only practicable road over the Ardennes on the western side of the Meuse.

The war languished for the next two years, while the Spanish and Austrians sorted out the complicated legacy of Charles v, who abdicated in 1555, his spirit broken by his failure at Metz. Ferdinand, the former emperor's brother, took over Austria and the claim to the Imperial crown, while Charles's son Philip received Spain, with the Netherlands, Franche-Comté, Milan, Naples and the New World.

The name of the new monarch was celebrated by Philippeville, a fortress which the Dutch engineer Sebastian van Noyen had just begun at an important road junction ten miles north of Mariembourg.

By marrying Queen Mary of England, Philip ii of Spain was able to conjure up an English contingent to help him to revive the struggle on the southern border of the Netherlands. In the late summer of 1557 he sent an army of fifty thousand Spaniards, Netherlanders, Germans and English against the fortress of Saint-Quentin on the upper Somme. The Duke of Guise and the better part of the French forces were away in Italy, and on 27 August the allies wrested the place from the weak garrison by storm.

The French troops from Italy returned at the end of the year, long after most people considered that the issue of the campaign had been settled. Guise, however, was not the kind of man to allow himself to be ruled by circumstances; instead he took up an old suggestion of Coligny's and turned against Calais.

Calais and the fat Terre d'Oye formed the last remnant of the old English empire in France, and posed a constant threat to the flank of French armies operating from the Boulogne salient against the Netherlands. The territory as a whole formed an oblong, roughly eight miles broad and eleven long, with the river Aa covering the east, and the fortresses of Ardres and Guines closing up the south-west. The Channel washed the northern side of the Terre d'Oye and the fortress of Calais, while the long inland side to the south was defended by a system of canals, forts and redoubts leaning on the village of Mark in the west centre. The strength of Calais was proverbial, for it had never undergone a serious attack since the fourteenth century. 'Thus the English were so boastful (as is their way) that they put up the following inscription over the town gates: "When the French besiege Calais, then we shall see iron and lead swim like cork"' (Branthôme, 1858–78, book I, part 2).

Guise did not concern himself with the brimming ditches on the landward front of the Terre d'Oye, but addressed himself directly to the town of Calais. Everything depended upon surprise, which in the event was total. On 1 January 1558 the French army presented itself before Calais, which was held by only five hundred troops and between two and three hundred armed citizens. Guise laid down a brief cannonade, then on the night of 5–6 January the French waded across the harbour and stormed the Castle of Calais, where the English had calculated on making their last stand. All the English counterattacks were beaten back, and on the evening of 6 January the town garrison capitulated for a free evacuation. Guines, the last English fortress on the Terre d'Oye, succumbed on 20 January, after eight days of cannonade.

The English were now excluded from the mainland of Europe, and they were never to return except as the allies of a major Continental power. Tavannes (1850, 214) rightly claims that the enterprise against Calais presents an example of the best way to exploit the principle of surprise in siege warfare: it was not a madcap escalade, but the sudden descent of a well-equipped army upon an unprepared fortress.

Guise granted his army no more than a brief rest before he wrenched the theatre of war back to the east and opened the main campaign of 1558 by laying siege to Thionville, a town sited nearly thirty miles down the Meuse from Metz. The operation involved the siege of a strong old fortress, which was amply furnished with artillery and held by between two and three thousand determined Walloons and Spaniards, and as such it constituted a more searching test of the French capacity than did the defence of Metz or the capture of Calais.

The siege got off to a bad start, but eventually the French were able to worm their way up to the defences of the Luxembourg Gate, on the west bank of the Meuse. The form of the trenches was a novel one, devised by the infantry commander Blaise de Montluc:

To begin with, the mistaken fancy of an engineer had led us to dig approaches which were a little too narrow. What I did was to make a little return (*arrière-coin*) every twenty paces, sometimes extending to the left and sometimes to the right. These extensions were wide enough to accommodate twelve or fifteen soldiers with their arquebuses and pikes. My object in building the returns was to permit the men to beat off any enemy who might capture the head of the sap and jump inside the trench (Montluc, 1571, 322–3).

Montluc's *arrière-coin* was one of the first attempts to endow siege approaches with the means of repelling counter-attacks. The device gradually evolved by way of the trench redoubts of the Dutch wars into Vauban's system of siege parallels, which remained in the textbooks of engineering schools into the twentieth century.

The French got close enough to take the outlying Tour-aux-Puces on 21 June, and they immediately 'attached' their English miners to the town wall behind. Early on 22 June they were making ready to explode their charges, when the garrison decided to capitulate.

The siege of Thionville represented the last significant episode of the war. The Peace of Câteau-Cambrésis, in April 1559, restored Thionville to the Empire, but confirmed France in possession of all the other conquests of recent years: Calais, Metz, Toul and Verdun. France now owned the beginnings of a defensible northern frontier, and the two flanks, which had once been the weakest sectors of all, had been converted into the strongest.

The first non-Italian practitioners of the new fortification

If we except Montluc's invention of the *arrière-coin*, the northern campaigns of the first half of the sixteenth century are surprisingly barren in technical advances. The theatre is nevertheless of some interest, because it witnessed the growth of the first native schools of the new engineering. By the middle of the century folk like the Germans, French, Netherlanders and English had absorbed most of the teachings of the Italian masters, and they began to wonder whether they could not do better themselves.

In France the confidence of native engineers was stimulated by the poor showing of the imported Italians in recent years. In 1545, for example, Antonio Melloni had contrived to immobilise the main French army for a full year before Boulogne, while he made and re-made Fort d'Outreau, an essential link in the chain of investment.

By the 1550s there existed a number of French engineers whose performance could be compared with that of the Italians, not always to the advantage of the latter. Thus while the French were fortifying the newly-won Three Bishoprics in 1552, the Sieur de Vieilleville decided to overrule the plans of Camillo Marini for the works at Verdun. Marini thereupon departed in a huff, fully expecting that Vieilleville would plead with him to return. He had no intentions of the sort, for

present in Verdun was the Sieur de Saint-Rémy, a French gentleman and a native of Provence, who had the reputation of being the most able fortress-engineer and the most admirable deviser of fireworks to be found anywhere in Europe. All of this redounds greatly to the glory of France, for the Italians like to think that they excel all the rest of Christianity in fortification (Vieilleville, 1850, 157–8).

Across the Rhine, the military architect Daniel Speckle (1546–89) also saw his quarrels with the Italians in terms of national prestige. The Germans, he said, had made useful inventions like printing and reliable mechanical clocks, and they had no reason to feel inferior alongside the Italians, who had elevated their rules of fortification to the status of holy writ.

Speckle could speak to a respectful audience, for his experience in fortress-building was unrivalled among the northern European architects of his time. He had served the Emperor and many of the German princes and cities, and he had a hand in the fortifying of Ulm, Colmar, Bâle, Bruck-an-der-Leitha, Komorn, Vienna, Prague, Ingolstadt,

20   Siege of Thionville. Assault on the Tour-aux-Puces 21 June 1558

Hanau, Schlettstadt, Hagenau and his native Strasbourg.

In 1567 he was called to testify before an Imperial commission, which was sitting at Augsburg to consider the defence of the Hungarian border against the Turks. He took this opportunity to declare that princes would place their lands in jeopardy, if they were so foolish as to apply the principles of Italian fortification in all their rigidity. In his last years Speckle put in order his own ideas on engineering, and in 1589 he published his famous *Architectura* (a second edition, published at Strasbourg in 1599, contains additional posthumous material).

Speckle states in his foreword that he was impelled to put pen to paper through the scorn he encountered among foreign engineers:

There was one Italian who not only laughed at us Germans, but knew how to make us appear contemptible and despicable in the eyes of princes and lords, as if we Germans were devoid of intelligence, brains and understanding, and were to be regarded as children alongside the Italians .... I also have in mind a certain Netherlander who, to be fair, was rather more modest in his claims. However the Italian and the Netherlander are absolutely at one in the way they devise their fortifications and rules. They derive all their fortress traces from old principles which nowadays have been replaced by much better ones.

Ironically enough, the eight 'systems' put forward by Speckle represented just so many sensible modifications of the prevailing Italian ideas on

21   Daniel Speckle

fortification. The underlying principles remained unchanged. (The further development of German fortification will be discussed in the next volume of the present work, *Siege Warfare II. The Fortress in the Age of Vauban and Frederick the Great*.)

The resentment of Speckle and the French was a sterile ground for the sprouting of new systems of fortification, or new methods of siege warfare. Fortification, like the other branches of the military art, did not burgeon afresh until it had received its drenching of blood and marsh-water in the wars between the Dutch rebels and the Spanish.

Four   The Eighty Years War in the Netherlands 1566–1648

The conditions of the struggle

'The war in the Netherlands is the biggest, bloodiest and most implacable of all the wars which have been waged since the beginning of the world' (quoted in Villa, 1904, 473). So exclaimed the Spanish councillor of state Fernando Giron in 1627, when the war between Spain and the young Dutch state had already lasted sixty years, and still had twenty more to run.

This struggle was of the first importance in the history of fortress warfare. These eight decades witnessed not just the further development of the new shapes of fortification which had first evolved in Italy, but the elevation of the siege attack to the status of a science. Such advances were given a European currency, for the Lowlands Wars were considered 'the nursery of the militia' (Hexham, 1642–3, dedication).

The human interest was also remarkable. The sieges of places like Haarlem and Ostend rivalled the most bitter episodes of the Turkish wars or the Peninsular War in desperate obstinacy, and they outmatched them in active, inventive bravery, which was a much rarer quality.

The ground

There are a number of geographical and military constants which go far to explain why the Eighty Years War was fought at such length and with such determination. Most obviously, there was the system of river barriers and associated obstacles – inundations, wastelands, forts and blockhouses – which cramped the movement of the field armies.

The Spanish Netherlands of the third quarter of the sixteenth century comprised present-day Holland and Belgium. Dutch nationhood had its roots in the natural redoubt formed by the seaward provinces of Holland and Zeeland. Here the rebels found a secure retreat during the crisis of the revolt in 1572 and 1573, for

it is almost impossible to enter either of those provinces by force: because not only the chief places, but even the commonest towns are environed either by the sea, rivers or lakes, or by earth, than which there can be none more low, or more miry (Bentivoglio, 1678, part I, book 4).

The Duke of Alva was counted one of the most experienced commanders of his time, but a year's campaigning was enough to disgust him with the conditions of war in that part of the world. Never in his life, he complained to the Duke of Savoy, had he found himself 'put to more trouble than in waging war against the rebels in the province of Holland, a land of dykes, ponds and difficult passages' (Alva, 1952, III, 381, letter of 6 May 1573).

Once they had weathered this first crisis, the rebels extended the borders of their 'redoubt' to cover the province of Utrecht and the western part of Gelderland, and formed an eminently defensible region which was cradled to the east by the river Ijssel, and to the south by the multiple barrier of the Rhine and Maas (lower Meuse) and their branches.

For all its length, this Maas-Rhine barrier was extremely difficult to penetrate. Westwards the Zeeland islands posed an almost insurmountable obstacle to the Spanish, who lacked the sea power of the rebels. In 1575 a very brave army actually managed to wade as far as the island of Schouwen, but there were natural limits to the amphibious capacity of even the tallest Spaniard. On the eastern sector the approaches were cramped by the independent Bishopric of Liège and the barren heaths of Kempen. There remained the centre, where the isle of Bommel, enclosed by the Maas and the Waal, formed the only convenient stepping-stone from Brabant to the northern provinces.

Offensively, the possession of the southern river barrier enabled the rebels to transfer the theatre of war from Flanders to the German border and back again with a facility that was denied to the Spanish, as Maurice of Nassau was going to prove so brilliantly in 1591.

To the south of the river complex stretched the wide provinces that make up the greater part of modern Belgium. Great cities like Bruges, Ghent, Tournai, Valenciennes and Oudenarde offered the rebellion very strong support. Brussels, though the nominal capital of Spanish rule, was one of the most restless places of all. The northern fringes of Brabant and Flanders lay within easy reach of short overland offensives launched from the rebel 'redoubt', and the Flemish coast down to Ostend and beyond was accessible to Dutch sea power.

Similarly Artois, the southernmost province, was vulnerable to France whenever that nation stood under anti-Spanish leaders. Spanish commanders dreaded any stirrings in that part of the world, for overland transport was so difficult that they were unable to deal with the French and Dutch simultaneously by a 'strategy of interior lines'. Any forces sent against France were committed in that direction for the rest of the campaign.

The career of rebellion in 'Belgium' was however fairly short. For one thing, the heartland province of Brabant was good open country, where the Spanish superiority in regular troops could be shown to the best advantage. Also the southern Netherlands were the theatre most open to the forces which came across the Rhine and middle Meuse from Germany, or by the long route from Spanish Italy by way of the Valtelline, and thence by parallel tracks through Franche-Comté, Lorraine and Luxembourg.

The most curious scene of war was certainly the remote north-eastern province of Groningen, which was cut off by the Zuider Zee from the crowded hysteria of the rebel cities. Tradition and authority were the things which counted in Groningen, and here more than anywhere else the Spanish cause enjoyed something like popular support from the start. In the Eighty Years War, as in most wars of 'liberation', much of the energies of the rebels was devoted to putting down people who wanted nothing of the delights which were being offered to them. So it was that this isolated theatre was disputed until the supporters of the Spanish finally lost heart in the 1590s, when Maurice of Nassau severed their communications with the south. As in Flanders and Brabant, the natural sympathies of the people had to give way before the forces of geography.

Lastly we must take account of the vital area of Overijssel and eastern Gelderland, which functioned as a strategic pivot around which all the other theatres of war revolved. Rather than resume their attempts to pierce the rebel 'redoubt' from the south, the Spaniards found that it was more worth their while to work their way further east and north across the Maas and Rhine, just above the points where they began to divide and re-divide to form the southern river barrier of the rebel fastness.

By this right-flanking movement the Spanish could cut off the rebels from the heretics of Germany, establish communication with the loyalists in Groningen, and arrive opposite the eastern flank of the 'redoubt'. Here their way was barred by the river Ijssel, which branched off from the Neder Rijn near Arnhem. The fortified towns of Doesburg, Zutphen and Deventer studded the right bank of the Ijssel, and eastwards the sodden plain towards Germany was commanded by the strongholds of Emmerich, Deutichem, Grol, Oldenzaal, Ootmarsum and Coevorden. These places apart, the Ijssel constituted a single, unsupported barrier, and gave the Spanish by far their easiest entry into the Dutch 'redoubt'. Only in 1589 did the states of Utrecht and Holland resolve to erect a second line of defence in the shape of the *Nieuwe Hollandse Waterlinie*, a tract

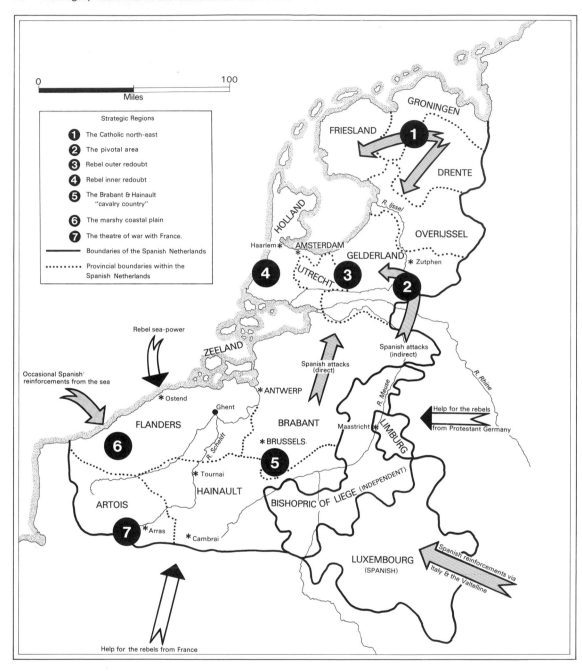

0 —————————————— 100
Miles

Strategic Regions

1 The Catholic north-east

2 The pivotal area

3 Rebel outer redoubt

4 Rebel inner redoubt

5 The Brabant & Hainault
"cavalry country"

6 The marshy coastal plain

7 The theatre of war with France.

————— Boundaries of the Spanish Netherlands

·········· Provincial boundaries within the
Spanish Netherlands

GRONINGEN

FRIESLAND

DRENTE

R. Ijssel

OVERIJSSEL

HOLLAND

Haarlem *   * AMSTERDAM

GELDERLAND   * Zutphen

UTRECHT

Rebel sea-power

ZEELAND

Spanish attacks
(direct)

Spanish attacks
(indirect)

R. Rhine

R. Meuse

Occasional Spanish
reinforcements from the sea

* Ostend

Ghent

* ANTWERP

FLANDERS

BRABANT

Maastricht *

LIMBURG

Help for the rebels
from Protestant Germany

* BRUSSELS

* Tournai

HAINAULT

ARTOIS

BISHOPRIC OF LIEGE (INDEPENDENT)

LUXEMBOURG
(SPANISH)

Spanish reinforcements via
Italy & the Valtelline

* Arras   * Cambrai

Help for the rebels from France

The Spanish Netherlands in the Eighty Years War: political and strategic

of inundations and forts which ran in front of Utrecht from the Zuider Zee near Naarden to the Lek.

Conversely, once the Spanish were thrown onto the defensive, as happened in the 1590s, it required no more than a brief Dutch offensive from the Ijssel to sever all communication between Brabant and the Catholics of Groningen.

All the provinces and river lines would have fallen easily enough if they had not been held down by fortresses of great tactical strength. The great cities of Artois, Brabant and Flanders owned large and fanatical populations, ample resources, stout old walls and some modern citadels. The Spanish therefore rarely attacked them direct, preferring to leave them to one side or to reduce them by blockade.

To begin with, the towns in the north were fortified by nothing more ambitious than earthen banks and decaying walls. But what these places lacked in conventional fortifications they more than supplied by the watery inaccessibility of their sites. Only at the apparent height of their success did the Spanish come to appreciate the size of the task still before them. The towns of Alkmaar and Haarlem absorbed the entire Spanish military effort in 1573, and it dawned upon the secretary to Governor Requesens that these two places were nevertheless the weakest of the many strongholds that had to be reduced:

The quantity of rebel towns and districts is so great that they embrace almost all of Holland and Zeeland, which are islands that can be reduced only with great difficulty and by naval forces. Indeed, if several towns decide to hold out, we shall never be able to take them. We who are on the spot can see all this with our own eyes, but the people at the Court of Spain have a dim and distant view (Prinsterer, 1857–9, 1st series V, 30).

The high water-table in the north-west Netherlands saturated the ground to within a couple of feet of the surface, which compelled the besiegers to build up high trench parapets out of gabions. Bernardo de Mendoza, a veteran of the sieges of Haarlem and Alkmaar, was convinced that

wet ditches offer more dangers to the attacker than dry ditches, in spite of the great difference of opinion which prevails on this point between the officers and the engineers – the engineers maintain that dry ditches are more effective, while the military take the opposite view (Mendoza, 1853, book XIII, chapter 2).

Many a stretch of ground, which seemed eminently suitable for siege approaches, could be flooded without warning when the defenders cut a dyke or opened a sluice, as happened to Mondragon's battery when he was attacking Fort Lillo at Antwerp in 1584. Simon Stevin, Prince Maurice's famous hydraulic engineer, defined two categories of sites which were particularly suitable for 'water manoeuvres' of this kind. The first embraced towns which stood beside the sea or on rivers which had a large tidal variation (Ostend, Sluis, Ijzendijk, Antwerp, Veere, Zierikzee, Willemstad, Geertruydenberg, Enkhuizen, etc.). The second consisted of places that stood on non-tidal stretches of river, but owned a tributary which flowed through or close by the walls (Doesburg, Zutphen, Deventer, Zwolle).

The armies

Both of the belligerents did their best to put powerful armies into the field, but as far as the results went there was little to choose in point of inefficiency between the Dutch system of trying to scrape together an entire new army every year (and often failing to raise any men at all), and the Spanish practice of holding together a large nucleus of force throughout the year, only to see the troops dissolve in mutinies when they were most needed. The most reliable troops, the native Spaniards (seldom more than 10,000 at any given time) and the Italians, were forced to take the long overland route from the Mediterranean to the Netherlands. Any attempt to make the passage by sea was attended with appalling risks, as was shown when Van Tromp broke Oqueno's fleet in 1639.

The Spanish commanders did not even have the free disposal of the loyal troops, for about 30,000 men or two-thirds of the army of Flanders were always tied down in the defence of

Fortresses in the northern Netherlands in the sixteenth and seventeenth centuries

a frontier which extends from Gravelines to Luxembourg, and from thence to Groningen, and which is made still more difficult to defend by being bordered by the sea and traversed by great rivers (Essen, 1933–7, V, 33, letter of Parma, 28 February 1585).

Some of the fortresses absorbed Spanish manpower like sponges, but many others valued municipal privileges so highly that they refused to admit garrisons or relinquish their keys to royal governors. In 1591, for instance, the strongly Catholic towns of Groningen and Nijmegen remained deaf to all the pleas of Verdugo and Parma, and, martyrs to their own particularist tendencies, they preferred to await the onset of the heretics alone: 'such was the feeling of distrust in those times, even among the most loyal populations' (Coloma, 1853, book IV). In 1584 local sentiments of the same kind cost Prince William of Orange eleven or twelve strong towns of the southern Netherlands, and the whole of the Pays de Waes.

Thus in the early decades of the rebellion neither the Spanish nor the Dutch could hope to possess a coherent fortress-frontier in the sense that the term was going to be understood under the rule of an absolutist monarch like Louis XIV.

With few and wretched troops like these, fighting in a 'strong' country of rivers and marshes, it was small wonder that war in the Netherlands was conducted according to its own rules. Spanish and rebel commanders came to shun encounters in the open field, and Cardinal Bentivoglio found a clear divergence from the French practice when he came to make a comparison between the generalship of Parma and Henry IV: 'The king (Henry) loved battles, it being the custom of the French to do so; the duke (Parma) was a well-wisher to industrious advantages, according to the manner of waging war in Flanders' (Bentivoglio, 1678, part I, book 5).

With battle ruled out, how well qualified were the Catholics and heretics to meet each other in the only kind of contest left to them, a war of sieges?

In the first decades of war the Spanish had no lack of expert technical advice, for the prestige of their army drew many talented engineers from Italy to serve under the ragged cross of Burgundy. Alva's right-hand man was Captain Bartolomeo Campi of Pesaro, whose work on the building of Paciotto's citadel at Antwerp led the duke to describe him to Philip II as one of the best men he had ever known, not just among engineers, but in any rank. Campi was killed at Haarlem in 1573, and his place was taken by the Florentine Chiappino Vitelli (1519–76), who had distinguished himself in the defence of Malta before transferring to the Spanish service. Following the departure of Alva, he served on in the Netherlands as Camp-Master-General of the army until his death at the siege of Zierikzee in 1576.

In the 1580s Parma found some of his best assistants among the most noble families of Italy – an indication of the high social standing of engineers in the Spanish service at the time. Rafael Barberino, the uncle of Pope Urban VIII no less, was consulted on technical details of fortress construction. The Chief Engineer of the army was the Milanese Gabrio Serbelloni, a relative of Pope Pius IV, and re-membered for having reported on the construction of St Peter's in Rome and thwarted a plot to scrap the designs of the aged Michelangelo. Less exalted in rank, but still very useful, were engineers like Scipione Campi, who soldiered on manfully regard-less of his father's death at Haarlem, or the two technicians Properzio Barozzi and Giambattista Piatti, who assisted at the sieges of Tournai in 1581 and Antwerp in 1584.

Parma's favourite helper was, however, the Netherlander, Master Hance. This gentleman had made the acquaintance of the Duke in unpromising circumstances, having been captured by him in a minor siege in 1578; but thereafter Parma

always kept him at his side, for he liked and respected him for his energy and ingenuity . . . . In addition to being a man of great intelligence, Hance was a very fine carpenter. He put in excellent service, and he never let his master down once in all the actions during the fifteen years he spent with Parma up to his death (Vazquez, 1879–80, book IX).

By the end of the sixteenth century the Spanish had absorbed enough of the foreign expertise to produce a short-lived but very creditable school of technical literature. Luis Collado brought out an artillery textbook in Italian in 1586, and then, growing more bold, he published a Spanish edition in 1592 (*Prática Manual de Artillería*, Milan). This was followed in 1613 by the publication of Diego Ufano's highly influential work (*Tratado de Artillería*, Brussels). Collado and Ufano compiled their useful tables of elevations and ranges from hard experience and practical experiments, and they despised Italians like Tartaglia as academic theorists.

In 1598 Captain Cristobal de Rojas ventured to publish the first Spanish book on military engineering, the *Teorica y Prática de Fortificacion* (Madrid). He modestly says that he would not have taken on the task if

any Spaniard had done it before me. But, seeing that our nation is more concerned with battering down forces and walls than in building them up . . . I have decided to blaze the trail (dedication).

The next year saw the publication of a rival work, the *Examen de Fortification* (Madrid) of Diego Gonzalez de Medina Barba. Unlike their cousins in the artillery, Rojas and Medina Barba did not attempt to break away from the prevailing Italian opinions on their subject.

In 1611 the distinguished gunner Cristobal de Lechuga brought together the two branches of technical knowledge in a comprehensive *Discorso de la Artillería . . . con un Tratado de Fortificacion* (Milan). The last Spanish author of note was Juan de Santans y Tapia, who drew heavily on the history of recent campaigns in order to present an up-to-date analysis of the state of the engineering art (*Tratado de Fortificacion Militar de Estos Tempos*, Brussels 1644).

However, we are still far distant from the circumstances of the eighteenth century, by when engineering had become an arcane art and field commanders had to depend on technicians for advice. Men like Alva, Parma, Spinola and Maurice of Nassau were themselves experts and innovators, and they were fully capable of taking their own counsel in engineering affairs.

Neither side commanded permanent units of engineering troops. The Spanish pioneers were attached to the artillery, and their main job was to clear the roads for the guns. For special purposes the Spanish had to recruit their labour beyond the bounds of the Netherlands. Thus in 1582 they began to make use of Bohemian sappers to build forts, and Spanish and Dutch alike hired quantities of master miners from the Bishopric of Liège. These were 'more skilled than the men from the other provinces on account of the many mines they dug to extract a certain black stone which is found around Liège. It goes by the name of "coal"' (Mendoza, 1853, book IX, chapter 3).

Parma discovered that the simplest expedient in routine fortress-building and siege work was to persuade his troops to dig in return for extra pay, though in this ambition he had to battle with the twisted pride of the Castilians, who regarded begging in the streets as more honourable than labouring for a reward. Prince Maurice had better luck with his Dutchmen; there was little that they would not do for money.

Throughout their wars the Spaniards were desperately short of artillery and transport. A particularly dangerous situation arose in 1574, after the guns from the southern towns had been lost in the many vessels which were sunk in the attempts to relieve Middleburg. Except for their sieges in Holland and Zeeland and on to the major rivers in the east, the Spanish were thrown entirely upon land transport, with all its costs and difficulties. Once inside the rebel 'redoubt' the facility of water transport was more than offset by the existence of thickets of fortresses on every side. At Alkmaar in 1573 the opening of the siege was fatally delayed because the guns were a fortnight late in arriving.

The Spanish conduct of war was profoundly influenced by the lack of an effective artillery train. The commanders knew that they could never subdue the rebellion by laying siege to every town that stood in their path. Instead they had to examine the means by which the Dutch were able to maintain the revolt – whether by trade or foreign help – and seek to cut off these channels at the points where they entered the Netherlands. When an individual fortress had to be taken, the Spanish invariably preferred to take the place by means of a generous bribe rather than incur the far greater cost of a formal siege.

Little is heard of individual Dutch engineers in the 1570s and 1580s. This is hardly surprising, for the insurrection was at first scattered and lacking in co-ordination. Sometimes there was skilled help immediately at hand, as when four hundred outlaws emerged from the woods of Flanders to help the revolt of the Zeeland towns in 1572: 'Some of these man had good understanding in the wars. Principally in fortification they did help the townsmen greatly, in such sort that they mounted their pieces in good order and mended their fortifications' (Williams, 1618, 57). More often the rebels had to learn by mistakes, like the escalade at the 'ignorant poor siege' of Goes in 1572.

The country people of the northern Netherlands remained generally aloof from the war, and they refused to work for the rebels even for pay. In October 1583, in an attempt to place affairs on a more regular footing, the States General ordered one thousand pioneers to be raised at the cost of Holland, Zeeland and Utrecht. By February the next year the scheme had produced just thirty men, and so orders went out to arrest all vagabonds and place them at the disposal of the Colonel of Pioneers, Hans Duyck. In the event, the problem of raising siege and fortress labour remained unsolved until the days of Maurice of Nassau. As far as the first decades of the rebellion are concerned, we must agree with Sir Henry Pelham as to 'what beastly pioneers the Dutchmen were' (Leycester, 1844, 401).

In contrast, the rebels rapidly evolved one of the most satisfactory garrison systems in the history of fortress warfare. In the first, heroic period of the rebellion, many towns owed their survival to the fact that there was still a spark of life in the old militia companies and guilds. More and more, however, the defence came to rest on the shoulders of paid garrison troops, the *waardgelders*, who were disbanded and re-hired annually, though often on the same terms and in the same numbers as in preceding years.

Although the ranks of the *waardgelders* included many invalids and aged veterans, the effectiveness of the companies was much greater than was the case with the generality of garrison troops in foreign services. The *waardgelder* officers were frequently transferred to the field army, and entire companies

sometimes followed them. All in all, the *waardgelder* system freed the Dutch armies from the responsibility of routine garrison duty, and offered them an occasional reserve in time of emergency. When a fortress was threatened with actual siege, the guilds and the *waardgelders* were of course bolstered up with troops of the line.

The Spaniards had no comparable system. Spanish armies spent the winter in whatever fortress towns would receive them, and otherwise the only stable garrison troops were represented by independent companies of regulars. In 1627 these companies lost what little status remained to them, when Philip IV ordered that all troops must come under the control of the generals of the field army. The authority of fortress governors was thereby diminished. A further step towards a more 'military' system was taken in 1634, with the institution of a regular annual rotation of garrisons.

Just as was the case with the garrison system, so the administration and financing of the Dutch fortresses showed a gradual departure from the local initiative which had been a feature of the beginnings of the revolt. Whereas in those early years nearly every town constituted a fortress under its own governor, this mighty officer was appointed in later times only to one of the *generaliteits-vestingen*, the border fortresses most recently taken from the Spanish. Right up to the end of the wars the individual provinces were loath to help to build or maintain distant fortresses. Sometimes, however, two neighbouring provinces would contribute towards a stronghold which served both their interests. In this way two-thirds of the costs of the upkeep of Coevorden were defrayed by Friesland, and one-third by Groningen.

The variety of rebel cannon was remarkable. Some of the guns were captured from the enemy, while others were manufactured privately by the towns, or (in the case of the iron pieces) bought from England and later from Sweden. The towns and provinces were not at all willing to yield up their artillery to the field army. Fortunately the availability of water transport enabled the rebel commanders to make the best use of whatever guns they had at hand. Also, the central authorities began to free themselves from their dependence on the goodwill of the towns. A quantity of artillery was held ready in the frontier fortresses, under the care of a small staff of permanent gunners, and in 1586 a *Meester-Generaal* was appointed to direct all the operations of the artillery service.

The Dutch were just as eager as their enemies to snatch a fortress if it could be done without the cost of a siege. Whereas the Spanish style was to suborn a governor, the Dutch liked to gain entrance to a town by stratagem. Thus Ypres fell to the heretics in 1578, after a waggon containing an unusually hairy 'bride' with 'bridesmaids' broke down by arrangement at the Messines Gate. Another famous *coup de main* gave the Dutch the fortress of Breda in 1590.

Atrocities

River lines, engineers, guns and fortresses went far to shape the events of the Eighty Years War, but they cannot tell us much about the ferocity and tenacity for which the sieges are chiefly remembered.

There is little need to dwell on the heroism of the Dutch, who were fighting for their religion and independence. The motivation of the Spanish is not quite so simple to explain. Many of their 'barbarities' appear a little less horrifying when we bear in mind that they were the lawful authorities, and that they were dealing with people who were triply damned by the custom of the time: as rebels, as heretics, and as fanatics who insisted on holding out long after the reasonable term of a defence had expired. Naarden was chastised in 1572 not just as a nest of Anabaptists but because the town had dared to 'maintain its opposition after the battery had been planted. This alone deprived it of consideration' (Mendoza, 1853, book VIII, chapter 10). Using the same argument Don John of Austria justified the blood-letting at Sichem in 1578.

At the same time the special relationship between sovereign and subject could act to the advantage of the rebels. On 22 October 1574 King Philip II rejected a scheme to inundate Holland by breaching the Maaslandsluis, for he claimed that such a deed would be an intolerable cruelty against his own peoples. As erring subjects, the Netherlands heretics were both less and more than other enemies.

It is not easy to judge whether the policy of slaughter was really effective. Vazquez (1879–80, book II) states that 'the wars in the Netherlands would have been less prolonged and bloody if the governors of those states had not been so merciful (so to speak) with the enemies of God and their Prince'. That was only to be expected from a Spaniard. Rather more weighty is the testimony of Sir Roger Williams, who had fought on both sides, and believed that Philip would have done well to throw all his authority behind Alva and his bloodthirsty methods: 'To say troth, fury and resolution well used or executed had been the only ways to suppress that nation' (Williams, 1618, 104).

On the other hand, the delight taken by the Dutch in exaggerating the tales of Spanish horror, when the reality was strong enough, seems to indicate that the rebellion flourished on harsh treatment. This was certainly the belief of Parma, who knew 'by experience that clemency is the only remedy with these people, and that the harsh punishments of earlier times merely served to embitter and exasperate them' (Essen, 1933–7, III, 189).

At no time in the struggle, not even in the bloody 1570s, did the opponents cease to regard each other with respect. Alva's tribute, in a letter of 17 January 1573, to the defenders of Haarlem, *defienden muy como soldados* (Alva, 1952, III, 282), is matched word-for-word by the exclamation of Count John of Nassau-Siegen at the siege of Coevorden in 1592, *sie haben sehr wohl, und als soldaten gebühret, gehalten* (letter of 3 September 1592, in Prinsterer, 1857–9, 2nd series I, 209).

Sieges were so cruel in the early decades of the war simply because the Dutch were determined to hold out to the utmost, even when they knew that the recognised custom of the time allowed the Spanish to exact the harshest retribution.

The war from the beginning of the revolt until the Twelve Years Truce 1566–1609

Alva and his citadels 1566–72

If fortifications had the power to restrain rebellion, then the great heretical insurrection of 1572 would never have engulfed the Spanish Netherlands.

22   Spanish massacre at Oudewater 1575 (Baudart, 1616)

There had been two scattered and badly co-ordinated outbursts of unrest in 1566–7 and 1568, which merely served notice on the Spaniards to do something to prevent a repetition, without seriously endangering their rule. The work of subjugation fell to the Duke of Alva, who had come to the Netherlands with an army in 1567. This tough-minded gentleman decided to impose a permanent curb on the disaffected towns by building citadels at Valenciennes, Ypres, Groningen and Flushing. The mightiest citadel of all was to be traced at Antwerp, 'since it was a powerful town which hitherto had been badly guarded, added to which many foreign merchants stayed and traded there each year' (Baudart, 1616, I, 140).

What Alva thought about citadels is most clearly shown in a memorandum which he drew up on 28 June 1568 on the subject of the fortification of Naples. He stresses two factors above all others: first, that the loyal forces must be free to enter the citadel and break into the town whenever they wish; and, second, that the citadel garrison must be able to cut off the townspeople from their sympathisers in the country.

The Antwerp site was chosen in consultation with Gabrio Serbelloni and Chiappino Vitelli, and the principal architect Paciotto of Urbino, who was renowned for the citadel which he had built for the Duke of Savoy at Turin. The Italian experts fixed on a location on the right (east) bank of the Scheldt immediately above Antwerp.

The work began on 1 November 1567 and it was

completed with astonishing speed. Paciotto wrote proudly to Duke Guidobaldo II of Urbino that he had

finished the citadel of Antwerp with its five large bastions and all the appurtenances in four months. I managed the progress of the work so well that the draught-animals and the carts were working right up to the end, which is saying quite a lot, as Your Grace knows (Promis, 1874, 714).

As transpired in the course of the Eighty Years War, the position of the citadel was admirably gauged to fulfil the first of the conditions laid down in Alva's memorandum, namely to be easy to reach from friendly territory. It proved to be less well positioned to meet the second requirement, to keep the enemy

away from the town. This would have demanded a site to the north of Antwerp, commanding the lower Scheldt and the approaches from the rebel Zeeland. The truth was that the choice of any site in 1567 was bound to be a gamble. With disaffection spread throughout the Netherlands, and Antwerp placed in the middle of the region, the Spanish had no indications as to the directions from which relief or attack were to be expected.

Contemporaries attached no such reservations to the design of the actual citadel, a 'perfect fortress' (Tavannes, 1850, 175), which earned Paciotto the title of the 'inventor of modern fortification' (Estrada, 1682, book I, chapter 7). Alva was delighted, and after a visit to the site in May 1569 he reported to Philip (3 June) that he could 'assure Your

23   Statue of Alva in the citadel of Antwerp. He is trampling upon Dutch rebels (Baudart, 1616)

24   The demolition of the Antwerp citadel

Majesty that it is one of the finest places in the world' (Alva, 1952, II, 93).

Alva left the townspeople in no doubt that he built the fort so as to hold them down. Thus, when the opportunity came in 1576, the townspeople threw themselves on the offending work with pick, crowbar and spade, 'regardless of the size, strength, beauty and excellence of construction which had earned it the title of the finest citadel in the Netherlands, if not of all Christianity' (Baudart, 1616, I, 250). The citadels of Ghent, Utrecht, Lille, Valenciennes, Béthune and Arras went the same way.

Interestingly enough, the triumphant Dutch authorities did not hesitate to build citadels of their own, if they would serve their purposes. In 1583 William of Orange placed a States garrison in the remnants of the Antwerp citadel and rebuilt the townward fronts, and in 1600 the States General went so far as to build a new citadel of their own in the town of Groningen, as a punishment for the citizens' refusal to pay their contributions. The French envoy was astonished at the decision, and exclaimed that 'even the Spanish Archdukes would have been prevented from taking such measures in the towns subject to them' (Prinsterer, 1857–9, 2nd series II, xxvii).

The heretics would never have had the opportunity to destroy or build citadels in the first place, but for the complete failure of Alva's fortifications to stem a new tide of rebellion which swept over the Netherlands in 1572. In April of that year gangs of ruffians and seamen gave the signal for a general rising by taking Brielle. This was followed by the revolt of the other towns of Holland, Zeeland and the northern provinces.

Alva had certainly begun his programme of citadel-building ambitiously enough, but such was the lack of money that only the works at Antwerp and Valenciennes were pushed ahead to near-completion. Among the other citadels, the fort at Flushing on the island of Walcheren was left unfinished, although the place was 'the only port and key of the Netherlands .... All men of any judgment may easily conceive that had they finished first the citadel of Flushing, Zeeland had never revolted' (Williams, 1618, 34). In these northern regions the Spanish could be sure only of Schiedam, Rotterdam, the citadel of Antwerp, and Rammekens Castle and Middelburg on Walcheren, where they had isolated garrisons which were powerless to influence the march of events outside their walls. The Spanish had therefore lost their hold on the strongest natural strategic redoubt of the Netherlands, and they were never to regain it.

During the same spring of 1572 the rebel parties in the south seized Valenciennes (despite its citadel) and Mons, thereby opening the way to their Huguenot friends in France.

The Spanish catastrophe of 1572 shows that fortifications, being fixed in purpose and site, never show to greater disadvantage than in the circumstances of a revolt. Rebels are by definition the people who hold the initiative at the beginning of an insurrection, and in the first heady weeks of revolution they have it in their power to overrun strongpoints that will cost the governmental forces years of effort to reduce to obedience. In 1572, as so often again in the revolutions of the nineteenth century, fortification served the ends of rebels rather than loyalists.

The Alva and Requesens offensives 1572–6

In 1572 Alva was faced with the task of recovering almost the whole of the Netherlands. His difficulties were compounded by the fact that for the next two years the Spanish had to divide their attention between this part of the world and the Turkish threat in the Mediterranean. Alva was urged by

some officers to concentrate at the citadel of Antwerp, but he wisely chose to go over to the attack and cut off the rebels from one of the most important of their 'base areas': Huguenot France. He took Valenciennes after a feeble defence, and on 23 June the Spaniards appeared before the hard blue stone ramparts of Mons.

Since the rebel Prince of Orange was bringing up powerful forces from Germany, Alva's engineer Chiappino Vitelli adopted the siege technique which had been applied by Prospero Colonna at Milan in 1522, and two years later by Francis I at Pavia, namely to entrench the besieging army in an improvised fortress of its own, with the inner side (countervallation) facing the garrison, and the outer perimeter (circumvallation) holding off any forces advancing to the relief. There was one important difference. Whereas Colonna and King Francis were content to occupy a chain of farmhouses, park walls and other strongpoints, Vitelli now threw up a coherent system of earthen forts and interconnecting ditches and banks. By this means the Spanish held the Prince of Orange at a distance, and they forced Mons to capitulate on 19 September.

Vitelli's siege lines were to become part of the basic vocabulary of fortress warfare for a couple of centuries to come. Mendoza (1853, book VII, chapter 11) describes the extraordinary scenes when

the town was being scourged by the fire of the duke's artillery, the besiegers were being cannonaded by the guns of the town, and the Spanish army had to endure the fire of the rebel field forces, which were in turn being hit by the Spanish troops . . . and all of this at the same time.

Such episodes were to be commonplace.

The Orangist army collapsed after the fall of Mons, and Alva advanced almost unopposed to punish the rebels in the northern provinces. His son, Don Fadrique of Toledo, staged an exemplary massacre at Zutphen, and the terrified rebel garrisons opened their gates all over the provinces of Overijssel, Gelderland and Utrecht.

Nothing had occurred to abate the confidence of the Spaniards by the time Don Fadrique and the advance guard arrived before Haarlem, in the heart of the province of Holland, on 11 December 1572.

The reduction of the town seemed more of an administrative than a military problem, for the defences consisted of an old twenty-foot high wall that was set with low round towers. A single modern outwork, a ravelin, stood before the Kruispoort on the northern side.

The Spanish opened an ill-prepared attack against the Kruispoort, 'not observing the military proceedings in sieges, and too scornfully neglecting to make their trenches, so as to draw near by degrees (as is usual) under their rampires' (Bentivoglio, 1678, part I, book 7). They made a scrappy attempt at a storm on 20 December, and met with the repulse they deserved.

By the New Year the attention of both Alva and the Prince of Orange was riveted on the struggle that was developing at Haarlem. Inside the town the rebels had 2,000 armed citizens (out of a population of 20,000) as well as about 4,000 troops. More important still the defenders owned an unrestricted communication with the towns of southern Holland by means of the channel which led south-westwards to the Haarlem Lake.

The Spaniards had 17,000 or 18,000 troops around Haarlem at the outset of the siege, but with the steady erosion caused by casualties, cold and disease, the size of the force sometimes sank to below half that number. Alva knew that a complete investment was out of the question. 'The town is very large,' he reported to King Philip on 8 January 1573, 'and there is nothing we can do to stop the enemy coming in and going out as they please. That is what makes them put up such a firm defence' (Alva, 1952, III, 274).

After the rebuff of 20 December the Spanish set about a formal siege. Under the direction of Bartolomeo Campi the trenches wormed towards the ravelin, and on 15 January 1573 the Dutch relinquished the work without a fight. Unfortunately the rearward defences proved to be stronger still. The Dutch had been pulling down a number of houses *inside* the walls, 'in which void room they entrenched the town . . . with rampart bastions and a large ditch thereto, making their old wall of the town (almost battered down about them) a counterscarp unto their new fortification' (Morgan, 1976, 115). A Spanish captain exclaimed: 'Who would believe that

we are no further forward than on the first day of the siege!' (Vazquez, 1879–80, book IX).

Disgusted with the labour of the last three weeks, Don Fadrique threw in a new assault on 31 January. The result was a still bloodier massacre than the episode of 20 December. Some of the officers were so downcast that they spoke out in favour of raising the siege. Alva and the other commanders, however, had no intention of marching tamely away. Also the feeling among the troops ran so high that whole companies swore never to move from the spot before Haarlem fell.

The soldiers willingly accepted all the toil as the price of satisfying a personal vendetta, for the war had become so cruel that there was no question of either side taking a man alive. A prisoner was allowed to live just long enough to permit the soldiers to extract some information from him (Mendoza, 1853, book IX, chapter 11).

The Spanish were forced to return to the laborious but tried method of systematic siege. They brought up coal miners from Liège to begin a war inside the ramparts with the rebel tunnellers, while, above ground, they drove the saps slowly forward to the breach.

Spring found the defiance of Haarlem undiminished. The heretics scornfully tossed loaves of bread to the famished Spaniards, and they infuriated the besiegers still more by planting statues from the plundered Catholic churches on the ramparts. On one occasion a pious soldier ran forward to rescue one of the images, and

since the figure was large and heavy, and the enemy poured a rain of bullets on him, he clasped the statue to him, rolled with it to the bottom of the breach, and by this means brought it back to the trenches (ibid.).

The blasphemous ebullience of the defenders was cut short when they learnt that on 28 May the Spaniards had defeated the rebel galley flotilla and immediately afterwards seized the Fort of Fuick, which commanded the entrance from the Haarlem Lake to the channel leading to the town. Now that the investment was complete, the great quantity of soldiers and townspeople, which had once been the mainstay of the defence, began to make visible daily inroads into the slender stock of provisions.

On 9 July 1573 the Spanish cavalry defeated an attempt by the rebel field army to break through to the relief. Four days later the starving town surrendered without conditions. Don Fadrique made his entry early on 14 July, and the Spaniards set about the systematic executions in which 1,735 of the garrison and the leading rebel citizens lost their lives. The first few hundred were beheaded by a squad of five executioners, who laboured until they could lift their arms no more. The rest of the condemned men were bound back-to-back in twos or threes, and flung into the river Spaarne.

The ten-month resistance of Haarlem can probably be counted the most obstinately disputed of all the rebel defences in the Eighty Years War, not excluding the epic siege of Ostend in 1601–4. From the technical aspect the episode is notable for the delay and losses inflicted on the Spanish by the defence of the ravelin, one of the earliest proofs of the value of outworks. More important still, the repeated failure of the assaults impressed on the Spaniards (or at least should have impressed on them) how dangerous it was to try to abridge the march of a siege. In Vauban's famous words '*la précipitation dans les sièges ne hâte point la prise des places*'. Unfortunately this was a truth which successive generations of Spanish commanders had to learn for themselves, whether at Haarlem in 1572–3, Maastricht in 1579, or Ostend in 1601. Only after the coming of Spinola to the Netherlands did the Spanish habitually undertake sieges by systematic approach.

As regards the strategic results, the 'recapture of Haarlem, as is the case in most long sieges, gave the Spanish a great deal of glory but not much benefit' (Estrada, 1682, part I, book 7). Alva dragged his mutinous army northwards to the siege of Alkmaar, which lay 'in an ill-favoured marsh far more unwholesome than Haarlem' (Williams, 1618, 91). The artillery was late in arriving, and the Dutch dug themselves in so strongly that the Spanish had to abandon the operation in the middle of October

Alva was not the least of the many casualties of this soggy campaign. Tormented by rheumatism, he turned over the governorship of the Netherlands to Don Luis de Requesens. The rule of Requesens began inauspiciously enough, with the capitulation on 18 February 1574 of the long-blockaded Spanish garrison of Middleburg, on the island of Walcheren. The rebels thereby completed their conquest of the Zeeland islands, and safeguarded the western or seaward flank of their strategic redoubt.

The gallant Requesens defeated and killed Count Louis of Nassau on the Mookerheide on 15 April 1574, but the rest of that campaigning season was spent in a fruitless blockade of the town of Leyden, which stood in the inundated country of southern central Holland.

The waters flowed again over their ancient site, among the trees and farmhouses, and a multitude of boats made their way through the drowned woods. It was like the Ancient Roman theatres, where forest scenes gave way to wonderful inundations, on which whole fleets did battle (Estrada, 1682, part I, book 7).

On 30 October 1574 Prince William of Orange broke through to the town with a flotilla of flatboats, and the Spanish raised the blockade forthwith.

Next year it was the Spaniards' turn to wet their feet. Putting on a bolder front than the state of his finances really justified, Requesens launched a two-pronged offensive against the rebel redoubt.

Baron Hierges assembled the troops for the right-hand thrust in the area north of the Maas-Waal river barrier, and then marched westwards, taking all the fortresses that stood in his way. Buren was the first to fall, and on 8 August 1575 he took the town of Oudewater by a bitterly-resisted assault. Schoonhoven and the forts at Krimpen went the same way, which brought Hierges to within sight of the islands of Holland and Zeeland. The rebels, however, had every confidence in their fortifications, a trust which on this occasion was not betrayed. Talking of the loss of Oudewater and Schoonhoven on 29 September 1575, William admitted that

some people were taken aback by the first impression, but they presently picked up courage and set to work with a good will to fortify the towns and see to whatever else was necessary for the defence of the country. Thus the enemy thereabouts lost all desire to press on and exploit their victory (Prinsterer, 1857–9, 1st series V, 280).

Hierges soon found himself penned in between the earthworks at Woerden on his right, and Zwindrecht and a number of other fortified islands to his left.

Meanwhile Requesens in person was directing the left-hand thrust, which was an advance northwards over the Zeeland islands. Lacking boats, he bravely waded the water from Tolen to Duiveland and thence to Schouwen. He took the town of Bommenede with little difficulty, and in October he laid siege to Zierikzee.

With Hierges almost at Rotterdam, and Requesens on Schouwen, the Spanish achieved their deepest penetration of the Dutch redoubt during the Eighty Years War. From then onwards the state of their cause deteriorated with such speed that the entire Netherlands were as good as lost to them within little more than a year. Already on 1 September Philip II was forced to issue a decree of bankruptcy, which left the army at Flanders without pay.

In the field things began to go wrong when the rebels recaptured the Krimpen forts early in 1576, which removed the threat to the mainland and reopened the navigation of the Lek branch of the Rhine. From the Spanish viewpoint 'this was a heavy blow to our prospects of reducing Holland' (Mendoza, 1853, book XV, chapter 1). To the south Zierikzee was still holding out when Requesens died from illness on 5 March 1576. By the time the place finally capitulated, on 13 July, the Spanish army was dissolving in mutiny. One body of troops seized Alost, as some compensation for their arrears of pay, while the disorderly garrison of the citadel of Antwerp vented their feelings on the city in the famous 'Spanish Fury' of 3–6 November.

In February 1577 the new Spanish governor-general, Don John of Austria, concluded a Perpetual Edict with the States General of the rebel provinces 'for the alleviating of the troubles aroused in these countries by the foreign forces' (quoted in Ten Raa, 1911, I, 43). In the months following this virtual capitulation the garrisons retreated from almost all the fortresses still in Spanish hands, and the 'foreign'

troops – Italians, Burgundians and native Spanish – were withdrawn from the Netherlands.

Don John and the few loyal Netherlandish troops were reduced to clinging on to the small foothold formed by the Duchy of Luxembourg and the province of Namur. They were near to eating themselves out of house and home by the time that active operations were resumed with the help of a new general, Alexander Farnese, Duke of Parma. Financial support was at last to be had in fair abundance, at least for the next few years. Hostilities were ended with the Turks, and in 1578 the first *Flota* arrived in Spain with gold from the New World.

The Parma offensives 1578–89

The coming of the Duke of Parma to the Netherlands in 1578 presented the rebels with the most formidable opponent they had yet encountered. Parma shared with Alva the gift of being able to see the theatre of war as a whole, but he far surpassed the Spaniard in his understanding of siege warfare. Parma had taken part in many sieges, most recently the attack on the Turkish fortress of Navarino in 1572, and he developed a knowledge of the theoretical side of engineering through his conversations with the leading Italian expert Francesco de' Marchi at Brussels in 1565. Parma indeed was one of the first officers to have the opportunity of reading the manuscript of the treatise *Della Architettura*, on which Marchi had been working for several years.

From his experience and his studies, Parma reached the conclusion that it was better to browbeat a fortress into surrender than to take it by siege. By applying this strategy to the small towns of the Netherlands, he was able to leave the larger fortresses as isolated pockets of resistance in a hostile countryside. He could then complete the sealing-off process by cutting the water communications and throwing up chains of forts.

Whenever Parma discovered that a formal siege was unavoidable, he followed an unvarying routine. His first step was to launch a wide cavalry sweep through the surrounding countryside, so confusing the enemy as to his intentions. He then focused the movement on the selected town, cutting it off from its neighbours, and driving the peasantry inside.

There were some towns, like Maastricht, Antwerp or Venlo, which were situated by major rivers, and so could not be sealed off by cavalry patrols or siege-forts. In such cases Parma completed the investment by throwing stout blockade-bridges across the water. The existence of a river could also influence Parma's choice of which side of the fortress to attack. In 1586, in the sieges of Grave, Venlo and Rijnberk, he went to the trouble of planting batteries on islands, so as to breach the weak river fronts of the town walls.

Parma had no intention of imitating the practice of Alva, who left the conduct of the siege of Haarlem to the over-inventive Don Fadrique, and that of Alkmaar to the Sieur de Noircarmes. From the first Parma set an example of activity which was worthy of his near-contemporary, the great Duke of Guise, visiting the most dangerous and inaccessible positions daily, whether they were saps, mine galleries or flooded camps. He was tortured as cruelly as Alva by 'gout', the curse of the southerners in the Netherlands, but he thought nothing of spending seven or eight hours at a stretch up to his waist in the water of an enemy fortress ditch.

The actual work of reconquering the Netherlands was begun in 1578, by the ailing Don John of Austria. He defeated the rebels in an encounter at Gembloux in January, and went on to expand his foothold by prosecuting a number of small sieges. Thus by the time of his death in October he had the satisfaction of knowing that he had firmly established his army on the upper Meuse in the 'quadrilateral lodgment' (Cardinal de Granvelle, 14 July 1578, in Prinsterer, 1857–9, 1st series VI, 413), formed by the strongholds of Mariembourg, Philippeville, Givet and Namur.

Parma succeeded in the governorship, and decided to march down the Meuse and devote the main effort of 1579 to the reduction of Maastricht, 'which was', wrote Vazquez (1879–80, book 3), 'the rebels' main fortified depôt and the path and entrance by which so many evil things entered the Netherlands'. The capture of this place would help to open up the eastern flank of the northern provinces and, as Vazquez implies, cut off one of the main avenues by which the rebels received help from Germany.

Parma drew his heavy guns and ammunition from Burgundy, Lorraine and the fortresses of the upper Meuse, and he pushed the early stages of his siege through the orderly sequence already outlined: first the cavalry sweep, and then the tighter investment by means of siege lines and blockade-bridges.

What Parma had not bargained for was the presence in Maastricht of the Lorrainer Sébastien Tapin, 'a valiant soldier and a great engineer, who performed many extraordinary and unprecedented feats in the defence of Maastricht' (ibid.). Thus Parma gravely underestimated the strength of the defences, and he lost 2,000 dead in a premature assault against the s'Hertogenbosch and Tongres Gates.

It was a pitiful sight to see the men who had been maimed by the fire of the artillery, muskets and arquebuses. Some lacked a leg, others an arm. Here there was a soldier whose guts were pouring from his body, and over there lay a man who had half his face torn away (quoted from Paolo Rinaldi's *Liber Relationum* in Essen, 1933–7, II, 165).

Parma accordingly set about a formal siege, all the time keeping Maastricht under a tight blockade. At last the defenders became so enfeebled that Parma was able to take the town by a *coup de main* on the night of 28–9 June. The Spanish themselves were starving, having been checked for 111 days before Maastricht, and now the streets ran red with blood as the exasperated soldiers revenged themselves for their miseries.

Parma carried away some unforgettable lessons from the siege of Maastricht. First, that he must always inspect the state of the fortifications and breaches in person. Second, he had to admit that 'still being somewhat unpractised, he had risked and lost all the bravest men of his army in bloody assaults. He finally learnt by experience, and saw that he would have to take towns foot by foot' (Tavannes, 1850, 33). Lastly, he made up his mind that his soldiers would never again want for ammunition, food, clothing, shelter or pay in the course of a siege. Vazquez wrote in 1614 that

25 Parma's assault of Tournai 1581. The fortifications are typical of the period – earthen bastions in front of old walls. The letter 'F' indicates the entrance to a mine gallery (P. Melchor de Novar, 1682)

from that day to this, there has always been ample ammunition in the trenches and batteries . . . The soldiers in the trenches and posts are so well provided . . . that they have no fear of ever having to undergo the hardships they knew at Maastricht (Vazquez, 1879–80, book III).

Parma spent the next three years in the work of reconciling the towns of the southern Netherlands by persuasion, threats or blockade. He was forced to go to the trouble of a siege only at Tournai in 1581 and Oudenarde in 1582.

While Parma was thus profitably engaged in the south, a new theatre of war came into being beyond the Zuider Zee. In 1580 the Catholic party in the north-eastern provinces rose in favour of Spain, and expelled the rebels from the towns of Groningen, Delfzijl, Coevorden and Oldenzaal. After this, Count Rennenberg and the mercurial Martin Schenck van Nydechem managed to hold the heretics at a distance until Parma sent his ablest officer to help them. The gentleman in question was Francisco Verdugo, 'a brave, courteous and very experienced soldier, who rose from the rank of musketeer, which he held at the siege of Haarlem, to the governorship of Frisia' (Baudart, 1616, I, 404).

In October 1583 Verdugo captured Zutphen by surprise, and with it attained the most significant of all the Spanish gains in the north-eastern theatre. The counter-revolution had now pushed far enough south to establish occasional but effective contact with the main Spanish body in 'Belgium', while the loyal provinces to the rear – Overijssel, Drente and Groningen – were given a fair measure of security against rebel raids. From the offensive aspect the possession of Zutphen placed the Spanish on the middle of the Ijssel, the eastern river barrier of the heretical strategic redoubt. Thus all the country between the rivers Ijssel and Rhine became 'daily infested and harassed by Spanish incursions' (Grotius, 1657, 137).

Not surprisingly, the rebels threw garrisons into Lochem and Dort, and tried to contain the Spanish inside Zutphen by building a great semi-circle of forts and inter-connecting lines on the western bank of the Ijssel. The fighting around Zutphen went on for seven whole years, and it flared up violently whenever the Spanish broke through to the fortress with their convoys of provisions.

Both sides prosecuted these sieges, diggings of entrenchments, skirmishes and other enterprises so enthusiastically and for so long that it seemed as if the prosperity or ruin of all the towns and provinces of the Netherlands hung upon the fate of Zutphen and its neighbourhood. The Dutch States threw most of their forces and revenues into this obstinate struggle, with the result that the best towns of Flanders and Brabant, and indeed almost the whole of these two important provinces fell into the hands of the Prince of Parma for lack of sufficient help and support (Baudart, 1616, I, 454).

Parma took full advantage of this diversion in the north-east. He sealed off Brussels, Malines and Ghent by forts and trenches, and in 1584 he proceeded to grasp the greatest prize of the southern Netherlands, the city of Antwerp. Ghent was certain to fall anyway, and if Parma took Antwerp as well he would complete the conquest of the Scheldt, which was the taproot of Brabant and Flanders, and he would bring the Spaniards once more close to the seaward flank of the Dutch strategic redoubt. The more active style of operations derived also from the fact that Philip II had by now absorbed his conquests of Portugal and the Azores, and was willing to devote more attention to the Netherlands.

The main Spanish army appeared before Antwerp on 3 July 1584. The place was surrounded by wide inundations, but Parma got off to a good start by seizing the important Koevenstein dyke on the right (eastern) bank of the Scheldt, and he determined to cut off the remaining path of relief by building one of his favourite blockade-bridges across the river below (north of) the city. By March 1585, after seven months of labour, the Spanish had closed off more than 1,000 yards of grey river water by means of a boom of boats extending from wooden jetties which were driven into the Scheldt from either bank. Unfortunately the defenders of Antwerp were hard at work on a scheme of their own.

The inventors of war machines were one of the less sane manifestations of the late Renaissance. They filled notebook after notebook with their fantastic designs, and they had been badgering

26 Siege of Oudenarde 1582. Parma (A) carries on with his meal despite the carnage wrought among the company by a cannon shot. The ball was fired by a drunken Spanish gunner (P. Melchor de Novar, 1682)

sensible military men for decades. Philip II had little time for such gadgetry (whatever its appeal for unstable people like Don Fadrique), and he used his courtiers and servants to keep at arm's length one of the more persistent of the tribe, the Mantuan engineer and mechanic Federigo Giambelli. This wit thereupon set sail for the northern Netherlands, muttering that 'the Spanish would one day hear him spoken of in a way that would make them regret that they had scorned his offers' (Essen, 1933–7, IV, 55).

Giambelli settled in Antwerp, married a local girl, and lent all his support to his adopted city when it came under siege. On his request, the city fathers agreed to let him stuff two boats with between 6,000 and 7,500 pounds of gunpowder each, and load them down with layers of masonry, gravestones, mill-stones, stone shot, scrap iron, beams and bricks.

On the night of 4–5 April 1585 the two 'infernal machines' swept down on the Spanish bridge with the ebb tide. One of the boats stranded herself on the bank, but the other lodged just where the Calloo jetty joined the bridge of boats. There she blew up with an ear-splitting explosion.

A minute later and miles away the good things that Giambelli had piled on board were still pattering to the ground. The western half of the bridge was shattered, and 800 of the Spanish soldiers were blown to pieces. The toll among the commanders was correspondingly heavy. Richebourg's body was found draped over the anchor-chain of a boat, while the remains of Robles de Billy were identified months later, plastered to a pile of the bridge.

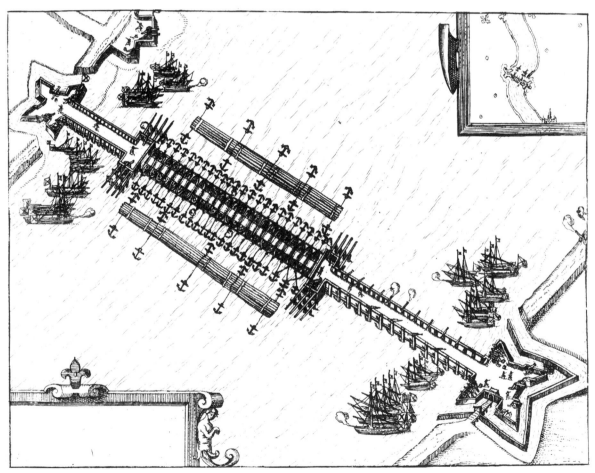

27   The Spanish bridge at Antwerp 1585 (Baudart, 1616)

28 Giambelli's infernal machine destroys the Spanish bridge. 'A' denotes Parma. 'C' is Ensign Vega (P. Melchor de Novar, 1682)

Unbelievably, the defenders of Antwerp were so stunned by the explosion that they did not venture down the Scheldt to see what damage had been caused. A fleet from Holland and Zeeland was waiting downstream, but the city never gave the rocket signal which would have summoned the armada up the river. Thus Parma was allowed to bar the way again by boats, rafts, piles and floating patrols.

On 26 May 1585 the Spanish threw back a determined attack on the Koevenstein dyke. Now that they were undisputed masters of the inundation as well as the Scheldt, they merely had to hold their positions and let starvation do their work for them. On 15 August Antwerp yielded by capitulation.

Since Brussels had already surrendered to a Spanish blockading force on 10 March, the reduction of Antwerp brought the area under Spanish control northwards to the approximate line which was going to be recognised in 1648 as the border between the Spanish Netherlands and the United Provinces. For that reason Parma may be called the creator of 'Belgium'.

Parma was full of admiration for the defenders of Antwerp: 'Thus we can appreciate the obstinacy and *brio* of these people, and the resourceful courage with which they use all kinds of devilish inventions against us' (ibid., IV, 73).

At the same time Parma was thoroughly vindicated in his decision to build the Scheldt bridge. The river barrier played an important part in delivering Antwerp from the rebels, and earned its place as a 'Catholic' siege device which was to be employed against the heretics at Ostend and again at La Rochelle in 1627–8.

Now that Parma had closed up to the southern river lines of the rebel strategic redoubt, and Verdugo had lodged himself on the Ijssel to the east, Queen Elizabeth of England felt obliged to intervene directly on behalf of the hard-pressed Dutch. She accordingly sent a contingent of 6,000 English troops to the northern provinces, and the rebels were persuaded to accept the Earl of Leicester as their governor-general. The English newcomers excelled when they were defending a breach or making an assault, but they were much less good at the more systematic work of fortress warfare. As Secretary Walsingham admitted, 'our captains, being but young, know not what belongeth to the defence of a town' (30 June 1586, Leycester, 1844, 328). Out of the 200 pioneers, a large number were 'householders and married men, and of body not fit for this service' (ibid., 86).

After a series of indecisive manoeuvres, Leicester and Parma ended up confronting each other on the old stamping-ground around Zutphen. The deadlock lasted until late January 1587, when Sir William Stanley and his garrison delivered to the Spanish the fortress of Deventer, the capital of Overijssel. Rowland Yorke followed his example, and admitted the Spanish to the fort on the west bank of the Ijssel immediately opposite Zutphen. These gains enabled Parma to consolidate and extend his hold on the Ijssel line, and by giving the Spanish the services of Stanley and his 'regiment of the wild Irish' they began centuries of association between Spain and the Wild Geese, 'excellent soldiers . . . who serve with the Spanish more willingly than do the troops of any other nation' (Coloma, 1853, book IV).

Following some bitter disagreements with the rebels, Leicester departed for home in December 1587, leaving his English troops leaderless but still scattered over the Netherlands in considerable numbers. Early in 1589 the long-unpaid English garrison of Geertruydenberg rose in rebellion; withstood a siege by the Dutch, and on 9 April

opened their gates to Parma. 'This is a considerable gain for the enemy,' wrote Count William Louis of Nassau on 23 April, 'for they have thereby gained all Brabant and are now completely secure against every raid and surprise attack' (Prinsterer, 1857–9, 2nd series I, 96).

King Philip wasted these years of magnificent opportunity, preferring to indulge in schemes of extending his rule to England and France. Parma was therefore diverted from the northern theatre, and ordered to prepare the southern Netherlands as a base for the invasion of England. He took Sluis in August 1587, after a difficult siege, and so won an outlet by which the Spanish boats from the Pays de Waes could reach the North Sea coast. All the effort was in vain, for the Great Armada of 1588 proved to be a disastrous failure. Parma was so discouraged that he confined his land campaigning of that year to a feeble and unsuccessful siege of Bergen-op-Zoom.

The second, and for Parma the fatal diversion was directed into France, where Philip wished to set himself up as the saviour of the Catholic League. In 1589, the year of the mutiny at Geertruydenberg, Parma was warned not to commit himself too deeply in the northern Netherlands. This was followed by positive orders to turn south, and over the next three summers the Spanish army was engaged in campaigns deep inside France. Parma was exhausted and disappointed, and he died at Arras on the night of 2–3 December 1592 before he could lead his troops into France on yet another misconceived invasion.

These diversions were doubly pernicious, for the Dutch now had the power to take the offensive. The credit was due to Prince Maurice of Nassau, second son of William the Silent, who gave the rebel provinces their first effective field army, and, more important still, adopted and developed the techniques of siege warfare as they had been worked out by people like Vitelli and Parma.

The offensives of Maurice of Nassau 1590–1600
The activity of Maurice of Nassau embraced every branch of the military art. He assembled reliable troops, paid them regularly and well, and reorganised them into the manageable tactical unit of the battalion.

As regards siege warfare his main contribution was to put things on a businesslike footing. For at least two generations commanders had been aware of the disadvantages of relying on the peasantry for siege labour, and commanders such as Montluc, Guise and Parma had taken up pick and shovel and shamed the soldiers into following their example. Maurice too was prepared to set to work in person, as befitted a student of the wars of ancient Rome, but he very soon discovered that the prospect of extra pay was the surest key to unlock his Dutchmen's hearts.

According to the settled procedure worked out by Maurice, the Dutch engineers used to send their requisitions for siege labour to the regimental quartermasters, who in turn were responsible for ordering the corresponding number of troops to the trenches. The pay was always generous, and in 'dangerous and hazardous situations' (quoted in Ten Raa, 1911, 283) it might soar to twenty times the normal rate.

On the whole the system of paid military labour worked well, though a contemporary grumbled that

the works which are performed by 'commanded' soldiers end up by being incomplete and very costly. They prove so expensive because all the soldiers are set to work, regardless of the fact that many of them have never held a shovel or spade before in their lives. The French are the worst of all, for they spend most of their time on the site in joking and playing. A single Frisian or other hard-working man will do more in a single day than four Frenchmen (ibid., II, 284).

There were further opportunities for abuse when civilian contractors set themselves up as inter-mediaries between the generals and the soldier-pioneers. The money was liable to stick in the palms of these middlemen, and the pioneers were left with 'little incentive to endure any great danger. All too often the siege works which involve risk are left incomplete, as happened here (at Oldenzaal in 1597), for whenever the town opened a heavy fire the workers ran away, leaving the gabions unfilled' (Duyck, 1862–6, 21 October 1597, book III).

Maurice set up a new hierarchy of officials to supervise the progress of all engineering works. The commies van de fortificatien stood at the bottom of the ladder, and the successive rungs were represented by ingenieurs (who received 300 florins per year) and controlleurs (who got one hundred more).

The whole machine was directed by Simon Stevin of Bruges, who had once been Maurice's tutor in mathematics and fortification, and was now appointed Quartermaster-General of the army. Stevin originated and directed the attacks in all the sieges at which he was present. Otherwise, as 'even Master Stevin cannot be everywhere' (quoted in Ten Raa, 1911, II, 284), the siege projects were put forward by the engineers on the spot and the most suitable scheme selected by the commanding general.

Stevin's work was not confined to the field. As well as composing valuable textbooks, he helped Maurice to draw up the engineer regulations of 1599 and 1606, and he worked out the exact and permanent dimensions of the Rhineland foot, a unit of measurement which remained in wide currency in northern European fortification well into the nineteenth century.

On 9 January 1600 Maurice and Stevin set up a chair of surveying and fortification at Leyden University. The instruction to the university stipulated that each period of teaching in surveying

is to last half an hour, and it is to be followed by a further half hour in which the lecturer will answer questions and elaborate on any points which were not understood in the first session. In their daily engineering business the pupils are to converse in the ordinary local speech, and speak little or no Latin. For that reason the lessons are to be held in Dutch, and not in Latin, French or any other foreign language (Duyck, 1862–6, II, lxxix).

Aspirant engineers attended the Leyden school in some numbers until a pedantic professor re-introduced Latin in 1668 and drove them away.

As far as garrisons were concerned, Maurice was content to extend the excellent waardgelder system. Seeing that the scheme had not caught on widely enough outside Holland, Maurice in 1596 ordered a total of 6,000 waardgelders to be raised in all seven of the provinces, so that the field army would not be sucked into the defence of remote fortresses.

In the time of Maurice the expenditure on

fortification rose steeply, both in absolute terms and in relation to the cost of the field army. Whereas just 100,000 florins were spent in 1596 (and about 350,000 on the field army), this sum climbed to 300,000 in 1600, and to half a million in 1606 (compared with 600,000 on the field army). Much of this money went towards realising the designs of Adriaan Anthonisz, a burgomaster of Alkmaar who emerged as one of Maurice's most talented fortress engineers.

Maurice was the first Dutch commander to have great quantities of engineering materials at his disposal. We learn as much from such incidental details as the mention of 10,000 iron-tipped stakes which the Dutch left behind when they raised the siege of Grol in 1595.

Artillery was also available in unprecedented quantity. Domestic manufacture on a large scale began with the setting-up of a cannon foundry by the city fathers of The Hague in 1590, and the stock of artillery and requisites was swollen still further by the capture of material in Spanish fortresses over the next decade. Thus conquest fed on conquest. While a respectable total of twenty-four cannon was employed against Deventer in 1591, an enormous park of no less than forty siege guns thundered against Steenwijk in the following year, discharging over 6,000 rounds in a single day.

In strategic terms what Maurice did in the 1590s was to consolidate and expand the southern border of the Dutch redoubt, and isolate and eliminate the Spanish and their supporters in the north-eastern provinces. He darted between these two theatres, making full use of his assets of interior lines and water communication, while the land-bound Spaniards were granted no time to move around the wider circuit to parry his blows.

With Parma and his army locked up in France in 1590, the few Spanish that were left in the Netherlands were incapable of withstanding Maurice's first offensive. He captured Breda by surprise on 4 March, then advanced deeper into Brabant, reducing Steenbergen, Rosendael, Oosterhout, Turnhout and Westerloo – a useful chain of conquests for the work of a single summer. Nijmegen was too hard a nut to crack, but Maurice nullified the place by building Fort Knodsenburg on

the opposite bank of the Waal, 'so that the Upper and Lower Betuwe will be free from raids, and the enemy will be prevented from making a sudden crossing there with his whole army and gaining a passage into Holland' (William Louis of Nassau, May 1590, Prinsterer, 1857–9, 2nd series II, 133–4).

Maurice's growing confidence was shown in his remarkable triple offensive of 1591. He first of all struck a blow in the vital strategic pivotal area of the Ijssel. On 27 May the Dutch threw a bridge of boats to an island opposite Zutphen, and on the next day a party of sailors helped the troops to plant thirty-two cannon there. 'This was done with a dexterity and a speed that were almost unbelievable. It goes to show that by using sailors we can plant a battery far more quickly and effectively than with horses' (Baudart, 1616, II, 153). The weak and badly-provisioned garrison surrendered on 30 May, and Parma had to write to Philip that 'we have just seen the enemy shut one of our remaining entries into Holland' (Essen, 1933–7, V, 317).

Deventer went the same way on 11 June, after the Dutch had battered it 'furiously and with the greatest speed' (Vazquez, 1879–80, book XV). The greater part of the Ijssel was now in the Dutch power, and the Spanish had to recognise that Maurice had taken

so many important places that any attempt to recapture them would involve us in heavy and endless costs, which are particularly inconvenient at the present time of general calamity and embarrassment. Added to which the Dutch have the habit of fortifying captured places so strongly and putting them in such a good state of defence that they become impregnable (ibid.).

Parma marched north to invest Knodsenburg. Maurice responded to the provocation, and the two armies glared at each other until, on 24 July, Parma received King Philip's order to march into France. He had to comply, leaving just 9,000 men scattered over Flanders and Brabant. Maurice reconcentrated his forces, landed on the southern shore of the Scheldt estuary, and on 24 September he had the impudence to take Hulst, scarcely sixteen miles from Antwerp.

After this, Maurice summoned up the resources

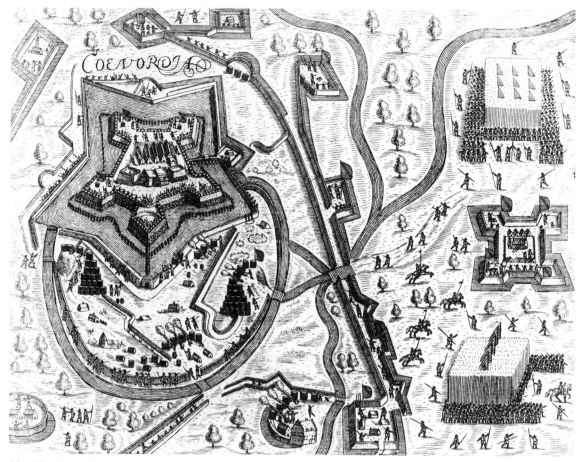

29 Maurice of Nassau's siege of Coevorden 1592 (Baudart, 1616)

to make the third and final offensive of that year. He re-embarked his troops, ferried them eastwards to Dordrecht, where they landed and began the overland march against Nijmegen. This place fell to the twenty-four-year-old Maurice on 21 October, representing the fourth major fortress he had taken in that eventful year.

In 1592 Maurice resolved to finish off the Catholic provinces in the north-east. He began on 28 May by laying siege to Steenwijk, which barred his entry to Friesland. On 24 June the large east bastion was blown into the air by a mine, which was 'a truly terrible sight' (Prinsterer, 1857–9, 2nd series I, 196), for 'bodies of men might have been seen hovering piecemeal in the air, the torn and divided limbs yet retaining their decaying vigour and motion'. All the

same the garrison held on with determination until the lack of provisions compelled them to capitulate on 4 July.

On 5 July 1592 Count John of Nassau-Siegen wrote that

it will be generally agreed that no such determined siege and defence has been seen since the beginning of the Netherlands wars, what with all the thunder of the heavy cannon, the continual labour of the soldiers on so many works and trenches, and all the mining and sapping. There was plenty to learn and see for anyone interested in the engineering trade (Prinsterer, 1857–9, 2nd series I, 198–9).

The Dutch were faced with difficult technical

problems at their next target, the five-bastioned marsh fort at Coevorden, 'knowing that it was a solid mass of earth, and that their artillery, however powerful, would have little effect' (Verdugo, 1610, book IX). The besiegers therefore drove forward a covered trench, almost identical with one which the Spanish had employed at Haarlem, and by 'attaching' their miner to the ramparts they forced the garrison to capitulate on 12 September. Anthonis Duyck (1862–6, book I) entered in his diary that this was a siege 'in which more than any other we may appreciate the power of the spade, and see that it can smash and conquer obstacles which withstand every other instrument of war'.

Maurice might have gone on to crush the north-eastern Catholics in his very next campaign if the southern party in the States General had not called him down to Brabant in 1593, so as to deal with the annoying fortress of Geertruydenberg. Having arrived before this place, he set 3,000 soldiers and pioneers to work to build the most ambitious of his siege lines up to that date:

The forts were raised very high with earth; the trenches and ditches were everywhere answerable; many great palisades were added for the greater security in divers places; and every fort was well furnished with artillery (Bentivoglio, 1678, part III, book I).

Notable persons came from all sides to see the sight, which aroused great expressions of admiration. Among them were even the Princess of Orange, one of the daughters of the Prince of Orange . . . and several other great ladies (Meteren, 1618, book XVII).

By turning his siege into a social event Maurice had anticipated one of the more charming customs of seventeenth- and eighteenth-century fortress warfare.

The Spanish commander Mansfield reconnoitred the lines, and found that

Maurice was so strongly dug in that it was quite impossible to attack him in his position . . . . Before arriving at the trenches the Spanish would have had to take four well-sited royal forts, all

amply provided with cannon and musketry (Carnero, 1625, book X, chapter 2).

Geertruydenberg capitulated in June, and Count William Louis of Nassau, in a letter of 19 June 1593, congratulated his brother Maurice on

a signal victory which proves that skilful direction and patient labour are more potent in warfare than brute force. This siege is to be hailed as a second Alesia [the Gallic fortress besieged by Caesar], and a significant restoration of the art of war of the Ancients (Prinsterer, 1857–9, 2nd series I, 245).

This compliment must have given Maurice a good deal of satisfaction, for his great ambition had been to get his soldiers to build siege works as skilfully and willingly as the legionaries of Ancient Rome.

Nothing stood between the north-eastern loyalists and their fate. In 1594 Maurice moved north and laid siege to the town of Groningen. The Spanish answered with a furious fire, 'and the shot churned up the surrounding fields so that it seemed as if they had been ploughed up, or turned over by a herd of swine' (Baudart, 1616, II, 204). The duel was sustained until the place capitulated on 22 July.

After taking a long pause to recruit his forces, Maurice exploited a new opportunity which opened up in 1597, when the new Spanish governor-general, Archduke Albert, led his army away to face the French in Artois. Maurice promptly captured Rijnberk and seven other fortresses, thus cutting a wide swathe along the borderland between Germany and the Netherlands, and pushing the Dutch holdings south-eastwards for more than fifty miles beyond the Ijssel. At the end of this campaign it was a common saying among the Dutch that 'the fence of the Netherlands is closed'.

Spain and France signed peace on 2 May 1598, and for the first time in eight years the Spanish were free to concentrate all their attention on the war against the Dutch. In the same year they took back Rijnberk, 'one of the most important towns for guarding the navigation of the Rhine' (Coloma, 1853, book XI).

In 1599, instead of exploiting their successes in the same promising direction, around the eastern flank, the Spanish made the mistake of probing the river lines that ran along the southern flank of the Dutch rebel redoubt. They thereby committed themselves to a war of attrition on the narrowest and strongest sector of the enemy frontier. Marching up the Waal, to a point where it briefly flowed with the Maas, the Spanish planted a strongpoint of their own, Fort St Andries, in the midst of the river barrier.

By a supreme irony, Fort St Andries was completed at almost the precise moment when the Spanish army dissolved in one of the most spectacular of its mutinies. Prince Maurice could therefore lay siege to the place in the spring of 1600 without the slightest danger of being interrupted. The garrison put up a creditable resistance, but finally disgraced itself by capitulating for a bribe in May. As Count William Louis of Nassau observed, 'this part of the frontier is now so firmly closed that the enemy must give up any thought of breaking through it' (5 May 1600, Prinsterer, 2nd series I, 10).

His confidence swelled by such an easy victory, Maurice made one of his extremely rare ventures into the open field, advancing in the midsummer of 1600 along the Flanders coast to besiege the Spanish privateer bases of Nieupoort and Dunkirk. Maurice beat the hastily-assembled Spanish forces at Nieupoort on 2 July, but discovered that his own army was unequal to either of the projected sieges. The Dutch army was therefore evacuated by sea in early August. Maurice was not to know that for the next three years the attention of all Europe was going to be fixed on the same Flemish dunes by the greatest of all the sieges of the Eighty Years War.

The siege of Ostend and the Spinola offensives 1601–8

Maurice's foray along the Flemish coast brought home to the Spanish the need of doing something about the Dutch coastal enclave at Ostend, which the enemy had been diligently fortifying for some years:

Quite apart from the fact that the Archduke Albert was denied the use of such a good port, the presence of the garrison compelled him to maintain a war in his own territory, added to

which the land had to bear the ruinous cost of paying an extra army – Flanders in particular was the prey of the soldiers, whereas in peacetime it was reckoned to make up a fourth part of the whole Seventeen Provinces in wealth (Haestens, 1615, 98).

Albert therefore decided to reduce Ostend. His ambition resulted in a contest which lasted for three years, and bears comparison with the sieges of Vienna in 1683 and of Stalingrad in 1943 for the interest which the rest of the world attached to its outcome.

Parma himself had never dared to tackle Ostend, which possessed free communication by sea to Zeeland and Holland, and was surrounded by water on almost every side. The sea ruled out all serious attacks against the Old Town, or northern portion of the fortress, while the landward fronts were protected by two tidal creeks: the Old Harbour on the western side, and the New Harbour or Geule (the present port of Ostend) on the eastern side.

The landward approaches represented 'a plashy moor (Vere, 1672, 126) on all sides except the coastal dunes. These sand hills offered the only tracts of dry ground over which siege guns could be brought close to the fortress, but if they chose this path of advance the Spanish would be presented with the problem of crossing the Old Harbour and the Geule at their deepest and widest points.

The man-made defences of Ostend consisted of two perimeters. The inner enceinte owned eight earthen bastions, in front of which was a broad and deep ditch of sea water. The bottom was 'a glutinous impermeable mud, which supported no vegetation . . . and always retained its water' (Montpleinchamp, 1693, 152). Beyond the ditch ran a very thick counterscarp, or rather outer enceinte, which conformed approximately to the trace of the inner enceinte, and consisted of long branches which ran forward into bastion-like salients. The works as a whole were high, well-flanked and strongly-palisaded, though built of a 'sandy and mouldered earth' (Vere, 1672, 121).

On 5 July 1601 the Spanish appeared before Ostend in the strength of about 12,000 men. Over the following months they proceeded to drive the defenders back from their positions in the marshes to the two enceintes. They simultaneously planted some heavy siege batteries in the western dunes, from where the guns kept up a heavy fire against the Sandhill Bastion, which stood at the north-west corner of the outer enceinte and overlooked the point where the Old Harbour entered the sea. The cannonade was so violent that the work

might rather have been called iron-hill than sand-hill: for it was stuck so full of bullets, that many of them tumbled down into the fausse-braye, and others, striking on their own bullets, breaking into pieces flew up into the air as high as a steeple (Hexham's account, Vere, 1672, 166).

The besiegers paid heavily for their gains. The newly-arrived troops from Spain and Italy perished miserably in the bitter weather, and they were cut down in scores by the fire from Ostend. 'The ground was strewn everywhere with arms, legs and hands . . . surgeons came out of the town, and brought back bags full of human fat which they had stripped from the bodies' (Haestens, 1615, 147). (This disgusting material was prized as a salve for wounds.)

Possibly as many as 2,000 men were lost on the single night of 7–8 January 1602, when the Spanish launched an assault along the beach at low water against the Sandhill Bastion. Archduke Albert had committed precisely the same mistake as Parma at Maastricht in 1579, throwing his men into the assault over open ground against prepared defences. All along the ramparts of Ostend lay the people who had paid for his error:

whole heaps of dead carcasses, forty or fifty upon a heap, stark naked, goodly young men, Spaniards and Italians: among whom, some (besides other marks to know them by) had their beards clean shaven off. There lay also upon the sand some dead horse, with baskets of hand-grenades; they left also behind them their scaling-ladders, great store of spades, and shovels, bills, hatchets, and axes and other materials (Hexham's account, Vere, 1672, 174).

For the rest of 1602 and the best part of 1603 the siege settled into a noisy but indecisive routine. The Spanish never again essayed an assault, but con-

tented themselves with cannonading the town from a high platform built on the western dunes.

Compared with the Spanish host, the garrison was not particularly big (in March 1602, for example, it stood at 7,000), but in compensation the defenders were continually reinforced and replenished from the sea. So sure, indeed, was the traffic that many civilian spectators, including women, made the trip to Ostend to view the siege.

This period was enlivened for the Spanish by the arrival in their camp of a present from the Pope, in the person of the engineer Pompeio Targone (1575–c. 1630). Targone had

a very ready wit, which made him apt for inventions in his calling: but having never till then passed from the theory to the practical part in military affairs, it was soon seen, that many of his imaginations did not upon trial prove such, as in appearance they promised to be (Bentivoglio, 1678, part III, book 7).

Targone bent his imagination to the task of pushing forward the approaches from the eastern dunes, but he failed dismally in every one of the devices he contrived: first a monstrous rolling gabion, then a floating battery, and finally a dyke which broke apart in the north-western storms.

Such was the state of affairs when the Spanish officers heard that yet another Italian dilettante was coming out to Ostend, not merely to invent siege engines but to take charge of the whole army. This gentleman was one Ambrogio Spinola, a scion of a wealthy Genoese family. The signs could hardly have been worse. Spinola was known to be devoid of all military experience, and to have been brought up in comfortable, not to say sumptuous surroundings. Moreover, the family had virtually bought the command for its pampered son, by offering to put the Spinola riches and credit at the disposal of the army in the Netherlands.

In one respect the Spanish expectations were fulfilled, for as soon as Spinola reached Ostend in the late summer of 1603 he charged a large proportion of the costs of the siege to his own account. As early as 10 December Archduke Albert could write to King Philip III that since Spinola had taken charge

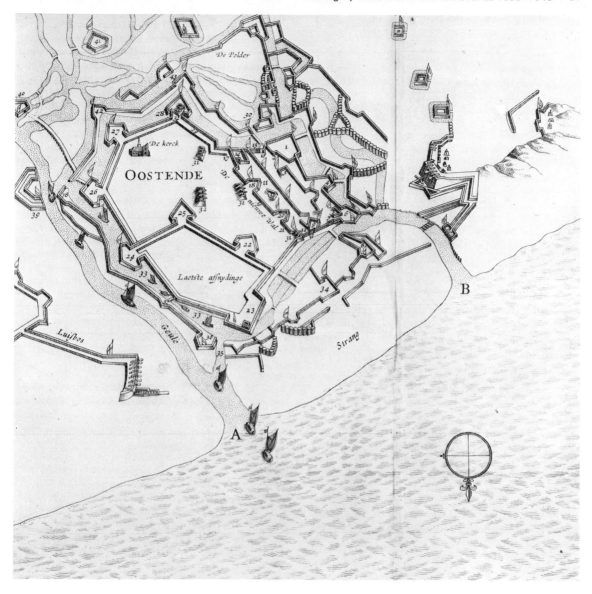

30 Siege of Ostend 1601–04. 8 = Sandhill Bastion; B = Old Harbour; 22–25 = the retrenchment (Dögen, 1647)

the siege has been progressing very quickly. With the help of the money which the said Marquis is providing . . . we have overcome many difficulties which hitherto impeded the course of the works. All of this gives us good cause to be optimistic (Villa, 1904, 73–4).

What was much more surprising was that Spinola proved to be that rarest of creatures, a man who had equipped himself to be a complete commander from the study of books. Not only did he show himself to be an expert engineer, but he won over the ordinary soldiers by leadership of the most direct and forceful kind. In the quiet of his library he had absorbed all the lessons which Parma and Archduke Albert had had to buy with the blood of their men.

Spinola's main objective was to force the crossing of the Old Harbour from the west. If he could gain the counterscarp on that side, he explained to the king, 'Your Majesty would have a guarantee that the town would be yours' (ibid., 76).

Reviving the ferocious emulation which had existed among the Habsburg contingents in the days of Charles V, Spinola arranged his Germans, Spanish, Italians, Burgundians and Walloons in order of battle along the bank of the Old Harbour from its mouth to the marshes behind the town. The troops then threw causeways of earth and fascines across the creek. This was a difficult and bloody business which was helped by screens of gabions, but not at all by the employment of the last of Targone's inventions, a mobile drawbridge mounted on four ten-foot wheels. A single cannon shot shattered one of the wheels and immobilised the machine for good.

Spinola was everywhere, 'exposing himself as much as any of the rest to all the labour and dangers, encouraging some, rewarding others' (Bentivoglio, 1678, part III, book 7). The Walloons and Burgundians were the first across, for the water was shallowest at the head of the creek, but the other contingents were not far behind, and on 4 April 1604 the besiegers surprised and took a number of redoubts on the counterscarp opposite the Sandhill Bastion. Maurice received the news in Holland with astonishment, and began to harbour his first fears as to the fate of Ostend.

Parma now undertook a second, formal siege of the inner enceinte. In the summer the Dutch were forced to abandon the inner rampart altogether, and they retired to a large bastioned retrenchment which they had heaped up in the north-eastern corner of the town.

In order to complete these fortifications the defenders had to dig up a number of dead bodies, and heap up the heads and bones of their late comrades like fascines. Since these works were made of dead bodies and freshly-dug earth, they could not offer adequate resistance to cannon-fire (Baudart, 1616, II, 340).

Unseasonable storms completed the Spaniards' work for them. The Dutch supply ships found it increasingly difficult to make their way into Ostend, and on 22 August a combination of tempest and high tide swamped the grisly retrenchment and carried large sections of it away.

The States General finally authorised the last governor, Daniel d'Hertaing, to seek a capitulation on good terms. He shipped off all the gunners, engineers, Spanish deserters, heretical preachers and other folk who were calculated to awake the Spanish ire, and then opened negotiations with Spinola. On 20 September 1604 he was granted a free evacuation for the remaining 3,000 men of his garrison.

Archduke Albert and the Infanta Isabella came from Ghent to view the conquest, but they could see

nothing but a misshapen chaos of earth, which hardly retained any show of the first Ostend. Ditches filled up, curtains beaten down, bulwarks torn in pieces, half-moons, flanks and redoubts so confused with one another, as one could not be distinguished from another; nor could it be known on which side the attack, or on which side the defence was (Bentivoglio, 1678, part III, book 7).

The scale of the struggle for Ostend resembled that of a war rather than a siege. The contest lasted three years, three months, three weeks, three days and three hours, and the losses of the Spanish from all causes are variously estimated at between 17,000 and 80,000 dead. The impartial Carnero (1625, book XV, chapter 10) puts the figure at 40,000, which seems a good average. The casualties of the Dutch are quite impossible to estimate, for their vessels made something like 3,000 round trips, bringing reinforcements to Ostend, and carrying away the sick and wounded to die or recover in their homeland.

The siege, long and costly though it was, must be accounted a major victory for the Spanish, for they had evicted the Dutch from their one remaining foothold in 'Belgium', and so completed the work which Parma had begun in the 1580s. The technical lessons were obvious enough: in the first place, that it was extremely difficult to take a fortress which could receive reinforcements and replenishment throughout the siege; then again, it was clear that an unprepared assault would almost certainly meet with a bloody repulse, and that it was essential to shelter the besieging troops with all the cover that earth and brushwood could provide.

Maurice and the Dutch field army had meanwhile been striving to draw the Spanish away from Ostend by reducing fortresses in other parts of the Netherlands, applying the technique of trying to break a stranglehold by stamping on the strangler's foot. Maurice captured Rijnberk in 1601, Grave the next year, and in 1603 he essayed a determined but vain siege of s'Hertogenbosch – all without persuading the Spanish to move from Ostend. At last in the spring of 1604 the Dutch army undertook a direct offensive along the Flanders coast. Sluis and its fine harbour fell to Maurice on 19 August 1604, hardly a month before the Spanish conquered Ostend.

If the siege of Ostend had established Spinola as a master of fortress warfare, then his capacity in the open field was proved beyond doubt in the brief (but for the Dutch extremely alarming) period of fighting which preceded the Twelve Years Truce. In 1605 Spinola took a leaf out of Maurice's book. He advanced threateningly on Sluis, then swung eastwards with 15,000 men, crossed the Rhine at Kaiserswörth, and in August reduced the fortresses of Oldenzaal and Lingen. For the first time in two decades the main Spanish striking-force had been transferred to the vital pivotal area east of the Ijssel, and Maurice spoke wonderingly of the movements of this 'flying devil' who seemed to read his thoughts like a crystal ball.

Grol fell to Spinola on 14 August 1606, so deepening the area of his conquests in Overijssel and eastern Gelderland. Heavy rains ruled out any exploitation westwards across the Ijssel, or northeastwards towards Friesland. Spinola accordingly turned on his tracks, and strengthened his hold on the middle Rhine by taking the much-disputed fortress of Rijnberk.

Despite his recent conquests, Spinola was one of the leading advocates of a truce with the Dutch. He knew that the Spanish finances could not possibly support the strain of further campaigns. A preliminary armistice was concluded in April 1607, which led to an agreement to conclude a truce with a term of twelve years dating from 1608. The demarcation confirmed the *status quo*, leaving the Dutch with a narrow foothold in northern Brabant and Flanders to the south of their river line; further east, the Spanish reaped the benefit of Spinola's recent successes, and retained Oldenzaal and Grol as tiny enclaves lodged on the borders of Germany and the Dutch provinces.

The defence and the attack in the early seventeenth century

The Spanish and Dutch contributed in equal measure to the great advances that were made in fortress warfare in the last quarter of the sixteenth century. 'The Method of Maurice of Nassau', with its labyrinthine siegeworks and its employment of soldier-pioneers was merely a continuation of what Parma had been doing in the 1580s. Conversely, the 'Netherlandish Fortification' originated with the Dutch, but was extensively applied by the Spanish, sometimes with the help of renegade rebel engineers. In the event, no combatant could make a significant advance in the attack or defence without seeing it rapidly copied by the enemy, and diffused over Europe by the countless foreign officers who served in the Netherlands.

The unity of Spanish and Dutch methods is due in part to the inspiration which both sides derived from the classical past. The Huguenot general Rohan (1850, 209) states that

the Ancient rules of attacking fortresses are the

same which are employed today. The siege of Alesia is the model which has been copied by the Prince of Parma, the Prince of Orange, and Marquis Spinola in order to prosecute their own sieges.

Netherlandish fortification

The salient characteristics of Dutch fortification were the employment of the earthen rampart and the wet ditch. These features met the most pressing demands of the theatre, which were for a kind of fortification that was suited to a flat terrain with a high water table, and for one which could be thrown up in a short time and at a low cost. Four stages of increasing elaboration may be traced in the evolution of this Netherlandish fortification.

First came improvised works which were added to medieval enceintes, like the horse-shoe retrenchments behind the breach at Haarlem.

Then there appeared more developed fortifications *à la Huguenote*, consisting of earthen ravelins and detached bastions of regular design, which were placed in front of the old town walls.

These appear in the 1570s at Oudenarde, Ghent, Bruges, Dunkirk and other large towns in the southern Netherlands.

After that the Dutch began to build complete earthen enceintes, with regular bastions and elaborate outworks, as at Ostend and Maurice's reconstruction of Coevorden.

Finally came complete permanent fortresses, which had their earthworks supported by low masonry scarps in demi-revetment. Coehoorn rebuilt Bergen-op-Zoom and other fortresses in this style in the later seventeenth century.

Co-existing with the fortresses proper were the small earthen redoubts, or *Schanzen*, which were built to command dykes or river crossings. Some of the most important chains of *Schanzen* were constructed by Maurice along the Waal and the Maas in 1599, so as to guard these river lines with the least possible number of men, and give warning by bonfires or shots whenever the Spanish ventured out of s'Hertogenbosch. The system was strengthened and extended in the winter of 1605–6.

The culmination of Maurice's achievement in fortification was represented by the third of the

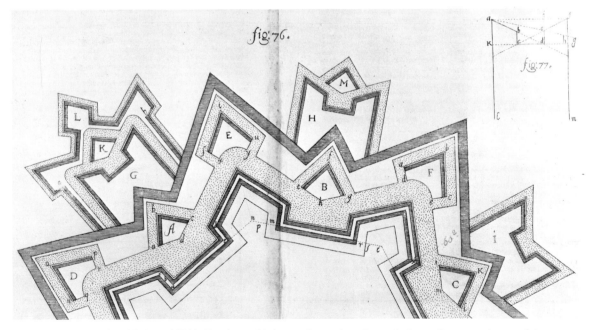

31   Dutch fortification (Freitag, 1631). Enceinte with fausse-braye, broad wet ditch, continuous outer enceinte (envelope), and elaborate detached works – ravelins (A, B, C), demi-lunes (D, E, C) and hornworks (G, H, I)

stages outlined above: the complete earthen fortress. It was the product of no individual engineer, but it had been foreshadowed in 1533 by the unrevetted fortifications which Count Henry of Nassau built at Breda, and it was expounded and developed by such writers as Samuel Marolois, Maurice's *Kastramentator* Simon Stevin, Hendrik Hondius, Adam Freitag and Andreas Cellarius (see the bibliography). At the present time the fortress of Heusden offers a fine example of this style.

The heart of the defence consisted of a thick earthen rampart, which possessed an unrevetted outer face descending at the 'natural slope' of the earth. This bank was protected against escalade by horizontal palisades called 'storm poles', and along the foot of the rampart there ran a low outer rampart, or fausse-braye, which gave the defenders complete command of the ditch.

This double enceinte was formed into curtains and bastions in imitation of the Italian model, but with the important difference that the trace was always devised with the range of musketry in mind. Thus the flanks of adjacent bastions were rarely spaced more than 250 yards apart, and usually stood at much closer intervals. The flank of the bastion met the curtain at right-angles, which made for a spacious gorge suitable for retrenchments. However, the bastion as a whole was long and etiolated, and the faces met in narrow salient angles of between sixty and seventy-five degrees. The sharply-inclined faces could therefore supplement the cross-fire of the flanks proper, leaving the main task of frontal defence to the curtain and the outworks. The flanks were sometimes straight and single, and sometimes retired and double after the Italian style.

The enceinte was surrounded by a wide wet ditch which offered the chief passive defence of Netherlandish fortification. The covered way, which ran along the outer rim, was unusually spacious by Italian standards.

Like the other elements of the fortress, the outworks represented a compound of Italian teaching and Netherlandish innovation. While the ravelin was a direct imitation of the Italian original, the Dutch far surpassed the southerners in their application of two other detached fortifications: the first was the demi-lune, a ravelin-like work which

was planted in front of the bastion; the second was the boldly-projecting hornwork, which was sited beyond the main ditch in order to occupy a patch of commanding ground, to provide additional flanking fire where it was badly needed. The sides of the hornwork were formed of two parallel or slightly diverging 'branches', and the 'head' was made up of a small front of two half-bastions, a connecting curtain and an outlying ravelin.

Of all the fortresses, the one at Coevorden was cited as a stronghold 'which, everything considered, . . . is without peer in the Netherlands' (quoted in Ten Raa, 1911, II, 391). In the days of the Spaniards it had been possible to make a circuit of the works four times in half an hour, but by the time Maurice completed the reconstruction in 1605 the place owned seven 'royal' bastions of characteristic Netherlandish design, with salient angles so acute that the 'lines of defence' (the imaginary inward projection of the faces) met the curtains almost in the centre. A thick fausse-braye gave onto a 180-foot wide wet ditch, which was set with a complete chain of ravelins and demi-lunes, each preceded by its own thirty-foot wide ditch. These outworks were shielded from hostile view by a glacis, and beyond that again ran an outer ditch brimming with water, then an outer glacis, and finally the marshes.

Netherlandish fortification possessed outstanding virtues. Its wet ditches and earthen ramparts endowed it with unsurpassable powers of passive resistance, while its multiple lines and elaborate outworks contributed an important extension of the principle of defence in depth to European fortification as a whole. In his *Discours Politiques et Militaires* (first published Bâle 1587) the Huguenot captain La Noue admitted that the Italians had been the first to reduce fortification to a science, but he claimed that they had to give way to the Netherlanders when it came to speed and economy of construction. As an example he cited the fortification of Ghent with earthen ramparts, ravelins and counterscarp in the late 1570s. The work lasted two years and cost 300,000 florins, whereas masonry fortification of the same proportions would have been at least twenty years in the making, and cost twenty times as much.

Dutch engineers and their imitators spread the notions of Netherlandish fortification throughout

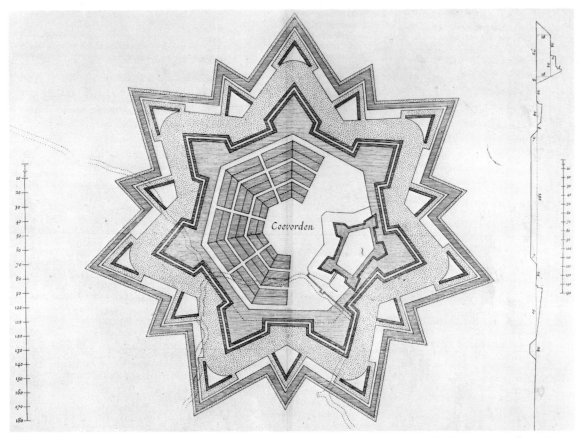

32 Coevorden as rebuilt by Maurice. Note the profile of the earthworks on the right-hand side of the plan, and the radial plan of the streets (Dögen, 1647)

Europe in the sixteenth and seventeenth centuries. Thus the enceintes of Berlin, Hamburg, Neisse, Danzig, Rostock and other cities displayed all the characteristic earthen ramparts, fausse-brayes and elaborate outworks. The French were enthusiastic for the hornwork, and, more remarkable still, the Venetians employed Netherlandish-trained engineers in the second half of the sixteenth century at Corfu, where they added ravelins, hornworks and the large San Dimitri outwork.

With such strong advantages to recommend it, how then did Netherlandish fortification come to be supplanted in European fashion by other, far more costly forms? The answer lies partly in a number of technical weaknesses. The elaborate outworks were not easy to defend by a small garrison, and once they were lost they offered the besieger some useful

lodgments where he could dig in. Then again, the wet ditches certainly offered a formidable obstacle to the attacker, but by the same token they hindered the supply and reinforcing of the covered way and the outworks. You could get to them only by means of rafts, or over timber bridges which could not be made too stout or broad without offering an avenue to the besieger. Once this wet ditch had been allowed to freeze, the storm-poles and the earthen slopes of the rampart offered only the feeblest obstacles to escalade. Every severe winter therefore threatened to deprive the Netherlandish fortress of its *Sturmfreiheit*, and ice-breaking became one of the first duties of the garrison.

Moreover, the Netherlandish fortifications were found to be singularly unfit to resist the forms of artillery attack which were perfected by Vauban in the later decades of the seventeenth century. The ricochet batteries discovered ideal targets in the long, easily-enfiladed branches of the hornworks and the faces of the sharply-pointed bastions, while the guns which were planted on the counterscarp could make short work of any defenders who were holding out in the low fausse-braye.

These were mere technical quibbles in comparison with two inherent limitations of the system. French and Venetians might borrow and adapt individual features for their own purposes, but the application of the Netherlandish form as a whole presupposed a level site, with a water table no more than six or seven feet below the surface. Such conditions were difficult to find outside the north European plain.

More serious still, the wooden palisades and earthen slopes of the Netherlandish system had to be constantly kept up, if the work were not to subside into a shapeless lump. As early as 1632 the deputies of the States General could make a tour of vital frontier strongholds, and find a place like Bergen-op-Zoom which was in 'a desolate condition' (quoted in Ten Raa, 1911, IV, 345). The Netherlandish system was in its essentials merely an elaborate field fortification, and the money you spent on it did not bear comparison as an enduring investment with the far higher sums demanded by a true permanent fortification with masonry revetments.

The march of the attack

The first thing that a besieging army did was to surround the fortress with a stronghold of its own. The evolution of the lines of circumvallation (facing the country) and countervallation (facing the fortress) has been indicated on earlier pages, from the first tentative experiments before Milan in 1522 and Pavia in 1524, to the more systematic application which dates from Alva's siege of Mons in 1572. The process was carried forward by Parma, and reached its full flowering in the enormous constructions of Maurice of Nassau. Part admiringly, part apprehensively, the French envoy Buzenval reported that the Dutch siege of Grave in 1602 was

begun and continued on a scale more befitting a great Sultan of Turkey than a small state which

owes its survival to the disorder which exists among its enemies, to some small economies and to a little help from its friends. The works which Prince Maurice has made before this place are truly gigantic. Every redoubt, no matter how small, has its own wet ditch and drawbridge, and the continuous line is so huge and vast that it takes nearly five hours to make the circuit (Prinsterer, 1857–9, 2nd series II, 153).

In the first half of the seventeenth century it was axiomatic that a line of investment, once established around a fortress, was impossible to break. Thus on 20 October 1627, reporting to Philip IV, Spinola justified his failure to attack the Dutch lines around Grol by harking back to Maurice's own hesitations twenty years before: 'The late Prince of Orange, who was a great soldier, came up to relieve Rijnberk while I was besieging it. He remained in the offing throughout the siege, but he saw that I was well dug in and so never ventured to attack' (Villa, 1904, 470).

Once the engineers and the commander of the siege army had settled on the point of attack, they began to build one or more square redoubts to act as the base for the operation.

These works and redoubts serve for a retreat to the workmen, if an enemy should make a great sally upon them: for being retreated into the said redoubts, they may resist an enemy, and stop him, till they are seconded; so that such redoubts are very necessary. For if the workmen had not a place to retreat into, they would be forced to betake themselves to their heels (Hexham, 1642–3, II, 22).

Between 200 and 500 'lusty soldiers' were then led after nightfall to within musket-range of the outworks of the fortress, and they were arranged by the engineers in a line roughly parallel to the covered way, with three or four men to every twelve feet. Companies of infantry were sent out ahead, and lay flat on the ground in readiness to ward off sorties. In the event of a very large sortie, the infantry and the workers would retire together to the protection of the corps de garde, a powerful body of infantry and cavalry standing in support behind.

With any luck the ground would be 'broken'

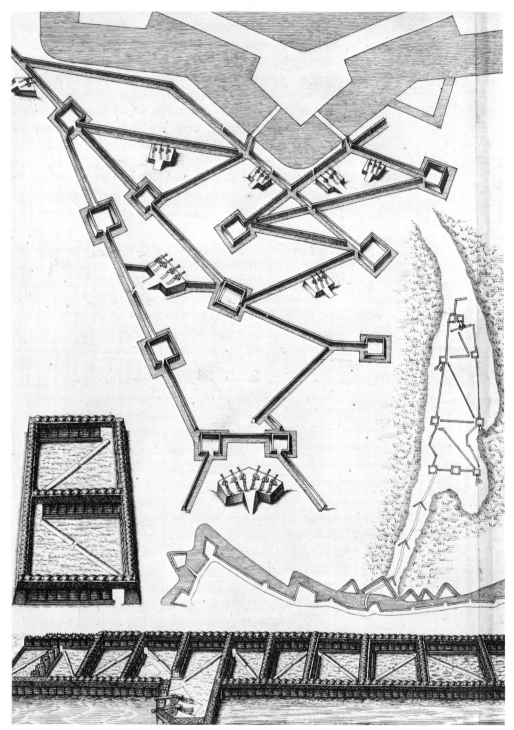

33   Progress of an attack, with trenches and redoubts. The figures at the bottom show how siegeworks could be built up with gabions across damp ground (Dögen, 1647)

unnoticed by the garrison, each soldier digging a trench three feet wide and three feet deep, and throwing the earth towards the fortress so as to make a parapet three feet high. In sandy ground, a firm parapet would have to be built by shovelling the soil into gabions (cylindrical wicker baskets, open top and bottom). Any defects which passed undetected in the night were made good on the next day, and the trenches were widened during the following nights and days to a breadth of anything between six and twelve feet, or sometimes even more if it was intended to draw carts and cannon through the trench rather than across the open ground. Sometimes the trenches were dug so deep that the side facing the fortress had to be recessed into a firing step to enable the musketeers to level their weapons over the parapet.

The next procedure was to extend the first trench towards the fortress by means of the smaller trenches known as 'saps'. The form and direction of the sap was dictated by the terrain. Over firm, clear ground the sap wound towards the fortress in a series of zig-zags, with the arms between 120 and 160 paces long, and the successive arms diminishing as the approach neared the covered way. If the terrain was so constricted by swamps or other obstacles as to leave no room for the zig-zags, then the only course was to follow the practice of Bartolomeo Campi before Haarlem in 1572 and run the sap straight at the fortress. In this case the sap would have to be directed under timber bridges or around traverses of gabions, in an attempt to diminish the casualties from enfilade fire. The work was still more laborious when the saps had to be directed over marshes or ground that was liable to intermittent flooding:

Having no firm foundation, the foundation of them is layed by filling up the water with bundles of boughs, brush, faggots and such like things, having earth cast upon them to settle them and make them lie fast, and the earth being brought upon wheelbarrows from some other place, a parapet is raised, and blinds set up, that the workmen and soldiers may work and be in more safety (ibid.).

All the while the garrison contested the issue with cannon, musketry and wall-pieces, but especially by launching powerful sorties which usually broke with devastating effect over these narrow saps. Infantry and cavalry repeatedly surged from the covered way and outworks, killing the workmen, and wrecking and filling in the trenches. The countervallation was too far away to lend effective support to the workmen, and the besiegers were forced to convert the actual approaches into defensive positions. This they did by studding the trenches every one or two hundred paces with square redoubts, each a miniature fortress, with sides about twenty-five paces long. Cavalry was stationed nearby, in hollows in the ground or behind breastworks, and it came out of hiding whenever the defenders' horse put in an appearance.

The closer the saps came to the fortress, the more bitterly was their progress contested. The heads of the saps had to be protected from fire, or at least from view, by screens of canvas or fascines, and by that very useful device the sap-roller, a stout and firmly-filled gabion, which the workers pushed in front of them as the saps advanced.

A special procedure was adopted at this vital stage of the siege. The men worked in threes, the leading worker digging a narrow furrow and planting gabions in a row, while the two men behind him made the sap successively deeper and wider, and filled the gabions with the spoil. The wise commander now made contracts to pay the workers handsomely for every stretch of sap completed. If he was generous enough the advance of the saps would rarely be delayed, even though two-thirds of the workers might be killed in the process.

The regular march of the sap attack came to an end when the head approached to within thirty paces of the covered way. Trenches were now dug to right and left, and the earth heaped up to form a high *cavalier de tranchée* or *Katze*, which served as a musketry position, and an assembly assault for the coming assault on the covered way.

The besieger undertook sap attacks of this kind in ones, twos or (as against s'Hertogenbosch in 1629) as many as four at a time.

The progress of the trenches was supported by artillery fire of various kinds. One of the most consistent features of our period is, in fact, the steady growth in both siege trains and fortress armament. For most of the sixteenth century all the work of the siege guns was carried out by a single unspecialised monster battery called the *batterie royale* or *Generalbatterie*, which was planted on a suitable hillock or an artificial *Geschützhügel*. The breastworks were usually built of tall and thick gabions, though woolsacks, sandbags or hurdles were sometimes used instead.

Within the *batterie royale* as many as thirty pieces were placed in line, about eight paces apart. The beastly construction was planted at a range of some 400 or 600 paces from the fortress, and from this site it kept up its fire throughout the siege, varying the target as circumstances demanded. In German lands the *Generalbatterie* retained its primitive simplicity until the last decades of the seventeenth century, but long before then the gunners of more advanced Western European lands had evolved smaller and more handy batteries, better adapted to deal with elaborate and well-screened fortifications.

The process of specialisation began at the turn of the sixteenth and seventeenth centuries. The *batterie royale* was now reduced in size, and supplemented by smaller batteries which were sited on either flank to assist their larger brother. This they did by bringing a cross-fire to bear on the breach, or searching out the retired flanks of the bastions.

As the glacis was piled ever higher and higher by military architects, so the batteries as a whole had to be moved much further forward than had been the case in earlier times, when they had to cope only with exposed walls. Writing in about 1620, Tavannes urged that the batteries should never be planted further than 200 paces from their target, and that in no event should the gunners open their breaching fire before they could see the base of the revetment.

When the target was a reasonably modern fortress, with closely spaced bastions, the leading authorities of the time held that the combined trench and artillery attack should be directed against the point of a bastion. They argued that it was a mistake to attack the curtain, the apparently easier target, for then the besiegers would find themselves in a fire-swept re-entrant between the bastions. As for the siting of the guns on the counterscarp, it was best to plant four or more heavy cannon opposite the bastion so as to make breaches near the salient angle, while placing supplementary batteries on either side in order to knock out the enemy cannon in the flanks of the adjacent bastions.

The rationalisation of siege artillery constitutes one of the main contributions of the Netherlands wars to fortress warfare. In 1609 the Spanish reduced the calibres of their cannon to four. These were the 48-pounder full cannon, nicknamed 'whistler' or 'wall-basher', the 24-pounder demi-cannon, the 10- or 12-pounder quarter cannon, and the 5- or 6-pounder eighth cannon. This reform was undertaken on the initiative of the Count de Buquoy, who was General of Artillery of the Spanish dominions, aided by the advice of the artillery experts Cristobal Lechuga and Diego Ufano.

It was easy to see, wrote Ufano, that the new cannon represented a great improvement, for

there was such diversity and confusion among the old pieces that it cost a good deal of trouble and effort to obtain their ammunition. Nowadays we have but a single range of artillery, all based on the full cannon and its fractions down to the eighth. It is truly remarkable to have reduced all our guns to these four calibres (Ufano, 1613, 14–15).

Out of all these pieces, the 24-pounder demi-cannon emerged as the king of siege warfare. It was the lightest gun which could be relied upon to breach masonry, yet round-for-round it did the job almost as effectively as the 48-pounder full cannon, while weighing little more than half as much, consuming half the charge of powder, taking up less space in the batteries and being much quicker to load. It held its dominating position for two and a half centuries until it was dethroned by the rifled artillery of the later Industrial Revolution.

In 1620 France adopted the 24-pounder and the 12-pounder in direct imitation of the Spanish practice. Maurice did the same, after he had conducted some experiments on the sands at Scheveningen to find out by how much he could reduce the length of the barrels without diminishing the range. The barrel of his demi-cannon weighed 4,500 pounds, which was actually 316 pounds lighter than the Spanish prototype.

As the seventeenth century wore on, the siege cannon received increasing help from its stubby

34 Battery shooting a breach from the counterscarp

Böltern den 20 August 1657 Attaquirt . vnd sich den 23

35   Siege of Münster by the German princes, 1657. A graphic representation of the chaos of the pre-Vauban sieges

cousin, the mortar, a weapon whose capacity was first demonstrated in the Netherlands at the Spanish siege of Wachtendonck in 1588. Ufano claimed that the mortar was a useful adjunct to the defensive, seeking out the enemy when they were lodged close under the ramparts, but most people maintained that the mortar was a heavily-biassed beast, which inclined strongly to the side of the attack. 'The mortar is useless and expensive in the defence of fortresses,' wrote a Frenchman, René Le Normant,

for the bomb rarely falls on a redoubt or other siege works, whereas it always finds its mark in a besieged town, providing it does not burst in the air or fall in some empty street or square. The bomb causes most havoc of all when it lands on the roof of a house or in the gutter separating the roofs of two dwellings. The weight of the bomb should therefore amount to at least 140 or 150

pounds, so that it will crash through the roof and the floors to the bottom of the house, where it will explode, bursting and burning the floors . . . and smashing and roasting the people within (Louis-Napoléon Bonaparte, 1851, II, 330).

We left the sap attack at the point where the besiegers had established their lodgment within a few yards of the covered way. They next set about evicting the defenders from the covered way, a task which was greatly facilitated by the invention of the hand-grenade: a powder-filled sphere of cast iron, bronze, thick glass (especially fashionable among the Spaniards), pottery or even wood.

Once in command of the covered way, the attackers had come within full view of the ditch and the enceinte beyond. As Tavannes put it (1850, 178), 'having arrived at the counterscarp, they count the town as being half taken'. Here also lay the first

severe test of the resolution of the defenders, for to
hold out any longer signified that they were willing
to withstand the breaching and assault of the main
rampart, a willingness which was less and less
evident with each succeeding decade of the seventeenth century.

The wet ditches of the Netherlands made high
demands on the skill of the siege engineers. Workers
and materials were first brought down to the level of
the ditch by way of a ramp or corridor which was cut
through the counterscarp. The men were then
employed on building whatever 'passage of the
ditch' the taste of the engineers had devised; perhaps
a bridge of barrels and planks, or a causeway
constructed by dint of piling earth or weighted
fascines into the ditch. In any well-managed siege,
the fortress artillery would by now have been

silenced. Precautions were nevertheless necessary
against the violent musketry which the defenders
invariably kept up until the end of the siege.
According to the severity of the case, the soldiers
crossing the bridge were protected by a canvas
screen, an earthen bank, or, in very obstinately-
disputed crossings, by a square-sectioned timber
gallery which was built over the bridge or causeway
and covered with earth.

The assault was delivered as soon as possible after
the bridge had been completed, providing the
rampart was unrevetted or had already been
effectively breached by the artillery. The latter was a
rare event until the time of Vauban. Failing this, the
miners had to be 'attached' to the rampart. They
burrowed through, then along, the interior side of
the revetment, and planted charges to blow the

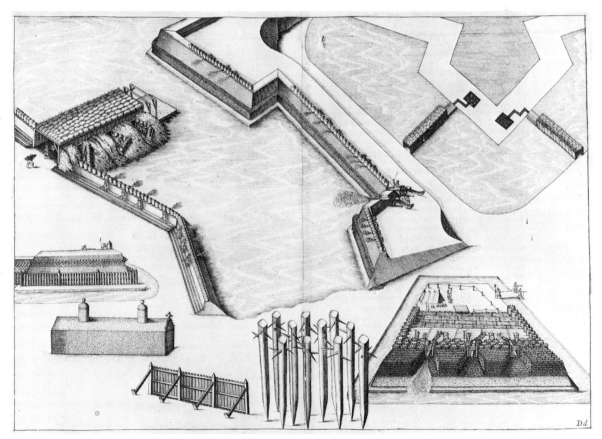

36 Final stage of a siege. The attackers are building a causeway across the outer ditch. We see further progress at the top right-hand corner, where two causeways have crossed the inner ditch, and mine chambers have been excavated in the rampart. The lower figures show batteries and obstructions used in siegework

masonry into the ditch. In the case of the Netherlands fortresses the inside of the rampart was often a
maze of beams and piles, which compelled the
miners to excavate the space for their charges by
cutting away the timbers, and extracting them with
the help of ropes and screws. In any event, they were
lucky if they avoided the attention of the defending
miners, and escaped the protracted and inconclusive
underground warfare of the kind which was waged at
Haarlem in 1573.

Various means of interior defence were open to
the garrison if it chose to hold out after the breach
was lost. The exit from the breach could be defended
by retrenchments such as the work at Haarlem in
1572–3, or the elaborate triple line at Maastricht in
1579. In a very exceptional case the defenders could
imitate the practice at Ostend in 1604, by abandoning the rampart altogether and retiring to a more
defensible perimeter in the interior. In the course of
the seventeenth century, however, more and more
engineers turned to the simple device of the 'gorge
retrenchment', a single earthwork which was built
across the neck of the bastion.

Of all the writers of the time, the Marshal de
Tavannes was probably the one who saw most
clearly the implications of the scientific attack as it
had been worked out by Spinola and Maurice of
Nassau:

Thirty years ago [he was writing in about 1620]
fortresses were so well provided with defences that
in the prevailing ignorance of the time were
regarded as impregnable, and even those which
were very weak were not at all easy to capture
(Tavannes, 1850, 178).

He cited the prolonged sieges of Maastricht, La
Rochelle and Sancerre.

Nowadays the besieger has gained the upper hand,
and the defence of fortresses has been so weakened
that we can see that without the help of an entire
army, and not just small detachments, they have
no hope of holding out .... Nowadays the
Spanish and Dutch officers have made the capture
of towns an art, and they can predict the duration
of resistance of a fortress, however strong, in terms
of days (ibid.).

The war from the end of the Twelve Years Truce until the Peace of Münster 1621–48

The last duel of Spinola and Maurice of Nassau 1621–5

In scale and cost, the second round of the struggle
between the Spanish and Dutch was in every way
the equal of the first encounters in the sixteenth
century. In most other respects, however, the
renewed war lacked the tension and the interest of
the earlier fighting. A general mood of confidence led
King Philip IV and his minister Olivares to renew the
war after the Twelve Years Truce expired in 1620.
This time the Spanish government aimed not to
bring down the Dutch republic by armed force, but
principally to re-open the navigation of the Scheldt,
and revive the commercial life of Antwerp and the
rest of the Spanish Netherlands. To that end the
Spaniards clamped embargoes on Dutch trade, and
committed the armada of Flanders to operations
against Dutch merchant shipping and the North Sea
fisheries. In the long term this strategy proved
highly effective.

On land, the official policy was one of a *guerra
defensiva*, which ultimately reduced the struggle to a
contest around the southern approaches to the
Maas-Waal line. On their side the Dutch lacked the
enterprise to emerge from the fortress zone and help
their French allies to finish off the Spanish in the
southern Netherlands. At no time was the existence
of the Dutch Republic at stake. Lacking the vital
spur to technical invention, both sides were content
to follow the routine which had been established in
earlier decades. The siege operations were consequently vast, predictable and somewhat dull.

Ambrogio Spinola, military commander of the
Spanish Netherlands, was the one man who retained
something of the fighting spirit of the olden times.
Indeed his aggressive strategies were irreconcilable
with the *guerra defensiva*, and for a time caused no
little consternation in Madrid.

Spinola did not have the supplies and the cash to
put all his schemes into immediate effect. He took
Jülich early in 1622, which made the Dutch nervous
for their eastern flank, but then turned against
Bergen-op-Zoom, the most westerly of the Brabant
fortresses held by the Dutch. Here Spinola bit off

more than he could chew. His mutinous and poorly-paid army managed to capture only a few outworks before a Dutch relieving force came up in the autumn and forced him to raise the siege.

Spinola spent some time in recruiting his strength, and then, to the horror of his own generals, he set the army down on 28 August 1624 before the inundations and bristling works of Breda, a rich town in north Brabant. Spinola hoped to reduce Breda by starvation, and he confined his active siege operations to long-range fire from a chain of strongly-built batteries. He stayed there through the winter and spring, keeping the town under bombardment and blockade, and holding the Dutch field army at arm's length.

Maurice of Nassau concluded that Breda was as good as lost, and took to his bed at The Hague. He died there on 23 April 1625 at the age of fifty-eight, asking to the very end what had happened to Breda, the town he had captured thirty-five years earlier when he began his chain of conquests. Since then he had taken thirty-eight towns and forty-five forts by siege, and five towns and ten forts by surprise. Twelve times he had relieved fortresses under enemy siege.

The seventy-two-year-old governor Justin of Nassau capitulated for a free evacuation on 2 June, and on 15 June he and the 3,500 remaining men of the garrison marched out with the honours of war. Spinola saluted the officers as they went by, 'and in particular the governor, a venerable old gentleman, with his wife and child, and Dom Emanuel de Portugal, with Count Maurice and his two base sons, who all returned the like courtesy, with modest composed countenances, bowing their colours with respect to Spinola, as they passed' (Hugo, 1626, 34).

Spanish artists captured something of the elation which was aroused by the reduction of Breda, the last great military achievement of the golden age of Spain. Lope de Vega composed a *Diálogo Militar* in honour of the Spanish commander, and years later, when Spain had much less occasion to celebrate, Spinola's friend Velázquez harked back to the happy events of 1625, and recorded on canvas the scene as his patron accepted the keys of Breda, and embraced Governor Justin in front of the two armies.

The campaigns of Frederick Henry the
Stedenzwinger *1626–47*

The Spanish capture of Breda was a memorable feat, but all that Spinola had to show for this two years of effort was the bringing down of a single Dutch fortress on the Brabant side of the Maas. So much for the ambitious plans he had outlined in 1621. This small gain was more than offset by events elsewhere. War broke out with England in 1624; this denied the Spanish supply ships and troop transports the shelter they used to find in the Downs before they made a dash for the Flemish coast. Worse still, the vital land route to the Netherlands became subject to a series of increasingly prolonged interruptions, beginning with the capture of the Valtelline by the Swiss heretics in 1624.

Isolated, unpaid and nearly forgotten, the Spanish forces were capable of putting up little more than a show of opposition against the Dutch in the period of nearly a quarter of a century which intervened between the capture of Breda and the Peace of Münster. All semblance of a contest was at an end, except for the Cardinal Infant's brave little offensives of 1635 and 1637, and the interest of the war came to centre around the question of whether the Dutch could summon up the necessary resolution and forces to take Spanish fortresses which were virtually theirs for the asking.

The command of the Dutch was assumed by Frederick Henry of Nassau, half-brother of the late Maurice. It was not long before the new chief earned the title of *Stedenzwinger*, or Conqueror of Towns. He began by reducing the footholds which Spinola had established in Gelderland and Overijssel in the last campaigns before the Twelve Years Truce. He took the fortress-depôt of Oldenzaal in 1626, and this led him on to crack the still harder nut of Grol in the following year.

In 1628 Spinola left for Spain for the last time. For years now he had been working for something like eighteen hours a day, bottling up all the affairs of the Netherlands in his head, and so his departure was followed by a long period of confusion. Thus far Frederick Henry had been content with closing the eastern gate of the United Provinces, but now he did not hesitate to cross the Maas and expand the Dutch holdings in 'Belgium'. His objective was the rich

Brabant town of s'Hertogenbosch, which was situated four miles south of the Isle of Bommel and on the direct route between Utrecht and the southern Netherlands.

Frederick Henry arrived before s'Hertogenbosch on 1 May 1629, and applied enormous resources to carrying out what was by now the established routine of sieges. He devoted no less than 28,000 troops to the operation, and disposed them in siege-lines that were eleven hours in circumference, and studded with six entrenched camps, nine major bastioned forts, and a dozen hornworks. Thus secured against disturbance, he placed 116 cannon in battery, dammed two rivers, and drove forward four separate sap attacks to bring about the final reduction of the fortress on 14 September. Carlos Coloma wrote to Spain that he was desolated 'to see the most Catholic and loyal city in the Netherlands fall into the hands of such people. And that without any hope of ever getting it back' (Villa, 1904, 564).

This misfortune was as nothing compared with the events of 1632, when the treacherous commander Hendrik van den Bergh invited all the non-Spanish soldiers in the southern Netherlands to liberate themselves *van de slaverie der Spaignaerden*. Venlo, Roermond and Maastricht opened their gates to the Dutch, thus almost severing the Spanish Netherlands from the Catholic powers of Germany, and accounting for the odd bulge which the Dutch border ever afterwards made south-eastwards to Maastricht. For the moment Frederick Henry did not dare to follow up his success by turning west against Brussels: he was at home among fortresses, dykes, rivers and marshes, but hated the thought of venturing into the open field.

In February 1635 the Dutch signed an alliance with the France of Cardinal Richelieu, which did something to spur Frederick Henry once more into motion. By that time, however, the enterprising Cardinal Infant Ferdinand and 11,000 fine Italian and Spanish troops had reached the theatre, where they were greeted with an outburst of popular enthusiasm.

The combined invasion force of 30,000 French and 20,000 Dutch duly met near Maastricht, and advanced by the direct path on Brussels. Any lingering affection for the Dutch in the southern Netherlands was however dispelled when the allies assaulted and burnt Tirelemont on 9 June 1635. This was followed by a vain siege of Louvain, which was prolonged until the news came that the allied communications with Maastricht were in jeopardy (see p. 124).

Having weathered the crisis, the Cardinal Infant went over at once to the counter-attack, and on 28 July he surprised the Schenckenschans, a fort which stood at the division of the Waal and the Neder-Rijn. He could not have chosen a better target, for the Spanish were now able to lay the eastern Dutch provinces under contribution, and harass the communications of Frederick Henry with his recent conquests on the middle Meuse and Rhine.

Frederick Henry devoted something like six months to the recapture of the Schenckenschans, first building redoubts to hem in the garrison, then throwing up to sixty bombs a day into the fort, until the governor capitulated on 29 April 1636. The siege was of some technical importance, for it marked an important stage in the turning of the Dutch towards bombardment as a means of siege attack, but the effort so exhausted the heretics that they undertook nothing of importance for the rest of the year. Thereafter Frederick Henry was content to launch short-winded and sporadic offensives, and he aimed at little more than winning ground in northern Brabant on either side of Antwerp.

In 1637, at least, the Dutch seemed to act in something like the old Nassau style, and wiped out the last memory of Spinola's conquest by retaking Breda on 10 October. The elation of the United Provinces was somewhat dimmed by a characteristic counter-stroke of the Cardinal Infant, who snapped up Venlo and Roermond while the Dutch were busy at their siege.

Frederick Henry remained supine until the progress of his French allies in southern Flanders called for some sympathetic movement on his part. All the same, despite the talk of *notabele entreprinse* and *groote dessein*, the Dutch did little more than launch brief forays into Spanish Flanders, which led to the reduction of Sas van Ghent in 1644 and of Hulst in 1645. The French were given a startling revelation of Frederick Henry's state of mind when, in 1646, Marshal de Grammont went to the Dutch

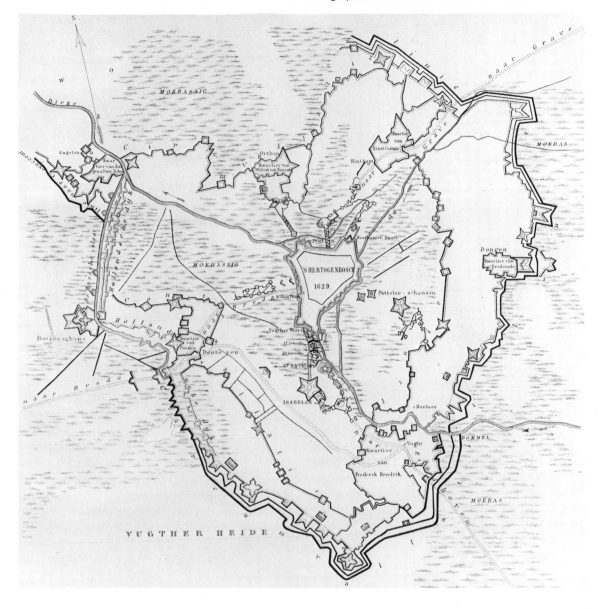

37 The siege of s'Hertogenbosch, 1629. Showing the extraordinary development of the Dutch siegeworks

camp to urge a move against Antwerp:

He was astounded when, wishing to get down to business and obtain his orders, Prince Frederick Henry took him by the hand, and after leading him wordlessly around the room, asked him whether he would like to dance an allemande with him, for the opportunity would never come again (Grammont, 1850, 269).

When Frederick Henry did get under way, he found that Ghent and Antwerp were skilfully covered by small Spanish forces. Thwarted in this direction, he moved east to the middle Meuse and sat down before Venlo on 11 October 1646. The result was the last and almost the feeblest siege of the Eighty Years War. The province of Holland refused to pay a penny towards the cost of the operation as long as Gelderland and Overijssel remained *defectueuse* in their contributions, and on 29 October the siege was raised without a single sod having been turned. Frederick Henry deserved a better end to his career.

On 15 May 1648 the Dutch provinces as 'Sovereign States' exchanged their ratification of the Peace of Münster with the Spanish. Beyond the Ijssel-Waal-Maas river cradle of the Dutch Republic, the United Provinces retained all the conquests of Maurice and Frederick Henry (save Venlo and Roermond), from the shot-ploughed works of Sas van Ghent and Hulst to the grassy mounds of Coevorden, trampled only by the gentle cows that gave the fortress its name. The rest of the Netherlands remained to the Spanish.

The decline of Dutch and Spanish military engineering

Until the middle of the seventeenth century the Spanish and Dutch retained the European prestige which they derived from their experience of fortress warfare in the Eighty Years War. Englishmen like Hexham and Ward could plunder the text and plates of Ufano's treatise on artillery, while the French for a brief period regarded themselves as humble pupils sitting at the feet of the Dutch.

A rather different story is told by the experienced Dutch officer Rüsensteen, who had travelled widely in Europe, and was not at all impressed by the state of engineering in his homeland by the end of the Eighty Years War. There were

but few alterations or diversities of attacks, seeing they are almost all of them made after the same manner . . . and this proceeds chiefly from the impression which many had, and still have, that the fortifications were at perfection, contrary to the experience and matter of fact in the late wars (Rüsensteen, 1654, 25–6).

The truth was that no single ruler or engineer could have prevented the Dutch and Spanish from resigning the lead in siege warfare to other nations. The long series of campaigns which began in 1621 was totally lacking in the urgency and drive to invention which marked the first bout of the wars, as we have seen, and the attempts by propagandists to hark back to the horrors of Alva and the Inquisition were more likely to make people laugh than shudder. There is more than a whiff of the perfumed air of the eighteenth century in episodes such as the cease-fire which was ordered at Breda in 1624 to allow Prince Ladislaus of Poland to inspect the rival lines, or in Frederick Henry's polite expression of admiration for the Spanish defence of Sas van Ghent twenty years later, when he knew very well that the feeble effort deserved nothing of the sort.

In Spain the decay of intellectual energy was already far advanced. Technical education was confined to a small number of private schools which were run by Italian masters, and few or none of their lay pupils seem to have entered the public service. Philip IV once complained that native Spaniards had no taste to serve in the artillery. As for the engineers, the military reforms of 1633 actually reduced the number to six ill-paid individuals, and by 1637 Philip was so short of help that he promised titles of nobility to any foreign experts who came to serve with the Spanish army in the Netherlands. The deficiency was never made up.

Far from the Spanish sending out experts to help in the defence of their outlying possessions, they actually lived parasitically on the same lands, and deprived them of native masters in order to prosecute works of civil and military engineering in the Peninsula. In 1624, 1637 and again in 1646 the Brussels administration was ordered to send some of the finest Netherlandish technicians to Spain: men like the engineers Abraham Melin and Pierre Goins, the hydraulic expert Pierre Baes, and the geometrician Jacques de Beste. A draft of miners was raised in 1639, and gunners were enlisted for Spain in 1644.

All of these measures proving inadequate, the king was forced to employ clergymen who had some knowledge of mathematics or the natural sciences: Dominicans like Roldan, or Jesuits like Isasi, Camosa and Lafalla. The names of no less than 151 such clerical 'engineers' were recorded between 1600 and 1675. Nowhere was there any attempt to create a corps of experts, and the engineers still corresponded direct, as individuals, with the king or the Council of War.

In these circumstances, the Spanish were quite unable to *institutionalise* their experience of fortress warfare. A commander such as Parma profited by the mistakes of his early sieges, while one of academic bent like Spinola could draw lessons from history, but if great men of this kind were lacking, there was no body of engineer officers who could step in and supply the deficiency. As the example of France was to show, the element of continuity was all-important in the process of building up a corps of proficient experts.

Five   The Apprenticeship of France 1560–1660

We have seen how, in the middle of the sixteenth century, the borders of France had marched forward alarmingly under the direction of Henry II. This advance had been made possible by a generation of able commanders, who had harnessed the resources of a full sixteen million subjects. Within a single decade, however, the divisive work of the Reformation had set these same captains at each other's throats, and established a sense of factionalism that was not to be eradicated for the best part of a century.

National interests were forgotten in the eagerness of the warring parties to admit foreign troops. English and German Protestants came to help the 'Hugenowses' in the 1560s, while the Spanish were invited to France in the 1580s and early 1590s, and again during the troubles of the Fronde in the middle of the next century.

The techniques of war itself could find no stable foundation, and the art of siege warfare, as practised by the French, entered a long period of stagnation or actual regression.

Darkness and false dawn 1562–1610

The early religious wars 1562–78
France was plagued by no less than nine separate wars of religion between 1562 and 1598. This was largely because armies lacked both the artillery and the money to follow up their victories in battle by taking castles and fortified towns.

In those times the towns used to hold out for six or seven months, because the art of the attack was so little understood, and the defenders were confident of being saved by one of the frequent changes in the face of public affairs (Tavannes, 1850, 424).

For many years the Huguenots simply could not make up their minds what to do about fortresses. In the early 1560s the Protestant commanders maintained that every effort should be devoted to keeping a powerful army in the field,

but when, as a result, they abandoned their strong fortresses in the provinces, they found themselves in a bad way, for they had deprived themselves of refuge (La Noue, 1850, 618).

On the offensive, the Huguenots suffered heavily from being denied the resources of central government and taxation. As La Noue sagely remarked,

what ruined the Huguenots was the shortage of artillery, ammunition and pioneers. When they sat down before one sector of a fortress they were unable to pursue the battering and the siege works with any energy, which gave the Catholics two or three days to prepare effective counter-measures. If they tried to plant new batteries somewhere else, the same thing happened again. It seems to me that Parma and his kind are the ones who excel in siegework, and that Protestants in general are at their best in the defence (ibid., 635).

Admiral Coligny, La Noue and the wiser heads among the Huguenots knew from history and their own experience how Imperial armies, strong ones, had been broken at the sieges of Padua in 1509 and Metz in 1552. They would therefore have preferred the victorious Protestant forces to march straight to their goal, without bothering themselves with irrelevant fortresses. Instead the Protestants chose to sit down before Chartres in 1568 and Poitiers in 1569, and lost the initiative just as surely as the decision to attack Saint-Jean d'Angely, later in 1569, deprived the Catholics of the fruits of their victory at Montcontour. As long as civil anarchy reigned, neither faction could really afford the luxury of a long siege.

The fortress therefore reigned supreme. As Palma-Cayet noted concerning Issoire, 'in the circumstances of civil war the master of this town is also the master of much of Auvergne, where he can levy taxes just as he wishes' (Palma-Cayet, 1850, 635). Likewise in the great towns the word 'citadel' proved to be as emotive a term in sixteenth-century France as it was in the contemporary Netherlands. Thus the citizens of Lyons ousted their governor the Duke of Nemours on 13 September 1593, complaining that 'as soon as Nemours takes a place, he turns it into a citadel in order to subjugate the townspeople' (Lestoile, 1850, 178).

The French stronghold came to assume a sinister life of its own, as the home of a fortress-based warlordism which gradually escaped from all control. By the 1590s many fortress governors ceased to have any interest in the victory of one party or another, and much less in the restoration of royal authority. A neutral observer commented that

they grew to like the pleasure of absolute command so much – with its delicious freedom to dispose of the royal revenues and the labour and sweat of the people, that they would rather have seen the kingdom go to ruin than give up this kind of life.

The mass of the nobility conceived a dislike of domestic peace,

for, in imitation of these great governors, there grew up a multitude of bandits and other people who waged local wars, and made their houses into

miniature frontier fortresses. When the king wanted to form an army, nobody responded to the call, unless it was to sally a few steps from their fortresses in order to take some more booty (Palma-Cayet, 1850, 294–5).

As regards the geography of the fortresses, Providence seemed to have disposed the three-quarters of a million Huguenots about France with the express purpose of setting the superior resources of the Papists at naught. The rapid spread of heresy through the main trading avenues had ensured that almost the whole of the periphery of France was studded with towns under Huguenot control. Protestantism was firmly rooted in the trading towns of Normandy, the Seine and the Channel coast, and reached out by way of Picardy to the rebels of the Netherlands. In the south-east was Lyons, which lay hard by the seat of Calvinism at Geneva, and was reckoned to be the greatest Protestant city in the whole of France. From there a host of heretical townships, with their stark and smelly little chapels, extended in a wide arc through Languedoc to the Navarre of Jeanne d'Albret (a patroness of the reformed religion) and then north-westwards by way of Guyenne and Poitou and thus back to Normandy.

Among all those seats of heresy, two fastnesses were so pre-eminent as to deserve the title of 'strategic redoubts'. These were the city of La Rochelle and the region of the Cevennes. They were situated about 250 miles apart at opposite ends of the Protestant perimeter, yet they held to the cause of the Reformation long after the other centres of resistance had been beaten down, and they eventually succumbed within a year of each other in 1628 and 1629.

La Rochelle, the north-western redoubt, was a large seaport inhabited by people 'accustomed to war and trade' (La Noue, 1850, 639). Landwards lay the fertile Pays d'Aunis which, closer to the fortress, gave way to the salt marshes and canals girdling the walls. Out to sea the twin islands of Ré and Oléron owned profitable salt-pans, and acted as outer bulwarks sheltering the roomy inner and outer harbours of La Rochelle from all winds except that from the west-south-west. Thus La Rochelle came

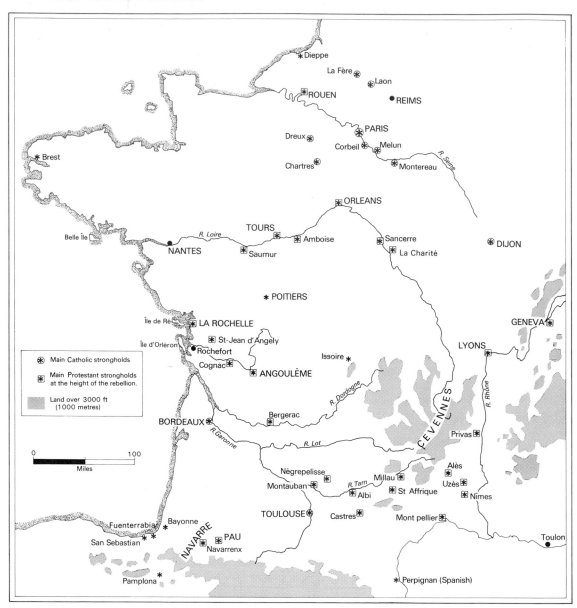

France in the Religious Wars

to provide French Protestantism with its lifeline to the heretics of foreign nations.

A grey, jagged country of thorn bushes and arid rocky soil, the Cevennes had offered a fitting theatre of war for the struggle between Catholics and heretics ever since the time of the Crusades against the Albigensians. The strongholds of Millau and Saint-Affrique, on the western slopes of the *massif*, were matched by the eastern bastions of Anduze and Alès, which faced onto the valley of the Rhône. The towns of this region were peopled with formidable opponents, 'all brave soldiers, most of whom had spent their youth in the Netherlands Wars, from which they returned as skilful and experienced soldiers' (Pointis, 1850, 501).

The Cevennes were responsible for halting the conquests of Admiral de Joyeuse in the dangerous Catholic offensive of 1568; they acted as the bridge by which arrived the reinforcements which enabled the northern Protestants to fight at Montcontour in 1569, they were the foundation of the party of the Duke of Rohan in the last days of independent, belligerent Protestantism in France. As Richelieu observed (1850, VII, 17), 'this country has furnished a passage for the Protestant armies ever since that party was formed in France'.

Northwards, the mountainous spur of the Vivarais reached out to the Protestants of Lyons and thus to the fountainhead of doctrine at Geneva. More important still, the Cevennes were connected with the other heretical redoubt, at La Rochelle, by means of an immensely deep belt of Protestant towns which as good as cut France in two. At the height of the prosperity of the Protestant cause, the heretics managed to command the line of the Loire itself, through their strongholds at La Charité, Orleans, Amboise, Tours, Saumur and Angers. To the south and rear of these precarious outposts stretched the far more solid chain that was represented by the strongpoints of Castres, Albi, Montauban, Bergerac, Chalais, Angoulême and Cognac.

France was therefore effectively encircled by a perimeter of Protestant towns, and bound across the middle by a wide band of fortresses which touched the Huguenot periphery at the redoubts of La Rochelle in the north-west and the Cevennes in the south-east.

In contrast, the cause of Catholicism held firm in a number of isolated but vitally important pockets which could hold only the most tenuous communication with one another. If there was a single reason for the eventual triumph of the True Faith, it was because it found its firmest support in the Ile de France and Paris. As Tavannes remarked, 'the capture of Paris or the person of the king is half the battle in a civil war – you can get the king to talk as you please, and the example of the capital is followed by most of the towns of the kingdom' (Tavannes, 1850, 250).

In the provinces, the activity of individual Catholic commanders encouraged the Romists to hold fast in useful flanking positions on either side of the Protestant belt. Thus the Catholics of Burgundy prevented the heretics from forming a continuous frontier along the eastern side of France. The ferocious Blaise de Montluc simultaneously encouraged the resistance of a constellation of towns in Upper Languedoc and Guyenne. By establishing Catholicism along the Garonne from Toulouse to Bordeaux he effectively planted a seed of destruction in the heretical south-west. But for his work in the 1560s the Protestants would have been free to face northwards, and keep up such an obstinate defence along the successive river lines of the Loire, Charente, Isle, Dordogne, Lot, Tarn and Garonne as to establish an independent Huguenot republic which would probably have survived long after the sixteenth century.

So much for the overview. When we come down to the actual sequence of events we find that grand strategic considerations were not always evident in the sporadic outbursts of violence which marked the first round of the religious wars, in 1562 and 1563.

The Huguenots were suspicious of the ascendancy of the Guise family over the young king Charles IX, and in the spring of 1562 they rose in a mass rebellion.

It was important for the Catholics to secure the outer approaches to the Ile de France, and, if possible, to gain the Norman ports by which English help could reach the Huguenots. Conversely, the Protestants wished to seize the same avenues and, by winning Paris, to secure the king and the seat of government. Neither side addressed itself to its object with any great consistency.

Protestant forces lunged towards Paris in March 1562 and again in December, but each time they shrank from pressing forward to their goal. The Duke of Guise on his side at first hesitated to attack Orleans, and instead laid siege to Rouen. The place was taken by storm on 26 October, but the siege had proved costly beyond the Catholics' expectations. In the course of one assault the king of Navarre, Antoine de Bourbon, became so excited that he had to turn aside from the foot of a scaling ladder to perform a natural function. While he was thus engaged, a musket ball dealt him a mortal wound:

Ami françois, le prince ici gissant, Vécut sans gloire et mourut en pissant.

His widow Jeanne d'Albret took over the guardianship of his young son, Henry of Navarre, and bent her efforts to turn him into as determined a Protestant as herself.

The Catholic cause suffered a still more grievous casualty on 18 February 1563, when the Duke of Guise was assassinated while riding behind the siege works he had laid before Orleans. He had been the greatest of all Henry II's captains, and the man France could least afford to lose. The will of the Catholics to continue the siege was broken, and in March they accepted a patched-up peace with the Huguenots.

The pattern of the first conflict was repeated in the wars of the later 1560s. In 1567 the Protestants once more wasted their opportunities of taking the king and Paris by surprise, and in the following two years they chose to expend their limited resources in the unsuccessful sieges of Chartres and Poitiers. On 3 October 1569 the Protestants were defeated at Montcontour, and the term of ascendancy expired.

Now, when the Catholics could have given chase to the broken Protestant armies and entered with them into La Rochelle, the Duke of Anjou and King Charles IX took over the command from Gaspard de Tavannes, and set in train a murderous six-week siege of Saint-Jean d'Angely, which stood on the outer approaches to the place. The heretical hosts were thus afforded the opportunity to re-assemble. In 1570 their leader Admiral Coligny left his base in the mountains of Languedoc and undertook an offensive which ranged through the length and breadth of France, threatened Paris, and induced Catherine de' Medici to conclude the Peace of Saint-Germain en Laye in August.

The St Bartholomew Massacre of 24 August 1572 for once delivered the initiative into the hands of the Catholics. This time they were sure that they ought to use it by striking a decisive blow against La Rochelle, and on 13 December the advance guard of the Catholic army duly appeared before the heretical seaport. Only now did they appreciate the magnitude of the task they had set themselves: the approaches were constricted by mile upon mile of fens, while strong bastions had recently been grafted onto the old walls.

The Catholics owned princes of the blood in plenty, as well as a powerful siege train, but nothing could compensate for the dozen years of anarchy which had supervened between the death of Henry II in 1559 and the present siege. An essential continuity in the art of managing sieges was lost, and, since the French officers could not agree among themselves as to what to do, Italian engineers began to reappear in force. Certain gentlemen by the names of Tosinghi, Piesque, Greghetto and Ramelli were entrusted with sounding out the fortress, and the direction of the siege was taken over by the Venetian engineer Scipione Vergano. He had built the bastions of La Rochelle for the Calvinists in 1569, and now he was hired by the Court to knock down his own handiwork. Vergano spent less than two months in the service of his new employers before he was struck dead by a musket ball on 18 April 1573.

La Rochelle withstood no less than eight major assaults, the last of which was bloodily repulsed on 12 June. By now the royal army had expended 34,000 cannon shot, and about 20,000 Catholic soldiers had been killed or disabled by enemy action and disease. King Charles opened negotiations with the garrison, and early in July he granted La Rochelle and the other major towns full liberty of conscience and the right to maintain garrisons. Not content with the advantages they had won, the Huguenots were encouraged by the successful resistance of La Rochelle to stage a series of sporadic rebellions which lasted until 1578.

The technical aspects of the Catholic failure were

more significant still, for they showed how far the French arms had declined since the great days of Henry II and Guise in the 1550s. Montluc remarked (1571, III, 434) that

from this siege the officers who were present, as well as those who came afterwards, may see that nowadays you must either starve strong fortresses into submission by blockade, or else reduce them foot-by-foot over a period of time. At La Rochelle we were very mistaken to have risked so many men in assaults, and still more misguided to have kept up such a bad watch that the place could be replenished with gunpowder by way of the sea.

The single innovation of any note had announced itself in the form of a dull thud, which had been heard every now and again from the Catholic trenches. This was the handiwork of the Sieur de Strozzi (a brother of Piero Strozzi) who was showing off to his comrades the first 'musket' to be used in warfare in France. This was the long, heavy-calibre handgun of Spanish invention, which was capable of considerable accuracy when you fired it from a forked rest. The soldiers were at first unwilling to take up the weapon, 'but, so as to win them over little by little, Strozzi had a page or lackey carry a musket about with him throughout the siege. Whenever Strozzi saw a good target, he fired' (Branthôme, 1858–78, book I, part 1). On one occasion Strozzi knocked over a horse at a range of five hundred paces. Several officers were impressed by the demonstration, and so the musket began to supplant the arquebus in the French armies.

Henry of Navarre and his struggle for Paris 1586–94

The resistance of La Rochelle secured that strategic redoubt for Protestantism for another half-century. From then onwards the balance of the wars gradually swung against the Catholic cause, weakened as it was by the creation of the moderate *Tiers Parti*. By the early 1590s Catholicism's own redoubt at Paris stood in the gravest peril.

The Protestant counter-offensive was promoted above all by the work of Henry of Navarre, son of Jeanne d'Albret and the Antoine de Bourbon who

had met such an undignified end at the siege of Rouen in 1562.

One of Henry's most formidable claims to leadership was his very wide experience of siege warfare. He was the man who was known to have made the most effective use of the petard, if he did not actually invent the device. This weapon was employed against gates, palisades and thin walls, and it offered the one contribution which later sixteenth-century France had to make to the vocabulary of fortress warfare. The petard was made up of a bell, usually of bronze, which was filled with a charge of fine powder calculated at about twelve pounds to every hundred pounds of metal. The bell was attached to a stout iron-bound beam by means of screws, chains or ropes, and bell and beam together were hung or propped against the target. A fuze leading to the base of the bell gave the petardiers (if they survived long enough) time to retire to a safe distance, and watch the force of the explosion propel the beam through the timber of the gate.

Henry first used the petard with notable success on the night of 5–6 May 1580, when he was pursuing a private feud against the town of Cahors, and it was not long before French petardiers became famous throughout Europe.

Henry was also a knowledgeable practitioner of fortress warfare on a larger scale, as he proved when he visited the siege of Laon in 1594 and rearranged the trenches in an expert fashion. More and more, however, he came to rely on the advice of his talented chief engineer Maximilian de Béthune, Marquis of Rosny and later Duke of Sully.

By the beginning of 1589 the Catholic city of Paris was in open rebellion, having suffered more than enough from the rival Henrician kings, whether the heretical Henry IV of Navarre, or the Henry III who had just staged a miniature St Bartholomew's Massacre of the Guise family at Blois.

In 1590 Henry of Navarre reduced the Seine crossings at Corbeil, Melun and Montereau, 'which were the keys to the food supplies to the capital, and the fall of which greatly forwarded the king's design, which was to starve the people of Paris so as to abate the enthusiasm behind their rebellions' (Lestoile, 1850, 15).

Eventually there was nothing left for the poor folk

of Paris to eat, 'not even grass or the skins of vermin; they had already eaten up the asses, the dogs, the rats, the bones of the dead which they ground up into a dust-like flour, and even the roofing-slates, which they stole, pounded down and swallowed with water' (ibid., 25).

Paris could not have held out much longer if the Prince of Parma, the Sobieski of the Catholic League, had not led a Spanish army from the Netherlands into France. Before this threat Henry prudently withdrew into Normandy.

Parma was forced to fall back in the winter to quarters in the Netherlands, which left Henry with a delectable freedom of action at the beginning of 1591. 'All the governors of the League towns knew that the king was going to descend on one fortress or another; they said he was like some bird of prey, waiting to swoop on his quarry' (Palma-Cayet, 1850, 269).

With the events of 1590 still fresh in his mind, Henry abandoned any idea of a new royal visit to Paris, and on 9 February he instead bestowed the honour of his presence on Chartres, which was 'one of the best fortresses of the League' (Lestoile, 1850, 52), and an important outwork of the Paris strategic redoubt since the earliest days of the religious wars. Henry determined on a cautious, formal siege, and he was greatly assisted in his design by the ingenuity of the engineer Claude de Chastillon, 'a brave and valiant gentleman who had a great understanding of mathematics, a science which it is well worth the while of nobles to master, if they wish to attain the highest military ranks' (Palma-Cayet, 1850, 269). The garrison of Chartres capitulated on 19 April 1591, as soon as the besiegers completed a bridge across the ditch.

Henry was less well advised when he listened to the urgings of the English, and decided to make the capture of Rouen his next objective. The place was peripheral to his main target at Paris, and the governor put up such a good defence that Henry's 35,000 were tied down there until Parma marched into France with another army of Spanish and relieved the place in the spring of 1592. On the return journey Parma made a diversion which enabled him to call in on his friends at Paris.

In 1593 Henry impudently sent an emissary to the Pope to represent that he had reduced the city of Paris to such a state that in order to survive it had to be relieved every year, whereas in the earlier wars it had been able to send help to royal armies and the entire kingdom. Orleans too was blockaded on all sides, and eked out a perilous existence. This town represented the League's one surviving passage over the Loire, the river which transversed, nay divided, the entire kingdom of France (ibid., 515).

In reality the position was one of stalemate. Henry knew very well that he could never be king of France until he was king of Paris, and since his blockades had repeatedly failed he took the only course open to him and made a solemn abjuration of heresy on 5 July 1593. Thus the Catholics were in a position to claim that they had conquered Henry at least as convincingly as he had conquered them. Paris came over to the king on 21 March 1594, and the other Catholic towns followed her example with a rush.

Henry pleased the towns by setting out to rule in a new style. Already in 1589 he had tried to win over Orleans by arguments that sound strange in the mouth of a sixteenth-century sovereign: 'If you complain that we wish to impose citadels and other unpleasant things upon you, I must admit that you have some little justice on your side . . . in these troubled times' (ibid., 144). In 1595, as established king, Henry went still further and delighted the citizens of Rouen by demolishing Fort Sainte-Catherine, wishing to 'have no other citadel at Rouen than the hearts of the townspeople' (ibid., 669).

No doubt these words and actions proceeded from the overflowing goodness of Henry's nature; at the same time it is just possible that he had examined the record of sixteenth-century warfare, and concluded that citadels were more successful in provoking revolts than in keeping them under.

Henry's war with Spain 1595–8

The character of Henry's campaigns changed fundamentally after he had been reconciled with all Frenchmen save the most implacable *Ligeurs*. What had been a civil war, with occasional foreign intervention, was transformed into a direct dynastic or national conflict along the borders of France and the Netherlands. Neither Henry nor his army were prepared for the change of style and tempo involved in war with a dangerous enemy like the Spanish. Strategic inconsequentiality of the kind that passed unnoticed during the religious wars was now liable to be punished very severely indeed.

Again and again the Spanish contrived to be the first in the field, snatching fortresses before Henry had time to respond: Doullens and Cambrai in 1595, Calais in 1596, and in the following year the Somme fortress of Amiens, where Henry had heaped up great quantities of artillery and ammunition.

Henry knew that his crown was loose upon his head if he failed to recapture Amiens. A Spaniard commented that

the loss of a single fortress would not have produced much effect in a land where the king was well-established and ruled by hereditary right. But things were different in France, for the memory of the recent wars was fresh, and there was still sympathy for the party of the League. The people, as always, were ready to incline to the stronger side (Coloma, 1853, book X).

Henry's first and wisest step was to put Sully in charge of the finances of the realm. This ingenious gentleman raised 300,000 *écus* from the notables in voluntary loans, and used the money to conclude ambitious contracts with merchants and waggoners. Thus the army that went to besiege Amiens was magnificently provided. Unfortunately, the conduct of the actual siege works proved to be so poor that more than six months passed before the place was forced to capitulate, on 19 September 1597.

At Vervins, on 2 May 1598, the deputies of the dying Philip II of Spain accorded Henry a peace on much better terms than he deserved for his performance in the last three years of campaigning. All the conquered Picardy fortresses were restored to the French; and Spanish military opinion was particularly outraged by the relinquishment of Calais, for 'it was astonishing to see a prince yield up a stronghold by which he could have assured all his provinces, or at least a good part of them' (ibid., book XI).

The reforms of Henry IV and Sully 1598–1610

The Peace of Vervins gave Henry the opportunity to put into effect the reforms for which the campaigns of the 1590s had given the spur. His instrument was his engineer Sully, who by the end of 1599 had accumulated the four offices of Grand Master of Artillery, Superintendent of Finances, Superintendent of Buildings and Superintendent of Fortifications. The King and his minister set themselves a number of ambitious tasks:

To ensure by good regulations, a kind of orderliness which could not be upset; to amass great quantities of money, weapons, artillery, ammunition and tools; to fortify the frontier towns; to try by means of new inventions to improve the arts of attacking and defending fortresses (Sully, 1850, 362).

The inferiority of the brigand-like French infantry had been proved by the ease with which Parma had frustrated Henry's projects against Paris, and by the devastating effect of the Spanish sorties from Amiens. In reply, Henry and Sully assembled a peacetime infantry force of unprecedented size, and sought to endow it with the 'Spanish' qualities of endurance and address.

During the 1590s the French gunners had performed rather more creditably than their cousins in the infantry. Even so, Henry doubted whether his artillery would be able to argue strongly enough with the rock-fortresses of the Duke of Savoy, if war ever broke out over the disputed ownership of the Marquisate of Saluzzo. In 1599 Sully therefore installed himself in the Paris Arsenal, which he found

badly-built, and almost bare of cannon, ammunition and weapons; in order to put things right, I summoned all the officers and dismissed four or five hundred of them, who were all creatures of the judiciary, the treasury and the administration (ibid., 322).

Sully put an end to the peculiar custom by which many cannon had been signed over to galley captains and other people as private individuals, and with this leakage stopped, he began to build up the stock of ordnance by purchase and state manufacture. He bought the metal for casting direct from the smelters, instead of by way of middlemen as before, and thus the treasury was able to support the enormous efforts which by 1605 had succeeded in assembling no less than four hundred pieces, 200,000 cannon shot and 4,000,000 pounds of gunpowder in the Paris and provincial arsenals.

Sully regulated the tactical employment of the guns by means of an *Instruction*, which was circulated among the gunners and engineers in manuscript. In this document Sully discussed the construction and arrangement of siege batteries in detail, and he was well up with the times when he advocated that a fortress should be attacked by the bastions rather than the curtains.

As early as 1599 the new stirrings at the Paris Arsenal induced the Duke of Savoy, of all unwelcome people, to pay the place a visit. At the sight of twenty gleaming new cannon, and the preparations to cast twenty more, the Duke asked what the French were going to do with so much ordnance. Sully replied with a steely-edged banter:

'Monsieur, it's intended to take Montmélian.'
He then asked me, 'Have you ever been there?'
'No, monsieur,' I said.
'I am not at all surprised,' he rejoined, 'otherwise you would not speak like that. Montmélian cannot be taken.'
'Very well, monsieur,' I added. 'I am willing to believe you, but I ask you not to put the king to the trouble of attacking it. If he orders me to take it, I shall certainly do so one way or another. But I hope it will never come to that, and that you and the king will part good friends' (ibid., 323).

This last pious wish was not fulfilled, for in 1600 the French invaded Savoy and settled the arguments over Saluzzo in their favour by force. In the process Sully took the fortresses of Charbonnières and Montmélian by dint of carving out battery-sites on the steep mountain slopes. Thus all the hard work for the artillery finally had its justification.

Since the days of Francis I, almost the only measure relating to the administration of French fortresses had been an instruction dating from 1567, which provided for the physical transfer of cash to individual fortresses. Otherwise the fortress gover-

nors were completely free to decide how repairs and constructions were to be carried out, and how the necessary money was to be spent. This arbitrary procedure was supplanted by the firm rules that were laid down in a *Règlement* of 1604. The engineers of each province were now expected to draw up annual projects for fortifications, and send them to Paris to be examined by Sully and a number of distinguished experts, who gave their judgment in the light of the needs of national strategy and within the bounds of a sum which was set apart each year for fortifications. After receiving Sully's approval the projects were put out to open tender, and the work carried out by the successful civilian contractor, who now replaced the governor as the employer of the labourers. The progress of the construction was carefully checked, and the finished works were finally accepted by a small committee made up of the provincial engineers and the provincial and fortress governors or their deputies. If need be, the contractor and his men could be set aside by soldier labourers in the interests of speed or economy.

To administer the new machine, Sully established a hierarchy of engineer ranks which roughly corresponded to the structure which Prince Maurice had set up in the United Provinces. At the top stood the *Surintendant des Fortifications*, in which post Sully had succeeded Incarville in 1599. Then came the newly-established *Directeurs des Fortifications* (*Ingénieurs du Roi* being an alternative title), each of whom was responsible for a single province, and below them the hard-worked *Contrôleurs Généraux* who acted as intermediaries while the construction projects were being shuttled to and fro between the fortresses and Paris. The *Contrôleurs Généraux* also had to see that the completed works conformed to the agreed designs, and were built of the specified materials. At the bottom of the pyramid lay the ordinary engineers, who kept an eye on the day-to-day building work.

In the last generation little thought had been given to the problems of national defence, as opposed to the throwing up of such works as were dictated by the chaotic religious wars. In 1604 the English traveller Robert Dallington wrote that 'if a man will look through all France, I think that he

38   Montmélian (De Fer, 1690–95)

shall not find any town half perfectly fortified, according to the rule of engineers' (Buisseret, 1968, 123).

Henry and Sully were already doing all that lay in their power to remedy this state of affairs. Between 1595 and May 1610 altogether 7,785,000 *livres* of state funds were expended on the building and repair of fortresses. The sum was swollen still further by the produce of local taxes such as the *taille* and customs and excise, which were set aside for specific works. These enormous funds were devoted to a systematic programme of fortress construction.

Existing strongholds were reinforced, and nearly thirty open towns converted into fortresses. Among them was Toulon, which was founded as a military port in 1594. Ambitious fortifications of white stone were raised at Grenoble, as a safeguard against Savoy and Franche-Comté, but the most pressing works of all were undertaken along the northern frontier, where the Spanish had caused so many alarms. The fortifications of Beauvais, Ham, Abbeville, Boulogne, Montreuil, Le Catelet, La Capelle, Ardres and Calais were all strengthened and extended, and a fine new citadel was built at Amiens after the town had been retaken from the Spanish.

Hand-in-hand with the construction of new works went the dismantling of old and superfluous ones. As early as 1593 Sully had recommended that the authorities ought to draw up a list of all royal and private fortresses and castles,

in which should be specified the places that are absolutely necessary for the defence and security of the realm, and those which can be demolished one by one as the governorships fall vacant, or when we have the opportunity of doing so without the danger of affronting persons of quality whom we do not wish to offend (Buisseret, 1968, 175).

A large number of demolitions were undertaken in the new century, by when Henry and Sully had little hesitation in 'offending' persons of even the 'highest quality'. In that way the royal revenues could be devoted to fewer and better fortresses, and the local malcontents were deprived of both provocation and places of refuge.

Perhaps the most impressive achievement of these years was the way that Italian technicians were almost completely replaced by native engineers like d'Espinai de Saint-Luc, who advanced the artillery to the counterscarp of Amiens in 1597, or the Claude de Chastillon who directed the sieges of Chartres (1591), Dreux (1593), Laon (1594), La Fère (1596), Amiens (1597), and Montmélian (1600).

The leading light among the new generation of

French engineers was Jean Errard de Bar-le-Duc (1554–1610). He had left his native Lorraine some time before 1588, and after completing his education in Italy he entered the service of Henry IV, for whom he designed and directed the building of northern and eastern fortresses. His most notable construction was the citadel of Amiens, which was founded in 1597 and finished by the time of his death in 1610. In 1614 work began on a powerful citadel at Verdun, which was traced entirely in accordance with Errard's maxims.

In 1594 Errard published *La Fortification Démonstrée et Réduicte en Art*, a work which was doubly important: it was printed at royal command, and it constituted the first important French book on fortification. Thus in the preface Errard addresses himself proudly to the nobility of France, proclaiming that the king had ordered him to

put in order and publish everything that is practised in fortification, so as to assist you gentlemen in your efforts to render yourselves able to perform worthily in the service of His Majesty and your country.

Errard's drawings are easy to read, and he wrote in a clear and simple style. He insisted that nobody could be called a true engineer unless he had taken part in the defence and attack of fortresses, and learnt to understand the action of artillery and the other arms. At the same time we must admit that Errard's designs offer a backward and inferior imitation of Italian styles. He showed little appreciation of the value of outworks. Also, he made the shoulder angles of his bastions into right angles, which produced a flank which met the curtain acutely, giving only the most inadequate command of the face of the adjacent bastion.

Still more to Errard's discredit is the fact that he took a decided step towards the overconfident stress on geometric properties which was to plague seventeenth- and eighteenth-century 'systems' of fortification. He boasted that he had dared to 'undertake something which no engineers up to now have so much as desired or attempted', and that he had arrived at 'geometrical proofs upon which everyone can rest with complete confidence'.

For all these failings, Errard's book remains a worthy monument to Henry IV, a king who was not content to strengthen his frontiers, but wished to lead his nation to a mastery of fortress warfare.

Decay and revival 1610–60

The collapse of the military art in France 1610–c. 53 Henry IV was assassinated in 1610; and his military machine was rapidly destroyed by the same forces of warlordism and religious faction that had wrecked the similar structure which his namesake, Henry II, had set up half a century earlier. The deterioration was most evident among the engineers and gunners, for they were the officers who were most dependent upon powerful financial support and continuity of direction.

Instead of having seasoned and dedicated experts at their disposal, the commanders were now plagued with hordes of 'volunteers' who served well enough in the field, but were 'completely useless in siege warfare, where things are carried on in a different way' (Fontenay-Mareuil, 1850, 159). Thus in 1635, when Richelieu was making ready for the French intervention in the Netherlands, he was in the humiliating position of having to explain to his Dutch allies that it would be unwise to commit the French army to a siege, because

we are not so accustomed to making large sieges as are the Dutch. If we fail at our first siege, I fear that we shall lose time and, worse still, undermine the ardour of our troops and the reputation of the royal arms (Richelieu, 1850, VII, 598).

When it came to the defensive, little reliance could now be placed on the frontier fortresses. Amongst other noblemen, the Duke of Luynes bought up governorships shamelessly after the death of Henry; in 1617 he went on to gain control of some of the most important strongholds of Picardy, and 'if he had lived rather longer, and if he had stayed in favour, his ambition would have extended to taking over all the fortresses of France' (Fontenay-Mareuil, 1850, 141). Other governors, less ambitious or corrupt, harboured shortcomings which remained undetected in the long period of external peace (Arnauld, 1850, 488).

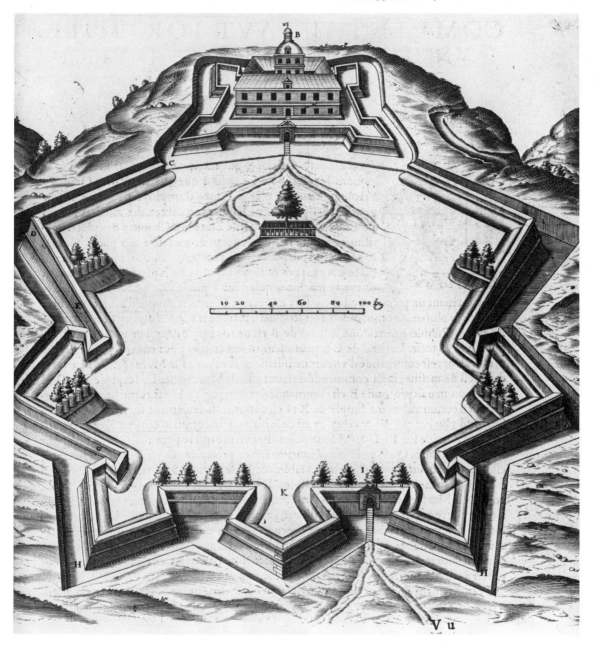

39 Errard's fortification. The lower bastions have the characteristic right-angled shoulders (Errard, 1594)

The end of the heretics 1621–2 and 1627–9

In 1621 the Huguenots rose in general revolt. This challenge was answered by something less than a dramatic demonstration of royal authority. On 1 June the young king Louis XIII appeared before Saint-Jean d'Angely, the outer shield of La Rochelle. Contrary to all expectations, the heretics capitulated after the feeblest of defences, 'at which everyone heaved a huge sigh of relief, for the prevailing ignorance about sieges was such that the Huguenots could have held out for a long time' (Fontenay-Mareuil, 1850, 160).

Perhaps wisely in the circumstances, Louis did not press on to La Rochelle. The royal army instead wandered off southwards, mopping up small towns as it went, and finally exhausting itself in a vain siege of the powerful stronghold of Montauban.

In 1622 the king's army pursued exactly the same progress. It crawled over Languedoc, reducing small towns against steadily increasing resistance and under ever less tolerable heat, and finally came to a halt before another large Protestant fortress, in this case Montpellier. On 10 October the Catholics were glad to bring the war to an end by an accord which confirmed the toleration established by the Edict of Nantes, and allowed the Protestants to retain the fortifications of La Rochelle and Montauban intact. The works of Montpellier were razed, in return for the king's promise never to build a citadel there.

Cardinal Richelieu, a new and mighty royal minister, came to power in 1623. Possibly his greatest achievement was to bring to an end the series of major religious wars which had plagued France for six decades. This he did by delivering decisive blows against the heretical redoubts of La Rochelle and the Cevennes.

The royal government gradually tightened its grip on the seaward approaches to La Rochelle, undeterred by the landing of a force of hostile English on the Isle of Ré in July 1627.

Although the Rochelais still hesitated to throw in their lot with the English, Cardinal Richelieu decided that he must finish with the Huguenots once and for all. A royal army under the command of the Duke of Angoulême came within sight of La Rochelle on 4 August 1627, and the king in person reached the camp on 12 October. The Catholic army was exceedingly well administered and fed, and it gradually grew in size to a strength of 22,000 men.

The English were expelled from the Isle of Ré in November, and Richelieu could now turn his whole attention to the work of reducing the heretical seaport. Not even the growing danger of a war with Spain was going to divert him from his purpose. He wrote that

if the king did not take La Rochelle this time, he would never be able to take it, and in that case the Rochelais and the Huguenots would have become more insolent than ever, and we would have been faced with annual wars against the Protestants and dissidents. If, on the other hand, the king did take La Rochelle, he would have perpetual internal peace, . . . he would be the most powerful king in Europe and the arbiter of Christianity (Richelieu, 1850, VII, 500).

The fortifications of La Rochelle were still stronger than they had been in the siege of 1572–3, and Richelieu had no intention of ruining the royal army by following the same procedures which had been adopted in that bloody operation. He instead sought to cut off the fortress from outside help by means of a dyke or bridge barrier, the device which had enabled the Prince of Parma to reduce so many heretical towns to reason in the 1570s and 1580s, and which the Spanish had employed again, with rather less success, in the great siege of Ostend. A relic of those wars was unearthed in the person of the irrepressible Pompeio Targone, who, as Richelieu says, 'proposed to bar the harbour channel by some novel inventions; however it was impossible to have much faith in him, since he gave little evidence that he knew what he was about' (ibid., VII, 501). Richelieu himself encouraged the faddish schemes of his familiar, the Capuchin Père Joseph. This warlike monk devised *'une terrible machine'* to travel up a sewage aqueduct into the city, and Richelieu was furious when the military men, after making some muddy reconnaissances, flatly refused to attempt the voyage.

Targone's schemes were broken by the winter storms, but the notion of barring the outer harbour was taken up by Metezeau, who was a royal architect, and the Parisian mason Tiriot. These

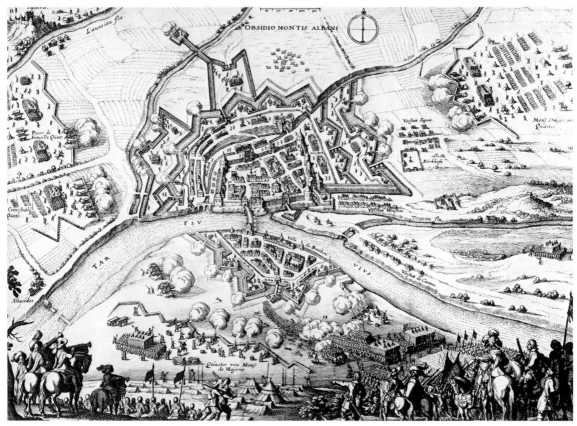

40   Siege of Montauban 1621 (Merian, 1646)

practical men managed to build two drystone jetties, each projecting two hundred yards from the capes on either side of the harbour entrance.

The royal forces established guns on the completed jetties, and they were able to beat off every attempt of the English fleets to break through to the relief of La Rochelle. The last duel of the kind was staged on 12 October 1628, and a Frenchman records that

our ears were deafened with the thunder of the cannon, and the sea was covered with a dense black cloud of smoke which was riven by gun-flashes. It was wonderful to see those monstrous ships, like some great floating houses, advance on our dyke one by one in beautiful order. As each of them drew near, it suddenly wore round, presented its beam and fired sixty or seventy guns simultaneously (Pointis, 1850, 546).

The failure of the English deprived La Rochelle of the hope which had been its only subsistence. Between 8,000 and 10,000 of the population of some 45,000 were already dead of starvation, and the survivors lacked the strength to carry off the bodies that lay in the houses and streets. On the ramparts it sometimes happened that half the number of a company on guard overnight would be found dead by the morning.

Negotiations for a capitulation opened on 27 October 1628, after the Huguenots had eaten the last of the grass, shoes and sword scabbards. The royal army made its entry on 30 October.

The end of the fifteen-month resistance of La Rochelle signified more than the subjugation of one of the redoubts of the Reformation in France: it put a term to the period of happy anarchy which had been enjoyed by military men of all religions and none. The loyal Bassompierre was not speaking

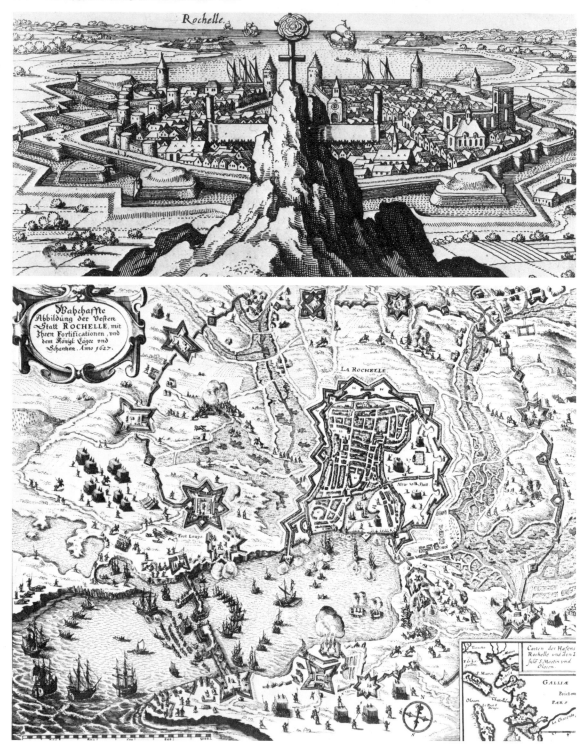

41, 42   La Rochelle

entirely in jest when he said 'I really think we are mad to want to take La Rochelle' (Fontenay-Mareuil, 1850, 199).

Sensing that their turn was next, the Protestants of the Cevennes had risen in rebellion under the leadership of the Duke of Rohan. Here again Richelieu wished to derive some benefit from the harsh lesson of the earlier religious wars, and he cast about for some alternative to the endless succession of sieges which had ruined the royal armies in the Midi in 1621 and 1622.

A novel yet practicable strategy was proposed by the Marquis des Portes, who described the southern Protestant fortresses as 'a chain which begins at Nîmes and Usez, and stretches across the Cevennes and the Rouergue to Castres and Montauban' (ibid., 31). It would be wrong, he said, to nibble at the western end of the chain as in 1621 and 1622, and give time for every small town to convert itself into a royal stronghold. Instead the royal army should strike at the centre of the chain at the links which were represented by the towns of Privas, Alès and Anduze, and so sever Castres and Montauban in Languedoc from the eastern bulwarks of the rebellion at Nîmes and Usez.

The scheme was put into effect in 1629, and a brief attack brought Louis into possession of Privas on 28 May. Alès shared its fate on 17 June, after a vigorous formal siege, and a feeling of alarm and despair spread so rapidly through the Protestant Midi that the small towns went under in rapid succession. Montauban opened its gates without a pretence of resistance, and on 27 September the Peace of Alès brought an end to Protestantism in France as an effective independent military power.

The dream of lightning victory 1629–36

With the end of civil, or at least religious discord, Richelieu had the opportunity of doing something to stay the disintegration of France's international standing which had proceeded unabated since 1562.

Beyond the Alps, the influence won by Francis I and Henry II had been eroded by the growing power of Savoy-Piedmont and Spain. We have already seen how Duke Emanuel Philibert of Savoy had fortified his frontiers, and persuaded the French to relinquish Turin in 1562. The process of capitulation was completed by Henry IV. In 1600, after his successful campaign against Savoy, he made a deal by which he ceded the Marquisate of Saluzzo to the Duke of Savoy, and gained in return the territory of Bresse with the fortress of Bourg. The acquisition of Bresse gave the city of Lyons a useful protective outpost to the north-east,

but the result of the treaty was to strengthen the authority of the Spaniards in Italy, and give them the means of attaining the mastery in that land. This was because the ownership of the Marquisate of Saluzzo was the real cause of the war between France and Savoy, and the issue at stake was whether or not the French could retain a foothold beyond the mountains, and keep alive among the Italians the hope that they could obtain help from France when they needed it (ibid.).

Eastwards again, the Habsburgs had forged a new and powerful link in their chain of empire. In 1603 the Spanish governor of the Milanese, Count Fuentes, began to build a fort at the point where the Adda flowed into Lake Como. Henry IV protested mightily, but he was unwilling to go so far as to declare war. Thus the Spaniards were suffered to complete their fort, and push out lines of earthworks to the mountain slopes on either side. The building of this 'Fort Fuentes' was of the greatest significance, for it secured for the Habsburgs the Valtelline (valley of the upper Adda), the vital funnel by which the resources of Spain and the Spanish duchy of Milan could be channelled through the Alps, and thence be dispatched in one direction towards the Netherlands, and in the other along the Inn and Danube to southern Germany and Austria.

France therefore emerged from the period of the religious wars to find herself contained to the east by a stone necklace of strongholds which extended from the new fortresses of the Duke of Savoy, by way of the Valtelline and the neutral but unfriendly Franche-Comté and Lorraine to the Spanish province of Artois, which bulged from the Netherlands to within one hundred miles of Paris.

Richelieu for some years entertained the hope that he could break the stranglehold by pursuing two strategies. The first was to lend judicious encouragement to belligerent foreign heretics like the Swedes or the Swiss of the Valtelline; and the other was to launch the French army on short but hard-hitting expeditions beyond the borders.

This policy of limited intervention certainly paid off handsomely in Italy, and Richelieu ignored the fears of people like Cardinal de Berulle, who set themselves against a breach with Spain, and 'highlighted the dangers by calling to mind the example of Henry IV, who lost all the Picardy frontier in two years' (ibid., 214).

The French army twice came across the Alps, in 1629 and 1630, pushing aside the forces of Savoy, and compelling the Spanish to raise their siege of the friendly fortress of Casale. This place represented a Mantuan enclave which was inserted between Piedmont and the Milanese – and thus caused great annoyance to the Duke of Savoy and the King of Spain. In their progress the French seized the fortress of Pinerolo, on one of the exits of the Mont-Genèvre Pass, and they retained the stronghold after

some hard bargaining with the Duke of Savoy. 'By acquiring this fortress,' said Rohan (1850, 614), 'the French have gained such an easy entry into Italy that . . . they will always be in a position to hold in check the Spanish forces in the Duchy of Milan.'

No less swift and decisive were the French invasions of Lorraine in 1631 and 1633. Lorraine was an independent duchy which owned the human talent, if not the geographical obstacles, to make itself the 'Savoy' of the French and German borderlands. Lorrainers had the reputation of being excellent draftsmen; and in the closing decades of the last century Duke Charles III had gathered together a circle of native and Italian engineers who significantly strengthened his frontiers, by, for example, fortifying the New Town at Nancy, which contained the famous ducal arsenal.

The most prominent of the Italians were probably Orfeo de'Galiani (1570–1611), who became first engineer and councillor of state in 1596, and planned and built the fortifications of the New Town of

43   Fort Fuentes. Vital link in the communications between the Habsburg lands of southern and northern Europe (Bodenehr)

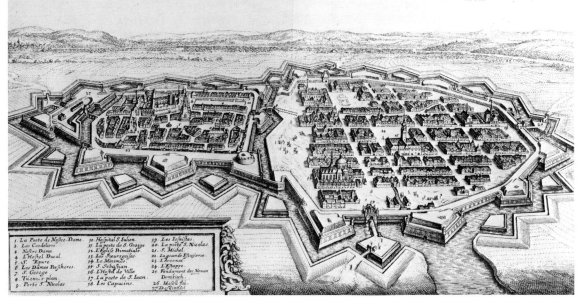

44 Nancy. The New Town is on the left (Zeiler, 1645)

Nancy. Among his compatriots in the ducal service were numbered Niccolo da Furli, Giovanni da Ponte, Ottaviano da Chiesi, and Giambattista degli Stabili, who succeeded Galiani as chief engineer. Appier de Bar-le-Duc, a born Lorrainer, helped Galiani to re-fortify Nancy. Appier's son, Jean Appier, better known by the name of 'Hanzelet', wrote one of the most important books of the time on the application of artillery to fortress warfare, *La Pyrotechnie de Hanzelet*, Pont-à-Mousson, 1630. The famous Jean Errard de Bar-le-Duc was born in Lorraine, and received his training in the duchy before he passed to the service of Henry IV of France. The mason Tiriot, who helped to build the dyke at La Rochelle, was probably also a Lorrainer by origin. Épinal was one of the leading European centres for the production of prints and cheap printed books, and the engraver Callot has left us with an enduring visual impression of the horrors of war in his time.

All the same, the next duke, Charles IV, was singularly unwise when he provoked Richelieu by allowing Imperial troops to hold and fortify the small town of Moyenvic.

The French seized the fortress of Marsal early in 1632, and in the next year they frightened Duke Charles into admitting their army into Nancy, and yielding up Stenay and Jametz on his northern borders. The denial of Lorraine gravely threatened the 'Spanish Road' from the Alps, and forced the Spanish to resort to local recruiting and risky sea voyages in order to keep up the level of their troops in the Netherlands.

Richelieu determined to mete out the same treatment, on a far more ambitious scale, to the Spanish Netherlands in 1635. In February of that year he concluded a treaty with the Dutch which provided for the partition of the Spanish territory, and paved the way for a joint plan of campaign.

The first achievement of the combined French and Dutch arms was the lawless sack and burning of Tirlemont on 9 June. Pointis and the other officers were disarmed by their own troops, and they had to watch the pillage as helpless spectators: 'I cannot tell you how horrified I was to see one of the poor nuns running about in a panic with a knife buried in her head. She cried out between her tears, "*Messieurs*, save my life, I beg you!"' (Pointis, 1850, 591).

It is not too much to say that the indiscipline of the armies at Tirlemont condemned France to a twenty-four-year European war with Spain. In the first place the horror of the event succeeded in ranging the people of the southern Netherlands firmly with the Spanish, while by destroying the town and the great quantities of stored grain the allies deprived themselves of a base from which they could have reduced the land to submission.

Louvain, the next objective on the road to Brussels, had no intention of sharing the fate of the sister city. The bellicosity of the citizens was inspired by the example of a pioneer company formed of Jesuits, and by Thomas Preston's regiment of Irish infantry, who accompanied each volley with terrible cries and fought with especial glee against the English companies in the Dutch service. The French and Dutch raised the siege on 4 July, rather than do battle with an army of relief which had arrived from Germany.

Balked in the Netherlands, Richelieu retained a last hope of a runaway victory in the old style by making an attack on that political oddity, Franche-Comté. This blessed land was lodged between Burgundy and the north-western flank of the Swiss Alps, and it was ruled with the lightest of possible reigns by its distant Spanish masters. It was free of all taxation from Spain, hence its name, but in an emergency it could provide for its own defence by raising loans to fill the fortress magazines with grain, and by forming a mobile corps of ten thousand troops, many of whom had served with Spinola in the Netherlands. Franche-Comté had been spared from war by a series of treaties dating back to 1552, but Richelieu was unable to resist the temptation of striking at this readily-accessible target, which was such an important link in the remaining Spanish overlands communications between Italy and the Netherlands.

Richelieu could not believe that any of the fortresses would hold out much more than a week against the expeditionary force of 10,500 men. The French left the fortress of Gray to one side and arrived before Dôle, the capital of Franche-Comté, on 27 May 1636. The result was a dismal humiliation. 'The courage of the Comtais was redoubled by the natural hate which they harboured for the French' (Richelieu, 1850, IX, 62), and under the direction of the Capuchin Père Eustache, 'one of the finest cannoneers of his time' (Montglat, 1850, 40), the crews of the guns in the bastion flanks destroyed all the galleries which the French tried to drive across the ditch. The siege was accordingly abandoned. A veteran remarked some time later that

the French in general did not have the experience which they acquired afterwards. It was enough for a man to have served in Holland for him to be listened to like a great oracle. The kind of officer who was then acclaimed as a great general would now be thought hardly fit to command a company (ibid., 41–2).

The French proved to be as incompetent on the defensive as they were in their sieges, and in 1636 the vengeful Spanish broke over the appallingly neglected Picardy frontier, taking the fortresses of La Capelle and Le Catelet against feeble resistance.

Thus Richelieu was finally disappointed in all the expedients with which he had tried to pursue an aggressive policy without involving France in a war on a European scale. The French had performed badly in their sieges in the Netherlands and Franche-Comté. Likewise war by proxy failed him with the defeat of the Swedes at Nördlingen in 1634, and the treachery of the Valtelline Protestants in 1637. France was therefore committed to a war on multiple fronts, a struggle which the disasters of 1636 had shown she was in no condition to wage.

The Italian theatre 1635–59

There were two French-garrisoned fortresses which made sure that the Duke of Savoy or his regent were bound to the interests of France for the duration of the war. These were the stronghold of Pinerolo, at the back door of Piedmont, and that of Casale, which was the shield of Piedmont towards the Spanish duchy of Milan. France therefore owned a foothold beyond the Alps, the prerequisite of making war in Italy.

For the rest of the story is one of restrictions and limitations, and all the accidents and misunderstandings which Clausewitz sums up in the word 'friction'. The French armies in Italy were small in the first place, and carried with them such little ammunition that if they wished to make a siege of any size they had to wait until further convoys came up from the rear. The Piedmontese were not too enthusiastic about helping the French out of their difficulties, as was only natural.

Even when the Piedmontese were willing to join in active operations, the freedom of allied action was still severely limited by the difficulty of carrying war into the Milanese area. The further they advanced the more the allies' right flank lay open to the Spanish forces grouped to the south, in the area where the Tanaro and Sesia flowed into the Po. There, at Alessandria, Valenza and Tortona, the Spanish held a triangle of fortresses from which they were never completely evicted in the course of the war.

The vain siege of Valenza in 1635 represented the one serious attempt to break the Spanish triangle before the allies were thrown onto the defensive, as the result of civil war in Piedmont. The Marquis of Leganés, the Spanish governor of the Milanese, captured Vercelli in the summer of 1637, and thereby breached the main line of Piedmont's defence north of the Po. The Spanish made further inroads into Piedmontese territory in 1639, and on 30 May 1640 an advance guard of Spanish and rebel Piedmontese troops came within sight of Turin.

The arrival of Leganés before Turin brought about a situation of mind-testing complexity. In the very midst of all the armies milling about Turin there resided a small kernel, a French garrison ensconced in Paciotto's famous citadel. The citadel was beset by 12,000 rebel Piedmontese under Prince Thomas of Savoy, holding the town walls of Turin, which were in turn laid under siege by Count Harcourt with 10,000 French. These were duly attacked in their lines by the 18,000 Spanish and rebels under Leganés. Thus we end up with four layers of warring forces.

In these circumstances the rebels in the town and the Spanish could establish no effective co-ordination, despite all the ingenuity of Leganés. He filled mortar bombs with flour, musket balls and every kind of food and ammunition. The vents were plugged with clay, and the bombs were shot from mortars and sailed over the French camp. The bombardiers aimed very carefully so that the missiles landed in the town, where they were solicitously retrieved. There was one bomb which contained a load of fat quails, together with a message from a Spaniard in Leganés' army to his mistress who lived in the town (Montglat, 1850, 99).

Finally on 20 September the town surrendered to the French, leaving Leganés with no alternative but to march away.

The triple siege of Turin in 1640 has earned a place in history on two accounts. As a technical curiosity, it represented the extreme but logical development of the system of siege lines which originated with Colonna and Alva in the sixteenth century. From the strategic aspect, it marked the beginning of the French counter-offensive which won back the land and people of Piedmont in the following years, not least by persuading the rebels back to the ducal party.

The progress of the French was temporarily interrupted by the outbreak of the civil wars of the *Fronde* in their homeland; but by the end of the campaigning season of 1658 they and their Piedmontese allies had advanced to the banks of the Ticino, just fifteen miles short of the city of Milan, the capital of Spanish Lombardy. The French commanders had every intention of going forth to capture Milan in the following year, but this final prize was denied to them by the death of the Duke of Modena, who had been a useful ally, and by the signing of the Peace of the Pyrenees.

The Pyrenean and Catalan theatres 1635–59

For the French, the war in the Pyrenees represented a somewhat tiresome distraction from the more interesting theatres of war in Italy, along the Rhine, and above all in the Netherlands. The southern scene of operations drew down the king and his army only once. That was in 1642, for the attack on Perpignan.

The Spanish could not afford to be so indifferent. From the beginning they were anxious about their outlying north-eastern counties of Cerdagne and Roussillon, which were stranded on the far side of the Pyrenees. Then there was the general crisis which followed the rebellion of the Catalans and Portuguese in 1640. The Spanish monarchy was now threatened with dismemberment, and so even small French contingents operating in the Peninsula could begin to exert a pressure out of all proportion to their numbers. The Spanish did not hesitate to put on foot armies of 40,000 and more, or summon up the best engineers of the southern Netherlands and stock the magazines with an abundance of material that would have been the wonder of a Spanish fortress governor in any other theatre of the war.

The conflict in the Pyrenees began tamely enough, with some cannonades and manoeuvrings in 1636 and 1638 on the far western flank of the mountains: the French were just as unwilling to besiege Pamplona as were the Spanish to march into France and try conclusions with Bayonne.

The combatants put much larger armies into the field in the County of Roussillon, at the eastern end of the chain, where the French stronghold of Leucate glowered across the brackish Etang de Malpas at the Spanish border fortress of Salses. The old but strong walls of Salses were the outer shield to the great fortress of Perpignan, the guardian of the Pyrenean passes:

Perpignan possessed extraordinary strategic value for Spain in her age-old struggle against France, and it constituted the first national fortress of Spain and one of the most important in all Europe. This place was prized, cared for, and visited in this capacity by the three great political figures who presided over the government of Spain and her dominions – namely Ferdinand the Catholic, Charles v and Philip ii (Sanabre, 1956, 221).

On 19 June 1639 Prince Henry of Condé wrested Salses from the Spanish, who at once took great offence and launched a very ambitious attempt to get it back. They recovered Salses on 6 January 1640, but at a cost which was nothing short of catastrophic. About 10,000 men died out of the 40,000 who made up the siege army, and the effort put such a strain on the resources and loyalty of Catalonia that the province burst into revolt.

Catalonia had not been ruled with any great harshness. The rebellion broke out in 1640 partly because the region was the natural base for Spanish campaigning in Roussillon, and partly because it had

preserved its privileges so long that it had only recently been subject to the process of Castilian-isation which the other provinces had undergone more gradually and less painfully over the earlier part of the century. Among other complaints, the Catalans resented the violation of their constitutions in the matter of fortification. For a start, the peculiar sanctity of private property in Catalan law was outraged by the razing of the nobles' castles on the excuse that they served as nests of bandits. Then in the public domain the Madrid government ordered the Catalan coat of arms to be struck down from the gates of fortresses and dockyards, and in 1639 it laid the whole province under a levy for fortress-building. As a committee of royal officials declared: 'No law can stand in the way of natural defence'. (For conditions in Catalonia see Elliott, 1963.) The final spark for the conflagration was supplied when the authorities billeted 9,000 troops on Catalonia in May 1640.

The revolt prospered mightily with the help of advisers and troops who were shipped from France. On 26 January 1641 the great seaport of Barcelona repulsed the Spanish army of the Marquis of los Vélez, and so the French columns were granted time to take over the fortresses. King Louis himself came south in 1642 to open an overland communication with Catalonia. A tight blockade starved Perpignan into submission on 9 September, and 'thus this important fortress, the strongest in Spain, fell into the hands of the French' (Montglat, 1850, 123). Salses shared the same fate a little later. Rosas succumbed in 1645, and with it the Spanish lost their only remaining strongpoint on the coastline between Roussillon and Barcelona. By then, however, events elsewhere had swung the strategic balance against the rebels and their French supporters.

Richelieu was disgraced in 1643, and he had to yield place as chief minister to Cardinal Mazarin, an Italian who was more interested in dabbling in the affairs of his homeland than in promoting rebellion in Spain. From then onwards the French commanders in the Peninsula were starved of resources and gradually forced onto the defensive.

Never did the French manage to prise loose the pincers by which the enemy gripped Catalonia; 1644

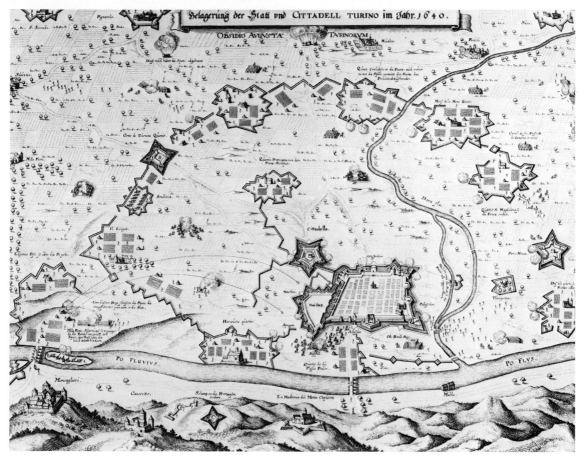

45 Siege of Turin, 1640. The French are in the citadel, the rebel Piedmontese are in the town, and Harcourt has thrown a line around the whole lot; the Spanish have emerged at the bottom left-hand corner, and are shooting food-filled mortar bombs to their friends in the town (Merian, 1692)

proved to be a particularly bad year. They failed in their attack against Tarragona, which offered the Spanish a stepping-stone for an advance northwards from Valencia up the Mediterranean coast; worse still, the French and rebels lost Lerida, which was ensconced on a nodal point of roads between Catalonia and the inland province of Aragon. The people of Lerida hated the Catalans, and thenceforward the Spanish found in them and their rock citadel a sure guard for Aragon, and a support for offensives eastwards into Catalonia.

The Spanish launched a further offensive in 1651, at a time when the wars of the *Fronde* had sucked most of the French troops back to their homeland. After enduring fourteen months of blockade, the starving population of Barcelona capitulated on 13 October 1652. Except for Rosas, all the other Catalan fortresses followed the example of the capital, and by the end of the year the French were back at the Pyrenees and Catalonia was re-instated as part of the Spanish monarchy.

The struggle for Portuguese independence 1580–1666
A sense of separate nationhood was also to be found on the far, western side of the Iberian peninsula, where the Portuguese were maintaining their centuries-old struggle against the Spanish. Portugal was remarkably lucky to have asserted any kind of independence, when we consider that she possessed

a common six-hundred-mile land border with her inveterate enemy. One reason for her survival was the fact that the Spanish were so often preoccupied with wars elsewhere. Another was the readiness of friendly powers – whether Sweden, Holland, England or France – to send weapons and advice when they were badly needed.

By itself, the fortified frontier of Portugal would never have succeeded in keeping out the Spanish. In the third quarter of the sixteenth century, when the danger was particularly acute, the Portuguese certainly did all they could to build up their artificial defences. Evora, the distant eastern outpost of Lisbon, was the scene of a rather clever feat of improvisation in 1570, when the Italian engineer Pompeio Ardicio added spacious bastions and two outlying forts to the ancient town walls. However it was easier to strengthen the fortress ramparts than to harden the resolve of the governors, most of whom were cowardly and corrupt. In 1580 the Spanish came over the border and overran the entire country, the towns everywhere opening their gates to the invaders.

During the sixty years of Spanish rule the Portuguese strongholds were stripped of their cannon and allowed to fall into decay. The wretched state of the fortresses made it easy for the Portuguese to rebel and win their country back again in 1640, but by the same token the Portuguese were forced to work hard to re-constitute their frontier with Spain. The new king, John IV, set up a permanent *Conselho de Guerra*, together with a special *Junta* to attend to the defence of the borders. The detailed direction of the most important works was entrusted to a Flemish Jesuit called Cosmander, who was a renowned mathematician.

During 1641 and 1642 the Portuguese bent their efforts to fortifying the province of Alentejo, which lay on the direct line of advance on Lisbon from the great Spanish fortress of Badajoz. Elvas stood in particular danger, for it was located on the main road only a dozen miles from Badajoz, though it could be given close support from the lateral strongholds of Campo Maior to the north and Olivenza to the south. Thanks to the limited supply capacity of seventeenth-century Spanish armies, the other dangerous route of invasion crossed the frontier only

a little over thirty miles to the north, between the Spanish fortress of Valencia de Alcantara and the Portuguese town of Castelo de Vide.

The 'war' was confined to inconclusive border incursions until 1657, when 8,500 Spaniards under the Duke of San Germano besieged and took Olivenza. Exploiting this breach on the southern flank of the Portuguese defences, Don John of Austria devastated the Alentejo in 1662 with 14,000 troops. In the following year he repeated the operation on a still more ambitious scale and managed to reduce Evora, which caused some panic in Lisbon. However, the remaining frontier fortresses were in good hands (in marked contrast to the state of affairs in 1580), and Don John was unable to get his supplies through from Badajoz. He began to extricate himself, but was overtaken and defeated by the army of the Conde de Villa Flôr at Ameixial on 8 June. In 1665 a last invasion by 23,000 troops was broken on the Portuguese positions at Montes Claros, and the war was prolonged by minor skirmishing until the Spanish recognised Portuguese independence in 1668.

The unusually heavy fighting of the early 1660s drew attention to the importance of building up both the field army and the passive defences, a work which was carried out with great energy by the minister Castelo Melhor, who was in office from 1662 to 1667.

The engineering personnel was overwhelmingly French, and one of Turenne's secretaries left a detailed description of the state of the Portuguese fortresses in November 1662, within five months of Castelo Melhor's coming to power. He found that the Upper Alentejo was considered the most vital sector of the frontier, and that the late King John IV (1640–56) had fortified Élvas with nine revetted bastions (with ravelins to match), a ditch cut out of the rock, and a detached fort on a nearby hill. The Frenchman correctly predicted that the Spanish would never be able to take it. The nearby fortress of Campo Maior was well suited to serve as an offensive base, but 'as far as its fortification is concerned the Portuguese have been led astray by unskilful engineers, who have begun (but not completed) several works which would require a great garrison' (Turenne, 1782, I, 574). The Duke of Schomberg, who was the most famous mercenary commander of his time, repeatedly had to dissuade the Portuguese from undertaking over-ambitious works.

The large fortress-depôt of Estremoz acted as a rearward support for all the Upper Alentejo fortresses, and the French observers saw 1,500 men toiling on the works. The access to Lisbon was protected by forts and redoubts which were disposed along the Tagus, and an ambitious project was set in train to defend the capital itself: 'The enceinte is intended to be of an incredible extent, containing much arable land and pasture, and capable of accommodating all the people for six leagues around with their families and cattle' (ibid., I, 578).

In 1666 Castelo Melhor hired the French engineer Allain Manesson Mallet to put the finishing touches to the programme. Mallet repaired and strengthened Evora and Estremoz, and made plans of all, or nearly all the new fortresses. He found that the gigantic new twenty-six-bastioned enceinte of Lisbon was nearly complete (Mallet, 1673).

The Rhenish theatre 1635–48
In earlier centuries the French had seen plenty of fighting in the Netherlands, in Italy and in the Pyrenees. By intervening in the Thirty Years War, however, the French had now opened up a major new theatre of operations on the eastern flank, where they proceeded to push their frontiers to the Rhine and make forays deep into Germany.

The war on the German theatre presented the French with two problems: first, how to seize and hold bridgeheads on the far (eastern) bank of the Rhine; and, after that, how to make headway on the further side against the forces of the Duke of Bavaria, to whom the Emperor devolved the main burden of defending the south-west flank of Germany.

Much useful groundwork was laid in the 1630s by the private army of the dispossessed Duke Bernhardt of Saxe-Weimar. The French lent this heretic encouragement and occasional armed support, and he boldly carved out a fief on both sides of the upper Rhine, from Saverne in Alsace to Rheinfelden on the confines of Switzerland.

The most important of Bernhardt's gains were made in 1638. He beat the Imperialists at Rheinfelden on 21 February, and went on to capture Freiburg, a fortress which was lodged in the spurs of the Black Forest, and commanded two parallel carriage roads which led over the watershed of the Black Forest to the regime of the Danube (the northern route via Furtwangen and Villingen: the southern via Neustadt). Towards the end of the campaign Bernhardt and the French joined in an attack on the nearby stronghold of Breisach, which capitulated on 14 September, after the garrison had been driven to eat rats, leather, and perhaps also a few corpses.

The capture of Breisach gave the French their first bridgehead on the right bank of the Rhine, together with the command of the fertile riverine plain and a secure communication with Freiburg, which lay fifteen miles to the east. Bernhardt died in 1639, and his legacy of fortress and troops fell to the French. The Spanish were distraught, for they had lost the use of the Rhine valley route for sending their troops from Italy to the Netherlands.

One of the constant factors of warfare in Germany was soon apparent. Rather than return to France at the approach of every winter, and so yield up the fruits of a year's campaigning, the French commanders found that it was much better to capture some of the towns on the far side of the Black Forest, and use them as quarters for their troops. As Turenne observed, the last months of the year were 'the time which decides so many things in Germany, because then you can gain command of a tract of territory in which you have all the winter to refresh and remake your army' (Turenne, 1782, I, 97). The disadvantage was that once the French were scattered over the little towns and villages, they became very vulnerable to any Imperial commander who was enterprising enough to take the field in the 'closed season'.

The Bavarian general Franz von Mercy surprised the French army in such a posture at the end of 1643, and he exploited his success by recapturing Freiburg and flinging the enemy back to the Rhine.

In compensation, the French shipped their siege train down the Rhine in the late summer of 1644, reducing the fortress of Philipsburg on 9 September, which gave them a second secure bridgehead on the east bank, about one hundred miles below their first bridgehead at Breisach. Over the next few weeks a host of brisk sieges and easy capitulations put them in possession of the course of the Rhine as far north as the confluence with the Moselle at Coblenz. All of this was the work of the two most dashing of the younger French commanders, Viscount Turenne and the Duke of Enghien (later Prince of Condé).

Thus the Rhenish campaign of 1644 vastly extended the base from which the French could fight in Germany. They now had the means of carrying their operations around what we might term the 'Bavarian block', the Black Forest and the broken wooded country of Württemberg, which were made so strong by nature and the mole-like labour of Mercy.

In 1646 and again in 1647 Turenne led a French army into central Germany, joined up with the Swedes and descended on Bavaria from the north. On both occasions the Bavarians fled into their fortresses as swiftly and instinctively as those pale sea-creatures that flit into rock crevices whenever a shadow falls across their pool. In 1646 Turenne wasted invaluable time when he reduced the little fortress of Rain and laid a vain siege to Augsburg. In the second campaign, however, he left the fortresses alone and revenged himself on the Bavarians by devastating their open country for three weeks – his pupil John Churchill was going to pursue the same course in 1704.

Now that Bavaria was overrun by the French, and the Swedes were before Prague, the deputies of the Emperor signed peace at Münster, on 24 October 1648. He ceded Alsace to France, together with Breisach and the isolated bridgehead of Philipsburg. He still refused to allow the French to interfere in German political affairs, though in return he agreed to disarm the German fortifications on the right bank of the Rhine, all the way from the Swiss border to the neighbourhood of Philipsburg. Appearances were saved, but the French had lodged themselves firmly on the Rhine and won their way to a century and a half of military intervention in Germany.

The Netherlands theatre 1637–48
We have already seen how the Spanish in the Netherlands responded to the first French aggression by launching their devastating counter-attack of 1636. Over the following years they continued to give the enemy a good run for their money.

Strategic geography was one of the reasons why the French were doing so badly. They were lucky only in the disposition of the Somme, which lay across the line of Spanish invasion for eighty miles (as the crow flies) from the Channel coast eastwards to Saint-Quentin. Unfortunately this western sector of the frontier was not a very good base for an offensive. The Boulogne–Calais salient ran to the north for sixty miles along the coast, but it offered only a narrow stretch of land for the assembly and feeding of armies, and gave on to Spanish Flanders, with its many river lines and modern fortresses.

Inland from the Boulogne–Calais salient, the Spanish province of Artois bulged threateningly towards to within a score of miles of the Somme. Several roads radiated over the province from its strategic centre at Arras, and gave the Spanish the command of the long chalk ridge of the Collines d'Artois, which deprived the French of access to the regime of the Scheldt. French armies taking the offensive into Artois and Hainault therefore had to haul their siege trains by land over the watershed.

Once the French arrived on the far side of the Collines d'Artois they found that the country was accessible enough (unlike the Flemish coastlands), but in compensation the towns were strong and large, and, as Richelieu knew, 'the nobility in those parts is numerous and brave, and all the people skilled in the use of arms' (Richelieu, 1850, VII, 338). The transition of the feelings of the Netherlands townsmen – from the hostility of the 1570s and 1580s to the unreserved loyalty shown in the middle decades of the seventeenth century – must surely be accounted one of the most remarkable achievements of Spanish rule. Condé for one was brought to despair by the sullen opposition of the Flemings, and in 1648 he complained to Mazarin: 'The enemy fortresses are defended by the townspeople as well as the garrisons, whereas in our fortresses the citizens are our mortal enemies' (D'Aumale, 1886–96), V, 585).

The Somme petered out just east of Saint-

Quentin, at a place calculated to cause the greatest danger to the French. A scarcely perceptible swell of ground, hardly five miles in width, separated the source of that river from the headwaters of the Oise, the valley of which provided the Spanish with an avenue leading directly to the Ile de France. A dense nest of fortresses (Cambrai, Valenciennes, Le Quesnoy, Landrecies, Avesnes) enabled the Spaniards to mass their forces on the approaches to the Oise, and threw a heavy responsibility on the exposed French strongholds of Le Catelet and La Capelle, which stood guard over the headwaters, and of Guise and La Fère, which were sited by the river itself.

An alternative means for the Spanish to open up the French frontier was to make a 'left-flanking' movement by way of the Ardennes, and then turn west through the wide gaps between the French fortresses along the Meuse. From there the Spanish could advance down the Aisne by way of Rethel towards the junction with the middle Oise at Compiègne. Spanish activity in this part of the world was to become particularly promising in the late 1640s and early 1650s, when Condé turned against the French crown and tried to form a private empire on the southern flanks of the Ardennes.

As some compensation, the French had the time and the resources to reduce the Spanish fortified frontier by a continuous 'crumbling' process which extended over several campaigns. The Spanish, on the other hand, were fighting the Dutch in the northern Netherlands, and they had limited means and leisure to devote to the war against the French. They accordingly pursued a strategy of rapid and well-timed penetrations. Characteristic of the Spanish irruptions into France were the moves designed to lend a hand to malcontents in Paris (1591, 1652), and the well-calculated spoiling attacks which repeatedly threw the French plans into disarray (the capture of Amiens in 1597, the offensive of 1636, the surprise of Courtrai in 1648. The capture of the Schenckenschans in 1635 was an example of the same technique as applied against the Dutch).

On passing to the sequence of events, we therefore find that the French were slow to recover from the impact of the unexpected Spanish counter-offensive of 1636. It was not until 1638 that they set about expanding the Boulogne–Calais salient, a task which was to occupy them, with one interruption in 1643, until the outbreak of the civil wars of the *Fronde*.

Richelieu recouped something of his lost prestige by taking the isolated little fortress of Hesdin in 1639. Arras, a much tougher proposition, was taken after a major siege in the following year, and the campaign of 1641 found the French engaged against the obstinately-defended fortress of Aire. This last operation gave the French the opportunity of demonstrating their growing professionalism in fortress warfare:

All the rules of the military art were observed at this siege. After spending forty days in reducing the outworks, we had to cross the ditch of the main rampart against a determined and inventive opposition from the Spanish, who were ceaselessly casting incendiary materials on our bridges. After that we had to 'attach' the miners to the bastions, blow up the bastion faces, and then undermine the gorge retrenchments and push further mines along the curtains between the bastions (Grammont, 1850, 250).

The place fell on 26 July, and with it the French gained additional security for Calais, and a useful post between the Lys and the Scarpe from where they could levy contributions deep inside Flanders.

A brave new Spanish commander, Francisco de Melo, set himself the task of redressing the losses of the last few years. He swung eastwards in 1643, in a bold attempt to open up the Champagne frontier of France, but he was halted on 13 May in the western Ardennes by the little fortress of Rocroi. Here, six days later, he was smashed beyond redemption by the army of the young Duke of Enghien. There could have been no more promising opening to the reign of the new king of France, Louis XIV.

The French exploited their victory by capturing all of Artois except Saint-Omer, and over the following years they proceeded to break into the Flemish plain against the opposition of some of the best-found and most modern fortresses of the Spanish Netherlands. The whole of 1644, for instance, was devoted to the work of reducing Gravelines, an undertaking which became 'a gulf into which gold and blood disappeared without trace' (D'Aumale, 1886–96, IV, 278).

After the fall of Gravelines the French remained lodged in coastal Flanders. Mardick was firmly in their grasp in August 1646, and in October Enghien reduced the important privateer port of Dunkirk after a model siege. He had made a careful study of siegecraft and fortification in his youth, and more than once he had acted as the chief engineer of his army.

The inland fortress of Ypres went the same way in May 1648, and when the Spanish moved forward for a counter-blow they were soundly beaten by the Prince of Condé (to use Enghien's new title) in the plain of Lens on 20 August.

Perhaps it would have been better for France if the Spanish had swept Condé aside and recovered Artois. As things were, Cardinal Mazarin was so heartened by the victory at Lens that he recalled the Swiss and French Guards to Court, and placed the refractory members of the Paris *Parlement* under arrest. There followed a civil war between the parties of the Court and the princely *Fronde*, which threw the French onto the defensive in Italy, spelt the ruin of the Catalan rebels, and once more laid open the northern frontiers of France after all the hard-won gains of recent years.

The Wars of the Fronde and the Netherlands theatre 1649–53

In the new bout of civil strife, best described by its popular title of the 'War of the Chamber Pots', the art military regressed to the standards of the most disorganised days of the religious wars of the sixteenth century. Thus the great Turenne was reduced to borrowing carriage horses from the courtiers and nobles in order to haul his siege guns into position before Etampes in 1652.

The year 1652 proved to be the decisive year of the struggle, if such a term can be applied to the various scamperings and posturings. Turenne, newly-reconciled with the party of the Court, stormed the rebel Condé's position just outside Paris at the Faubourg Saint-Antoine, and compelled the dissidents to flee through the city to safety.

Paris still refused to allow the royalists inside, but Turenne refused to listen to talk of evacuating the Court to Lyons, even when a roving army of Spaniards and Lorrainers marched through Picardy to the help of the rebels. For six weeks Turenne stood firm in his entrenched camp at Villeneuve Saint-Georges, which he had skilfully sited at the confluence of the Seine and Yères about ten miles above Paris. Condé did not dare to attack the position, despite his superior forces.

By now the Parisians were becoming weary of the hostilities, and on 21 October they welcomed Turenne and young King Louis into the city with wild acclamations. Condé with the Spanish and Lorrainers stole away into Champagne.

The civil war was now extinct, save for isolated troubles in Burgundy and Guyenne. Condé still maintained a private army on the Meuse with the help of the Spanish, but Bordeaux, the only other refuge of princely faction, capitulated to the royalists at the end of July 1653.

The return of Guyenne to obedience put an end to the civil war. France was no longer divided, and she began to unite her forces to make war on the Spanish, and recover the losses sustained in the Netherlands during the time of the troubles (Montglat, 1850, 170).

By the middle of 1653 these 'losses sustained' amounted to the fortresses of Ypres, Hirson, Le Catelet, Gravelines and Dunkirk. They were severe enough, to be sure, but they did not amount to a dangerous inroad into the heartland of northern France. In August the Spaniards certainly marched some way through Picardy in the company of Condé, but they were unwilling to prosecute a major siege so far from the Netherlands, 'whence it is difficult to bring up provisions and ammunition' (Fuensaldaña, 1880–8, 575).

The Spanish called off their advance, and they were content to reduce the fortress of Rocroi in the Ardennes – a wholly peripheral gain compared with the prize offered by Paris. They had lost their one remaining chance of snatching a decision before the contest was taken up again, on radically different terms, by a reunited France.

The relief of Arras and the end of the war in the North 1654–9

After the manifold frustrations of recent years, Condé's vanity was outraged beyond all measure in June 1654, when Cardinal Mazarin sent an army to besiege Stenay in the heart of his Meuse empire. Condé cast about for a suitable object upon which to vent his anger, and he committed his Spanish friends to no less an enterprise than the attack of Arras, which was the capital of Artois and the key to all the conquests made by the French beyond the boundaries of 1635. The trenches were duly opened on the night of 14–15 July.

The Spanish army was a badly-balanced one, for it owned only 14,000 infantry as opposed to 18,000 cavalry. The line of circumvallation (facing the country) was therefore constructed with unusual care. The actual siege approaches were by no means so impressive, for the Netherlandish-Spanish techniques of fortress warfare, as perfected by Maurice of Nassau and Spinola, had by now become an exhausting routine into which the besiegers were prepared to throw a great deal of effort but very little imagination. Like the mountains that laboured to produce the mouse, the Spanish countervallation at Arras contorted itself into a multitude of bends, branches, spurs and diamond-shaped redoubts, but it contrived to throw out nothing more impressive than two trench attacks.

Once the rebel fortress of Stenay had fallen, on 5 August, all the French forces were free to march to take part in the interesting events around Arras. By the middle of the month 22,000 French were massed outside the Spanish lines under the triple command of the marshals Turenne, Hocquincourt and Ferté.

Turenne was already defying seventeenth-century practice by refusing to leave the neighbourhood of Arras, when he could have compensated himself by capturing some Spanish town; he knew very well that no other fortress was quite as valuable as Arras. As August wore on, Turenne came to believe that he must defy convention still further, and he persuaded his colleagues to take the bold step of attacking the Spanish in their lines of circumvallation. Recent wars had revealed the kind of fate reserved for the few commanders who were rash enough to make the attempt (Frederick Henry

of Nassau at Breda in 1625, Leganés at Turin in 1640), and wise men like Spinola preferred to leave an enemy siege army sedulously alone once it had thrown up its lines. Turenne, however, was convinced that it was imperative to make the attempt, for word had come through that the garrison of Arras was running out of gunpowder.

Turenne had clear ideas as to how to improve on the performance of earlier times. He calculated that the best moment for the attack was at night, for then the besiegers scattered their forces in order to hold the entire length of their lines, whereas in daytime they could observe the preparations for the assault and concentrate their defence on the threatened sector. A night attack brought with it the risk of confusion and delays, but Turenne was confident that he could retain control if he assembled the troops in three columns on a common start-line, then launched them in a concerted assault against a single sector of the entrenchments. The chosen portion of the circumvallation lay on the south-east, facing Eloi, where the Spanish forces were at their weakest.

The French army moved forward between midnight and one o'clock on the morning of 25 August 1654. The scene is described by the refugee Duke of York:

We had in our march thither a very still fair night, besides the benefit of the moon, which set as favourably for us as we could desire, that is, just as we came to the place appointed. As the moon went down, it began to blow very fresh and grew exceeding dark, in so much that the enemy could neither see nor hear us, as otherwise they might; and they were the more surprised when the first news they had of us, was to find us within half cannon shot of them. I remember not to have seen a finer sight of the nature, than was that of our foot when they were in one battle, and began to march towards the lines; for then uncovering at once their lighted matches, they made a glorious show, which appeared the more by reason of the wind, which kindled them and made them blaze through the darkness of the night (James II, 1962, 179).

There was some hesitation when the French

columns first reached the circumvallation, but they encountered no serious opposition and by dawn the infantry had cleared the passages and the cavalry could begin to lead in their horses. The Spanish abandoned their positions and fled towards Douai like a flock of sheep, leaving behind two or three thousand casualties and prisoners. The French themselves lost just two or three hundred killed.

Turenne's spectacular and economical victory helped to discredit the system of siege lines which engineers had evolved over the last hundred years. No less importantly, the relief of Arras preserved for France the freedom to carry the war beyond the chalk watershed of northern France into the Netherlands plain.

More heartening still was the clear evidence that the French were getting the better of the Spanish in the techniques of fortress warfare. A French officer toured the Spanish siegeworks after the battle and concluded that

the general opinion is very much in error when it claims that the Spanish surpass other nations in their talent for attacking fortresses. . . . They left a good example of their handiwork in the enormous diggings in front of Arras. I saw what they had done, and I must say that I could recognise no trace of this incomparable intelligence. Although they employed their most able men on the works, they committed so many mistakes that I truly believe that our most middling apprentices would have surpassed them (Turenne, 1782, II, 282–3).

The relief of Arras therefore took its place as one of the several manifestations of the change in French fortunes which occurred in 1653 and 1654, the years when the nation began to fight once more as a united force, and when an aspirant engineer named Vauban exchanged the rebel service for the king's.

Turenne prosecuted the work of chasing the Spaniards over the next four years. On the eastern flank, the avenues to the headwaters of the Somme and the Oise were sealed off by the capture of Le Quesnoy at the end of 1654, and by the reduction in the following year of Le Catelet, Landrecies, Condé and Saint-Ghislain. The Duke of Condé was provoked into making a number of counter-attacks. Now that the breaking of siege lines was in fashion,

he boldly smashed Ferté's army before Valenciennes in 1656, and cut his way into the beleaguered citadel of Cambrai in 1657.

The French resumed their offensive in the autumn of 1657, with the help of 6,000 Ironsides from the England of Oliver Cromwell, with whom Cardinal Mazarin had concluded an alliance. Turenne, it must be admitted, was not over-impressed with his new comrades-in-arms. On their side the English displayed impatience with the Continental methods of systematic siege approaches, and they noticed that when they suggested a hearty assault on Ypres the marshal 'fell into a passion, stamping with his feet, and shaking his locks and grinning with his teeth' (Firth, 1921, 176).

Still, these unlikely allies contrived to reduce Mardick in 1657, and on 14 June 1658 they convincingly defeated the Spanish army outside Dunkirk. The Spanish never again dared to show their faces in the open field.

The abandoned fortresses fell one by one: Dunkirk first, on 23 June, then the nearby towns of Bergues, Dixmude, Furnes and Gravelines in a rapid series of capitulations. Finally, Turenne raged unopposed over inland Flanders, and seized Oudenarde, Menin and Ypres, a suitably impressive ending to a great war which had endured for the last eight years of the reign of Louis XIII, and the first sixteen of Louis XIV's.

The Peace of the Pyrenees 1659

If the settlement of 1659 managed to put an end to a quarter-century of fighting between France and Spain, the clauses nevertheless placed France in a position to reopen hostilities on more favourable terms than ever before.

1   The Pyrenean frontier: The counties of Roussillon and Cerdagne were annexed by the French, which brought their borders up to the eastern Pyrenees, and freed Languedoc from the danger of Spanish incursions which had existed from the days of Francis I. Perpignan, Salses and Collioure were the main places which came into their ownership.

2   Italy: The French were recognised in possession of Pinerolo, and thereby retained the freedom to move into Italy in any future war. Mazarin had

offered to conquer Geneva on behalf of Savoy, in return for annexing the county of Nice, but Duke Charles Emanuel was already too chagrined at the loss of Pinerolo to be willing to fall in with the deal. 'It is bad enough to have one foot nailed down', he said. 'I should like to keep the other one free' (Saluces, 1817–18, IV, 334).

3   The Netherlands: Here France gained a broad belt of fortresses which stretched from the Channel coast at Gravelines all the way to the Moselle at Thionville, by way of Bourbourg, Saint-Venant, Lillers, Béthune, Lens, Arras, Bapaume, Landrecies, Avesnes, Mariembourg, Philippeville and Montmédy. These annexations eliminated the dangerous Artesian 'bulge', and placed France firmly on the 'forward slope' of the Netherlands border. The French now had their outposts on the Sambre and the northern flank of the Ardennes, and, more important still, they owned fortified depôts like Arras (on the Scarpe) which enabled them to bring siege trains against the Flemish fortresses by water transport.

The precursors of Vauban

The fortified border

In fortress building, as in so many other fields of governmental activity, all sense of purpose seemed to vanish with the murder of Henry IV in 1610. Royal construction of every kind remained in abeyance during the first two decades of the reign of his successor, Louis XIII, and in 1627 a member of an assembly of notables ventured to complain that 'we know the present king well enough in his capacity as destroyer of fortresses, but we have yet to see him build any up' (Bassompierre, 1850, 259).

Not until the outbreak of war with Spain in 1635 did Louis begin to emulate the work of Henry IV or Francis I. According to Richelieu, the aim of the new programme of building was to strengthen the subordinate frontiers by artificial obstacles, so as to have a free hand to concentrate the field forces in the eastern Netherlands.

The Provençal coast was duly attended to (though Richelieu admits that he forgot about the Iles de Lérins), and

His Majesty ordered the strengthening of the towns of Dijon, Auxonne, Saint-Jean-de-Losne, Bellegarde and Châlons, so that these places should be secure against surprise attack and able to put up a long defence in the event of a siege. His Majesty took these measures because he heeded the warning of the Prince [Henri de Condé?] that the authorities had been very negligent in fortifying Burgundy, for it had always been left in peace, even during the old wars between France and the Empire – the result was that Burgundy was by now the least defensible province of the kingdom. His Majesty also devoted very careful attention to the Picardy frontier. Finding the town of Péronne in a very bad state, even though it had always been reckoned very strong, he traced some designs with his own hand, and raised a number of fine works which have made this stronghold into one of the most redoubtable in the kingdom. . . . As for Champagne, although Lorraine covered most of it and held the enemy at a distance, His Majesty ordered the authorities to strengthen some of the fortresses lying near Luxembourg and Burgundy (Richelieu, 1850, VIII, 259).

This fine programme did nothing for La Capelle and Le Catelet, which were the fortresses which actually bore the brunt of the Spanish onslaught in 1636.

In the course of time most of the works mentioned by Richelieu were demolished or overlaid by accretions. For one of the most complete extant examples of a fortress of the period of Louis XIII we have to travel to the lonely Atlantic coast opposite the Ile d'Oléron at Brouage, where a stronghold in the shape of an irregular square was built to the designs of Pierre d'Argencourt.

It was to Louis XIII's credit that he kept alive the highly-centralised structure of engineer administration which had been created by Sully. Unfortunately, this inheritance failed to survive the minority of the next king, Louis XIV. In those turbulent years the supreme post of Surintendant des Fortifications became lost among the many functions of Secretary of State, and in 1645 Michel Le Tellier disrupted the hierarchy of command when he created Intendants de Fortifications who had authority over the administration of one or several

provinces. Sometimes a number of such in-
tendancies fell into the grasp of a single bureaucratic
pluralist who had no engineering knowledge what-
soever. By the most absurd arrangement of all, the
coastal fortresses were whisked away and placed
under the separate authority of the Minister of
Marine.

The only semblance of informed command was
provided by Louis-Nicolas Chevalier de Clerville
(1610–77), who directed all the important sieges of
the 1650s. He was rewarded in 1658 or the following
year with the title of *Commissaire-Général des
Fortifications et Réparations des Villes de France*.
Rather unfairly, Clerville is now remembered only
for his patronage of the young Vauban. He took that
fledgling engineer with him to the second siege of
Sainte-Menehould in 1653, and allowed his pupil
more and more responsibility, despite a history of
disagreements which began at the siege of Mardick
in 1657, and flared up again with the construction of
the citadel of Lille in 1668. By that time the fame of
the apprentice had already exceeded that of the
master.

The literature of fortification

By the middle of the seventeenth century the
appetite of the public for knowledge of *castraméta-
tion* was fed and stimulated by a flood of books produced by authors of the most widely-differing
qualifications, ranging from one-eyed veterans like
Pagan to the clerical geometricians (for example,
Silvère de Bitainvieu, Milliet de Châles, Père
Bourdin, Georges Fournier) who gathered at Metz
for the instruction of noble youth. Already in 1615
the soldier Vignère exclaimed that so many books
had been written on fortification that they would
almost be enough to re-stock the famous vanished
libraries of Alexandria and Constantinople:

Everyone likes to get out his pencil and sketch a
system of fortification, whether he is a painter, art-
dealer, mason, cabinet-maker or an architect. They
seem to imagine that it is enough to dream up a
fortress design in your head, and know how to
describe a straight line and a curve on paper with
the help of a ruler and compasses. They do not

appreciate that a knowledge of engineering is
derived from long experience of sieges (Vignère,
1615, 629).

Among the better-qualified writers we must place
the Sieur de Fabre (*Les Practiques du Sieur Fabre sur
l'Ordre et Reigle de Fortifier, Attaquer et Défendre les
Places*, Paris 1629). He belonged to the older
generation of Louis XIII's officers, and in 1626 he had
designed some forts in the Valtelline which he
describes as being preferred to the original works
which had been constructed on the same site by the
Venetian engineer Tensini. Fabre was recalled by
French engineers of the eighteenth century for
having pointed out the strength possessed by several
fronts of fortification when they were built along a
straight line.

Blaise Francois Comte de Pagan (1604–65) was
another author who escapes the charge of dilet-
tantism. This old warhorse had won the esteem of
the king in twenty-one sieges, and having been
blinded in one eye in the religious wars of the 1620s
he lost his sight altogether while campaigning in
Portugal in 1642. Pagan devised the simple methods
of tracing fortification which were followed by
Vauban, and he argued more passionately than
anyone before his time that the bastion must be the
chief point of the defence, to which all else must be
subordinated.

Such is the fame of Vauban, that it is easy to forget
that probably the most influential French writer in
the marshal's own time was actually the Chevalier de
Ville (1596–1656), whose *Fortifications* went through
many printings in the course of almost half a
century from 1629. Vauban's writings, in contrast,
became known only gradually through unauthentic
pirated editions, or through manuscripts which were
circulated among a small public of engineers.

De Ville wrote interestingly and well. He was a
down-to-earth soldier like Pagan, but he avoided the
obsessive stress on the bastion which had alienated
so many people from Pagan's work. Borrowing
freely from foreign motifs, he laid out an enceinte in
the Italian style, with obtuse-angled bastions, and he
protected it by the powerful outworks which he
believed were vital for a protracted defence. These
outworks consisted partly of the ravelins which had

been devised by the Italians in the last century, and partly of that newer Dutch invention, the hornwork.

At the same time de Ville was determined to simplify the earlier designs. He believed that orillons were superfluous, and he objected particularly strongly to the practice of housing guns in casemated bastion flanks:

In earlier times the cannon used to be lodged in two storeys of covered casemates in the flanks. This method had fallen out of use, on account of the grave defects which were observed in these constructions. After the artillery was fired the smoke filled the chamber so thickly that despite all the air vents it was impossible to stay inside, or see

well enough to reload. Also, the concussion of the cannon shook the whole fabric, and when the enemy fired at the lower storey of casemates the gun crews were killed or wounded by the splinters and débris, and a few rounds sufficed to reduce the structure to ruins. Once the bottom storey collapsed the upper tier fell down as well (De Ville, 1629, 1675 edn, book I, part I, chapter XXV, 5).

The proportions of de Ville's traces were simple and sensible, and were based on the effective range of the musket. At the same time he was realistic enough to point out that the fortress designer must always give priority to the demands of the site.

46   One of the bastions of Montmédy, a Habsburg fortress fronting onto Lorraine, where Charles V began a programme of reconstruction in 1545. By 1657 Montmédy was the only remaining Spanish stronghold on the north-eastern borders of France. It fell to Louis XIV on 4 August of that year, after fifty-seven days of heroic defence. The young Vauban helped to direct the siege. Montmédy is in an excellent state of preservation, and conveys a strong sense of romantic history.

For all his persuasiveness de Ville belongs to an older generation, you might almost think an older century, from that of the rational Vauban, who was to be the servant of a united France. The confusions of civil and religious war echo in every line of the pages which de Ville devotes to his surprises and seditions, escalades and petards. He believed that no man could be taken at his word, though he held that the most reliable governors were to be found among noblemen of modest ambition. Lacking confidence in his own experience and reasoning, he felt compelled to bolster up his arguments by constant references to classical antiquity and the Old Testament. Still, we must be grateful for such practical hints as the advice as to the best way of disposing of a sentry who is guarding a wharf: you ask him for a hand up from a boat, then you pull him into the water over your head.

The state of the siege attack

The self-confidence of French engineers was sapped by the disruptions caused by two long royal minorities, and by the puniness of their efforts in comparison with the mighty sieges that were directed by Spinola and Frederick Henry of Nassau. For a long time French military men were content with having achieved passable imitations of the Netherlandish practice, as in the sieges of Aire in 1641 and Gravelines in 1644. Likewise the new twelve- and twenty-four-pounder cannon were deliberately patterned on the Spanish and Dutch models, when they were not actually purchased direct from Holland.

The explosive mortar bomb was a further importation from the Netherlands, having been introduced at the siege of La Mothe in Lorraine in 1634 through the agency of the Englishman Thomas Malthus, who learnt the employment of bombs during his service with the Dutch (Malthus, 1629).

Malthus was killed by a random musket shot at the second siege of Gravelines in 1658, but thirty years later nearly all the French bombardier officers still counted themselves his disciples, much to the dismay of the scientifically-minded writer Blondel:

All his knowledge was derived entirely from experience, and he had not the slightest

acquaintance with mathematics. . . . He adjusted his mortars by a process of luck and rough calculation, making a guess as to the range, and elevating the barrel accordingly (Blondel, 1685, 6–7).

A few Frenchmen were dissatisfied with the laborious Netherlandish siege procedures. The Abbé Arnauld remembered how as a soldier he had been consumed with frustration at the siege of Damvillers in 1636, an operation that was 'dragged out by the fancy of the Marshal de Châtillon, who got it into his head to attack the place in the Dutch manner . . . we almost failed in the operation because we spent an inordinate amount of time sapping down to the bottom of the ditch by a covered gallery' (Arnauld, 1850, 492).

The elaborate Netherlandish countervallations required whole armies to build and guard them, yet the actual siege approaches, the object of the whole enterprise, were narrow and isolated. In particular, the approaches offered poor start-lines for an assault, as was amply demonstrated at the siege of Rosas in 1645, where an unsuccessful storm by the French prompted Marshal du Plessis to say

how dangerous it is to set out from any distance in order to establish a lodgment. It is essential to have near the objective some kind of line from where we may support the enterprise by fire. You cannot leave a communication trench to attack a large enemy-fortified front without having a similar position of your own close by (Plessis, 1850, 376–7).

The Sieur de Puységur reached the same conclusion from his study of the Turkish wars: 'I am all for the Turkish practice, according to which they attack by successive parallel lines which occupy the same width as the front of the fortress which is under attack' (Puységur, *Instructions Militaires*, 1690, II, 645). A parallel trench was proposed by a certain Le Maine-Chabaud at the siege of Montpellier in 1621, and such works were actually carried out by French engineers at Gravelines in 1644 and Duncannon in Ireland in 1645. Essays of this kind nevertheless remained isolated aberrations from the usual march of the attack, and it was left to Vauban to turn the idea of the siege parallel into a systematic routine of fortress warfare.

Vauban believed that the lack of any continuity in the engineering trade was the reason why the sieges in his youth tended to be so bloody and long-drawn-out:

Engineers were very rare birds in France in those days. . . . They survived such a short time that it was seldom that you came across one who had seen five or six sieges, and still more remarkable to encounter a veteran who had served in as many sieges as this without having been incapacitated by wounds at the beginning of each operation or when it was only half-way through. Since the engineers were prevented from seeing the sieges right through to the end, they had no means of improving their knowledge (Vauban, (1704) 1829 edn, 56–7).

There were certain campaigns, like the ones in the Netherlands in 1648 and in the Pyrenees in 1654, when the commanders were left without a single live engineer.

While they still breathed, the engineers used to spend their mayfly days in arguing such questions as to whether it was better to attack the strongest or the weakest front of a fortress. Such folk exercised no great influence on commanders like Turenne, Condé or Plessis, who believed that they were perfectly competent to manage their sieges in person. The Duke of York was convinced that

no general ought wholly to confide in any engineer for the carrying on of a trench, it not being reasonable to believe, that one who is always there will hazard or expose himself as far as officers, who are to take their turns, and who are pushed on by emulation (James II, 1962, 151–3).

When we look back on the state of fortress warfare in the 1640s and 1650s it is clear enough that without the determination of a single individual, namely Vauban, who set out to remedy all the deficiencies he had observed, the French would never have gone on to make their name as the greatest takers and builders of fortresses in modern history.

At the same time Vauban's achievement was founded on a solid basis. The earlier generation of soldiers had won new and advantageous borders, and they had begun, however clumsily, to get the better of the Spanish in siege warfare; their contemporaries Pagan and Ville had combined and simplified the most useful features of the Italian and Netherlandish traces, and demonstrated that the good engineer must adapt his fortifications to the nature of the ground. Lastly, the young Louis XIV was in the process of creating an enduring political unity, the best guarantee that he would preside over a military renaissance that was going to be longer-lasting than those which had flowered so briefly in the times of Henry II and Henry IV.

Six · The English Civil War and the Subjugation of Ireland

The Tudors

Henrician and Elizabethan fortification

'They are persuaded according to the opinion of the Lacedemonians, that fortifying of towns doth more hurt than good.' Sir Thomas Wilson's comment (Boynton, 1967, 126) on English statesmen could have been applied equally well to the sentiments of most Englishmen throughout the centuries which followed the perfection of artillery.

Lacking the constant spur of a long land frontier, the English bestirred themselves to throw up fortifications only when some concatenation of events elevated a Continental power into a major naval threat. There was no opportunity for a school of native engineering to evolve, and so the fortifications represented just so many isolated models of fashions in Continental military architecture, from the three tub-like 'reinforced castle' towers of the eastern wall of Hull, dating from 1541, to the 'polygonal' forts that were built along Portsdown Hill in the early 1860s.

England entered the late-Renaissance period with one such bout of energy. This was when the highly-centralised Tudor state, as personified in Henry VIII, confiscated the monasteries and tapped the increasing wealth of the merchant classes. The king devoted the proceeds to a programme of coastal defence, to establishing arms factories and building up a powerful navy. He set up an interesting though short-lived seat of military architecture in his Office of Works, a department where men like John Rogers, Sir Richard Lee and Sir Henry Cavendish made their transition from master-masons to fully-fledged architects, and equipped themselves to take the place of their Bohemian master Stefan von Haschenperg. The Office of Works was proficient enough to accomplish a rapid and complete change from the 'reinforced castle' style of its earlier essays to the new Italian bastioned system, which was possibly first attempted by the English at Boulogne in 1545.

Sad to record, the English architects responded rather less well to the challenge set them by Henry's daughter Queen Mary, when she commissioned Lee to fortify the north-eastern gate of her kingdom at Berwick-upon-Tweed, the only side on which the mainland of England possessed a land frontier with a foreign power, Scotland. Lee drew up his plans in 1558, but nobody was quite sure how to carry them out on the ground. The Italian architects Giovanni Portarini and Jacopo Contio were therefore called in to sort out the muddle.

English fortification languished until, in 1583, Queen Elizabeth I ordered John Hawkins, Sir John Gilbert, Sir Francis Drake and Sir Richard Grenville to inspect the defences of the south coast. Replacements were found for men such as the Portsmouth gunners who were 'by age and impotency by no ways serviceable' (ibid., 128), and between 1586 and 1588 imposing new works were built at Dover and Great Yarmouth.

Although the Great Armada of 1588 failed to land the Spanish army in England, the work of fortification went on unabated with the help of foreign engineers such as the celebrated Federigo Giambelli of the Antwerp 'infernal machines' (see p. 78), who completed Carisbrooke Castle between 1597 and 1601 in a most advanced style with flanks traced on the 'razing system'. Another of the foreign experts, Paul Ive, was responsible for some work on Pendennis Castle and the publication in 1589 of *The Practice of Fortification*, the first 'English' book on military engineering. It seems as if the four decades which had supervened since the great days of the Henrician Office of Works had been more than enough to break the continuity of native military architecture.

As for active siege warfare, Henry VII's attack on Boulogne in 1544 (see p. 47) had been the last occasion on which English forces had disputed a fortress with Continental powers on equal terms. The loss of Calais in 1558 cast a pall over the last days of Queen Mary, and the siege was too brief and too catastrophic (see p. 53) to provide any useful lessons as to how a defence should be conducted.

The reign of Mary's heretical half-sister Elizabeth opened a little more auspiciously, with a successful but costly operation in 1560 which evicted 4,000 Frenchmen who had ensconced themselves at Leith, the port of Edinburgh.

For the rest of the century the hostilities in the northern theatre were confined to unauthorised feuds and cattle raids. Decisive operations were out of the question, for the landowners could always seek refuge in their strong old castles, and the local siege techniques did not extend beyond a few attempts to blow in the 'yetts' (iron-bound doors) with charges of powder. The types of fortification ranged from the massive English feudal strongholds of Naworth, Alnwick and Warkworth and the Scots counterparts at Home and Caerlaverock, down to the narrow tower-houses or 'peel towers' of the minor gentry. Camden noted that 'there is not a man amongst them of the better sort that hath not his little tower or pile' (Tough, 1928, 38).

In Scotland the 'official' fortresses did not differ in kind from the minor castles. The power of artillery failed to produce any noticeable change in Scots fortification until the royal architects built the Half-Moon Battery at Edinburgh Castle in 1574, an essay

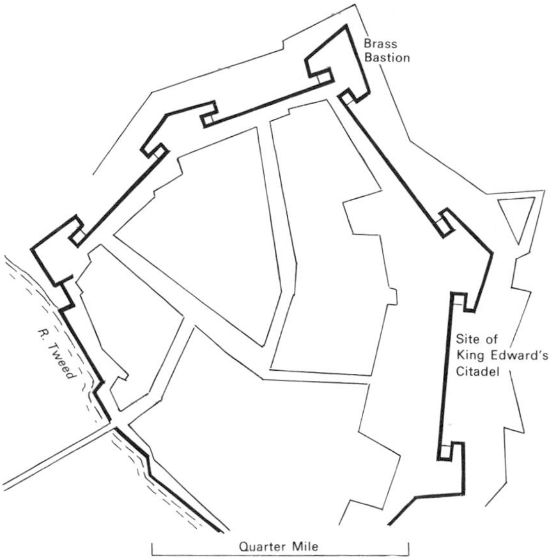

47 Berwick-upon-Tweed. The mis-shapen Brass Bastion at the north-east corner indicates the lack of expertise of the English engineers of the time

in the 'reinforced castle' style which had gone out of fashion on the Continent more than half a century before.

The Elizabethan wars in Ireland 1568–1602

In the sixteenth century both the Netherlands and Ireland witnessed prolonged rebellions against foreign rule. The two revolts were embittered by national and religious hatred, but there the resemblance ceases. Whereas the Dutch uprising was the work of a settled and prosperous society, which rapidly organised a financial and administrative base for its struggle, the Irish rebellion took place in one of the wildest and most remote lands of Europe, and was carried on for many decades by a 'backward' semi-tribal population.

The towns, ports and scattered garrisons therefore gave a secure refuge to the English colonists, and when the English went over to the counter-attack their walls furnished the punitive columns with secure bases from where they could subjugate the neighbouring countryside.

Sea power was another powerful asset which lay at the disposal of the English. It enabled the authorities

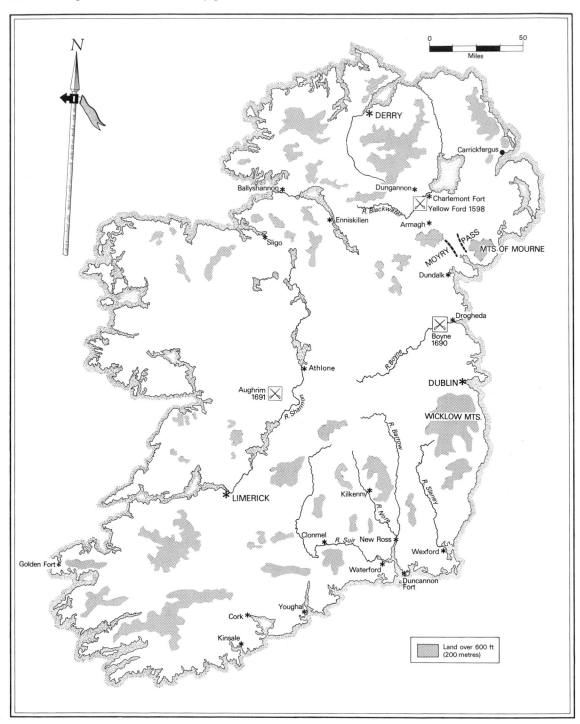

N

0   50
Miles

* DERRY

Carrickfergus ●

Ballyshannon *

Dungannon *
* Charlemont Fort
☒ Yellow Ford 1598
R. Blackwater

* Enniskillen

Armagh *

MOYRY PASS
MTS. OF MOURNE

* Sligo

Dundalk *

☒ Drogheda *
Boyne
1690

R. Boyne

* Athlone

Aughrim ☒
1691

DUBLIN *

R. Shannon

WICKLOW MTS.

R. Barrow

* LIMERICK

Kilkenny *

R. Slaney

R. Nore

Clonmel * R. Suir New Ross *

Wexford *

Golden Fort *

Waterford *
Duncannon
Fort

Youghal *

Cork *

Land over 600 ft
(200 metres)

Kinsale *

Ireland

to maintain soldiers, townspeople and settlers at scattered points around the periphery of the island, and allowed the English commanders to employ heavy guns which they could never have dragged over the wild and trackless countryside inland. English armies were able to sweep over the midland plain after landing on the flat eastern coastline between the Mountains of Mourne and the Wicklow Mountains, or after they had set foot on the shores of the south-eastern rivers: the Slaney, the Barrow, the Nore and the Suir. Even the mountainous flanks of the island could be attacked by sea-borne forces which came up the Ulster loughs and the Kerry bays.

For decades on end the Irish rebels managed to brave all these disadvantages by having recourse to the extremely potent weapon of guerrilla warfare. In 1612 Sir John Davies observed that the first settlers had made a strategic mistake when they established their castles and towns only in the fertile plains, 'and turned the Irish into the woods and mountains, which, as they were proper places for outlaws and thieves, so were they their natural castles and fortifications' (Davies, 1612).

By the 1590s the guerrillas had become formidable opponents, for the Ulster chieftan Hugh O'Neill, second Earl of Tyrone, had built up a modern Irish infantry and armed it with muskets which he bought from Scotland with Spanish gold. Lord Deputy Mountjoy admitted in 1602 that the Irish had become better shots than the English, a circumstance which stood them in better stead than 'any squadrons of pikes or artificial fortifications of towns' (Hayes-McCoy, 1969, 111–12).

The delicate balance was upset, to the disadvantage of the Irish, by the foreign friends who came to their help in the sixteenth and seventeenth centuries. The trouble was that neither party could offer the other their assistance in any useful form, even when the Spaniards who arrived in Ireland belonged to Spinola's generation, and the French to Vauban's.

In the first place, it was difficult to co-ordinate the action of foreign expeditions and native uprisings across hundreds of miles of ocean which were swept by English squadrons. Thus in 1580 the papal officer Bastian di San Joseppi and his engineer Angelucci could land at Smerwick in Dingle Bay, build the elegant *Castell d'Oro* with its two half-bastions, then undergo a siege and die with the whole expedition – all without one Irishman rising in their favour. Likewise Del Aguila's far more powerful Spanish expedition of 1601 arrived at a time and a place which were of the least possible assistance to O'Neill's rebellion. The forces and spirit of the Irish had already been battered by Mountjoy and Carew, the most skilful of their opponents; worse still, the Spanish chose to land at a harbour in the extreme south of Ireland, a site which was readily accessible to English sea power, and which compelled O'Neill to forsake his Ulster fastness, execute a march down the length of Ireland, and finally do battle in the open field in an attempt to break a major siege.

Once they were ashore, the foreign commanders and engineers found no sure basis for the rational calculations which served them so well in Continental wars. Del Aguila could establish no effective tactical concert with the Irish. Likewise, a French convoy sailed for the relief of Limerick in 1691, and discovered that it was two weeks too late: Patrick Sarsfield had surrendered the place to the Williamites simply because he and his now landless officers wished to pursue their fortunes on the Continent. Nowhere could foreign engineers find the essential requirements for siege warfare. General Rosen exclaimed that Vauban himself could not have taken Derry with the materials available in 1689. It was going to be the same story in Scotland, where the Highlanders proved to be useless in the sieges which their foreign officers tried to prosecute in the rebellion of 1745–6.

If the Continental powers were to intervene effectively in favour of Irish rebels or Scots Jacobites, they needed to have the support of a Celtic machinery of government. Such an organisation simply did not exist. In its absence there could be no question of raising and equipping reliable field forces, let alone supplying the continuous centralised direction which was essential for the creation of the engineer and artillery services. Small wonder that Irish soldiers proved more formidable abroad than in their homeland, or that foreign engineers performed well below their best when they were sent to promote rebellions in the British Isles.

Examining the course of events, we discover that

the earlier, less general or well-co-ordinated Irish uprisings revealed some basic truths concerning fortifications and guerrilla warfare. In the rebellions of James Fitzmaurice Fitzgerald (1568–73) and the Earl of Desmond (1579–83) the Irish chose at first to cling to a tactical defensive behind castle walls. This mistake permitted Colonel Humphrey Gilbert in 1569 and Sir William Pelham in 1580 to make stately progress up to the Irish strongholds, batter down the defences, and massacre the concentrated garrisons. Only then did the rebels break into bands and take to the bogs and hills.

Hugh O'Neill, the last and the greatest of this generation of rebels, meditated for some time whether he ought to convert his castle at Dungannon into a great fortress with the help of a foreign engineer. In 1595, at the outset of his own revolt, he cast these thoughts aside and dismantled the castle on hearing that the English had put some guns ashore at the head of Carlingford Lough. Somewhat inconsistently, he went on to plant a rather badly-designed bridgehead fortification (of two round towers and a connecting curtain) on the banks of the Blackwater, a river which guarded the access to the heart of Ulster from the south.

In 1597 Lord Burgh, the English Lord Deputy, responded to the provocation by storming into the Irish work by way of its weak riverside front. To consolidate his victory and hold open a path into O'Neill's territories, Burgh established a fort of his own nearby. In his own words the work was 'tender to me as my first begotten child' (Simms, 1955, 214), but he robbed his offspring of most of its value by abandoning Armagh, which was the intermediate station on the road back to Newry.

Whole armies were therefore required to push through supplies and reinforcements to the isolated fort. The last column of relief, comprising 4,000 men under Sir Henry Bagenal, was harried and finally engulfed by O'Neill's skirmishers at the Battle of the Yellow Ford on 14 August 1598. This catastrophe was staged within sight of the Blackwater Fort, and the garrison promptly surrendered to the rebels without resistance. The episode is an object-lesson in the misapplication of fortifications to the sub-jugation of a guerrilla uprising, and is strongly reminiscent of the strategy of the French in Indo-China in 1950 and 1952, when they clung on to isolated posts deep inside Viet-Minh territory, and ended by losing garrisons and relief columns together.

In 1600 a new Lord Deputy came to Ireland in the person of Lord Mountjoy, who was probably the most professional soldier of Elizabeth's reign. Showing an impressive grasp of the conditions of Irish warfare, he swept the cultivated areas of the north free of crops and cattle, and sent expeditionary forces around by sea to penetrate O'Neill's Ulster fastness from the rear. The main army took the south-eastern overland route by way of the Moyry Pass, where O'Neill was waiting behind multiple lines of entrenchments. The English threw in their attacks on 2 and 3 October, but they were checked in the midst of a labyrinth of walls, banks, palisades, thorn abatis and drystone flanking works. O'Neill evacuated the pass later in the month, at a time of his own choosing, and Mountjoy had to report that in building such defences 'these barbarous people . . . had far exceeded their custom and our expectation' (Hayes-McCoy, 1969, 34).

O'Neill was given temporary relief when a Spanish expedition arrived in the south of Ireland. The commander, Del Aguila, put about 3,400 troops ashore on 21 September 1601 at Kinsale, whereupon the warring parties forsook Ulster and streamed down to the new theatre of operations. Mountjoy was the first to reach Kinsale, and at the end of September he made a reconnaissance which told him that the Spanish were unlikely to emerge from their beach-head.

Mountjoy made it his first priority to capture the harbour castles and cut off Kinsale town from the sea. He planted three cannon against Rincurren Castle, and 'that the artillery might play as well by night as day, himself did take and score out his ground-marks, and with his quadrant took the true level, so as the want of daylight was no hindrance' (Stafford, 1633, 206). The garrison of 150 men surrendered on 1 November. The English fleet could now penetrate up the Bandon, and with the help of the land forces it reduced Castle Ny Park to submission on the 20th.

Mountjoy kept his army of 7,500 men extremely well provisioned, and he put on a bold face against

O'Neill and his 6,500 rebels, who arrived outside the camp on 21 December. The English had to suspend active siege operations, but Mountjoy was so alert that he was able to frustrate a joint attack which Del Aguila and O'Neill sought to carry out on Christmas Eve.

Del Aguila was so shattered by the experience that on 2 January 1602 he agreed to yield up Kinsale in return for a free evacuation of his force back to their homeland.

Leaving Carew to pacify Munster, Mountjoy followed O'Neill back to the old stamping-ground in Ulster. While Docwra reduced Ballyshannon, the most important rebel stronghold on Donegal Bay, Mountjoy advanced with an army of 3,500 men to the Blackwater in June and planted a new work, Fort Charlemont, on that much-disputed strategic barrier. O'Neill was aware that the Irish could never stage a repetition of the Battle of the Yellow Ford, for the new fort was strong and well supported, and so in 1603 he came to terms with the English.

It was not long before the Irish regretted their bargain. Life in a pacified and anglicised Ireland became intolerable for O'Neill and the Ulster aristocracy, as the last natural leaders of Gaelic Ireland, and in 1607, in 'The Flight of the Earls', they sought refuge on the Continent.

The siege of Kinsale deserves to be numbered among the decisive contests of history. It was less bloody and spectacular than a Waterloo or a Vicksburg, but in its consequences it bears comparison with the victories of Cortés or Pizarro in the New World: like those actions it signified the end of an ancient order of things, with the one essential difference that the Gaelic-Norman Irish life of the sixteenth century was a fast-evolving culture and not a static one.

The English Civil War

The military and strategic setting
By the 1640s England, or rather individual Englishmen, had accumulated a wide if ill-assorted knowledge of warfare. The intervention of English contingents on the Continent had been sporadic and not particularly happy, but the wars in Ireland had provided a useful school for the rough-and-ready sieges of small strongholds which were to become so prominent in the English Civil War. Thus in 1595 the governor of Connaught had been seized with the inspiration of uprooting the rood screen of Sligo Abbey, covering it with hides, mounting it on wheels, and using the contraption as an improvised tank against the rebels in Sligo Castle. Similar machines were widely employed in the English Civil War under the name of 'sows', from the forest of soldiers' legs which dangled from the innards of the beast like piglets' trotters.

Unfortunately, the Irish campaigns could give the English little appreciation of Continental standards of military engineering. The Earl of Orrery complained that, in comparison with France, the art of entrenching was practically unknown in England: 'I have seen eminent commanders there, when they came with armies for the war of Ireland, so great strangers to the rules of it, as their camps appeared to me like fairs' (Orrery, 1677, 129).

More far-reaching was the influence of the Holland of Frederick Henry and the Sweden of Gustavus Adolphus, both of which powers were passing through a significantly 'brutalist' phase of fortress warfare. Gustavus, if he attacked a place at all, liked to dispose of it in an accelerated siege of a few days, while the Dutch had recently brought the art of mortar bombardment to a high pitch in the siege of the Schenckenschans in 1636 (see p. 102).

The experience of these northern wars was transmitted to Britain by individual soldiers who had sometimes reached very high rank in the Protestant armies. From the Swedish service came men such as the redoubtable Major-General Skippon, who was to be the saviour of Parliamentary London, or Alexander Leslie, Earl of Leven, who had been governor of Stralsund and other Baltic fortresses between 1628 and 1631. Fairfax, Goring and the royal brothers Rupert and Maurice had served under Frederick Henry of Nassau at his siege of Breda in 1637, and other English veterans of the Netherlands service made so bold as to set themselves up as experts in siegecraft when they returned to their homeland. Shaftesbury said of the Parliamentarian Sir Walter Earle that he valued himself upon the sieges and service he had been in; his garden (at Charborough) was cut into redoubts and works representing these places, his house hung with the maps of those sieges and fights which had been most famous in those parts (Bayley, 1910, 102).

(Miniature fortification was something of an English hobby – doubtless the expression of an instinct that was starved in a more than ordinarily peaceful land. Earle's military garden was matched by the tiny bastioned enceinte of stone around the palace of Penshurst in Kent, by the eighteenth-century battery at Newstead Abbey in Nottinghamshire, by the elaborate confections of Corporal Trim as described in *Tristram Shandy*, and by the fortifications built for Queen Victoria's children at Osborne. The ha-ha, or sunken wall, first appeared as a field fortification of turves and storm poles which was cast about the Home Park at Stowe in 1719 by the first Viscount Graham, a veteran of the siege of Lille in 1708. This barrier was extended by Vanbrugh and his garden designer Bridgeman, and in later years similar works (though carried out in masonry) appear at Blenheim, Haughton, Kensington, Eastbury and other places where Bridgeman's influence was felt. As late as 1847 the Earl of Ross relieved the distress of his tenants in County Offaly by employing them to build a 'Vauban' fortification around Birr House to the designs of Colonel Richard Myddleton, a Peninsular soldier.)

When, however, Earle renewed his acquaintance with warfare at the siege of Corfe Castle in 1643, his nerve gave way after his hat was pierced by a musket ball. A little later he was seen dressed in a bear's skin and creeping on all fours around the sides of the castle hill, evidently in the hope of being mistaken for a large dog.

English military literature reflected the experience of English soldiers abroad. Most authors would have held with Ward (1639, book I, 72) that the Netherlandish way of fortification was the 'most absolutest manner that can be invented', and for decades the English military writers were content to plunder shamelessly from the textbooks then in fashion in the Netherlands. Norton, Hexham and such later writers as Venn and Binning mined

enthusiastically in the famous artillery manual of Diego Ufano (see p. 64), and copied his plates without a hint of acknowledgment. The new French school of fortification was much less well-known in England than the Dutch, and was probably first described in B. Gerbier's *Interpreter of Fortification* of 1648, which was a simple edition of the traces of Pagan and Ville, with parallel English and French texts on facing pages.

The one English authority who enjoyed any prestige on the Continent was the much-travelled Thomas Malthus, who had introduced the explosive mortar bomb into the French service (see p. 138). He put together a book on the subject 'at some broken hours while I followed the wars', for the benefit of the French, and in 1629 he brought out an English edition so as 'to confound and ruinate rebels and their habitations; so that afterwards empires, kingdoms, and commonwealths may the better live in peace and tranquillity' (Malthus, 1629, preface).

British military authors are noticeably reticent concerning the way their own civil wars were conducted. As early as 1677 a writer such as Roger Boyle, Earl of Orrery, could show himself completely under the influence of contemporary French feats of arms, and use not a single example from England's own recent wars. Perhaps the British authors did not have an analytical turn of mind, or perhaps they found that the experience of the civil wars was too painful to be written about in a detached kind of way.

There remained the problem of how to apply the Continental methods in the very different circumstances of the English civil wars, where at the start the only sources of manpower were the county militia and the town trained bands. At the Parliamentarian siege of Newark in 1644 'the poor old gentleman' Sir John Meldrum suffered extreme frustration for, 'having commanded abroad, and been used to deal with officers that understood the discipline of war, [he] was confounded among those who knew not how to obey any orders, but disputed all his commands' (Hutchinson, 1885, 318–19).

The warring parties imported a number of foreign engineers in an attempt to make native fortresses and sieges conform more closely to the Continental pattern. In 1642 Prince Rupert helped to begin the process by bringing a number of engineers and gunners with him to England. The most famous of these experts was the Walloon Sir Bernard de Gomme (1620–85), who was constantly in Rupert's suite, and was responsible for such important undertakings as the siege and re-fortification of Bristol in 1643. In 1645 Gomme was rewarded with the official titles of Engineer-General and Quartermaster-General, and following the Restoration he returned to his adopted land and designed the forts at Tilbury and Plymouth. Among the other foreign Royalists may be mentioned the gunner Bartholomew de la Roche, who was one of Gomme's companions on his original voyage to England, and the Swedish engineer Beckmann, who took a hand in fortifying the royal capital at Oxford.

The rebel pamphleteers found something sinister in 'the subtle art of the foreign engineers' (Godwin, 1904, 230) who were employed by the Royalists, but Parliament itself relied a great deal upon foreign specialists in the black ways of fortress warfare. The hard-drinking Dutchman John Dalbier became the Quartermaster-General of Essex's army, and directed the sieges of Basing House and Donnington Castle. In later years Dalbier was eclipsed by one Peter Manteau van Dalem, who was awarded the rank of Engineer-General of the New Model Army, with charge over an establishment of one engineer, one engineer extraordinary, one chief gunner, two ordinary engineers, one captain of pioneers, one master gunner of the field, and a company of common pioneers. Possibly out of resentment against Manteau, Colonel Dalbier declared for the Royalists in the Second Civil War. He met a hero's death in the action of St Neot's in 1648, and his former comrades rewarded him by cutting his body to pieces and planting the head on a pole.

For mine warfare, at least, the armies did not need to look abroad for expert help. For some time now the more adventurous English and Scots miners had gone off to serve in the French armies, and when war broke out in Britain the mineral miners of the Mendips and Derbyshire and the colliers of Staffordshire and Scotland adapted themselves readily to the demands of military mining.

The English employed their labour on fortifications and siegeworks in much the same way as the Netherlanders. The soldier considered that the status of full-time pioneer was the ultimate degradation, but he set to work willingly enough when he was offered a bonus at the going rate of one shilling a day. When the hearts of townspeople were actively engaged in the defence, they too were ready to lend a hand in engineering works.

Parliament was fortunate to have money and war materials in fair abundance. In the first place, the rebels enjoyed the unhampered use of the sea, which gave them easy access to foreign munitions, and enabled them to put ashore the naval demi-cannon which swung the balance of fortress warfare in their favour in remote theatres such as Scotland in 1650 and Ireland in 1651. An unjust Providence likewise made certain that the twenty-seven furnaces and forty-two forges of the Wealden iron industry were firmly in the Parliamentarian grasp.

The Royalists were by no means so advantageously placed. Their imported arms had first to survive the voyage from Holland or Saint Malo, and then be transported across disputed country to the armies or fortresses where they were most needed. This was a particularly perilous process for the munitions which came from the Yorkshire ports to Oxford across the Midlands plain.

To meet the cost of building their fortresses and keeping up their garrisons, the Royalists were thrown upon such fast-diminishing assets as the treasure of their noble supporters, or the goodwill of the parishes of the areas under their control. Many a Royalist stronghold was indissolubly linked with the name of the magnate who had beggared himself for its defence: St Michael's Mount with Francis Bassett, the fort at Dennis Head with Sir Richard Vyvyan, or Basing House with the Marquess of Winchester. The Parliament commanded the resources of London, and did not need to call upon its supporters for such hard sacrifices.

As with the civil and religious wars in the Netherlands and France, we find that in the English Civil War the rival parties scattered over the kingdom with no great regard for coherence or military logic. The painful 'sorting-out' process endured in this case until the end of the war. To make any sense of the unresolved chaos, it is useful to simplify the holdings of King and Parliament into

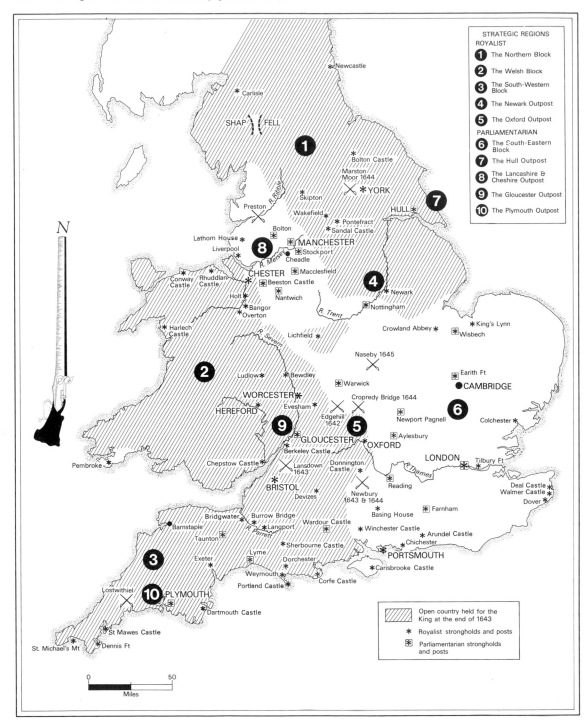

STRATEGIC REGIONS
ROYALIST
1 The Northern Block
2 The Welsh Block
3 The South-Western Block
4 The Newark Outpost
5 The Oxford Outpost
PARLIAMENTARIAN
6 The South-Eastern Block
7 The Hull Outpost
8 The Lancashire & Cheshire Outpost
9 The Gloucester Outpost
10 The Plymouth Outpost

*Newcastle
*Carlisle
SHAP)(FELL
1
*Bolton Castle
*Marston Moor 1644
*Skipton
*YORK
Preston
Wakefield
HULL
7
*Pontefract
*Sandal Castle
Lathom House
Bolton
8 MANCHESTER
Liverpool
*Stockport
Cheadle
Conway Castle
Rhuddlan Castle
CHESTER
*Macclesfield
Beeston Castle
4
Holt
Nantwich
*Newark
Bangor
Overton
R. Trent
*Nottingham
Harlech Castle
*Lichfield
*King's Lynn
Crowland Abbey *
*Wisbech
Naseby 1645
*Earith Ft
2
Ludlow *
*Bewdley
*Warwick
CAMBRIDGE
WORCESTER
Cropredy Bridge 1644
6
HEREFORD
Evesham
Edgehill 1642
Newport Pagnell
Colchester
9
5
Berkeley Castle
GLOUCESTER
OXFORD
Aylesbury
Chepstow Castle
Lansdown 1643
Donnington Castle
LONDON
Tilbury Ft
R. Thames
Pembroke
Reading
Deal Castle
Walmer Castle
BRISTOL
Devizes
Newbury 1643 & 1644
Farnham
Dover
Bridgwater
Burrow Bridge
Wardour Castle
Basing House
Barnstaple
Langport
Winchester Castle
Arundel Castle
Taunton
Sherbourne Castle
Chichester
3
Exeter
Lyme
Dorchester
PORTSMOUTH
Weymouth
Corfe Castle
Carisbrooke Castle
Lostwithiel
10 PLYMOUTH
Portland Castle
Dartmouth Castle
St Mawes Castle
St. Michael's Mt
Dennis Ft

N

Miles
0   50

Open country held for the King at the end of 1643
* Royalist strongholds and posts
Parliamentarian strongholds and posts

England and Wales in the Civil War

'blocks' (areas of solid support) and 'outposts' (garrisons or groups of garrisons planted in enemy territory).

The Royalist 'blocks' were scattered around the periphery of the island, and were divided into three by the indentations of the Bristol Channel and Liverpool Bay. Beginning in the south-west, the royal duchy of Cornwall offered a constant affront to right-minded Parliamentarians. The 'Cevennes' of the English Civil War, it was the channel by which the arms of France came to the Royalists; it bred a formidable infantry, which the Parliamentarians hated almost as much as they did the Irish; it was the base for the Western offensive of 1642–3 which gave the Royalists the open country of Devon, Somerset and Dorset and the great port of Bristol; lastly, when the Royalists were thrown onto the defensive, the region showed its potentialities as a strategic redoubt, for the River Parrett, with its garrisons at Bridgwater, Borough Bridge and Langport, presented a barrier to the enemy advance where the south-western peninsula narrowed between Bridgwater Bay and Lyme Bay. Sir Richard Grenville did not consider that all was lost, even after the Parrett line had been forced in 1645, for he hoped to make reality of every Cornishman's dream and

cut a deep trench from Barnstaple to the south sea, for the space of nearly forty miles, by which, he said, he would defend all Cornwall, and so much of Devon, against the world (Clarendon, 1826, book IX).

Northwards across the Bristol Channel lay Wales, the greatest in size of all the Royalist 'blocks'. It was eminently defensible in itself, being studded with Edwardian castles on all the major avenues, and it was cushioned in the direction of the English Midlands by the Royalist English border counties of Monmouth, Herefordshire, Worcestershire and Shropshire. This frontier region was stiffened by a belt of castles which ran northwards along the lines of the Severn and the Dee from Chepstow to Chester. This last town was doubly important, for it covered North Wales and held open the Dee for the landing of reinforcements from Ireland.

The counties of north-eastern England, the domains of the loyal Earl of Newcastle, were isolated from the other Royalist 'blocks' by the hostile north Midlands, the fortified Pennine passes and the waters of the Irish Sea and Liverpool Bay. The Royalist cause in that part of the world underwent extremes of fortune. In 1643 the fertile Vale of York was flooded by the advance of the Catholic Whitecoats of Northumberland and Durham, who evicted the Fairfaxes from the clothing towns of the West Riding, and forced them to execute a dangerous march to the shelter of Hull. There the Parliamentarians bided their time and gathered strength until the military balance was swung against the Royalists when the Scots irrupted into the back door of Newcastle's military kingdom. By May 1645 the Royalists in Yorkshire held only the isolated garrisons of Skipton, Pontefract, Scarborough, Sandal and Bolton.

Beyond their south-western, Welsh and north-eastern 'blocks' the Royalists held three 'outposts' deep inside the inimical Midlands plain. Lichfield in Staffordshire represented by far the smallest of them, but its garrisons performed the useful function of escorting convoys and couriers across the exceptionally dangerous region of the upper Trent. The lower reaches of that unprepossessing water were commanded by the powerful royal fortress of Newark, impudently sitting in the midst of the Parliamentarians of the eastern Midlands, and commanding the point where the Great North Road passed over the Trent. Since the bridge at Newark constituted the lowest permanent crossing of the river, the influence of the fortress was felt down the whole course as far as the confluence with the Humber more than seventy miles to the north.

The area of Oxford corresponded closest of all to what nineteenth-century strategists would have called a 'fortified region'. The city was girdled by a wide ring of posts, the garrisons of which led an exciting but not unduly dangerous life, preying on couriers and military and commercial traffic, organising parish contributions, and collecting information about enemy designs. If need be, they could assist friendly armies by taking on board their sick troops and surplus artillery.

In Oxford itself the university and town were burdened with the full apparatus of a royal capital in wartime: fortifications, royal suites, courts of justice, a mint, arms manufactories and magazines. The presence of the royal army at Oxford constituted an enduring threat to the rival capital at London, and from this central position Prince Rupert was able to intervene in other theatres of action, exploiting Wilmot's victory at Roundaway Down in 1643, and moving north in the next year to help the distressed Royalists in Cheshire and Lancashire. The Speaker of Parliament complained that 'the advantage of that place, situate in the heart of the kingdom, hath enabled the enemy to have ill influence upon this city [London] and counties adjoining, and to infest all other parts' (Varley, 1932, 131).

In marked contrast to the scattered 'blocks' of Royalist support, the base of Parliamentarian power was concentrated in the single mass of south-eastern counties which were ranged behind a line running approximately from the Solent to the Wash. London stood at the heart of the region, and possessed excellent communications to the wide semi-circle of border strongpoints: places like Farnham, the favourite haunt of the Parliamentarian general Sir William Waller, or Newport Pagnell in Buckinghamshire, which was held by Sir Samuel Luke in order to 'feel the pulse of the Cavaliers'.

On the other hand the Parliamentarian strategic 'outposts' were more numerous and still more dispersed than the corresponding Royalist strong-

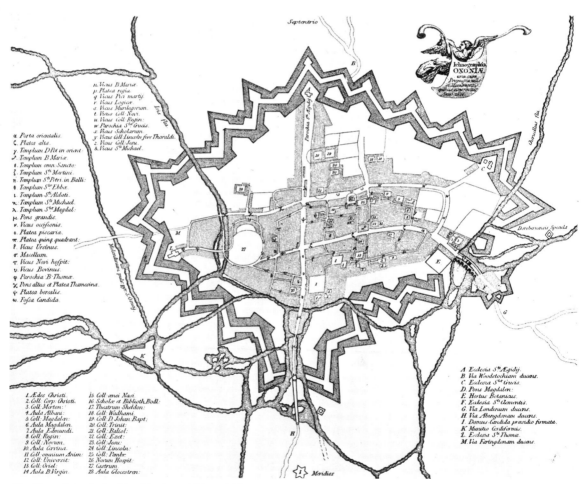

48 Plan of the Oxford fortifications. This ambitious scheme was never completed. Some sectors of the zig-zag envelope were probably the only works actually carried out on the ground. The bastion-like salients of the envelope strongly resemble the works at Ostend (Rallingson, 1648)

points. In the far south-west a Parliamentarian garrison was ensconced in Plymouth, at the mouth of the Tamar, which had the effect of tying down a large proportion of the Cornish Royalists before they could debouch into the rest of the kingdom. The Dorset port of Lyme and (from 1644) the Somerset town of Taunton played a no less valuable role, for they were sited at the rear of the line of the Parrett, just where the Royalists were most concerned about preserving the integrity of the country between the Bristol Channel and the English Channel.

A similarly disruptive function was performed by Colonel Edward Massey's strongpoint of Gloucester, which was described by one of its garrison as

the block-house to the river of Severn, and a bar to all passages between Worcester, Bristol and the sea; the stopping of intercourse between Oxford and Wales; the key to open the passage upon the Welsh and their frontiers, and the lock and bar to keep out their incursions; the only refuge and safety for the Parliament party and their friends in this part of the kingdom; and the enemy's sole hindrance to the command of the whole west (Corbet, n.d., 150).

Wedged between the Royalist 'blocks' of Wales and the north-east were the extraordinarily active Parliamentarians of Cheshire and Lancashire. The Cheshire squire Sir William Brereton rallied the Puritans of the local towns at the outset of the war, and before long he was using his native county as a base for forays into Staffordshire, Lancashire and Wales. Thus the Royalists of North Wales and the reinforcements from Ireland were bottled up at Chester, and prevented from entering the Midland plain.

The adjoining county of Lancashire was the setting for a miniature Thirty Years War, for religious feelings were polarised around the 'Genevas' of Manchester and Bolton on the one side, and the party of the Stanleys and the other Catholic families on the other. The Parliamentarians rapidly gained the upper hand, and made the county into an almost impenetrable bulwark which deterred every Royalist force except Rupert's army in 1644. The hired German engineer John Rosworm helped the Puritans to shut the Pennine passes, while the plain to the south was closed off by the Mersey and a broad band of the marshy wastes which went by the names of 'mosses' or 'carrs'. The one secure bridging point was at Stockport, where sandstone hills compressed the upper Mersey into a valley. The other two sides of the Lancashire strategic box were formed by the Irish Sea to the west, and by the line of the Ribble, which lay athwart the route of invasion from Scotland.

Even in Yorkshire, at the height of the Royalist successes of 1643, the Parliamentarians managed to cling on to Hull. This foothold represented in many ways the north-eastern counterpart of Plymouth in the West Countries, for both these places were fortress-ports sited far from the main centres of Parliamentarian power, but which stood on deep estuaries and were easy to help from the sea.

The campaigns, 1642–8 and 1650–1

The roots of the English Civil War lie deep within history, but hostilities were precipitated by the arguments as to which party, the king's or the Parliament's, was to have the control of the fortresses of the realm.

The events of the autumn of 1642 came close to deciding the war in favour of the royal party at the outset. The inconclusive battle at Edgehill on 23 October did nothing to stay the march of the king's army from the north Midlands, and the Cavaliers went on to occupy Oxford and push as far as the gravel plain immediately to the west of London. The fortunes of Parliament now rested in the hands of Major-General Skippon, who gathered 24,000 men in the path of the royal advance at Turnham Green, and began to fortify the capital. 'The daily musters and shows of all sorts of Londoners here were wondrous commendable, in marching to the fields and outworks ... with great alacrity, carrying on their shoulders iron mattocks, and wooden shovels; with roaring drums, flying colours and girded swords' (William Lithgow, Ross, 1887, 160–8). The rival armies came face to face on 13 November, but rather than accept the fight the Royalists turned back to Oxford.

Throughout 1643 both parties groped their way towards an understanding of fortress warfare. This

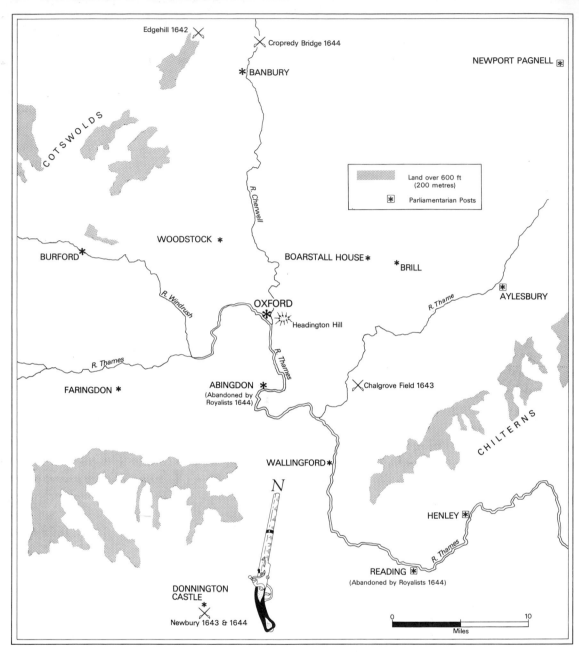

Edgehill 1642 ✕

✕ Cropredy Bridge 1644

NEWPORT PAGNELL ⊞

✱ BANBURY

C O T S W O L D S

R. Cherwell

	Land over 600 ft
	(200 metres)
⊞	Parliamentarian Posts

WOODSTOCK ✱

BOARSTALL HOUSE ✱

✱ BRILL

BURFORD ✱

R. Windrush

R. Thame

AYLESBURY ⊞

OXFORD
✱
Headington Hill

R. Thames

R. Thames

ABINGDON ✱
(Abandoned by
Royalists 1644)

✕ Chalgrove Field 1643

FARINGDON ✱

C H I L T E R N S

WALLINGFORD ✱

N

HENLEY ⊞

R. Thames

DONNINGTON
CASTLE
✱
Newbury 1643 & 1644

READING ⊞
(Abandoned by Royalists 1644)

0   10
Miles

Oxford and its satellite posts

process put the Royalists at a decided disadvantage, for they were the attacking party, and it is more difficult for an improvised force to take a position than defend it. Thus the Royalists failed in all their plans for a concentric advance from the scattered blocks against the Parliamentarian south.

The Earl of Newcastle marched from the Catholic north-east with about 15,000 men, but was brought up short by the defiant garrison of Hull. He attacked the place in a singularly inept fashion, then raised the siege on 11 October. Parliament therefore retained Hull as a base for the eventual re-conquest of Yorkshire.

In the south-west the Royalists were conducting their war in a rather more enterprising manner. By dint of reducing the smaller Parliamentary towns, and leaving the larger ones blockaded, the Royalist commander Sir Ralph Hopton fought his way through Devon, Somerset and Dorset and emerged on the open chalk country of Wiltshire. The Royalists twice beat the Parliamentarians in the course of July, and Prince Rupert came up with a small force from Oxford in order to exploit the success. The united force of Cavaliers then swung north against Bristol.

Bristol was the major port of south-west England, and the Parliamentarians had recently covered the surrounding hills with entrenchments and redoubts. All the same, Prince Rupert deliberately rejected the technique of formal siege, declaring 'the soldiers fitter for any brisk attempt than for a dull patient design; and that the army would be more weakened by the latter than the former' (Clarendon, 1826, book VII).

The assault was undertaken on 26 July 1643. The Cornish regiments were shattered when they tried to attack the south-eastern defences, but the main force of the Royalists burst through the line between Windmill Hill and Brandon Hill Fort, to the west of the city, and the resistance of the garrison collapsed.

Demoralisation spread through the Parliamentarian west, but two circumstances still gave the Royalists cause for concern. One was that they were unable to browbeat the ports of Lyme and Plymouth into surrendering. The other was the memory of the more than 500 Cornishmen who had lost their lives in the assault on Bristol; the king's armies were no longer willing to risk such a bloodbath in the attack of a city again.

We left King Charles I at Oxford with the central army. Since the Earl of Newcastle was still (in July) far distant in the north, and the south-western Royalists had occupations of their own, the King decided that he could best employ his time by retracing his steps to the west Midlands and eliminating the troublesome garrison on the Severn crossing at Gloucester. The capture of this place might make Parliament more amenable to terms, and in any event it would encourage the Welsh troops to cross the Severn and come to the help of their fellow-Royalists in England.

The royal army came before Gloucester on 9 August 1643. With the lessons of Bristol in mind, the Royalists subjected the town to an elaborate formal siege and 'their preparations seemed tedious, yet were effectual and certain, and tended withal to save the lives of their men' (Corbet, n.d., 46).

Unfortunately, the tempo of the whole operation was far too slow, and ignored the fact that an army of relief under the Earl of Essex was pounding up the road from London. There were no lines of circumvallation which might have checked Essex's progress, and on 5 September Charles and his army marched away to confront the enemy force, leaving Massey in undisputed possession of Gloucester for the rest of the war:

And it must be confessed, that governor gave a stop to the career of the king's good success, and from his pertinacious defence of that place the Parliament had time to recover their broken forces, and more broken spirits; and may acknowledge to this rise the greatness to which they afterwards aspired (Clarendon, 1826, book VII).

Meanwhile Charles and Essex hastened back east from Gloucester, in a race to be the first to control the communications with London. The two armies battled indecisively at Newbury on 20 September, and the campaign ended as it had begun, with the king back at Oxford, and the Parliamentarians still in command of Gloucester and London.

The general lack of proficiency in siege warfare went far to shape the events of 1644, which was the transitional year of the war. The New Year found the Royalist general Byron and a newly-landed contingent of Irish troops stuck fast before Nantwich, the refuge of the Cheshire Parliamentarians. Byron was still committed to the siege when Sir Thomas Fairfax came hastening from Yorkshire and beat him decisively on 25 January. That was the end of Byron and his 'Irish' army.

It was now the Parliamentarians' turn to lose their way. While Sir Thomas Fairfax wasted several weeks in Lancashire, laying ungallant siege to the Countess of Derby in her home at Lathom, Sir John Meldrum and 7,000 men were sitting down before the stronghold of the north Midland Royalists at Newark, and devoted more time to prosecuting their own squabbles than to reducing the fortress (see p. 146). The rest of the king's enemies in the north were grouped around the royal city of York. The huge investing force comprised not just Lord Ferdinando Fairfax and his English Parliamentarians, but the 20,000 Scots Covenanters of Alexander Leslie with their enormous artillery park of more than one hundred pieces. Such was the situation which presented Prince Rupert with the opportunity of turning the balance of the war in favour of his royal uncle.

Advancing north from Oxford with 6,500 troops, Rupert first of all descended on the rear of Meldrum's army, compelling him to surrender on 21 March. From Newark the Royalists swung northwestwards to bring help to the hard-pressed king's men in Lancashire. Rupert crossed the Mersey bridge at Stockport on 25 May, then relieved Lathom House and chased the besieging force into Bolton. The Puritans of Bolton were crazy enough to hang an Irish trooper from their walls, which provoked Rupert into storming the town on 28 May and cutting down 1,600 of the defenders. Rupert seized and garrisoned Liverpool, then continued his zig-zag course by marching east over the Pennines and relieving Sir Charles Lucas at York.

As was typical of this war, the siege force at York had not bothered to dig any lines of circumvallation. However, the Parliamentarians managed to dispute the open field near the city, and on 2 July they beat Rupert on Marston Moor. Rupert had to return to the south in August, and as soon as he was gone the Parliamentarians began to regain their ascendancy over the northern Royalists.

Meanwhile the south-western Royalists had provoked an outburst of activity by laying siege to Lyme. Prince Maurice clapped himself down before the town in March with 6,000 men and an excellent siege train, but he launched repeated assaults and consumed 500 barrels of powder without making any progress.

Once again a long and ineffective siege gave rise to a whole campaign. The Parliamentarians broke up their threatening concentration around Oxford, and the Earl of Essex raced off westwards with the major part of the army and brought relief to Lyme in June. Inspired by his easy success, Essex plunged deep into the hostile south-west and was trapped by the Royalists at the small Cornish port of Lostwithiel. On 1 September the Parliamentarians bought an evacuation at the price of yielding up their arms. King Charles might now have converted the long Royalist blockade of nearby Plymouth into an active attack, but he tamely brought the royal army back to the Oxford region. He was never to be presented with such an opportunity again.

The campaigns of 1645 brought some fundamental changes in the aspect of the war. Most strikingly, the defeat of the Royalist central army at Naseby 'proved the deciding battle, the king's party after this time never making any considerable opposition' (Ludlow, 1890, I, 123). Hardly less important was the success of the New Model Army in building up an effective engineer establishment (see p. 147) and a powerful artillery train. For the first time in the war we notice an army that was capable not just of beating the enemy in the open field, but of taking castles and towns in a systematic fashion.

During the campaign of Naseby the south-western Royalists had been paralysed by the need to blockade Plymouth, Lyme and Taunton. The Cavalier commander Goring was therefore unable to collect his forces before Thomas Fairfax irrupted into the west with the victorious New Model. Fairfax beat Goring at Langport on 10 July and relieved Taunton. He then began the more lengthy business of bringing down all the royal strongholds which stood between him and the Parliamentarian south-east.

Bridgwater was the first place on Fairfax's list, for

it was the main royal magazine of the south-west, and occupied a commanding position on the line of the Parrett. On 21 July the eastern side of the town was assaulted over eight ten-yard-long mobile bridges which had been devised by the Master of the Ordnance General Hammond, 'a gentleman of a most dextrous and ripe invention for all such things' (Markham, 1870, 239). The Royalists found a temporary refuge in the part of the town on the west bank of the Parrett, but Fairfax pursued them mercilessly with his mortar bombs, and on 25 July he received the surrender of 2,000 men and about forty cannon.

As if to display the army's newly-found mastery of fortress warfare, Fairfax decided to reduce Sherborne Castle in Dorset by a complete formal siege. The walls were battered by heavy naval guns from Plymouth, and burrowed into by miners from the Mendip Hills. Finally, on 15 August, the Parliamentarians burst from their trenches and took the castle by storm.

Bristol, the greatest prize of the south-west, fell to Parliament unexpectedly easily, for Prince Rupert threw in the sponge on 10 September after Fairfax had won his way into Prior's Hill Fort in two hours of hand-to-hand fighting.

While Fairfax stayed behind to complete the conquest of the west, Lieutenant-General Oliver Cromwell was sent ahead with the task of clearing the royal garrisons along the passages to London. In less than one month Cromwell reduced the castles of Devizes, Berkeley and Winchester, and on 11 October 1645 he joined Colonel Dalbier in his siege of Basing House in Hampshire.

This little place had earned its title of 'Loyalty House' during prolonged sieges in 1643 and 1644, and it now held a microcosm of all that the Puritans most abhorred in Cavalier England. There were Romish priests, high-born ladies, gifted men of the arts, and a garrison of 300 Catholics. At five in the morning of 14 October the Parliamentarians made their general assault. In the words of *The Kingdome's Weekly Post*:

Immediately the dreadful battery began, the great guns discharged their choleric errand with great execution; many wide breaches were made in an instant, and the besieged immediately marshalled themselves, and stood like a new wall to defend those breaches; our men in full bodies and with great resolution came on. The dispute was long and sharp, the enemy, for aught I can learn, desired no quarter, and I believe they had but little offered them. You must remember what they were. They were most of them Papists, therefore our muskets and swords did show but little compassion, and the House being at length subdued did now satisfy for his treason and rebellion by the blood of the defenders.

Throughout the kingdom the other royal strongholds were going under one by one. Chester had been under intermittent blockade by the Parliamentarians of Cheshire and Staffordshire since the end of the last year, and after the king's army was defeated on Rowton Heath nearby on 24 September the Parliamentarians closed in and subjected the town to a bombardment. The mortar bombs worked to terrible effect among the tall buildings of wattle and timber, and one of the garrison recalls how

our houses like so many splitting vessels crash their supporters and burst themselves in sunder through the very violence of these descending firebrands . . . two houses in the Watergate skip joint from joint and create an earthquake, the main posts jostle each other, while the frighted casemates fly for fear (Morris, 1924, 234).

The morale of the garrison and the Royalist merchants was nevertheless unshaken, and it was starvation, not the fear of fire and storm, which forced the town to capitulate on 3 February 1646. The fall of Chester opened the northern avenue into Wales, and by the following autumn every major garrison of the Principality save Harlech had succumbed to the Parliamentarians.

After Naseby the broken Royalists of the north Midlands had rallied at Newark, where they dug themselves in in a most elaborate manner under the direction of Lord Belasyse.

In 1646, 16,000 Parliamentarians and Scots paid Newark the compliment of subjecting it to the most elaborate siege of the war. Belasyse had no high opinion of the Scottish siegeworks, but he had to

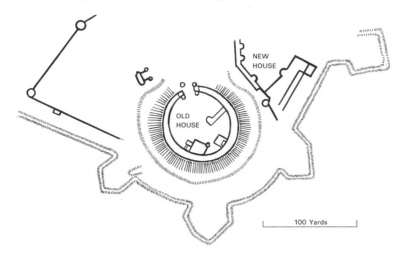

49 Basing House. Earthen bastions have been cast up around the medieval fortifications

NEW HOUSE

OLD HOUSE

100 Yards

admire the performance of Colonel Poyntz and his English contingent, who 'drew a line about the town, and made a very regular entrenchment and approaches in such a soldier-like manner as none of them who had attempted the place before had done' (Hutchinson, 1885, II, 91). Poyntz had learnt his trade in the Imperial service in the Thirty Years War.

Newark capitulated upon receipt of an order from the king, and the garrison marched out on 8 May 1646. At that very moment a further Parliamentarian army was testing the defences of Oxford, the seat of Royalism. On 13 May Thomas Fairfax completed a great fort on Headington Hill, from where his gunners duelled inconclusively with the fortress artillery until a cease-fire was proclaimed at the end of the month.

King Charles had escaped from Oxford shortly before the Parliamentarian blockade had closed in, and on 16 June 1646, from his doubtful refuge with the Scots at Newcastle, he issued a final order to all his remaining garrisons to relinquish their posts.

A brief experience of Parliamentarian rule was enough to provoke a widespread rebellion in 1648 which goes by the name of the Second Civil War. In May the situation appeared extremely grave for Parliament, with Cromwell's army committed in Wales to the siege of Pembroke Castle, a hostile Scots army making ready to invade the north-west,

and Thomas Fairfax confronted by uprisings in Kent and Essex.

By the end of September the crisis had been overcome, partly through Cromwell's victory over the Scots at Preston, and partly as a result of the prolonged blockades which had brought Pembroke and Colchester to submission. Active siege warfare hardly made an appearance. Fairfax's bombardment of Colchester did little to hasten the capitulation of 27 August, and the Parliamentarian siege artillery scored a notable success only in Colonel Richard's operations along the Kentish coast, where his mortar bombs caused great havoc in the small confines of the Henrician castles of Walmer, Deal and Sandown.

The heavy guns were used to great effect in the Scottish campaign of 1650, when Cromwell and his Lieutenant-General of Ordnance George Monk were exploiting the victory over the Scots field forces at Dunbar. Using mortars and naval demi-cannon shipped from England, the army rapidly reduced Edinburgh Castle, and the strongholds of Dirleton, Borthwick and Tantallon. At Stirling Castle, which guarded the vitally important entrance to the Highlands, the clansmen forced the governor to surrender after two mortars had lobbed twenty-four bombs into their midst.

After this campaign the English tried to impose their rule on Scotland by casting up a series of forts, beginning with a stone-revetted hexagonal citadel at Ayr. Similar forts were built at Inverness, Inverlochy, Perth and Leith, and small strongpoints were established at a score of other sites. These fortifications represent the first appearance of the bastion trace in Scotland.

Cromwell displayed a further aspect of his generalship in his final campaign, when he faced the irruption of King Charles II and the Scots in 1651. The invasion came to a halt at Worcester, where the Royalists stopped to add elaborate earthworks to the town walls. Cromwell had no intention of obliging the enemy by attacking them in their defences. Instead he bridged the Severn, fought and won the battle of 2 September on the west bank, and easily overran the fortifications in the subsequent rout.

The defence and the attack in the English Civil Wars
The fortress warfare of the English Civil Wars is astounding in its variety and vigour. The English borrowed nearly every device known to Continental engineers, and leavened the mixture with some peculiar notions of their own.

Sometimes the English seemed to be bent on displaying in four short years all the metamorphoses which Netherlandish fortification had undergone in twice that number of decades. The primitive fortification *à la Huguenote* of the Brabant towns of the 1570s has an obvious parallel in the bastions which were added to the walls of King's Lynn and Worcester. At the other end of the scale, the Royalists began to surround their capital at Oxford with a new double enceinte, designed on a scale which surpassed the very similar works at Ostend. Newark was fortified in the same style but on a less ambitious plan.

Between the two extremes we find that many important towns were fortified in what can only be described as a characteristically English fashion: namely, with trench lines which were reinforced every few hundred yards with square redoubts or bastioned forts. Such works were thrown up at Bristol, Chester, Plymouth and upon the largest scale of all at London, which possessed a continuous line on both banks of the Thames, studded with nine major bastioned forts, and thirteen redoubts and

hornworks. The inspiration for these works must have come from the siege lines then in vogue on the Continent.

Free-standing bastioned forts were liberally scattered around towns in order to cover dead ground or hold the enemy at a distance. 'Sconces' of this kind were built at Reading, Worcester, Newark, York and in front of the Carliol Tower at Newcastle, where there was a work 'standing champion-like commanding the fields' (Terry, 1899, 293). As was the case with every known fortification built during the Civil Wars, these forts were entirely of earthen construction, though often shored up with a timber revetment, and they depended for their *Sturmfreiheit* on palisades and storm poles.

The squire and his tame clergyman had been the pillars of English rural society since Saxon times, and it was natural that the two bases of their respective activities – the manor house and the parish church – should often have been sited within easy reach of one another. This arrangement, however convenient in peacetime, became little short of disastrous in a civil war, for many an otherwise eminently defensible castle or house was dangerously overlooked by a tall church tower. Sometimes the defenders went to the trouble of incorporating such towers in the fortified perimeter, as at Abbotsbury House in Wiltshire or at Westbury in the Forest of Dean; in some places the tower fell into the hands of the besiegers, as at Berkeley and Basing, and proved an annoyance to the garrison; very occasionally the defenders made so bold as to demolish the thing altogether, as happened at Boarstall House in Buckinghamshire.

At Lichfield the Royalists took on the difficult task of fortifying the entire cathedral area. They selected the moat around the close as their main line of defence, and supported it by building earthen banks, piercing loopholes in the bordering houses, and mounting artillery in the main cathedral tower. The Royalist Captain Cromwell (a relative of the infamous Oliver) turned the ditches and marshes around Crowland Abbey to similar advantage, and thereby condemned the Parliamentarian besiegers to months of amphibious warfare.

The defence of such positions was conducted with all the energy and determination characteristic of the

1   Bulwark on the hill at north end of Gravel Lane
2   Hornwork near windmill in Whitechapel Road
3   Redoubt near Brick Lane
4   Redoubt in Hackney Road, Shoreditch
5   Redoubt in Kingsland Road, Shoreditch
6   Battery and breastwork at Mount Hill
7   Battery and breastwork at St John's Street end
8   Redoubt near Islington Pound
9   Fort at the New River, Upper Pond
10   Battery and breastwork on the hill east of Black
     Mary's Hole
11   Two batteries and a breastwork at Bedford House

12   Redoubt near St Giles' Pound
13   Fort at the east end of Tyburn Road
14   Fort across the road at Wardour Street
15   Bulwark at Oliver's Mount
16   Fort at Hyde Park Corner
17   Redoubt and battery on Constitution Hill
18   Court of Guard at Chelsea turnpike
19   Battery and breastwork in Toothill fields
20   Fort at Vauxhall
21   Fort at the Dog and Duck in St George's Fields
22   Fort near end of Blackman Street
23   Redoubt near Lock Hospital in Kent Street

50   The fortifications of London (from Vertue's map)

seventeenth century. Governors were held up to their duty by a harsh code of conduct, and the Parliamentarians shot Captain Steel for yielding up Beeston Castle in 1644 just as readily as the Royalists executed Colonel Windebank for losing the almost indefensible Bletchington House in 1645. Religious or racial differences often signified a defence to the death.

Contemporary opinion was divided as to whether it was a good thing to tie down so many troops in guarding strongpoints. The Parliamentary Sprigge was exasperated at seeing Fairfax's field army turn aside to save a town like Taunton:

The slight retrenching and garrisoning of many towns of no great strength by nature and situation, though it may serve for the present securing of particular counties, and particular men's estates from plundering parties, yet they are prejudicial to the public, and to the main of the wars (Sprigge, 1647, 14).

In an extreme case every single company in a given area might be absorbed into the defence of fortifications, as happened on the lower Severn between 1643 and 1645, when Colonel Massey's command was entirely committed to guarding Gloucester and the satellite strongpoints at Tewkesbury, Sudeley, Newnham, Beverstone and Slimbridge.

All the same, the commanders probably had no alternative but to scatter their forces so widely. The major garrisons served as the backbone of the 'blocks' and 'outposts', while the smaller ones commanded the countryside and tapped its resources of fodder, parish revenues and recruits. The Royalist dependence on the smaller garrisons actually increased from about the middle of 1645, for then at least half of the proceeds of the regular parish contributions was diverted to keeping up the field forces. The garrisons made up the difference by resorting to plunder and free quarters.

By Continental standards the English proved very incompetent in some important branches of siegework. The cannon in particular were directed with little skill. Mortars were employed almost as freely as the long guns (after all, the Englishman Malthus had introduced the explosive bomb to France), but the effect was strictly determined by the nature of the target. Mortar bombs did little to hasten the surrender of towns, or even of houses like Basing which had extensive open courtyards. It was a different story when the fortifications were small and enclosed (Devizes Castle in 1645, the Downs castles in 1648, Stirling Castle in 1650, and Elizabeth Castle in Jersey in 1651).

Royalists and Parliamentarians alike remained strangely addicted to the generalised bombardment of towns. The noise and the spectacle were gratifying, but when the towns chose to surrender it was almost invariably because the garrison and the people were running out of food, or because they feared that they were about to be taken by storm. The cannonade played little or no part in the decision (King's Lynn and Devizes in 1643, Lyme in 1644, Chester in 1645, Worcester in 1646, and Colchester in 1648). Fairfax's bombardment of Bridgwater in 1645 offers one significant exception, for there the defenders were crammed into a single quarter of the town.

The Civil War revealed that the English were almost the last people in the West to use bows and arrows and employ medieval siege-machines like the 'sow'. The English were also very much behind the times in their unwillingness to cast up lines of circumvallation, and consequently the approach of an army of relief almost invariably precipitated a major crisis. The besiegers either had to abandon their operation and retreat to safety (Gloucester in 1643), or they had to accept the risk of fighting it out in the open field (Devizes in 1643, Nantwich and York in 1644, Taunton and Chester in 1645). Both courses were drastic enough, to be sure, but if the besiegers simply stayed where they were they were liable to be wedged between the fortress and the army of relief and forced to surrender (Newark in 1644). Mining proved to be one single form of regular siege warfare in which the English excelled their Continental contemporaries.

One of the alternatives to a proper siege was to sit down before a town and starve it into surrender, as happened at Colchester and Limerick. When time was short the Roundheads preferred to storm into a town without more ado. They threw their troops into assaults at Bristol, Drogheda and Wexford, and they would have liked to do the same thing at

Dunkirk in 1658. The violent assault held an intrinsic appeal for a commander like Sir Thomas Fairfax who was

still for action in field or fortification, esteeming nothing unfeasible for God, and for man to do in God's strength, if they would be up and doing; and thus his success hath run through a line cross to that of the old soldiery, of long sieges and slow approaches (ibid., 322).

The Irish Confederacy and 'The Curse of Cromwell'

Following the decisive defeat of Tyrone (see p. 145), the English hastened to fortify the most vulnerable points on the southern and western coasts of Ireland. They built forts on the shipping channels at Cork and Kinsale, and planted citadels to overawe the towns of Cork and Galway. In the north-east they held down the much-contested line of the Blackwater by Mountjoy's fort of Charlemont, which was reconstructed in more permanent form in 1622. These Jacobean forts were usually square, four-bastioned, and executed in full revetment with masonry embrasures. Paul Ive designed the forts at Castle Park and Haulbowline, but the execution of the programme as a whole lay in the hands of the active Sir Josias Bodley (c. 1550–1617).

More significantly still, a large colony of Protestant English and Lowland Scots was settled in Ulster. From 1609 the strategic centre of the new plantation was formed by Derry, which was fortified in simple but adequate style with the help of the City of London. From being the greatest redoubt of the rebellion, Ulster was transformed into a bulwark of alien rule.

The balance was restored in some measure when experienced Catholic Irish soldiers returned from the wars on the Continent. Among these captains were the Don Richardo Burke, who was 'much esteemed for his judgement in mathematics and a good ingeniere' (quoted in Loeber, 1977, 33), the Preston brothers, who had saved Louvain for the Spanish in 1635, the Owen Rowe O'Neill who had defended Arras in 1640, and the physician Owen Shiel who had seen how the Spanish organised their magnificent military hospital at Malines. In the

literary field, Captain Gerat Barry's *Discourse of Military Discipline* was published at Brussels in 1634, and had the distinction of being probably the first military manual to emanate from an Irish author. The Third Book contains an up-to-date and well-illustrated discussion on fortification. It is not without interest that Barry could write of such a thing as 'our Irish nation' (p. 210), for the days were past when the 'old' Irish used to fight among themselves with the same cheerful insouciance as they did against the English.

The Irish rebelled in 1641, and carried out a general massacre of the English settlers. The original quarrel was soon transformed by the wider issues which came to the fore in the English Civil War, and the barbaric simplicities of 1641 were succeeded by years of truces, treacheries and reconciliations which gradually heaped together the 'old' Irish, the Catholic English settlers, the Protestant English Royalists and ultimately even the Covenanting Ulster Scots in a highly unstable alliance against Parliamentarian England.

There was, however, no Irish 'state' whose support might have permitted the Catholic veterans of the Spanish service to set about ambitious sieges or build modern fortifications. These officers had to be satisfied with teaching their troops how to throw up retrenchments behind breached walls in the old Netherlandish style. The Earl of Castlehaven later reviewed the innumerable sieges of this period, and rightly concluded that the capture of the Parliamentarian stronghold of Duncannon on 19 March 1645, with the help of the French engineer Lalue, was the only one worthy of the name.

But for the help of their newly-found Protestant friends, the Catholics would probably have never gained entry to the larger coastal towns, or the two guardian fortresses of the Shannon: at Athlone in the midland plain, and at Limerick nearly seventy miles downstream. By the spring of 1649 the Earl of Ormonde had succeeded in rallying almost the whole of Ireland behind the royal cause,

yet one thing happened tending very much to the preservation of Dublin, and those few places [Derry and Dundalk] that were kept for the Parliament, which was, that Owen Roe O'Neill who was general of the Old Irish . . . could by no means be brought to a conjunction with the English (Ludlow, 1890, I, 227).

In August 1649 the allies' term of grace elapsed, for in that month Michael Jones smashed the forces blockading Dublin, and Oliver Cromwell sailed up the Liffey with his army and a siege train of a dozen cannon. These guns opened fire against Drogheda on 9 September and made two breaches, which were taken with storm and slaughter on the evening of 11 September.

By reducing Drogheda, the Parliamentarians had interposed a barrier between Monro's Ulstermen and Ormonde's Royalists, and it was now safe for Cromwell to execute his cherished 'southern design' of mastering the Leinster and Munster ports and depriving Prince Rupert's fleet of shelter. Wexford was taken on 11 October by the same technique of battering, assault and massacre which had brought down Drogheda. New Ross followed on 19 October, so opening the passage across the Barrow into Munster. The ports of Cork and Youghal thereupon declared in favour of the Parliamentarian cause.

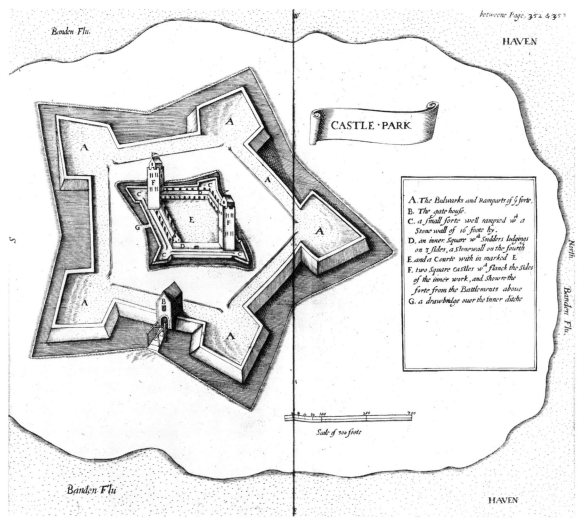

51   Castle Park on the Bandon at Kinsale. Typical Jacobean fort (Stafford, 1633)

Cromwell wrote to Parliament in April 1650 that

those towns that are to be reduced, especially one or two of them, if we should proceed by the rules of other states, would cost you more money than this army hath had since we came over. I hope, through the blessing of God, they will come cheaper to you (Firth, 1921, 173).

By that he meant that he was in the process of applying against the inland towns the same crude methods he had used against Drogheda and Wexford. Cromwell's hasty methods are certainly open to criticism on military grounds, but the harsh, clear and consistent custom of the time gave him every justification for cutting down a garrison which dared to withstand a storm.

After losing many men at the ancient Norman town of Kilkenny, in a vain assault on an interior retrenchment, Cromwell moderated his tone and persuaded the garrison to yield up the place on 28 March in return for a free evacuation. Instead of learning by experience, he proceeded to throw away 2,000 men on May in a storm against a very similar retrenchment at Clonmel. The Cromwellians had to admit 'there was never seen so hot a storm, of so long continuance, and so gallantly defended, either in England or in Ireland' (Baldock, 1899, 418–19). The Irish, however, had exhausted all their ammunition in the process, and the governor, Major-General Hugh Dubh O'Neill, 'an old surly Spanish soldier' (Buchan, 1934, 350), led them silently out of Clonmel on the following night. Cromwell's entry was an empty triumph.

The troublesome Scots now forced Cromwell to return across the Irish Sea. While he was away the troops that he left behind succeeded in breaking the back of resistance in Ireland. Bishop MacMahon with the field army of the Irish was defeated at Scarrifhollis, on 21 June; this left the Shannon as the last coherent line of Irish defence. In the south, the long-blockaded stronghold of Waterford capitulated on 10 August.

On 2 June 1651 Cromwell's successor Ireton forced the line of the Shannon into Connaught at O'Brien's Bridge, and closed in on Limerick from the west. Abandoning Cromwell's crude and costly method of attacking fortresses, Ireton used against Limerick the same combination of bombardment and blockade which Fairfax had employed against Colchester in 1648. The operation came to a sudden and altogether unexpected end. A new consignment of artillery arrived from the navy and the nearby garrisons, and Ireton was able to plant a breaching battery against the one sector of the wall of Irish Town which was devoid of an earthen backing. The masonry collapsed forthwith, and on 27 October 1651 Hugh Dubh O'Neill capitulated for a free evacuation. The 1,200 surviving members of the garrison marched out on the 29th, two or three of them dropping dead of the plague within sight of the Cromwellians. Ireton, the last casualty of the siege, died of a lung infection on 7 November.

The Irish prolonged their resistance into 1652 by a few isolated garrisons, but more especially by a number of roving bands. As the Parliamentary Commissioners for Ireland reported on 8 June:

Their [bog] fastnesses are better to them in point of strength than walled towns
1   because they cannot be besieged in them.
2   Because they can draw all their strength out of them to act their designs without hazarding the loss of the place (Ludlow, 1890, I, 498).

The Commissioners went on to make the extravagant suggestion that Leinster should be made safe for colonisation by fortifying the lines of the Boyne and Barrow. Such pessimism was unwarranted, for the Irish had already bled themselves white in the open field and in defending towns, and they were in no state to wage protracted guerrilla warfare on the sixteenth-century model.

Seven   The Baltic Empires

The Danish stranglehold

Dane and Swede: the first combats

In 1397 a tenuous union of the three Scandinavian kingdoms of Denmark, Norway and Sweden was established under the leadership of Denmark. The arrangements were incomplete and unsatisfactory from the start, but the notion of a composite Nordic state survived until the early sixteenth century, when it expired amid a series of revolts, betrayals and massacres.

The newly-reborn Swedish kingdom was a tender child, for Denmark-Norway pressed in from every landward side, and the rule of the native Vasa dynasty was confined to an area of Baltic coastland and the wild and hilly country around Lake Vättern. To the south the provinces of Blekinge, Scania (Scåne) and Halland were held by the Danish crown, and gave the Danish troops a wide and relatively fertile base of operations. Northwards the Norwegian provinces of Jämtland and Härjedalen projected deeply into what we have come to accept as the 'Swedish' side of the great Scandinavian watershed.

The semi-circle of hostile territory was broken only by a narrow strip of Swedish land which ran along the south bank of the Göta River and reached the Kattegat at Älvsborg, between Halland and the Norwegian province of Baahuslen. This westward-facing strip of coast, scarcely a dozen miles wide, constituted Sweden's one outlet to western Europe.

In the first century of its existence the Vasa dynasty was unable to widen the narrow corridor. The Seven Years War (1563–70) was the first Scandinavian conflict in which modern cannon were used to any extent, but the Swedes failed when they besieged Akershus in 1569, and they made at least five unsuccessful attacks on the island castle of Baahus. Conversely, the Danes put large armies of mercenaries into the field, and found that they were unable to maintain them in the wilds of Sweden. In December 1570 the warring parties made peace and agreed to return all their conquests.

The Danish armies made some rather more solid gains in the Kalmar War of 1611–12. In the first campaign an army of 6,000 troops contrived to reduce Kalmar, which was the principal fortress of Sweden's Baltic coast. Älvsborg went the same way in 1612, and in January the next year the Danes gained an advantageous peace on the understanding that they were to hold Älvsborg until the Swedes paid one million riksdalers' ransom. Much to the Danish surprise and chagrin their rivals managed to raise the money, and Älvsborg had to be returned in 1619.

Early Scandinavian fortress-building

The first Swedish essays in artillery fortification were represented by the lake strongholds of Gripsholm (1537) and Vadstena (1545), which were built in a mean and stunted 'reinforced castle' style by German architects at the command of Gustav Vasa.

The Italianate bastion style came to Sweden

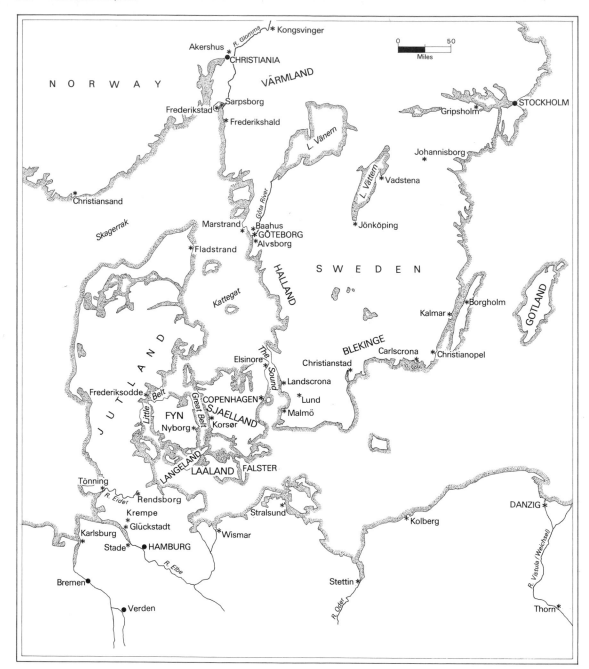

Denmark, with south Norway and south Sweden

during the reign of John III (1568–92), the patron of the four Milanese brothers who arrived in Sweden under the mysterious name of 'Paar'. The Paars were responsible for some work on the castle of Borgholm, on the isle of Öland, and in the 1580s they fortified Kalmar according to the most modern ideas. They built very well, and despite the unfortunate events of 1611 the chancellor Axel Oxenstierna could describe Kalmar as the 'strongest town not just of Småland but of all Sweden' (Generalstaben, 1936–8, I, 180). In the next century the Italian style of fortification was supplanted by the Dutch. It was the favoured manner of Gustavus Adolphus and his engineers, being eminently suited to the rapid fortification of a camp or the strengthening of an old town enceinte.

Swedish defensive strategy first assumed a recognisable shape in the reign of the inspired military reformer Erik XIV (1560–8). In the heart of his country Erik founded the fortress of Jönköping, at the southern end of Lake Vättern, as a central assembly point from where he could move against the flank of the Danes whether they were marching up the east or west shores of the lake. He strengthened Älvsborg, and made new fortifications at Revel to protect Sweden's foothold across the Baltic in Estonia (see p. 167). Finland was secured for the Swedes by Viborg and Kexsholm, the portals towards the Slavonic east, and by the fortress-port of Sandhamn (Helsingfors, Helsinki) which Gustav Vasa had founded in 1550. The reign of Charles IX (1599–1612) was notable for the laying-out of the city of Göteborg (Gothenberg) hard by the castle of Älvsborg, a provocative act which hastened the outbreak of the Kalmar War.

All of this time, however, the machinery of Swedish engineering administration remained in a primitive state, and the king had to see to things himself whenever he wished to garrison or equip a fortress.

Sweden as yet presented no serious challenge to the Danish *dominium maris Baltici*. The king of Denmark commanded every entrance to the Baltic from the western seas, and he maintained extensive fortifications, as well as a mercenary army and a powerful navy from the proceeds of the tolls he exacted from ships passing through the Great Belt (the channel between the islands of Fyn and Sjaelland) and the Sound (between Sjaelland and the Scandinavian mainland).

Military architecture was considerably more advanced in Denmark than in poor and remote Sweden. King Christian III certainly built the grim fortress-palace of Malmöhus in 'reinforced castle' style on the Sound in 1536, but he was almost immediately afterwards converted to Italian ideas, and went on to commission works in the bastioned style at Tønderhus, Ribershus and Landskrona. Frederick II (1559–88) made unauthorised passages of the Sound uncomfortably dangerous, if not altogether impossible, by constructing the great fortress of Kronborg at Helsingør (Elsinore), where every vessel was ordered to anchor and pay dues before being allowed to pass. Frederick was responsible also for founding Fredrikstad, which was the first of the bastioned towns of Norway and an important intermediate position between Baahus and Akershus.

Fortress-building, and indeed every kind of architecture, flourished in the long reign (1596–1648) of the expansive and popular Christian IV. He made large defensive works at Copenhagen, and laid out no less than fifteen new towns. He thereby hoped to give an impulse to commercial life (which had been strangled by the privileges of the existing towns) as well as to add to the strength of his realm. Typically, he took advantage of a devastating fire at Oslo in 1624 to rename the city 'Christiania' and move it to a new site closer beneath the Akershus citadel.

The new fortress towns of Christianstad in Scania and Christianopel in Blekinge acted as barriers against the southward advance of the Swedes. There were similar outposts on the German flank of the Danish empire: on the Baltic side of the base of the Jutish peninsula the fort of Christianspris (built 1631–8) served to bar the entrance to the Kiel inlet; the counterpart on the western side was the newly-strengthened and beautified Elbe fortress of Glückstadt, which exacted dues from the river traffic of the unwilling merchants of Hamburg.

A number of well-sited fortresses helped to preserve the articulation of the scattered elements of the Danish empire. Most notably, there existed a chain of strongholds which bound the islands

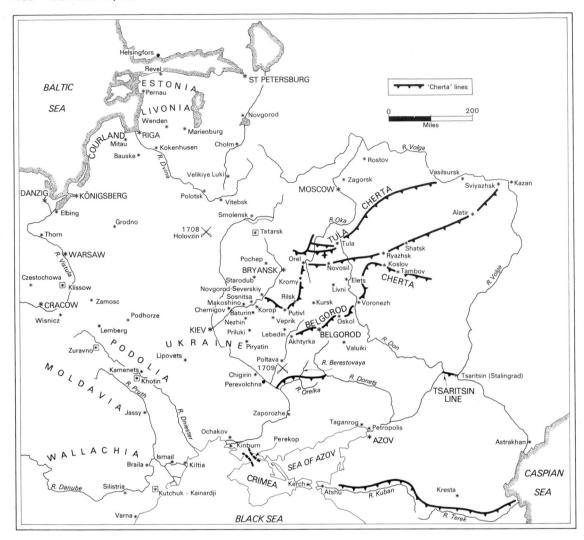

BALTIC
SEA

Helsingfors
Revel
ESTONIA
ST PETERSBURG
Pernau
LIVONIA
Novgorod
Wenden
COURLAND
Marienburg
RIGA
Mitau
Cholm
Kokenhusen
Bauske
R. Dvina
Velikiye Luki
Rostov
R. Volga
DANZIG
KÖNIGSBERG
Polotsk
Vitebsk
Vasilsursk
Elbing
Smolensk
Zagorsk
MOSCOW
Sviyazhsk
Kazan
Grodno
Tatarsk
R. Oka
CHERTA
Alatir
1708
Holovzin
Thorn
R. Vistula
WARSAW
Pochep
TULA
Tula
Shatsk
Czestochowa
BRYANSK
Orel
Ryazhsk
Klissow
Starodub
Kromy
Novosil
Koslov
Tambov
Novgorod-Severskiy
Rilsk
Elets
CHERTA
R. Volga
CRACOW
Sosnitsa
Makoshino
Livni
Kursk
Wisnicz
Chernigov
Baturin
Korop
Putivl
Voronezh
Podhorze
Nezhin
Veprik
BELGOROD
Lemberg
KIEV
Priluki
Lebedin
Oskol
Zamosc
UKRAINE
Piryatin
Akhtyrka
BELGOROD
R. Don
Zuravno
Lipovets
Valuiki
PODOLIA
Poltava
1709
R. Berestovaya
Kamenets
Chigirin
Tsaritsin (Stalingrad)
Khotin
Perevolchna
R. Donets
TSARITSIN
MOLDAVIA
R. Pruth
R. Orelka
LINE
Jassy
Zaporozhe
Taganrog
Petropolis
Astrakhan
Ochakov
Perekop
AZOV
WALLACHIA
Ismail
Kinburn
SEA OF AZOV
Braila
Kiltia
CRIMEA
CASPIAN
R. Danube
Silistria
Kerch
Atshu
R. Kuban
Kresta
SEA
Kutchuk - Kainardji
R. Terek
Varna
BLACK SEA

'Cherta' lines

0   200
Miles

Poland and western Russia

between Jutland and the Scandinavian mainland into the strategic equivalent of a continuous bridge. Bersodde (the later Fredericia) protected the short passage between Jutland and the island of Fyn. On the far side of Fyn the fortress of Nyborg was the point of departure for the voyage across the Great Belt to Korsør on the island of Sjaelland, from where the route lay overland to Copenhagen, the capital of Denmark.

Later events left the city of Copenhagen stranded like twentieth-century Vienna, with its back to its own land and facing a vanished empire. In the early seventeenth century, however, Copenhagen acted as a central entrepôt of the Danish dominions, and together with Frederiksborg it formed the link between the Danish islands and the Scandinavian mainland to the east of the Sound.

Norway was isolated from the rest of the empire by the waters of the Skagerrak, and by the Swedish fortress of Älvsborg which so annoyingly interrupted the overland route between Baahuslen and Halland. Everything therefore rested upon the Danish command of the seas. On the Danish side the most northerly starting-point for the journey was offered by the Jutish harbour of Fladstrand, which was sited about twenty miles south of the Skaw Point. From here vessels could make the 180-mile voyage to Oslo, or the shorter journeys to Fredrikstad (the *point d'appui* of the Norwegian flotilla), and the harbours of Larvik and Christianssand on the north-western shore of the Skagerrak.

The Danish fortress system must be regarded as one of the most comprehensively useful in history. Not only did the strongholds guard an elaborate network of communications, but they made a direct contribution to the empire's economy by exacting tolls and occupying commercially advantageous sites.

The advance and retreat of Old Muscovy

The struggle for the Baltic approaches

On the eastern side of the Baltic we encounter the struggling state of Muscovy, which laboured under geographical disadvantages which were every bit as severe as Sweden's. The western border was extremely ragged, and the Muscovites had to contend with the Poles and Lithuanians for the possession of the fortress-town of Smolensk, which commanded the main road from western Europe to Moscow. Along the coast to the north the obstructive Poles and Lithuanians were helped by another hostile power, the Livonian Knights of the Sword. The Swedes held the eastern end of the Gulf of Finland, and it was their ambition to plant bridge-heads on the southern shore of the Baltic as well.

Grand Prince Ivan III (1462–1505) gave the impulse to a series of spectacular but illusory Muscovite successes at the turn of the fifteenth and sixteenth centuries. In 1478 he captured the ancient trading city of Novgorod, where the Volkhov left Lake Ilmen. After this encouraging start he proceeded in 1492 to found the town of Ivangorod near the mouth of the Narva, thus opening a corridor to the Baltic. The Muscovites reduced Pskov in 1510, which gave them the command of the route around the southern shore of Lake Peipus; and three years later they crowned their conquests by taking Smolensk. The Lithuanians formally ceded Smolensk and its neighbourhood in 1522.

Muscovy dangerously overreached itself in the reign of Ivan IV the Terrible (1533–84). He launched a full-scale invasion of Livonia in 1558, and another of White Russia in 1562, but this career of aggression provoked a number of political and strategic revolutions in Baltic affairs, all of which were most unfavourable to Muscovy. The Swedes took over the protectorship of the Estonian port of Revel in 1561, and so began their one-and-a-half-century story of empire in the south-eastern Baltic. The siege techniques of the Muscovites were too crude to enable them to winkle the intruders out, and Ivan's armies vainly attacked Revel in 1570 and again in 1577. The Swedes then went over to the counter-attack, and their enterprising commander Pontius de la Gardie effectively sealed off Muscovy from the Baltic by taking Narva and Ivangorod in 1581. After years of desultory fighting, the Muscovites abandoned all claims on Estonia in 1595.

Livonia and Lithuania incorporated themselves in Poland, again in response to the Muscovite threat, and from 1575 to 1586 this newly-strengthened composite state was directed by the formidable King

Stephen Batory, who brought the Polish artillery up to the standards of the West, and hired large numbers of Hungarian and German mercenaries. Batory recovered Polotsk in 1579, and in the next year he penetrated Russian territory and took Velikie Luki and Cholm.

On 18 August 1581 the Poles sat down before Pskov. Batory divided the siegeworks into Lithuanian, German, Polish and Hungarian 'attacks', as befitted the composition of his army, but all the fury of the Poles and all the cunning of the mercenaries proved to be of no avail against the stalwart and active garrison. In Batory's words:

When they are defending towns the Russians give no thought to their lives. They steadfastly man the walls and defend the ditch, fighting night and day regardless of whether they have been torn by shot or steel or hurled into the air by mines, or whether their rations have run out and they are dying of hunger. They will not surrender, for their one concern is the welfare of the realm (Laskovskii, 1858–65, 206–7).

Batory was forced to convert the siege into a blockade, which lasted until the truce of 15 January 1582, by which the Muscovites recognised the Poles as masters of Livonia and Dorpat. Well over a century was to pass before the Russians were in a state to resume their drive to the Baltic.

Nothing could have been further than empire-building from the Muscovites' minds in the late 1590s and the 1600s. The Russian state dissolved in anarchy after the direct line of the old tsars died out in 1598, and more than once in the ensuing 'Time of Troubles' the independence of Muscovy hung upon a couple of beleaguered fortresses.

With Polish encouragement, the supporters of the pretender Dmitry invaded Russia from the Ukraine in the autumn of 1604. The fortress of Kromy declared in their favour, which gave them a strongpoint on the direct line of communication

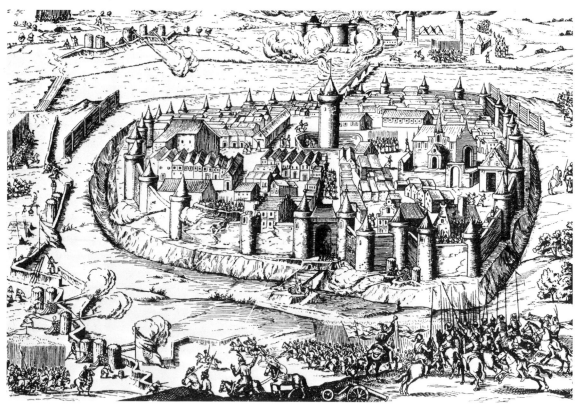

52 Siege of Smolensk, 1609–11

between the loyal army and Moscow, and so the recapture of this place became a matter of the first urgency for the new tsar, Boris Godunov.

Godunov's attempt on Kromy was beaten back in March 1605, largely owing to the activity of the 300 Cossacks in the garrison.

They encircled the town with a ditch, and heaped up a rampart, on the reverse slope of which they dug earth lodgments where they were hidden from gunfire like mice in their holes (Razin, 1963, III, 78).

The failure destroyed Godunov's credit, and he died in misery on 13 April. The Muscovites attempted to make a new siege of Kromy, but this fresh effort caused their army to disintegrate altogether. The path to the capital now stood open, and Dmitry entered Moscow without opposition on 10 June.

The brief reign of the pretender ended when the boyars rose in rebellion in May 1606. This energetic action earned the Muscovites little reprieve. In December they had to fend off an attack by 33,000 peasants, serfs and Cossacks, and in the four years from 1608 they were fighting for their independence against a sustained onslaught of the Poles.

The effective opposition was confined to Moscow and its most important strategic outposts. The fortified Troitse-Sergiev Monastery at Zagorsk, forty-four miles north-east of Moscow, underwent nearly sixteen months of blockade and assaults before the Poles marched away in January 1610. Meanwhile another force of 12,000 Poles had begun an epic siege of Smolensk on 19 September 1609. The contest was a fair trial of strength, for Smolensk was an immense new fortress which had been built between 1586 and 1602 by the architect Fedor Savelev. The walls were four miles in circuit, and rose to a height of between forty and sixty feet, or to nearly seventy feet in the case of the thirty-eight towers. The foundations were dug more than twelve feet deep, and a system of revetted listening galleries projected almost ten yards from the foot of the walls. The whole made up probably the largest construction project of the sixteenth century.

The eye-witness writes that

the Muscovites were very much on their guard, and not a single one of our mine approaches could be concealed from them, for their experienced and skilful engineers had excavated secret galleries beneath the earth. . . . By this means the Muscovites dug under the foundations and out from the fortress. They burst into our mines and grappled with the miners, or they drove under our galleries and blew them up with gunpowder, which ruined the works and buried and suffocated the men (Laskovskii, 1858–65, I, 249).

Countermines of this kind were exploded with particularly devastating results on 16 January and 14 February 1610.

Smolensk withstood almost a year and a half of mining, cannonade and investment, until the garrison was reduced to 200 men. At last the Poles detected two weak spots in the southern walls, where they managed to effect great breaches, and on the night of 2–3 June 1611 the besiegers surged forward once again. Some of the Poles poured through the breaches, while others scaled up eighty ladders 'so wide that five or six men could mount abreast, and as tall as the highest trees in the forest' (Razin, 1963, III, 166). The defenders were overwhelmed, and the wounded governor was carried away to be tortured.

The prolonged defences of Smolensk and the Troitse-Sergiev Monastery were of supreme importance, for during the second half of 1610 they had represented the only centres of organised Muscovite resistance. Moscow itself had fallen immediately after the boyars' field army had been routed at Klushino on 24 June.

On 18 March 1611, while a large part of the Polish army was still held fast by Smolensk, the Polish garrison in Moscow tried to force a number of draymen to transport some guns from the walls of the Kitai-Gorod. This represented an intolerable affront to civil pride, and the foreigners at once had a revolution on their hands. The 3,000 Polish troops fell back to the Kremlin, and Moscow became the focus of a national revival. In November 1612 the Muscovites accepted the surrender of the Kremlin from the collection of cannibalistic scarecrows which was all that was left of the garrison, and early the next year a crowd in Red Square acclaimed the boyar Michael Romanov as the first tsar of a new dynasty.

Muscovite military engineering

Until the second half of the fifteenth century, military architecture in Muscovy made the minimum of concessions to the power of artillery. Kremlins and town fortifications were built almost universally of timber, with irregularly-spaced towers, and only in the design of the gates do we find any attempt to secure better protection against missiles. This took the form of a clumsy device by which the entrance passage described a corridor between two parallel walls.

The spell was broken by Grand Prince Ivan III, who sent missions to Italy in 1474, 1488 and 1499 to recruit engineers and artists. Ivan was rewarded with a fine crop of Italian experts, who were confusingly endowed by the Muscovites with the common surname 'Fryazin' ('Frank'), the generic term for Westerners.

Under the Italian influence fortifications of masonry became more common (see below), and towers were disposed in a more systematic and even fashion than in the past. In some places, indeed, the whole fortress was laid out as a regular oblong, as at Ivangorod (1492–1610) and with the Kremlin of Tula (1507–20), although the irregular plan remained the more common (Smolensk, the Troitse-Sergiev Monastery).

The most enduring monument of the work of the Italians is represented by the present Moscow Kremlin, which was built between 1485 and 1499 in a style resembling the Sforza Castle at Milan, which was the home town of at least two of the imported architects: Pietro Antonio Solario and Alevisio da Milano. The Kremlin towers were roofed and decorated in the early seventeenth century, the most spectacular being the 190-foot-high Spaaskaya Tower, which was completed in 1625 by the Scots architect and clockmaker Christopher Galloway.

The Italian engineers began to go out of fashion in the sixteenth century when the Muscovites turned against 'Latinity', the influence of the Catholic West. The Kitai-Gorod, which adjoined the Moscow Kremlin, was fortified (1534–8) with low walls and squat towers which bore some resemblance to the German 'reinforced castles' of the time. After this the Muscovites lost all contact with Western engineering thought, and, like the Moghuls of India,

they sought to nullify the power of artillery by building immensely high and thick walls. Thus the Moscow Belyi-Gorod was enclosed between 1586 and 1593 with walls that were decidedly more archaic in aspect than the Kitai-Gorod perimeter of half a century before.

Moscow was just one of the many towns which possessed a kremlin citadel as well as urban walls:

During the whole period of Russian history up to the eighteenth century the kremlin of the Russian town was a complex of fortifications which held the organs of political, administrative and clerical power. It guarded the principal shrine of the neighbourhood, it contained the repository of the treasures of the townsfolk as well as supplies of every kind, and, finally, it served as the chief refuge of the population in time of war (Tverskoi, 1953, 108).

Whether in kremlin walls or town enceintes, the Russians concentrated the power of the defence in tall, multi-storied towers. These towers were of widely-differing design. In fact we frequently come across oblong and circular ground-plans co-existing in the same fortress. The interior space of the towers was cramped and awkwardly-shaped, and so it was rarely possible to accommodate more than a couple of guns on the same storey. Further guns were housed under the rampart-walkways of the curtain walls in heavily-arched casemates, open to the rear. However, even the largest fortresses were armed in a very paltry fashion – in 1610 Smolensk owned no more than ten pieces of heavy calibre.

The wealthier and the larger of the monasteries were fortified like the towns, and they acted rather in the way of the detached forts of the nineteenth-century engineers, adding significantly to the strength of the secular fortresses of their neighbourhood.

As for building materials, brick became a popular medium after Ridolfo Fieravanti taught the Muscovites the art of brickmaking in the later fifteenth century and organised the manufacture on a large scale. The Moscow Kremlin and Kitai-Gorod were entirely of this material, while the Tula kremlin and the Smolensk enceinte were of compound construction, the upper part being of brick, and the

53 One of the Smolensk towers

lower fourteen or eighteen feet built of stone as a protection against mining.

Timber was almost everywhere available in abundance. It was used extensively for the stockaded enceintes of the towns facing the Tartar East, and for defending suburbs and other less vital parts of fortresses in western Russia. The deacon and engineer Ivan Vyrodkov invented an interesting variation on the conventional timber fortress in 1551, when he assembled a stronghold out of prefabricated parts at Sviyazhsk, as a base for the advance on Kazan. He employed the same technique in 1557 to run up a fort at the mouth of the Narva in three months.

Half-way between the prefabricated fortress and a siege machine comes the *gulyai-gorod*, which was an arrangement of mobile timber screens. The Muscovites made their first recorded use of the device in 1522, and they employed it again in their unsuccessful siege of Kazan in 1530.

As a defensive expedient, the *gulyai-gorod* proved its worth when it helped to defend the southern approaches of Moscow against the Tartars in 1591, and against the serfs in 1606. The official Ivan Timofeev records that in appearance

it was like a wooden town . . . it was set up in the same way as the defensive enclosure of a city, and the sections were arranged like shields. Each part measured about five feet wide and more than six feet high, and these sections were joined like the

integral parts of a body, the connections being formed by iron chains . . . it was large enough to accommodate a sizeable army, with all its requisites and as great a quantity of artillery as was necessary (Razin, 1963, III, 78).

The sections could be opened up to permit a counter-attack to pass through. They were transported across country on wheels in summer and upon sledge-runners in the winter.

As we might have expected, the Soviets hail the *gulyai-gorod* as 'an independent invention of native Russians' (Pankov, 1952, 37). All the same the inspiration probably came from the *Wagenburg* of the Hussites of fifteenth-century Bohemia.

Most of the Muscovite fortresses possessed semi-permanent garrisons of regular troops. Among these were numbered the *streltsy*, or musketeers, who were distributed among the fortresses in packets of about one hundred each. The artillery was served by staffs who lived in special villages, where they tilled plots of land and exercised crafts rather after the style of the Turkish garrison Janissaries. The musketeers and gunners were aided by establishments of blacksmiths and other tradesmen, and by specialised troops who saw to the defence of the gates from the flanking towers.

In time of siege the town was usually swarming with fugitive troops and refugee peasants, not to mention armed townspeople who were eager to join in the defence. Warfare in these Eastern theatres

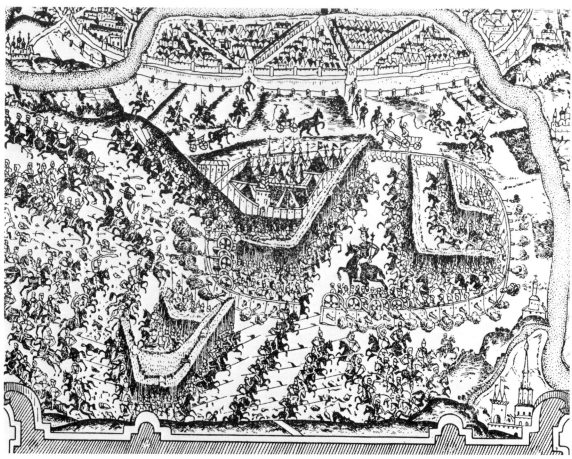

54   The *gulyai-gorod* at Moscow, 1606

therefore bore an elemental character, and the history of the defence of Russian fortresses is full of examples of repeated sorties, energetic counter-mining, fanatically-disputed breaches, the construction of massive improvised works, and other deeds which demanded a prodigal expenditure of labour and blood. The German merchant Samuel Kiechel observed in 1586:

The Russian people offer more resistance in fortresses and towns than in the open field. They are industrious, they can survive with little material support, they put up with bad food and drink, and they endure hunger and thirst more easily than other nations (Adelung, 1846, I, 374).

Muscovite sieges display no great consistency of style. Their attack on the Tartar fortress of Kazan in 1552, for example, was by Western standards a curious amalgam of medieval and Renaissance practice. The place was very efficiently invested on the evening of 23 August: as the chronicler Kurbskii says, 'they cut off all the paths and avenues to Kazan from the country side, and not a single person could leave or get into the town' (Razin, 1963, II, 360).

The impression of modernity was, however, somewhat spoilt when Ivan Vyrodkov was inspired to build a forty-foot high siege tower, which he stuffed with no less than ten heavy guns and fifty wall pieces.

On 26 September the sap attack reached the edge of the ditch, and the Muscovites proceeded to 'attach' miners to the Arsk and Nogaisk Gates (the

Russians had first seen gunpowder mines used in 1535, when the Poles breached the wall of Starodub). The charges were exploded at three in the morning of 2 October, and the Muscovites exploited the surprise by making a general cannonade and launching a successful assault in six widely-separated columns.

Ivan the Terrible's armies again resorted to trench approaches at Dorpat in 1558, and at Revel in 1570, where they had the help of a contingent of German mercenaries. Formal attacks of this kind were nevertheless rare, and the Muscovites preferred to use the crude technique of cannonade and storm (Viborg 1558, Marienburg 1560, Fellin 1560, Revel 1577, and Wenden 1578).

Muscovite artillery, like Muscovite military architecture, was imposing rather than advanced. Gunpowder probably came to Muscovy direct from the East, either by trade or through information extracted from Tartar prisoners, and so the Western influence on artillery remained minimal, despite the presence of a few European gunfounders.

The massive Muscovite bombards of the first half of the sixteenth century merely gave way to trunnioned versions of the same weapons, the most celebrated surviving specimen being the Tsar

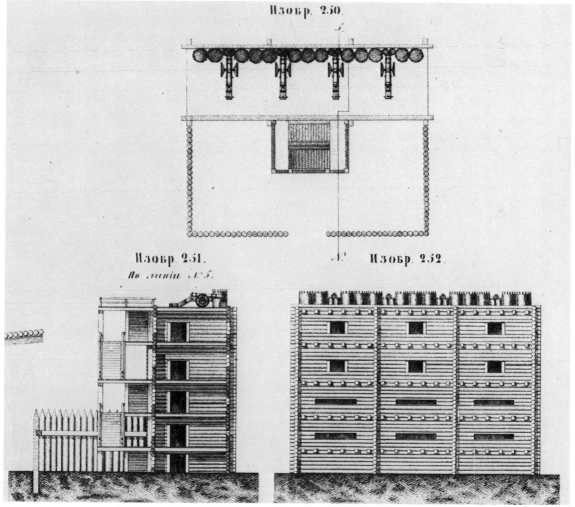

55 Vyrodkov's prefabricated siege tower at Kazan, 1552

Cannon in the Moscow Kremlin, which was cast by Master Andrei Chokov in 1585–6. The barrel of this monster is an untapered cylinder more than five yards long, and it has a gigantic bore of thirty-five inches.

As we have seen, the early tsars hauled great quantities of guns about with them on their campaigns, but mounted comparatively few large pieces in their fortresses.

The first sign of a revival of interest in Western military techniques probably dates from 1606, when one of the princes Shuiskii commissioned Onisim Mikhailov to draw up a compendium based on the best European methods. Mikhailov pursued his researches in several languages, and in 1621 he finally produced the 663-page manuscript which makes up his *Code of Military and Artillery Practice and Other Affairs Relating to the Art of War*. The treatment of fortification and gunnery was very extensive, and for more than fifty years the *Code* remained the only comprehensive source of information on the ways that war was fought in the West.

Foreign officers began to arrive in considerable numbers under the early Romanovs, and in 1618 the bastion system made its début in Russia when the Earth Town at Moscow was fortified on unmistakably Dutch lines. A certain 'Just Matson' is known to have strengthened the vast earthen perimeter of Novgorod in modern style in 1632, and in the same year Jan Cornelius van Rodenburg built the nine-bastioned fortress of Rostov Velikii. Less happily, Rodenburg was responsible for directing the unsuccessful siege of Smolensk in 1633. After the second, successful attack on Smolensk in 1654, this fortress was given an outer perimeter consisting of covered way, palisades and glacis.

The Age of Gustavus Adolphus

Apprenticeship in the East

Sweden's intervention in Baltic affairs in the 'Time of Troubles' was not particularly happy. Pontius de la Gardie snatched a few towns by his impudence and his petards, but the Swedes did not fare very well against garrisons which were determined to put up a good defence. The Poles successfully held Riga against a Swedish attack in 1600, and three years later they drove the Protestant invaders back to Revel and Narva.

The name of Gustavus Adolphus (1612–32) is associated with the beginning of an aggressive drive that was going to last a whole century, and carry the terror of the Swedish arms from the Alps to the Black Sea basin. However, the young king was doubly unfortunate at the start of his military career, for he was desperately short of engineers and ammunition for his artillery, and he was unlucky enough to arrive on the scene just when the Muscovites were beginning to climb out of their years of anarchy.

In 1614 Gustavus reduced the Russian fortress of Gdov, near Lake Peipus, after an inordinately long siege, and in the following year he failed altogether against Pskov. Gustavus turned his back on Russia, and from 1617 onwards he systematically expanded the Swedish foothold on the Baltic shore southwards from Estonia through the Polish territories of Livonia and Lithuania. By 1621 he was ready for the siege of Riga, which was a Polish city-port of 30,000 people, and the gateway to the Baltic cornlands and the trade of north-western Russia. The business of the siege as a whole was managed much better than the affair at Pskov, and Riga capitulated on 15 September.

The profitable attack on Riga had given Gustavus the opportunity to become acquainted with two young gentlemen who were to become the foremost Swedish commanders of the next generation. The eighteen-year-old page Lennart Torstensson had been carrying an order to a colonel when he noticed that the circumstances in which the message had been composed had been overtaken by events. Torstensson boldly amended the instructions, delivered them to the colonel, and reported back to the king. Gustavus exclaimed: 'You took a risk there! You might have answered with your life! But unless I am very much mistaken your action is the sign of a good general. All is forgiven!' (Tingsten, 1932, 293).

Another future field-marshal, Johan Banér, so distinguished himself in an assault on 9 September that he was appointed colonel on the spot. At twenty-five he was the youngest officer of that rank in the army.

By taking Riga, Gustavus had won the command of the mouth of the Dvina. He recruited his strength and moved forward once more in 1625, gaining the whole of the lower course of the river and some of the territory on the far side. He consolidated his conquest by planting large garrisons in Kokenhusen, Mitau, Bauske and Birze, and he issued a stream of ferocious orders to the new commandants. We encounter such gentle sentiments as 'If you deliver up your fortress you shall be unfailingly sent to the gallows,' or (according to another formula) 'you shall be hanged without more ado'.

The next bound took Gustavus across Lithuania to the regime of the Vistula. He made Elbing his principal depôt in the new theatre of operations, and overran the open country and the smaller towns. He did not feel equal to reducing the great port of Danzig, the Polish protectorate on the lower Vistula. Instead he cunningly obstructed the commerce by planting the fort of Danziger Haupt, 'the foothold of our estate in Prussia' (Steckzén, 1939, 81), beside one of the mouths of the river.

The Swedes prosecuted their war in this part of the world until 1629, when the battered and discouraged Poles ceded Livonia, and the Elector of Brandenburg surrendered most of the East Prussian coast.

Over the last years Gustavus had gained more than territory alone. He had learnt how useful it was to gather information about enemy fortresses from talkative traitors and by close person reconnaissance; he had seen that the best way to bring down a wall was to concentrate artillery fire against a narrow sector; lastly, he had evolved an exceedingly effective strategy by which he controlled river lines and routes of communication by means of fortified depôts and towns.

The Swedes in Germany

In 1618 the loose fabric of the dominion of the Austrian Habsburgs was rent by religious faction. The Protestants got the upper hand in Bohemia and the associated territories of Moravia and Silesia, and in 1619 they chose Frederick the Elector Palatine as their king. However, the Imperial forces defeated the heretics at the Battle of the White Mountain on 8 November 1620, and the Bohemian capital of Prague opened its gates without resistance. In 1622 the Imperialists and Spanish marched into Germany to attack the Palatinate itself, and in the autumn of the next year Frederick was forced to make an armistice. Frankenthal, his last stronghold, had been abandoned by its English garrison on the orders of King James I.

The resurgence of Habsburg power was countered by an alliance of France, Holland, England, Sweden, Denmark, Brandenburg and some of the smaller Protestant princes of Germany. This impressive array soon fell apart under the blows of the Imperial general Karl Albrecht von Wallenstein, who was a master of strategy, tactics and field engineering. Amongst other accomplishments he was particularly skilful at building fortified posts at great speed. In April 1626 the German Protestant general Mansfield chose to attack one of these works, a bridgehead on the Elbe near Dessau, and was repulsed with the loss of more than one third of his 18,000 men. The action at Dessau was all the more significant because in August the other Imperial commander, Tilly, defeated Christian IV of Denmark at Lutter.

The Catholic victories at Dessau and Lutter effectively broke the Protestant armies, and Wallenstein's thoughts now turned to the domination of the Baltic: 'There are twenty-eight ports in Pomerania, and we must put garrisons in them all' (Steckzén, 1939, 86). For the last few decades, in fact, warfare in the Baltic had focussed on the fortified ports of the southern shore, which were gradually losing their independence and falling into the grip of the belligerent powers. 'From then onwards they functioned as an integral part of the region's military resources, serving variously as corner stones of territorial defence, strategic sally ports, or advanced military bastions' (Schnitter, 1973, 2). Wismar, one of the finest of the natural harbours, was forced to admit a garrison in the autumn of 1627. Unfortunately the other towns opposed Wallenstein's demands, and in 1628 the lagoon-girt port of Stralsund withstood a full-scale siege with the help of Danish and Swedish troops.

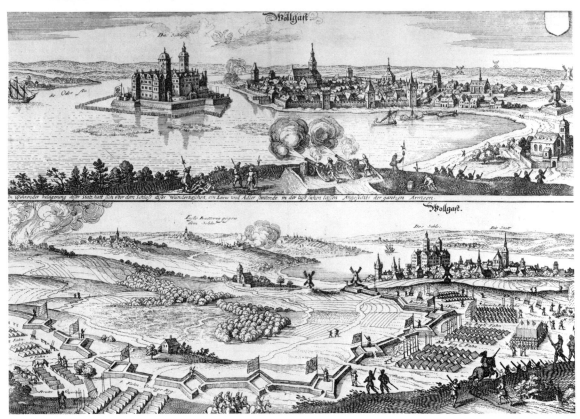

56   Gustavus's siege of Wolgast in Pomerania, 1630 (Merian, 1639)

The resistance of Stralsund wrecked the schemes of Wallenstein and the Spanish to base a Catholic fleet in the Baltic, and brought about an accord between Denmark and Sweden. The Danes certainly abandoned this unnatural alliance in the following year, but the Swedes had made their first intervention in the German war, and the Emperor was shortly to be confronted by a Protestant king who was in every way a far more dangerous opponent that the genial Christian IV of Denmark.

The Emperor was under the illusion that the war in Germany was as good as over, and he turned his attention to counteracting French influence in Italy, leaving 40,000 troops scattered widely among the German towns. Everything therefore favoured a full-scale Swedish intervention in Germany. The Danes, however, still gave Gustavus some cause for anxiety, and he was careful to secure his strategic rear against his fellow-heretics by driving ahead a programme of works at Älvsborg, Jönköping, Kalmar and the new fortress of Johannisborg in Norrköping.

Gustavus resolved to make his effort, not from Stralsund (which did not lie on a river) but further to the east up the great avenue of the Oder. Once in command of the lower reaches of this river he would be advantageously placed on the flank of the Imperial positions in Mecklenburg and Western Pomerania, and he would probably be able to frighten the Protestant electors of Brandenburg and Saxony into joining him as vassal-allies.

On 10 July 1630 Gustavus gained a peaceful entry to the city of Stettin, which stood forty miles up the Oder, the townspeople crowding the streets for a sight of the famous Swedish army and its simply-clad king, 'a gentle-mannered, affable gentleman who was ready to chat with anybody' (Roberts, 1953–8, I, 346). After this first success Gustavus

57 Tilly's siege of Magdeburg, 1631. The storming of the Zollschanze (Merian, 1643)

widened his German bridgehead by prosecuting a series of little sieges in eastern and western Pomerania.

The way for the southward thrust, directly up the Oder, was opened by the storming of Greifenhagen, twelve miles above Stettin, on Christmas Day 1630. The Imperial commander Tilly was now hard pressed, for he had to cope with a Protestant rebellion in Magdeburg, a strong city on the middle Elbe, as well as doing something to check Gustavus's advance up the Oder. In the early spring of 1631 the Swedes penetrated a further dozen miles upstream and planted an entrenched camp on the crossing at Schwedt. From this base Gustavus moved against the city of Frankfurt-an-der-Oder, which he took by storm on 3 April. The victorious Swedes massacred the garrison and plundered the citizens, and the Scots mercenary Monro comments that he 'did never see officers less obeyed' (Generalstaben,

1936–8, III, 417). Frankfurt was a Protestant town, and the unbridled sack was an indication of what the rest of Germany might expect from the Swedes.

The capture of Frankfurt gave Gustavus the command of eighty miles of the Oder, and he had every reason to expect that his steady progress into northern central Germany would bring relief to the beleaguered city of Magdeburg. But all the king's calculations were thrown out by the recklessness of the garrison, which was firing away its ammunition in an extravagant fashion. The Protestants ran out of gunpowder on 10 May, just when the Imperialists launched their final assault and the walls were 'black with men and scaling ladders' (Monro, 1637, 34). The Catholic troops poured into the streets, and in the afternoon the horrors of the scene were compounded by a fire which laid the ravished city in ashes. Altogether the storm, the massacre and the conflagration cost the lives of about 25,000 people.

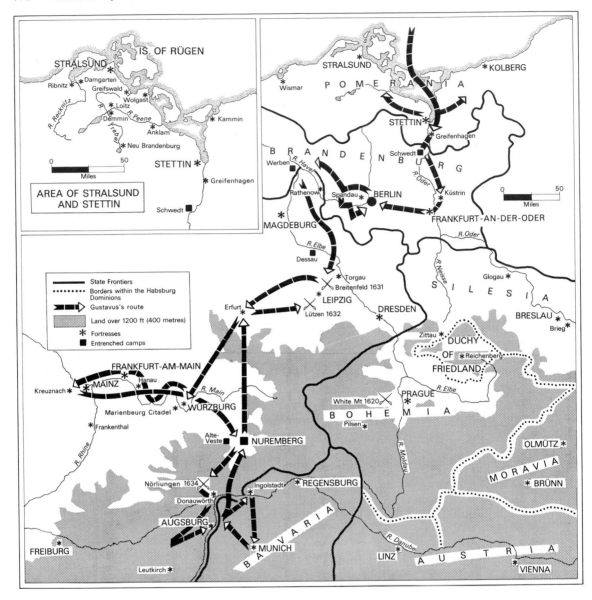

Central Europe in the Thirty Years War

The blaze at least was a kind of horrible accident, for history shows that the towns of this part of the world burnt very well – as was proved by the devastation of Gotha in 1632, the bombardment of the Saxon towns in the Seven Years War, and the destruction of Dresden in 1945.

Tilly had eliminated the *centrum mali* of German heretical rebellion, but in the process he had actually lost irreplaceable ground in his war against the Swedes. Wallenstein (whom he had supplanted in command) was too jealous to send him supplies, and since the magazines in Magdeburg were burnt out he was left with no alternative but to retire southwards to the Thuringian passes.

The events at Magdeburg provided the first impulse which launched Gustavus on the great anti-clockwise circuit which he traced from the Oder to the Elbe, thence down the Main to the Rhine, and finally along the upper Danube and into the heart of Bavaria.

Gustavus had already browbeaten the Elector of Brandenburg into admitting a Swedish garrison to Küstrin and placing Spandau under Swedish command, and now that he held the lower Oder firmly garrisoned he swung west to the Elbe, the second of the great rivers of the north German plain. As usual he felt his way forward by stages, building entrenched base-camps as he went. The next of these positions was planted at Werben, between the Elbe and the Havel, where the Swedes skilfully adapted the old town walls and the river dykes.

Both the town wall and the leaguer wall were so thick and firm of old earth, faced up with new, that no cartow [shot from a demi-cannon] could enter into it. The bulwarks on which the batteries were made for the cannon were also very strong and formally built, and they flanked one another, so that none could find but folly in pressing to enter by storm. And betwixt the flankers were left voids, for letting troops of horse in and out (Generalstaben, 1936–8, IV, 257).

The Elbe offered unlimited, if slightly corpse-flavoured, drinking water, and there was ample pasturage for the horses along the water meadows. The man responsible for these admirable arrangements was the royal cartographer Olof Hansson

Örnehufvud, whose services were much in demand now that Gustavus had marched off the maps he had brought from Sweden.

From Werben Gustavus hastened to join forces with Elector John George of Saxony, who had decided to throw in his lot with the Swedes and Brandenburgers. On 7 September the united army defeated the Imperialists at Breitenfeld, and the Protestant forces were free to fan out in all directions. Banér planted himself amid the abandoned ruins of Magdeburg, while von Arnim took an army of Saxons into Silesia and Bohemia. Erfurt, in the dead centre of the German road network, was occupied by a Swedish force on 22 September.

Gustavus himself led the main body of the Swedish army south-westward against the Main and the middle Rhine. The rich towns and fertile countryside would sustain him through the winter, and form a solid block of territory between the Bavarians to the east and the Spanish in Lorraine to the west.

Gustavus made the episcopal fortress of Würzburg his first objective, for 'he knew, whoever was master of Würzburg, he commanded the whole river of the Main, and consequently whole Franconia' (Monro, 1637, 51). The Swedes rushed the citadel on 8 October, and hewed down the garrison in the heat of combat.

After this bloody deed Gustavus marched on to the middle Rhine and evicted the small garrisons of Spanish auxiliaries which had been in undisputed possession of this area for the last ten years. The city of Mainz capitulated on 11 December, and the nearby post of Kreuznach was taken by storm on 21 February the next year. There was something almost unnatural in the ease with which so many fortresses were falling to Gustavus, and 'the Imperialists obliged the Swedes by spreading the rumour that in the king's army there were certain Lapps, who cast a spell upon their enemies and prevented them from offering any resistance' (ibid., 81).

As his goal for 1632 Gustavus conceived nothing less than invading Bavaria and Austria down the valley of the Danube from the west. No ordinary camp, no Schwedt or Werben, would have been equal to the magnitude of the operation. He accordingly aimed to make a defensible base out of the entire tract of land which lay between the Danube on the north, the River Lech on the east and the foothills of the Alps to the south. On 27 March the Swedes stormed into Donauwörth, which was the westernmost and most isolated of the Bavarian fortresses, and in the first week of April they gained possession of the line of the Lech. As the last prize the wealthy Protestant city of Augsburg yielded on 10 April, offering Gustavus the opportunity to

continue with his ambition of forming the region into such a *sedem belli*, with the facility of the two cities of Ulm and Augsburg and the angle formed by the Lech and the Danube, that if he were thrown onto the defensive the enemy would scarcely be able to force him out (Spanheim, 1634, 86).

Far from going over to the counter-offensive, the Bavarians retreated down the Danube to the powerful and modern fortress of Ingolstadt. Gustavus appeared before the place on 19 April, and the next day, according to his custom, he rode in to make a close reconnaissance. 'The gunners of Ingolstadt realised that the royal party signified something out of the ordinary, and they judged their aim so well that a shot carried away the crupper of the king's horse and covered him with blood and dust' (Droysen, 1869–70, II, 548). The fortress proved to be manifestly too strong to be taken.

The disappointing reconnaissance of 20 April 1632 represents the end of Gustavus's almost unbroken run of success. Thereafter the king gradually lost the initiative: his siege techniques were founded on *coup d'oeil*, fraud and impudence, which had served him very well in the past, but were unequal to the taking of fortresses in the Catholic heartland.

After the failure at Ingolstadt, Gustavus wasted precious time in clearing small pockets of resistance in southern Bavaria and Swabia. Wallenstein seized the opportunity to bring an Imperial army down from Bohemia to join Duke Maximilian of Bavaria and form an army of 48,000 men. Gustavus responded in characteristic fashion by concentrating at the Protestant city of Nuremberg in the second half of June, where he threw up a spacious entrenched camp to the designs of Örnehufvud.

Wallenstein was no mean engineer himself, and he countered by carving out a rival camp a short distance to the west.

Gustavus shrank from making a direct assault on Wallenstein's position, and in the second half of September he resumed his indecisive manoeuvres in the open field. Wallenstein promptly struck camp and launched a completely unexpected invasion of Saxony. Gustavus came panting after, but could not persuade the Elector John George to leave the security of his fortresses. Unsupported by their allies, the Swedes managed to beat the Catholic host at Lützen on 6 November 1632. However, Gustavus was lost to view during some bitter cavalry fighting, and after the battle his body was retrieved from beneath a pile of dead. A ball had drilled his temple, the same shot that was to rid Europe of another troublesome Swedish king less than a century later.

The death of Gustavus brought no immediate relief to the Catholic cause, for in 1633 Gustav Horn and the young Duke Bernard of Saxe-Weimar penetrated as far down the Danube as Passau, and the self-willed and overmighty Wallenstein hatched plots to take his army over to the Swedes.

By now, in fact, Wallenstein had become not just a 'fortress-based warlord' of a kind we have already encountered in the French Wars of Religion, but the greatest and most dangerous of the 'military enterprisers' of his time. His power was founded on his domain of Friedland, which was carved out of former Protestant estates in the cornlands of northern Bohemia. He assembled the produce of this private empire at the fortified depôt of Reichenberg, and transported it over the mountains by way of Zittau to the theatre of war in north Germany. Wallenstein paid his troops (and repaid himself) by instituting a severe but well-regulated programme of extractions from German towns. He financed his powerful artillery train by the same means. Thus Wallenstein was able to support the unprecedentedly large host of 140,000 men without having to call on the Emperor for a penny.

The crisis was resolved by the assassination of Wallenstein on 25 February 1634, and the rout of Horn and Weimar at Nördlingen six months later. Gustavus's legacy of empire began to crumble away. No man, perhaps not even Gustavus himself, could

58 Gustavus is checked at Ingolstadt 20 April 1632 (Merian, 1667)

have long held together the Protestant armies of 175,000 men, or maintained the Swedish dominion of the best part of Germany.

In the two years following the Battle of Nördlingen the Catholics recovered the major towns of southern and central Germany. Their run of success provoked France, nominally the 'first daughter of the Church', into entering the war as a full ally of Protestant Sweden, a misfortune that was to some extent offset by the return of Brandenburg and Saxony to the Imperial fold. More clearly than ever before, the conflict had become a struggle of the Germans against foreign invasion.

The Swedes consolidated themselves in Pomerania and on the lower Elbe, whence their ravaging armies made forays into central Germany and the Protestant dominions. However, the work of the Imperial bureaucracy and the Baroque Counter-Reformation had won back the allegiance and hearts of many people who in earlier times would have welcomed the Swedes as their liberators. Now we encounter unmistakable signs of popular resistance

to the invaders. Thus the adventurous Banér was repulsed in 1639 by Prague, which had been the very seat of heretical disaffection one generation earlier. His grim and single-minded successor Torstensson captured Olmütz in June 1642 and pushed his cavalry to within twenty-five miles of Vienna, but he did not dare to hold his positions for any length of time, for there were unreduced garrisons and indignant populations in his rear, most notably at Brieg in Silesia. It was much the same story in 1645, when Torstensson expended 8,000 of his men and the best part of the campaigning season in a vain siege of the Moravian fortress of Brünn, which was held by the ex-Huguenot Souches, and a garrison of 1,500 soldiers, armed citizens and students.

A scratch force of the same kind foiled the last Swedish venture of the war, which was the attack on Prague in 1648. The Swedes broke into the Klein-Seite by surprise on 16 July, but the townspeople and the garrison held out on the east bank of the Moldau until 22 October, when news came that peace had been concluded at Münster.

By the terms of the peace the Swedes retained the northernmost and most tenable parts of their German empire. Most importantly they remained masters of West Pomerania with Stralsund and Stettin, which gave them a wide and readily-accessible bridgehead on the German coast, and helped to divert the growing military resources of Brandenburg to wars in the north for the next seven decades.

Swedish military engineering in the period of the Thirty Years War

Gustavus (like Napoleon) habitually based his offensive strategy upon carefully fortified lines of advance. As early as 1622 the Polish commander Radziwill complained that he could make no headway against an enemy such as Gustavus who 'like a mole fights underground, and who being weaker in cavalry protects himself against it by trenches and bastions' (Spanheim, 1634, 280).

In the Thirty Years War Gustavus went on to fortify bridgeheads and river crossings as a matter of routine, and he based each successive bound upon camps like the ones at Stettin, Schwedt, Werben and Nuremberg. Thus in Germany nowadays the term Schwedenschanze is applied as freely (and as inaccurately) to ancient earthworks as the title 'Caesar's Camp' in England.

When it was a question of supporting his armies, Gustavus's digging entered the realm of grand strategy:

The base of operations was the source from which the royal army sustained itself during offensive operations, and drew reinforcements during pauses in the campaigns; it also formed a fortified zone to which the army could fall back in the event of a reverse (Roberts, 1953–8, II, 200).

As for the towns, Gustavus scattered the Swedish garrisons like the spore of some monstrous parasite across northern Europe from the Dutch border to Poland and from the Baltic to the Alps. Where they were not excised, these cancerous growths continued to sap the resources of the land until the end of the Thirty Years War, and in some places well beyond.

Gustavus defined the laws of plunder in a code of regulations which he published at Mainz in 1632. He accepted the sacking of a stormed town as unavoidable and legitimate, though he stipulated that the enemy had to be completely overpowered before the proceedings could start, and that the regiments were to confine their activities to the districts assigned to them, sparing the churches, hospitals and any other large buildings which might prove useful for the support of the army. These limits, and they were wide ones, were set only from considerations of military expediency.

The fall of the town was merely the beginning of the purgatory. The events at Augsburg may be taken as less harrowing than most, for this was a mainly Protestant city and it had submitted by capitulation. The alien rule began when Gustavus staged a ceremonial entry on 14 April 1632 and exacted an oath of loyalty to the Swedish crown. Since the Catholic priests refused to become traitors, the Swedes expelled all the popish clergy and closed down all but one of their churches. There was a significantly high proportion of Catholics in the force of 3,000 citizens which was rounded up each week to work on the new fortifications.

The officers and men were billeted upon the householders of Augsburg, who had to provide their unwanted guests with generous helpings of food and wine: every lieutenant-colonel, at every mealtime, was entitled to draw six full meals, as well as six pounds of bread and four measures of wine. By August most of the citizens were bankrupt. The garrison at first made a loud show of piety, bawling out long psalms in Swedish or Finnish in the streets every afternoon. This gave way to a regime of violence, in which Gustav Horn's army descended on the already impoverished city and plundered it to make up for arrears of pay. The northerners made off with almost everything that was not nailed or bolted down.

From a total of 80,000 in 1632, the population of Augsburg sank to less than 18,000 three years later. The missing 62,000 had wandered away, died of disease or fallen victim to the Swedes. One girl was unwise enough to watch the Swedes parading below the windows of her father's house, and was shot dead by a playful musketeer.

Gustavus was seldom satisfied with the town

59 The Swedish fortifications at Augsburg (Zeiler, 1643)

fortifications he found in Germany. He therefore made his quartermaster-general Frans de Traytorrens responsible for re-fortifying the cities of Stettin and Stralsund and their satellite strongholds (Ribnitz, Demmin, Neu-Brandenburg, Kolberg, Landsberg, Greifswald, Loitz, Wolgast, Anklam, Damm, Stargard and Küstrin). The next zone of fortifications, on the upper Oder and the Spree and the Havel, was strengthened by Olof Örnehufvud (Frankfurt, Crossen, Spandau, Brandenburg and Rathenow). The works in Franconia were largely the responsibility of Field-Marshal Horn.

In some places the Swedes built so ambitiously that they virtually created new fortresses. At Würzburg, Gustavus extended the ramparts of the Marienberg westwards along the citadel ridge and northwards down the steep slope facing the Main.

The 700 corpses from the fighting of October 1631 provided a convenient filling for the bastion of St Michael. Since much of the new work at Würzburg was in masonry the defences were not reasonably complete until August 1634.

Downstream at Mainz, Örnehufvud cast up three entrenched camps, and created the six-bastioned fortress-town of Gustavsburg on the left bank of the Main at its confluence with the Rhine. This *place royale* received its municipal charter in the name of Queen Christina in December 1633.

Both Gustavus and Traytorrens had a hand in the gigantic new works at Augsburg. The old town wall was strengthened with bastions and ravelins, and the whole was placed within an earthen envelope of twenty-two bastions.

The predominant influence on the design of

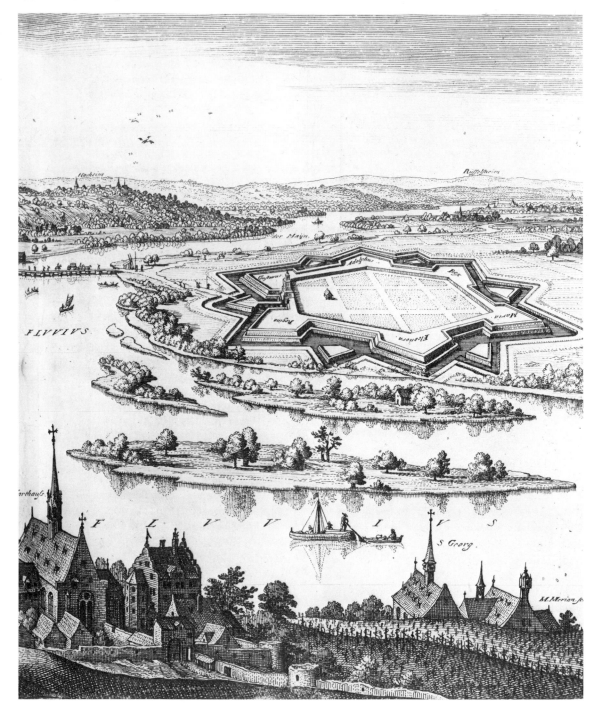

60   Fort Gustavusburg at Mainz (Merian, 1637)

Gustavus's fortifications was Dutch. Charles IX had sent Swedish officers to learn the art of war in Holland, and Gustavus was careful to keep up the tradition. According to Chancellor Oxenstierna he 'established the manner of Prince Maurice of Orange as the rule from the very beginning' (Generalstaben, 1936–8, IV, 312). Among the officers who received a practical training in Holland were Jacob de la Gardie, Nils Stiernsköld, Gustav Horn, Harald Stake, Lars Kagg and Gustav Lewenhaupt. In turn many Dutch officers served with the Swedish army, which strengthened the ties still further. The famous military and hydraulic engineer Simon Stevin probably visited Sweden in the course of his travels. His works were certainly widely read in that country, and his system of sluices was applied at Göteborg and Jönköping.

Olof Örnehufvud (1600–44) eventually assumed the leading place among the Swedish engineers. In his youth his outstanding talent for technical matters had brought him to the attention of Gustavus, who ordered the royal secretary Andreas Bureas to give him instruction in engineering and riding. Olof amply fulfilled his promise in the German wars. From the beginning of 1632 he functioned as acting quartermaster-general, and on 11 June 1635 Queen Christina confirmed him in this post with authority 'over all the fortifications'.

It was Örnehufvud who presided over the creation of the Swedish engineering corps. He won the engineer officers a recognised position in the state service in 1635, and six year later they achieved their final independence from the gunners and were brigaded together under Örnehufvud as quartermaster-general. Örnehufvud died in the Scanian campaign of 1644, as one of the many victims of the epidemic which was sweeping through Horn's army. His work was continued by the energetic Johan Andersson Lenoes, who was ennobled in 1646 under the name of Wärnschioldh, and held the office of quartermaster-general for the next three decades. During his administration the duties and conditions of the engineering service were first regulated, in the *Instruction* of 11 July 1653.

Gustavus did much to improve the efficiency of the artillery, the other technical arm. He brought the many private foundries of bronze ordnance under state supervision, and entrusted the manufacture of iron cannon to a closely-controlled private monopoly. By 1630 Sweden was self-sufficient in arms manufacture, and Gustavus could take to Germany an impressive siege train of two 48-pounders, six 36-pounders, and twenty-five 24-pounders. Paradoxically enough, Gustavus's ways of making war were so speedy that he never had the time to bring anything like this quantity of artillery to bear against a fortress. Monro comments:

Against either town or fort, I never did see in His Majesty's time one breach shot or entered, his fortune being such, and his diligence so great, that his enemies did ever parley before they would abide the fury of his cannon; as at Brandenburg, Demmin, Frankfurt, Mainz, Dönauworth, Augsburg and divers more; and in my opinion, the terror the cannon breeds is as much to be feared as the execution that follows (Monro, 1637, 211–12).

According to another British writer:

this was his order, mostly, in taking of a town: he would not stand entrenching and building redoubts at a mile's distance, but clap down with his army presently, about cannon-shot from it. There would he begin his approaches, get to their walls, batter, and storm presently: and if he saw the place were not by a running pull to be taken, he would not lose above five or six days before it, but rise and to another (Firth, 1921, 172).

The Danish catastrophe

'Torstensson's War' 1643–5

Denmark's intervention in the Thirty Years War was short and unhappy. As we have seen, in 1630 the Swedes assumed the role of the Protestant champion, and they threw back the Catholic forces from the Baltic and terrorised central Germany and the Imperial lands until the end of the war. With powerful and battle-hardened armies at hand, it was easy enough for the Swedes to deal with the Danes, who provoked them to war in 1643 by raising the Sound shipping tolls.

Turning aside for a moment from the war in Germany, Torstensson invaded Holstein from the south in December and overran all the province except the fortresses of Glückstadt and Krempe. Early in 1644 Horn broke into Scania and Halland, taking Helsingborg, Lund and Landskrona in rapid succession. Norway would have gone the same way but for the active viceroy Sehested, who reorganised the peasant militia and entrusted the frontier defence to the pastor Kjeld Stub, who was an amateur engineer. The Swedes paid this warlike priest the compliment of nicknaming him 'skansebyggeren', which sounds very rude to English ears but merely means 'the builder of fortifications'.

At the disastrous treaty of Brömsebro in 1645 the Danes had to yield the Baltic islands of Gotland and Ösel, the extensive Norwegian provinces of Jämtland and Härjedalen, and the province of Halland on the Scandinavian mainland immediately opposite Copenhagen. This last loss was the most significant of all, for the Swedes now had about ninety miles of westward-facing coastland to add to the wedge of territory they already owned at Älvsborg-Göteborg. Denmark's borders were placed in further peril through some of the provisions of the Peace of Munster in 1648, through which the Swedes acquired the bishoprics of Bremen and Verden on the left bank of the lower Elbe. The Swedes thereby

61   Storm of Frederiksodde, 23/24 October 1657. By Merian (1667) from a sketch by Dahlberg, it shows the great depth of a storming column

won a permanent base for the invasion of Holstein and the Jutish peninsula from the south.

The war of 1657–60

With exceeding foolishness the Danish National Assembly launched the kingdom on a war of revenge with Sweden in 1657. This fitted in only too well with the schemes of the ambitious new king of Sweden, Charles x Gustavus (1654–60), who aimed to secure the dominion of the Baltic. Using Bremen and Verden as the base for his offensive, Charles Gustavus by-passed Glückstadt and Krempe and struck deep into Jutland. The Danes withdrew their main forces to the islands, but left 6,000 men in the newly-rebuilt fortress of Frederiksodde (Bersodde, Fredericia) to guard the passage from Jutland across the Little Belt to the island of Fyn. The Swedes stormed into the place on the night of 23–4 October, and cut down one thousand of the defenders before the slaughter ceased.

The winter of 1657–8 froze the water around the Danish islands so hard that the Swedish career of conquest continued unchecked. In January 1658 an army of 10,000 boldly struck out from Jutland across the ice, using the islands of Brandsö, Fyn, Langeland, Laaland and Falster as stepping stones on the way to Sjaelland.

Copenhagen, on the far side of Sjaelland, was in no state to resist an attack from the landward side. 'The fortifications of the city were much decayed, partly through security [i.e., over-confidence], not having seen an enemy in a hundred years, partly through parsimony to avoid an expense supposed needless' (Manley, 1670, 7). However, King Frederick III of Denmark used the crisis as an opportunity to win the bourgeoisie over to his side and break the power of the nobles who had been mismanaging affairs since 1648. Thus Copenhagen was defended by enraged and determined citizens, and not just by dispirited mercenaries as was the case in most Danish fortresses.

The Swedish aggression had provoked a hostile response all over northern Europe, and on 29 October a Dutch fleet of seventy warships and supply vessels forced the Sound and got into Copenhagen. This reverse caused Charles Gustavus to turn the siege into a blockade.

The position of the Swedes in Denmark was becoming less and less tenable. They made a vain assault on Copenhagen on 10 February 1659, which cost them perhaps as many as 3,000 dead, and nine months later several thousand of their troops on Fyn had to capitulate to an allied army of Danes, Dutch, Poles, Brandenburgers and Austrians.

In Norway the erosion of the south-eastern border by the Swedes was finally halted by the resistance of Frederikshald (Halden), where the Danish-Norwegian forces had begun to fortify the Frederiksten rock. The Swedes raised the third and last of their sieges of this place on 22 February 1660, on hearing that Charles Gustavus had died of fever and frustration at Göteborg.

The Danish victories were purely defensive ones, and after they were deserted by their allies the Danes had to buy peace in May 1660 at a very high price indeed. They recognised the Swedes as masters of the Norwegian county of Baahuslen and the Danish provinces of Scania and Blekinge. In other words the lowland zone of the great Scandinavian peninsula had been yielded to the hereditary enemy, and the dominion of the Danes was confined to two widely-separated fragments of their former empire: the kingdom of Norway to the north, and the Jutish peninsula and the associated islands to the south.

Sweden's Polish adventure

The bloody work of earlier generations had given the Swedes the territories of Estonia, Livonia, West Pomerania and Bremen and Verden, all of which offered magnificent bases for intervening in the affairs of northern and eastern Europe. In the decade after the Thirty Years War Poland seemed to offer the most suitable target for further aggressions, for the central authority of this kingdom was weakened by a factious nobility, and the eastern borders were being overrun by Russians and Cossacks. Smolensk, the main bastion, fell to the Russians in 1654 after a three-month siege.

In 1655 Charles X Gustavus accordingly invaded Poland with an overwhelming force of 50,000 men. He entered Warsaw without opposition on 29 August, and found an arsenal full of artillery which had been assembled in the reign of the industrious Ladislaus IV (1632–48). At Cracow, in the south, the Poles put up a two-week resistance, then slipped away on 9 October.

The Swedes subsisted their garrisons in Poland by the same means they had employed in Germany in the Thirty Years War, and they might have planted themselves in the land for a whole generation if they had not provoked their hosts into an outburst of national and religious feeling. The monastery of Jasna Gora near Czestochowa repelled the heretics in a manner that was deemed miraculous, and in 1656 a general insurrection evicted the Swedes from southern and western Poland.

The Polish king John Casimir advanced on Warsaw in midsummer, undismayed by the fact that he had hardly any infantry or cannon at hand. He made the mounted nobles yield up their hordes of servants in order to fill up the storm columns which he repeatedly threw at the walls, and the garrison was so unnerved by the experience that it capitulated on 20 June. Warsaw fell to the enemy twice more: to the Swedes and their unwilling Brandenburger allies in the following month, and to the Transylvanians in 1657; but both of these alien occupations were short-lived, for the garrisons had to be withdrawn so as to check the ravages of the Poles in the open country.

By now Sweden had become type-cast as the 'bad man' of Europe, and for the next three generations the Swedish commanders had a very hard fight on their hands to maintain the provinces and the fortress-ports on the far side of the Baltic. In our period we see only the beginning of the struggle.

A combined army of Austrians and Poles reduced the Vistula fortress of Thorn in December 1658, after a prolonged and very noisy siege, and in August the next year the Austrians invaded Swedish Pomerania and laid siege to Stettin. Everything was made ready for a general storm, but on the day before the great event the Swedes sallied forth and destroyed all the siege material. The Imperialists marched disconsolately away.

The resistance of Stettin helped to earn the Swedes a reprieve, and in 1660 the peace settlement of Oliva maintained the integrity of their trans-Baltic empire. The Poles now had their hands free for the fight against Russia, and they campaigned

with fair success until an internal revolt and the growing danger from Turkey forced them to make peace at Andrusovo in 1667. The key border fortress of Smolensk was left in the possession of the Muscovites.

Military engineering in Poland
The Italian style of fortification seems to have been introduced to Poland by Simone Genga (c. 1530–96), who followed Stephen Batory from Transylvania to Poland after that gentleman had been elected king in 1575. Amongst other services, Simone is known to have assisted the Poles in the siege of Pskov in 1581, as well as building a fort on the lower Dvina in order to cut off the city of Riga from the sea. His countryman Bernardo Morando

62 Siege of the monastery at Czestochowa, 1655. The image of Our Lady, at the top right-hand corner, is revered as a relic of Polish nationhood (Bodenehr)

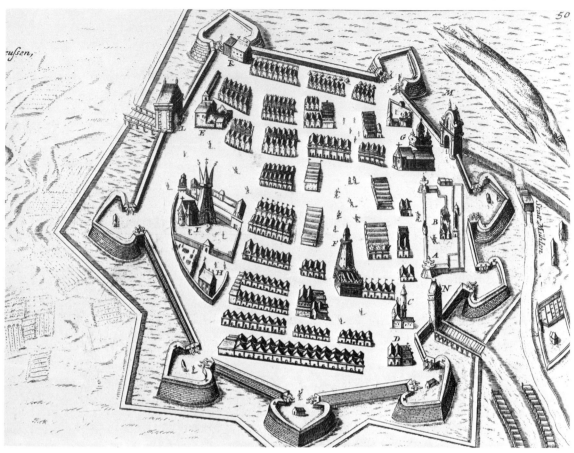

63 Zamosc (Bodenehr)

laid out the walls and town of Zamosc in modern style in 1578, and we also encounter a strong Italian influence in the fortifications at Grodno.

Where bastion fortification was most prolific was in the defensible country mansions which the great Polish magnates built from the middle decades of the seventeenth century onwards. In some places the 'civilian' buildings nestled inside a bastioned enceinte, as at Wisnicz or Łancut; elsewhere, as at Podhorce and Krzyztopor, the house was perched directly on top of the fortifications in imitation of the Farnese Palace at Caprarola. These secular strongholds were rivalled, if not excelled, by the powerful bastioned enceinte which was built at the monastery of Jasna Gora ('Mountain of light') near Czestochowa in about 1650.

State fortresses assume a secondary role in Polish history. The French traveller Blondel observed in 1684 that

the Poles put all their resources into their armies, and shun almost all fortresses. There are just two strongholds which they regard as impregnable: namely, Vitebsk in Lithuania against the Russians, and Kamenets in Podolia against the Turks. But we in France would not hold them in anything like such high esteem. At the very most they are fit only to withstand *coups de main* (Blondel, 1684, 10).

Eight   The Sultan and his Enemies

It is a useful experiment to turn the map of the Euro-Asian land mass on its side, and view the terrain from the east. With the familiar shapes now lost, Europe appears as a mere appendix to a huge and gradually narrowing peninsula. When the sites of battles and sieges are marked on the ground, the quarrels of the Spanish, French, Dutch, Germans and Danes take on an almost peripheral character, and the eye is drawn more and more to the Turkish Empire, as the epicentre of shock waves whose furthest tremors may be traced as far as the Atlantic in one direction and Moghul India in the other.

In strategic terms we shall see the boundaries of this great central power move rapidly to their greatest extent in the sixteenth century, and then undergo a long series of irregular contractions and expansions from a perimeter of strategic equilibrium about 9,000 miles long, extending from southern Arabia to Egypt, then along the north African coast to the central Mediterranean, and north again through the Adriatic and the Balkans to the Danube basin in central Hungary. From Hungary the border swung eastwards in a gentle curve across the Carpathians and then down the Ukranian river lines to the Black Sea. On the far side of the Black Sea we take up the border again in the tangled mountains of Georgia and Armenia, and follow its return across the basin of the Tigris and Euphrates to the Arabian Desert and the Red Sea.

On some stretches of this huge border, such as the frontier with Persia, the Turks stood from the beginning in direct confrontation with a powerful enemy. More frequently, Turkey and its foes reached out towards each other across an intermediate zone of nomadic tribes or small kingdoms, which were eventually absorbed by one or other of the warring parties. This was the case in the wars with Austria, Poland and Russia. We begin, however, with a glance at the process by which the Turks eliminated the island strongholds which the impudent Venetians and Knights of St John had planted in the eastern Mediterranean, in some places within sight of the coast of Asiatic Turkey.

The eastern Mediterranean
The extraordinarily close relationship between fortress and galley in the Mediterranean has been comprehensively explored by J. F. Guilmartin. He shows that on the tactical level a galley could attack a shore defence by landing an assault party, or manoeuvring with its oars into a position from where it could use its powerful bow armament to the most telling effect. More often, however, galleys combined in large fleets to carry powerful expeditions to their targets. 'The manpower and armament of a besieging fleet's galleys were convertible. They could be used on land or at sea as the occasion demanded. This was a salient characteristic of war in the sixteenth-century Mediterranean' (Guilmartin, 1974, 77). The Ottoman galleys in particular were designed to transport siege artillery. When they served the defensive, galleys could back onto a beach hard under shore guns, like Barbarossa at Prevesa in

1543, or they could land relief forces at some unguarded cove. Suitable points for such a disembarkation were not easy to find on small islands.

In the realm of strategy, galleys proved to be extremely short-winded beasts. These slightly-built vessels were incapable of taking to the water at all in the winter, and during the summer campaigning season they had to keep putting into port to take on water and provisions for their large crews. This lack of sea-keeping ability confined offensive operations to short hops from one harbour to the next, and greatly diminished the effects of naval victories by making it impossible to maintain a blockade of a port.

From the Turkish point of view the eastern Mediterranean in particular was annoyingly cluttered with a constellation of hostile islands and harbours, from where Christian corsairs plagued the sea communications with Egypt and raided the mainland of the Levant. The Venetians had garrisons planted along the Dalmatian coast of the Adriatic, around the Morea (the southern half of Greece, below the Isthmus of Corinth), on the island of Crete and, from 1489, on the former kingdom of Cyprus. Bolder still, the Knights of St John were ensconced on Rhodes, just over ten miles from the mainland of Anatolia.

The credit for the survival of posts like these is due to the Italian mastery of the arts of defence and fortification. Without such a proficiency the scattered pinpoints of Christian power would have been lost before relief expeditions could arrive on the scene. Certainly geography and resources offered little enough help by themselves. For a start, the islands of the eastern Mediterranean were usually monocultures, specialising in the cultivation of the vine, and even such a large colony as Candia (on Crete) was incapable of supporting itself for more than a few months of the year. Then again, the settled population of the colonies was surprisingly small, and the regular garrisons were weaker still. In the great siege of 1522, for instance, Rhodes was held by just 180 Knights and 1,500 auxiliaries.

The work of routing out the infidels was first seriously undertaken by Sultan Suleiman the Lawgiver (rules 1520–66), the man who was going to push the boundaries of Turkey to their maximum tenable limit by conquering Aden, Baghdad, Tabriz, Rhodes, Belgrade and Temesvár.

The Turkish expansion was the natural product of a predatory society. Subject Christian peoples had to yield up children for the Sultan's service. Many of these folk became privileged slaves or minor officials, others were brought up as Janissaries (professional soldiers), while a few ended up as commanders and ministers of state. These men in their turn hoped to make their fortunes by advancing their master's borders still further. In this work they were given enthusiastic help by disreputable gunners, engineers and other renegades from the Christian West.

Suleiman did much to institutionalise the process. He expanded the corps of *Topdshis* (gunners) to a strength of 3,000, of whom three hundred were *Kumbadshi*, the Christian renegades who served the siege pieces. Likewise he regulated siege procedure and life in the trenches by his Janissary regulations, a code which stayed in force until the nineteenth century.

Rhodes was the first Christian possession in the Mediterranean to feel the new-found power of Suleiman's siege machine. He evicted the Knights of St John from the island in a mighty siege in 1522, and in the process he showed just how much effort and blood he was willing to expend in order to capture a single stronghold. The Turks launched twenty assaults and fired away 85,000 iron and stone shot, while the conscript pioneers from the Balkan provinces helped to throw up two immense siege cavaliers and dig no less than fifty-four mine tunnels.

The Venetians, when their turn came, were able to call on Spanish aid, and they managed to survive in the worst of Suleiman's amphibious offensives in the 1530s. In the peace of 1540 the Venetians had to cede their last surviving Morean fortresses, at Nauplia and Malvasia, but they retained Corfu, which had been defended with style and dash in 1537, together with Zante, Crete and Cyprus.

It is now time to take up again the story of the Knights of St John. In 1530 the Emperor Charles V presented them with the island of Malta, as a new fortress-home in place of Rhodes. The strategic importance of this rocky island was immense. Whereas Rhodes had been a peripheral point, a raiding base and a means of holding down a concentration of the Turkish fleet, Malta served the vital purpose of helping to constrict the central Mediterranean bottleneck between Sicily and Tunisia. Moreover the ports of Moslem north Africa were few and insecure, and as long as the Knights held Malta they denied the Turks a stepping-stone for the invasion of Sicily and southern Italy, and a useful staging-station on the way to the western Mediterranean.

Almost as soon as they entered into possession the Knights began to fortify the Grand Harbour on the north-east side of Malta, and in 1558 the newly-elected Grand Master Jean Parisot de la Vallette borrowed the gifted architect Bartolomeo Genga from the Duke of Urbino to help to complete the defences.

The works certainly needed every possible reinforcement, for Malta was situated close enough to Constantinople to permit the Ottomans to mount a major expedition. On 19 May 1565 the leading elements of no less than 30,000 Turks landed on Malta. On the next day the Turkish commander,

Grand Vizier Mustafa, made the fateful decision to begin the siege of the Grand Harbour works by attacking the isolated Fort St Elmo. He needed to gain this point if his expedition was to have the use of the convenient Marsamuscetto inlet. The objective was taken only on 23 June, after the Turks

had spent over thirty days in attempting to reduce the fort. It had cost them 18,000 rounds of cannon and basilisk shot, as well as the loss of some 6,000 men (Balbi, 1568, 91).

As Mustafa stood among the ruins and looked across the Grand Harbour he exclaimed: 'The son cost us dearly enough. What will be the price of the father?'

Moving around to the southern side of the Grand Harbour, the Turks cast up a great semi-circular trench around the landward fronts of the two fortified peninsulas that made up the main fortress. They then bludgeoned their way forward by alternating cannonades and assaults. On 15 July a particularly ambitious land and naval attack was beaten off, but this reverse did not deter them from

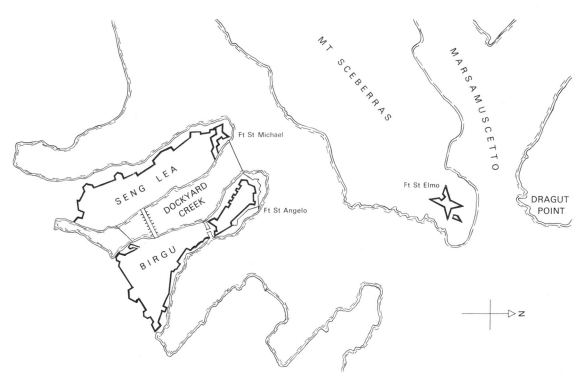

64   The Grand Harbour at Malta, 1565

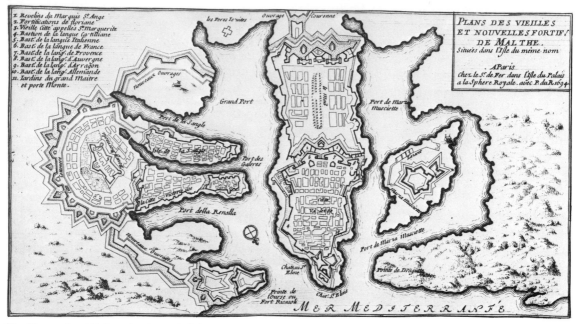

65   The works at Valletta by the end of the seventeenth century

throwing in further storms on 2, 7 and 21 August, which won them a number of lodgments in the ramparts.

The siege was proving excessively strenuous and bloody, even by Turkish standards, and Mustafa's resolution finally broke when the Spanish viceroy of Sicily landed 8,500 troops in Mellieha Bay in the north of the island. The Turks at once abandoned the batteries, and their last vessel left Malta on 9 September. The achievement of the splendid veteran La Vallette and his men were applauded as far away as heretical England, where Queen Elizabeth had written that 'if the Turks should prevail against the isle of Malta, it is uncertain what further peril might follow to the rest of Christendom'.

The siege capabilities of sixteenth-century Turkey were so formidable that they provoked an epidemic of fortress-building all over the Christian Mediterranean. The Knights of Malta had been lucky to survive the siege of 1565, and almost all the sovereigns of Europe promised help in one form or another to enable them to cover or neutralise the high ground which dominated the existing defences.

Working from the rough ideas of La Vallette, the chief papal engineer Francesco Laparelli planned to enclose the landward end of the Sceberras peninsula by a line of four bastions. The foundation stone was laid on 28 March 1566, and by 1571 the fortifications were so advanced that the headquarters of the Order was moved to the new town of Valletta, which was built on Sceberras ridge behind the protection of the new line.

The Christian fortifications in the Mediterranean were all the more imposing for having been built during the great age of Italian military engineering. In 1538 Michele di Sanmicheli was sent by the Venetian Senate to view the fortifications of Crete, where he designed the new enceinte of Candia. Isolated bastions in Sanmicheli's style are to be found at the other Cretan fortresses of Canea and Rettimo, though the master was so busy that he had to delegate most of the work to his assistants. He was fortunate to find an able pupil in his nephew Gian Girolamo, who 'thus became so proficient that he could be trusted to carry out any difficult project of fortification, an art of which he was very fond' (Vasari, 1550, part III).

Gian Girolamo skilfully interpreted the designs which his uncle drew up for the enlargement of Corfu, for the construction of the San Niccolo fortress at Sebenico, and for the extensive works at the Dalmatian fortress of Zara. Many of these strongholds were of the nature of colonial outposts, and so the Venetian engineers had to undertake works of civil engineering to support the local population. At Zara, for instance, the Sanmichelis built the famous cistern of Cinque Pozzi, where spring water and rainwater were filtered through sand, and stored in five inter-connecting underground reservoirs.

Three months' work in the heat of Cyprus killed off Gian Girolamo in 1558. Michele was shattered by the news, and he followed his nephew to the grave in 1559. Fortunately several gifted engineers were at hand to carry on the work, and Luigi Brugnoli, Gian Girolamo's brother-in-law, provided a strong element of family continuity. He had been working on the fortification of Famagusta during Gian Girolamo's last illness, and he had received a complete collection of designs from the dying man.

At Nicosia, the inland capital of Cyprus, things were in the hands of Giulio Savorgnano, who pulled down the old walls and made a three-mile enceinte on modern lines:

He fortified it with eleven bastions, set at equal distances in such a manner that each defended the other with its cannon. He chose as many of the best-qualified gentlemen: to every one of which he committed the care of carrying forward a bastion, and permitted them for a recompense to call them

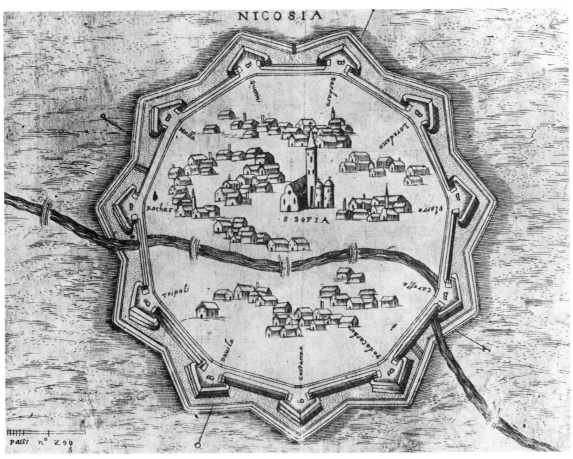

66 Nicosia

after their names. . . . This enterprise was prosecuted with such a diligence as surprised all people (Graziani in Cobham, 1899, 14).

All of Savorgnano's good work went for nothing after a host of 70,000 Turks descended on Cyprus in July 1570. His magnificent fortress at Nicosia fell to a storm on 8 September, largely owing to the insouciance of the Venetian commander and the Cypriot nobles; this left the ill-assorted fortifications of Famagusta on the east coast as the only bulwarks against the invaders.

The Turks camped around Famagusta during the winter, and they opened their formal siege of the place in mid-April 1571:

The ditches and shelters were so many, and so well arranged, that the whole army could be drawn up within, and though quite close to the city, every man would be under cover, buried as it were, out of sight among these mounds of earth, and anyone standing on the city walls would see nothing of the attacking force but the tops of their tents (Paruta in Cobham, 1895, 35–6).

The Venetian co-commanders Bragadino and Baglione put up a magnificent defence, but they were powerless to halt the mole-like advance of the Turks. The engineer Giovanni Mormori reports that;

having burrowed until they reached the level of the floor of the ditch, the enemy pierced a hole in the counterscarp revetment and threw out quantities of earth, little by little, until they had made a double traverse which extended to the rampart . . . they then entered the traverse with woolsacks and fascines, so as to protect themselves from the fire of our flanks (Promis, 1862, 120).

Techniques like this were as effective as anything the West had to show for the next century.

By the end of 157 days of 'open trenches' the defenders had run through their resources, and on 1 August the Venetians yielded Famagusta in return for a free evacuation. Four days later the Turks went back on their word and seized the wretched troops as galley slaves. Bragadino himself had his ears and nose cut off, and he was made to carry baskets of earth to help to repair the fortifications. 'At last he

was drawn into the market place, and being hung up by the heels like a sheep was flayed alive' (Graziani in Cobham, 1899, 17).

In this way the Turks added Cyprus to the list of offshore islands which they had conquered from the Christians. The issue was unaffected by the Western victory in the sea battle of Lepanto on 7 October 1571, for the Turks promptly fitted out a new force of galleys and held it as a 'fleet in being' in the fortified harbour of Modon in the Morea. Rather than risk further losses, Venice deserted her Spanish allies and made peace in 1573. The Venetians renounced Cyprus for good, and retained the important Ionian island of Zante only upon payment of a tribute.

The contest between Turkey and the Venetians was resumed three generations later, and it was going to last, with some intermissions, until the peace settlement of 1718.

Already in 1619 the Spanish envoy Don Alfonso reported to Philip III that the Turks were determined to destroy the Venetian seapower altogether, and that their blow would take the form of an attack on Crete,

for the possession of this island is the only means by which they may free themselves of the ravages of the Western pirates, for whom this island offers such a convenient refuge. Once masters of this important position, the Turks merely need to watch the channel which separates Crete from Zerigo in order to deny the access to the Archipelago to all hostile vessels (Zinkeisen, 1854–7, IV, 194–5).

The threat materialised in 1645, when 75,000 Turks under the renegade Mascovich descended on Crete. Thus the Venetians, much against their will, were plunged into a general Mediterranean war.

On the Venetian land frontier in Dalmatia the fight went unexpectedly well for the Republic, thanks to the energy and good sense of the General Proveditore Leonardo Foscolo and the help of the local townspeople and tribesmen. In 1647 the Turks besieged Sebenico, 'but were bravely repulsed by the valour of the inhabitants, the very women exceeding the imbecility of their sex' (Rycaut, 'Reign of the Sultan Ibrahim', 1679–80, 28). Foscolo retaliated in the following year by taking the powerful and important border fortress of Clissa. The Turkish threat to Spalatro and the coastlands was now considerably eased, and an uneventful stalemate lasted in Dalmatia until the end of the war. The Turks never attempted to launch anything in the nature of a major offensive, for the country was barren and studded with fortresses, and lay within easy reach of reinforcements from Venice.

The Venetians fared much worse on Crete itself, which was the last obstacle to the complete Turkish domination of the Levant seas, and, according to the commentator Framenti, 'the outer wall of all the states of the Mediterranean, and, indeed, Christendom's one bulwark against the Ottoman forces' (Zinkeisen, 1854–7, IV, 555). Canea succumbed in 1645, Rettimo went under in the next year, and in 1648 and 1649 Candia itself came under siege.

The best part of the next two decades was spent in a strange contest: while the Turks on Crete kept up the investment of Candia on the landward side, the Venetians resorted to a bold forward defence that was based upon a continual naval blockade of the Dardanelles. On 22 June 1657 the Captain General of the Sea, Mocenigo, threw back a Turkish squadron which attempted to escape from the Dardanelles, and he was prevented from penetrating the weakly-defended straits only by a lucky Turkish bomb which penetrated the magazine of his flagship and blew the craft to pieces.

The Grand Vizier Mehmed Köprülü took the hint, and in 1659 he set the men of the fleet to work on building two castles on the European side of the Dardanelles to complement the works which already stood on the Asiatic side. The two new castles were called Sedd el Bahr (Rampart of the Sea) and Kilid Bahr (Key of the Sea), and they were designed on a square plan, with round towers at the corners, and a continuous row of casemates running along the base of the towers and curtains. The architect, Mustafaaga, exacted building materials from the neighbouring villages, or at least expected fat bribes in lieu thereof, and even the Straits commander was moved to protest when this ferocious tribesman beat an innocent man to death. Mustafaaga simply replied: 'It has to be done'.

The sequel lies outside the view of the present work. There is space here only to mention the bare fact that the Turks took to the sea with more and more confidence over the following years, and that in 1669 they finally reduced Candia after the place had been subjected to the longest and most considerable siege of the wars between the Ottoman Empire and the West.

The western Mediterranean

At times the clash between the Christian and Moslem faiths seemed uncomfortably like a competition between rival piratical concerns. We have seen how the Christian forays in the Levant were answered by the Turkish attacks on the bases at Rhodes, Malta and Cyprus. It was therefore fitting that in the western Mediterranean the Barbary corsairs should keep up the good work by launching raids against the European islands and coastline.

In 1544 the Barbary adventurer Khaireddin (Barbarossa) devastated Elba and the coasts of Tuscany and Naples, and although the corsairs were never able to repeat the enterprise on quite the same scale, they managed to keep southern Europe in a state of alarm for centuries to come. Braudel, the historian of the Mediterranean, writes that

The Balearics, Corsica, Sicily and Sardinia . . . were literally fortresses under siege. The authorities had to make constant provision for their defence, constructing watch towers to give timely warning of the appearance of corsairs or suspicious-looking vessels, and building and rebuilding fortifications. The islands had to be equipped with artillery, whether the cannon were sent from the mainland, or their manufacture entrusted to local founders. . . . Finally, the islands had to be provided with garrisons and reinforcements to hold the coastline upon the approach of fine weather and with it the season for military operations. Spain did not find it altogether easy to hold Sardinia, or even to guarantee an island which lay as near as Minorca (Braudel, 1949, 121–2).

The states of the Christian Mediterranean met the danger in characteristic fashions. The Genoese had been great tower-builders ever since the distant days of their first commercial penetration of the eastern Mediterranean and the Black Sea, and now they applied the same means of defence closer at home. On Corsica the new generation of Genoese towers were designed on a circular trace which distinguished them from the older square towers which dominated the villages. One of the new works, a tower on Mortella Bay, became famous in history for putting up an impressive performance against a squadron of the Royal Navy in 1794, and thereby inspiring the British to build scores of imitative 'Martello Towers' along the shores of the British Isles in the 1800s.

The papacy naturally adopted a grander style, employing some of Italy's foremost architects to build the beautifully-dressed works at Civitavecchia, Ostia and the mouth of the Tiber. Just as typically, the Spaniards adopted vast schemes of defence which never seemed to reach completion. On Sicily, for example, the modernisation of the medieval enceinte of Catania was begun in 1541 and took sixty-six years to complete. Even Messina, the most important rallying-point of the Spanish galleys, was not satisfactorily fortified until the

1680s. In fact no systematic attempt was made to update Spain's Italian fortifications as a whole. As early as 1540 the Spaniards had renounced this extremely expensive course and shifted their resources from the land to the sea, preferring to build up a powerful galley fleet.

On the mainland of Spain Giambattista Antonelli set to work in the early 1570s, fortifying possible landing sites in Valencia and Granada with little towers. This programme too was never completed, partly because the danger from the Turks receded after 1577, but more especially because the attention of the Spaniards was forcibly drawn to their Atlantic coast, which came under English attack in the 1580s. In 1577 the Mediterranean still claimed 37 per cent of Spain's expenditure on fortification, but by 1611 this proportion had sunk to 17 per cent.

Meanwhile on the southern shore of the Mediterranean both the Christians and the Moslem corsairs were busy carving out enclaves at the expense of the native North American dynasties. The process had begun in the fifteenth century, when the Portuguese seized Ceuta and Tangier and the Spanish conquered Melilla. In the sixteenth century the

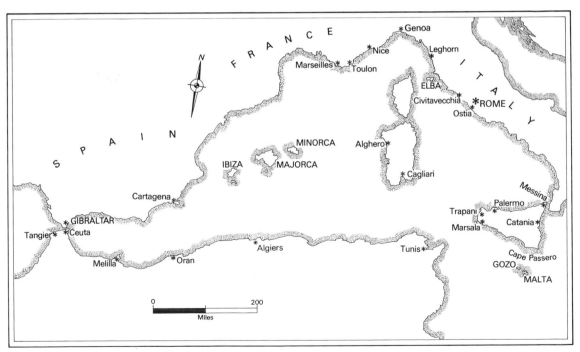

Western Mediterranean

Spaniards strode eastwards along the coast. They took Oran and neighbouring Mers-el-Kebir in 1509, and in the following year Tripoli was captured by Pedro Navarro and delivered by Charles V to the Knights of St John. Andrea Doria and a mixed force of Spanish, Portuguese and Genoese wrested Tunis and its harbour fort of Goletta from Khaireddin in 1534, and obligingly returned them to the native dynasty. This success helped to push Charles V into a disastrous expedition in 1541 against Algiers, which held the single remaining Turkish garrison on the Barbary Coast.

After the failure at Algiers only the megalomania of Don John of Austria could have persuaded the Spanish to come once more to the help of the native Tunisians in 1573. The Spanish duly expelled the Algerians from Tunis, and planted 4,000 Spanish and Italian troops in the Goletta. This precious force was lost when Oulodj Ali appeared with 20,000 Turks in 1574 and swamped both the Goletta and Tunis. Oulodj was greatly helped in his enterprise by a French-born engineer, who had been rescued by an Algerian galley while he was on his way to be tried by the Inquisition at Naples. His offence, a hideous one, was to have eaten meat on a day of abstinence.

Otherwise, Philip II of Spain renounced the policy of great expeditions, and busied himself instead with improving the works and administration of the Spanish fortifications on the Moroccan coast. Giambattista Antonelli laid down new plans for Mers-el-Kebir in the 1560s, and by the end of the century it formed a fortified complex with Oran, which made the position one of the strongest in the Mediterranean. The soldier and mason Diego Suárez rightly claimed that it was an architectural achievement which matched the Escorial.

The double fortress of Oran and Mers-el-Kebir also had the distinction of being the only enclave of Spanish North Africa which was to any degree self-supporting in produce. Little alleviation for the garrisons was provided by the ever-popular *razzias*, or plundering raids into the hinterland, for they were conducted as much for sport and personal profit as for the benefit of the troops.

In every way the Spanish investment on the far side of the Mediterranean was an expensive one. The distance from Europe made engineering work exceedingly costly, the doomed fort of Goletta setting the Spaniards back by 50,000 ducats in 1566, and double that quantity in the next year. Also the Spanish were compelled to maintain about 5,000 troops at all times in the North African garrisons. The force seems small enough at first sight, but it exceeded the garrisons of Naples and Sicily, and it cost as much as keeping up thirty galleys.

The strategic equilibrium of north Africa, as established in the 1570s, scarcely changed until the nineteenth century, when it was upset by the great punitive expeditions of the Western navies and the coming of the French. Meanwhile the unsuccessful Moslem sieges of the Spanish fortresses came to be accepted as almost annual events.

Confrontation on the Danube

In contrast with the complexity of Mediterranean affairs, the story of the wars on the Danube is simply that of the advance of the Turks up that great river to the frontiers of central Europe. In the process the Turks and Austrians came face to face, and people like the Hungarians and Transylvanians were reduced to the status of clients of the warring parties.

Two Turkish pushes were all that were needed to bring down the old buffer kingdom of Hungary-Bohemia. Suleiman opened hostilities in 1521, and reduced Belgrade by a characteristic process of blockade, cannonade, sapping, mining and assault. He moved forward again in 1526, and destroyed King Louis of Hungary and his faction-ridden army at Mohács on 29 August, whereupon the old kingdom of Hungary dissolved. Suleiman entered Ofen (Buda) without resistance on 10 September, and set up a puppet king. After this catastrophe Bohemia and the still-resisting portions of western Hungary took the only course open to them, and placed themselves under the rule of Anne, the late king's sister, and her husband Archduke Ferdinand of Austria.

By reducing Hungary the Turks as good as laid open the south-eastern flank of central Europe. The Danube offered them an avenue by way of Belgrade and Ofen to Austria, while there were tributaries which sprouted off in all kinds of tempting direc-

POLAND

CARPATHIAN MTS

Kamenets ✳   ⊞ Khotin

TRANSYLVANIA

Klausenburg ✳
Karlsburg ✳
Kronstadt ✳
Hermannstadt ✳

Grosswardein ✳

R. Maros

Arad ✳

Mehadia ✳

Orsova ⊛
Iron Gate
Widdin

R. Danube

WALLACHIA

R. Morava
Nissa ✳

BANAT OF TEMESVAR
Temesvar ✳

Szegedin ●

Zenta ⊠

Szalankemen ✳
Peterwardein ⊛
Semendria ●
✳⊞ BELGRADE

SERBIA

Kaschau ✳

Erlau ✳

R. Theiss

OFEN (BUDA) ✳

HUNGARY

Neutra ✳
Neuhäusel ✳
Komorn ✳
Gran ✳

R. Neutra
R. Waag

Leopoldstadt ✳

Raab ✳

AUSTRIA

R. Danube

VIENNA ✳

Graz ●

St Gotthard ⊠

Mohacs ⊠

R. Drava

Kanizsa ✳
Serinvár ✳

R. Raab
R. Mur

Warasdin ✳
R. Drava

CROATIA

R. Kulpa
Karlstadt ✳

Esseg ✳
Suleimān's Bridge

R. Drava

R. Sava

R. Bosna

BOSNIA

Travnik ✳

Gradisca ●
Banjaluka ✳

R. Verbas
R. Una

Land over 3000 ft
(1000 metres)

0   100
Miles

The theatre of war on the Danube

tions: on the left bank the Theiss snaked around and into the Principality of Transylvania, and on the right bank the regime of the Sava gave access to Bosnia, the hinterland of Venetian Dalmatia, and Croatia.

The single inconvenience was presented by the marshy-banked Drava, in western Hungary, a river which interfered with movement up the right bank of the Danube and led only to the Styrian Alps. Even Suleiman could not move mountains, but he managed to surmount the obstacle of the Drava by dint of building a 6,000-yard-long fortified wooden bridge across the marshes and river at Esseg. This very considerable feat of engineering earned the Turks a freedom of manoeuvre which was denied to the Austrians.

Hungarian roads are scarcely worth mentioning. In the summer the armies could move across the plains and the dried-up marshes with little difficulty. In the spring and autumn the tracks were bottomless and unusable. In the winter everyone stayed at home.

The western limit of effective Turkish campaigning was demonstrated surprisingly soon after the conquest of Hungary. In the autumn of 1529 Suleiman led an army of 125,000 Turks and Hungarians into Austria for the siege of Vienna. This was a very different affair from the attacks on Belgrade or Rhodes, for now Suleiman was acting at the end of an overstretched line of communications. The Turks effected several mine breaches in the thin and badly-maintained medieval wall at the Kärntnertor, on the southern side of the city, but the defenders had an entrenchment behind the breached enceinte, and they beat off a final despairing assault on 13 October. Starving and sickly, the Turks decamped two nights later.

The sporadic wars of the rest of the century merely confirmed how difficult it was for the rival armies to campaign at any great distance from their bases. Ferdinand was repelled from Esseg in 1537, and in 1541 the Austrian general Roggendorf made a vain attack on Buda, which was held by 2,500 hostile Hungarians. The Hungarians had been employing Italian condottieri and architects since medieval times, and the malcontents in Buda were greatly assisted by one Domenico da Bologna, who 'fortified

the city with bastions, and surrounded the walls with deep and wide ditches which were furnished with casemates and other rearward defences, such as you may see at Piacenza, Padua, Milan, Trevigli and many other fortresses in Italy' (Maggiorotti, 1933–9, II, 100).

Suleiman hastened up to the relief, drove away the Imperialists, and formally annexed Buda and the whole of occupied Hungary to the Turkish Empire. This was no more than a legal recognition of an already-existing strategic reality, for geography permitted the Turks to fight at a decided advantage in central Hungary. In 1540, for instance, the convenience of river transport enabled them to transport forty very heavy pieces to the attack on Gran; in 1552 thirty-six of the same guns were still serviceable, and were put to good use at the sieges of Erlau and Temesvár; these exploits left twenty-four cannon in a fit condition to fire, and they were straight away transported to Szolnok, where their arrival persuaded the garrison to surrender.

The Turks were prevented from consolidating their rule only because trouble broke out in the Principality of Transylvania, to the north-east, and because Suleiman, like most of the Turkish sultans, used to curtail his campaigning seasons on the approach of winter and go back all the way to Constantinople to manage political affairs.

On 1 May 1566 the seventy-two-year-old Suleiman left his capital to begin a fresh year's campaigning, but it was more than three months before he could arrive at his intended target, the provocatively-active fortress of Szigeth near the Drava. Suleiman died in his tent of natural causes on the night of 5–6 September, but his Grand Vizier wisely withheld the news from the army until the Turks reduced the place on 8 September.

Peace was made in 1568, and a calm settled over divided Hungary until the disreputable pair of Sultan Murad III and Grand Vizier Sinan re-opened hostilities in 1593. The Austrians countered by making an alliance with the Transylvanians, a move which endangered the whole right flank of Turkish Hungary, and compelled the Ottomans to make their main effort against the strategic corridor by which Austrian help could reach the Transylvanians. The situation is strongly reminiscent of the struggle that

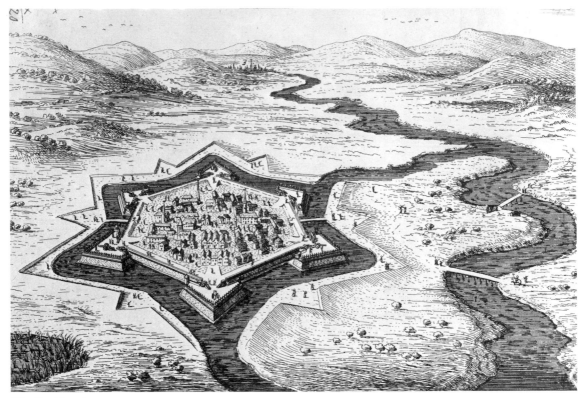

67   Neuhäusel

was taking place at the same time between the Spanish and Dutch for the area of the Ijssel.

Erlau, one of the 'corridor' fortresses, fell through the treachery of its mercenary garrison in 1596, though Grosswardein bravely repulsed the Turks two years later. The Turks could not attain a convincing military success, but they gradually detached the Transylvanian magnates from the Habsburgs, and in 1606 they forced Austria to conclude the disadvantageous Peace of Zitva-Torok. The Turks retained the border fortresses of Erlau, Gran, Kanizsa and Stühlweissenburg, and confined the Austrian holdings in Hungary to a forty-mile-wide strip running along its western frontier. Transylvania preserved an anarchical independence until the Turks invaded in 1613 and installed a sympathetic king.

The settlement of 1606 afforded the pitifully small remnant of Christian Hungary little respite. The countryside was devastated by the Turks in 1622,

while the Transylvanians swept in on three separate occasions (1623–4, 1626 and 1644–5).

With the extinction of Hungary as an independent power in the 1520s, the borders of Austria with the Turks became in effect the borders of Western Europe. Austria's existing system of defence in no way lived up to the new responsibilities that were placed upon it. Vienna was surrounded by a crumbling medieval wall, as we have seen, and the central government was so hard up that before the great siege of 1529 it had left the work of strengthening the place to the city fathers.

A much more far-reaching re-fortification of Vienna was carried out on a plan submitted by Count Nicholas von Salm and the Superintendent of Buildings Hermes Schallauzer on 13 January 1548. The eleven bastions were to be of brick, and they were designed on a rather crabbed Italian trace with angular orillons and narrow retired flanks. Significantly, the state now took a more direct interest in

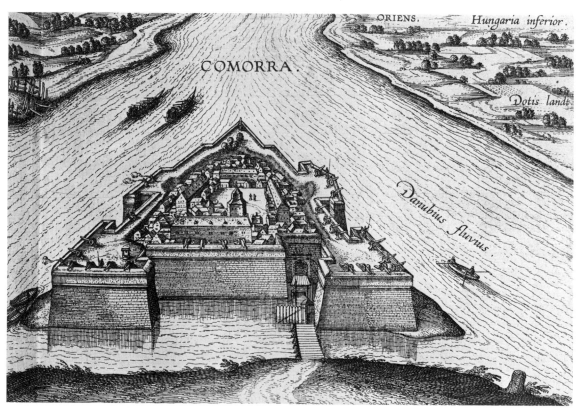

the proceedings, and the Treasury contributed half the cost of construction, which by 1560 already amounted to 600,000 florins.

Elsewhere along the Austrian frontier proper the defence rested upon castles or little fortified towns like Hainburg, Theben, Bruck-an-der-Leitha, Radkersburg, Leithaburg, Scharfeneck, Eichbüchel, Otten, Ebenstein and Kirschlag. Of these, only Hainburg, Bruck and Radkersburg were useful enough to survive as active posts into the seventeenth or eighteenth centuries. Long before then the military border had been pushed a short but vital distance beyond the political frontier of Austria.

North of the Danube we encounter the not particularly convincing line that was formed by the River Neutra with its fortresses of Neuhäusel and Neutra. It was fortunate for the Austrians that this was a roundabout route for the Turks to take, if they wished to pose a serious threat to Vienna.

On the south bank of the Danube the north-easternmost projections of the Alps funnelled the Turkish advance into a complex of marshes and winding water-courses. Among the artificial defences on this side, the fortress of Komorn occupied a supremely important position at the junction of the three waterways of the Danube, the Little Danube arm and the Neutra, and guarded the access to the enormous island of Grosse Schütt. If the Turks moved around the southern flank of the Grosse Schütt they would be stopped short by the stronghold of Raab, situated on the river of the same name, which was the most important of the south bank tributaries of the Danube in the frontier region. Behind the Raab a wide tract of marshes slid imperceptibly into the shallow and swampy Neusiedler See.

The Austrians assiduously re-fortified the region from the middle of the sixteenth century onwards, carrying out the works in a variety of styles. The designs for Raab were drawn up by Pietro Fer-

68 Komorn

rabosco (*c.* 1512–*c.* 69) and Bernardo Gaballio, and the construction was completed in 1564 under the aegis of Schallauzer. At the sister fortress of Komorn both Ferrabosco and the rabidly anti-Italian Daniel Speckle are known to have taken a hand in the building, which must have produced some interesting differences of opinion. The recruiting net was cast particularly widely by the Emperor Maximilian II (1564–76), who drew in such luminaries of the Italian engineering Renaissance as Francesco de'Marchi and Carlo Theti. The distinguished expert Cataneo is mentioned as having been in the Imperial service in 1583.

The major strongholds like Raab and Komorn were supplemented by eighty or so smaller 'official' fortresses, including many villages or small towns that were fortified in 'palanka' style with timber and earth.

In all of these places the western Hungarians did little more than go through the motions of providing for their own defence. The works were originally built and maintained from the proceeds of a tax upon labour and holdings of land. The field and fortress militia, or *miles nativus*, was raised by the same means. Unfortunately the Hungarian nobles were adept at placing all the burdens on the peasants, and in the last quarter of the sixteenth century it became evident that the Hungarians were unequal to safeguarding the major fortresses. The Archduchy of Austria therefore took over the maintenance of Raab, while Bohemia and Moravia jointly supported Komorn. Tactical considerations also played a part in bringing about a virtual military occupation of Hungary by the Imperialists. Komorn, like many other places, was held by an Austrian force 'which is esteemed to be more faithful than a Hungarian, who naturally love liberty and do not care to be long in garrison' (Journal of Jacob Richards, BM Stowe Mss 447). By 1662 there were 18,000 of the *miles extraneus, Germanus* in the Hungarian strongholds.

Where the Hungarian spirit of self-help was most evident was in the private strongholds of the Hungarian nobility. Some of these places owned extensive perimeters on a bastion trace, and were well-adapted to a variety of sites, from the high Burgenland crag of the Esterhazy castle of Forchtenstein, to the Danube bank above Pressburg where Count Traun had his palace of Petronell.

A different organisation was adopted along the right flank of Austria's border, from the middle Drava and the middle Sava to the mountains above the Adriatic. With official encouragement, many Serbian and German refugees from the Turks settled in the area and accepted lands and various privileges in return for the obligation of military service. By 1552, in the words of Nicholas Zriny, the region of the Windischland had become the 'outer rampart' of Styria and therefore of all the Hereditary Lands. In 1578 the Brucker Libell gave the settlements of this *Militärgrenze* an organised form, and at the same time the noble assemblies of Styria, Carinthia and Carniola clubbed together to pay for the building of the fortress of Carlstadt on the River Kulpa.

The outermost line of this 'Croatian' border was secured against plague-ridden travellers and the penetration of bands by means of a long chain of timber watch-towers (*Tschardaken*), which were supplemented at intervals by small forts of earth.

Russia's steppe frontier

Russia eventually became the nearest and most dangerous of Turkey's enemies, yet in the sixteenth century those two powers had hardly begun to feel out to each other, and were still separated by hundreds of miles of steppe and forest. In so far as Turkey and Muscovy came into conflict, it was occasionally and indirectly, when one party or another incited the wandering peoples of the intermediate zone, the Tartars and the Cossacks.

The Cossacks sprang from the Christian outlaws, hunters and fishermen who had found refuge on the lower reaches of the great Ukrainian rivers. The most important of their settlements was represented by the Sech (stronghold) of Zaporozhe, which was founded by the Starosta (Elder) Dmitri Vishnevetsky in 1557 on an island of the Dnieper below the great rapids. In the 1570s Poland and Muscovy began to subsidise the more biddable of these Cossacks as 'registered' men, and from this time the defensive organisation of the Ukraine took on a faint resemblance to the Austrian *Militärgrenze*, which proceeded from the same principle of setting up intermediate peoples as a buffer against the Turks.

However, the Cossacks and Tartars were hardly the most responsive instruments of policy, and their tangled affairs were complicated still further by the rivalry between Muscovite and Pole. In 1512 the Poles had gone so far as to bribe a Tartar faction to make a raid on Moscow, and until the 1620s the 'registered' Cossacks tended to look to the Poles rather than the Russians for their powder, shot and cash.

In the sixteenth century the Muscovites certainly owed their eastern and southern expansion almost entirely to their own efforts. For generations any move of the sort had been blocked by the hostile Tartar Khanate of Kazan, which had been founded in 1438 on the Volga 420 miles due east of Moscow. In successive campaigns the Muscovites had clawed their way along the Volga, but they were always checked short of their goal, and had to be content with establishing fortress-depôts along the river. Thus the fortress of Vasilsursk, 160 miles upstream from Kazan, was founded in 1523. Likewise Ivan the Terrible was repulsed from Kazan in 1550, but on the retreat managed to plant the depôt of Sviyazhsk, just fifteen miles short of the Tartar fortress.

This cumulative strategy laid the foundation of the great siege of 1552, when Kazan fell to a Russian army of 50,000 men and 150 guns (see pp. 172–3). The strategic importance of the conquest of Kazan was of the first order, for it opened to Russian trading and military penetration the routes to Siberia, India, Persia and Azerbaidzhan. The speed with which the Russians exploited the opportunity is illustrated by the fact that as early as 1556 they annexed Astrakhan, which was sited almost one thousand miles down the Volga from Kazan, and about fifty miles from the Caspian Sea. The Turks saw that it was important to do something drastic to stay the Russian progress, and in 1569 they sent 30,000 troops to help the Crimean Tartars to retake Astrakhan. The garrison repelled every attack, and only 7,000 Turks survived to return home.

These deep and narrow advances down the great rivers were supplemented by a characteristically Russian system of linear defence, the Cherta (border). The Cherta was designed to protect the zones of settlement, and it consisted of chains of wooden watch-towers, forts and fortified towns, which were linked by lines of ditches, palisades or abatis. Wherever possible the line made use of such natural obstacles as rivers, marshes, lakes and woods. The authorities prohibited the felling of forests in such border areas, for they served to hide the people in time of danger.

The Cherta underwent its first significant expansion in the middle of the sixteenth century, when Ivan the Terrible reinforced the old Tula line, then built a new defensive curtain which extended about 700 miles from Novgorod-Severskii to the Volga by way of Putivl, Rilsk, Orel, Novosil, Ryazhsk, Shatsk and Alatir. By Western European standards the line was extremely weak, but it was usually quite adequate for the task of containing people like the Tartars, who shrank from any kind of formal siege.

Towards the end of the sixteenth century the Muscovite state and all its institutions were disrupted by anarchy and foreign invasions. Ivan's Cherta sank into decay, and in 1591 the Tartar Khan Kazy-Girei broke through the line, by-passed Tula, and actually lay for a few days before Moscow. Tsar Boris Godunov thereupon turned his back on the Swedes and managed to drive the Tartars away, but he appreciated that he could not afford such dangerous diversions in the future. In 1592 Godunov repaired the existing Cherta, and over the following years he extended the border 150 miles south into the steppe by three stages, namely, the fortress groups of (1) Kromy, Livni and Elets; (2) Kursk, Oskol and Voronezh; and (3) Belgorod and Valuiki. Two special armies were assigned to defend the new lines.

The Cherta languished during the long wars against the Poles and Swedes, many of the works being ravaged in the period of Tartar raiding which lasted from 1606 to 1617. The frontier might well have collapsed altogether but for the assistance of Peter Sahaidachany, who was chief of the 'registered' Cossacks. In 1621, however, Sahaidachany was mortally wounded while rescuing the Polish army which the Turks had surrounded at Choczim, and in the next year the southern Russian settlements were ravaged by yet another Tartar raid. Moscow put the blame on the 'foolishness, neglig-

69　Cherta fortifications

ence, . . . imbecility and stupidity' of the Ukrainian voevods (Razin, 1963, III, 228).

In the late 1630s and in the 1640s the new Belgorod Cherta gave the border some degree of protection. This new line began at Akhtyrka in the west, and ran eastwards for 360 miles by way of Belgorod, Voronezh, and Kozlov to Tambov. The Belgorod Cherta represented an advance of only about eighty miles on the border of Godonov's time, but the forward defence was guaranteed by a frontier army which stood under united command, while in the rear a constellation of heavily-guarded towns secured the agricultural settlements. In 1637, for instance, no less than 13,991 troops are recorded as holding just eleven of the many towns along the Oka.

By conquering Astrakhan at the end of the sixteenth century the Muscovites had arrived at the shores of the Caspian, as we have seen, but the tsars were very slow to execute a parallel advance further to the west to the Black Sea. The Turks were careful to guard the exits of the great rivers, and at Azov, on the estuary of the Don, they held a fortress which for decades presented a barrier to Cossack penetration, while offering the Nogai Tartars a support for their raids into the Ukraine. The Turks were well aware that the mouth of the Don was just five days' good sailing from Constantinople, and they fortified Azov with a masonry wall of eleven towers, together with an interior ditch and earthen rampart. The garrison stood at 4,000 Janissaries.

The Don Cossacks could not afford to take the same detached view of the monstrous Azov establishment as did the Muscovites, and in 1637 they joined forces with their fellow Cossacks from the Dnieper and set about the siege.

The united force arrived before Azov on 21 April 1637, and the Cossacks made 'a great trench, and filled gabions with earth, and they sapped so close to the walls of the town on all sides that the combatants could throw stones at each other' (ibid., III, 232).

After several weeks the Cossacks, being poor people, ran through their resources, and they were delighted when Moscow sent help in the form of gunpowder, provisions, cash and the German engineer Meister Johann. At eight in the morning of 18 June 'Master Ivan' exploded a mine, and the Cossacks stormed into the fortress.

The Cossacks took care to hold their new conquest strongly garrisoned, and they built up the walls with earth-filled coffers. Azov gave them their entry to the Black Sea, and for five blessed years Russia as a whole was spared the depredations of the Crimean and Nogai Tartars. An embarrassed Moscow tried to explain to the Turks that the Cossacks had taken the place 'without the order of our Tsar' (ibid., III, 234).

In 1641 Azov successfully withstood a siege by some 60,000 Turks and Tartars, thanks largely to the skill of the Cossacks in counter-mining. However, the maintenance of a fortress was not the business of a semi-nomadic people, and the Cossacks naturally turned to the Russians for assistance. The rudimentary Muscovite state, feudal and beset by enemies, was quite incapable of taking on the responsibility, and the Russians had to advise their Cossack friends to abandon the place.

The Turks promptly re-occupied Azov and restored the demolished fortifications, and in 1661 Mehmed Köprülü and the Sultana Valide planted the new stronghold of Sedd-el-Islam nearby at the mouth of the Don. In later generations it was going to cost the Russians thousands of men and years of campaigning to win their way to the same Black Sea shores.

In marked contrast with the halting, almost unwilling push of the Russians to the south, parties of Muscovites and Cossacks staked out the tsar's claims eastwards in the earlier seventeenth century across 4,000 miles of Siberian steppe, forest and mountain in one of the most extraordinary territorial penetrations of history. The advance was consolidated by the establishing of a number of military or fur-trading posts which became the nuclei of future settlements: Tomsk in 1604, Kuznetsk in 1618, Eniseisk in 1619, and Yakutsk in 1632. Finally in 1639 the Cossack Moskvitin led a party to the Pacific.

In south-eastern Siberia the Russian activity in the basin of the Amur led to the founding of Irkutsk in 1652 and Nerchinsk in 1654, and brought about a period of friction with China which lasted until 1689 and the signing of the Treaty of Nerchinsk; this defined the Yablonovy Mountains as the border between the two empires. The almost inconceivably remote Pacific peninsula of Kamchatka was penetrated in 1697, which gave the tsar an outpost one-third of the way around the world from Moscow.

The Persian heretics

When Europe enjoyed a respite from Turkish pressure, it was often because the Sultan was engaged in war with Persia, which was ruled by the heretical dynasty of Sefavi.

The Persian theatre of war was dominated by the Pontine and Armenian mountains, which formed a rocky link between the southern shores of the Black Sea and the Caspian, and for decades the influence of physical geography reigned supreme over every other military consideration. Ambitious Turkish expeditions repeatedly captured such important strongpoints as Tabriz, Erzerum and Erivan, and the Turks just as often lost them again through the weakness of the fortifications and because it was difficult to support the garrisons at the end of long lines of communication.

The Turks finally undertook an extensive programme of fortress-building which gave some stability to the frontier. In 1579 they secured a fertile upland valley by constructing a city wall and castle at Kars. Three years later Ferhad, the seraskier (commander) in the wars against the Persians, rebuilt the works at Erivan on the upper Arras as a double castle sporting fifty-one towers and 2,478 loopholes. Lastly in 1585 the Grand Vizier Osman Pasha established the Turkish intention to stay in Tabriz, the Persian capital, by building a city wall in the extraordinarily short time of thirty-five days.

The three fortresses of Kars, Erivan and Tabriz placed the Turks in échelon in the heart of Persia, and in 1590 Shah Abbas had to accede to the Ottoman demands. By the end of the century, therefore, the Persians had been evicted from the mountains of Caucasia, and were thrown back to the

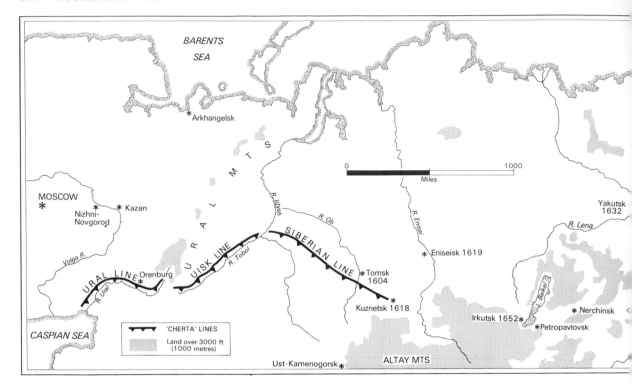

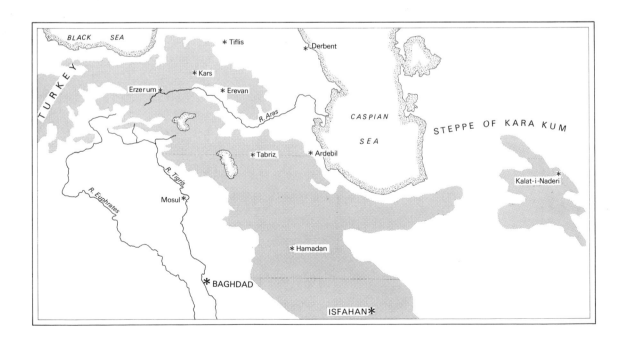

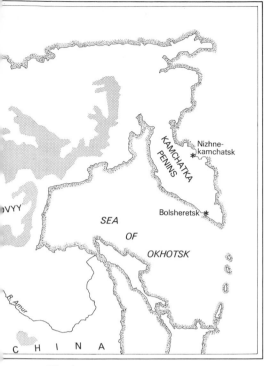

Siberia

Left Persia

southern shores of the Caspian and the basin of the Tigris and Euphrates.

This state of affairs was remedied by Shah Abbas (1587–1629), who was the last of the great men of the Sefavi dynasty. Between 1603 and 1607 he won back Tabriz, Erivan, Derbent, Tiflis and Kars, and in 1612 he forced the Turks to confirm his gains. Abbas proceeded to found a new capital, Isfahan, in a remote but fertile plain half-way between the Caspian and the Persian Gulf. The walls of mud brick extended for more than eleven miles, but even this perimeter proved to be far too cramped to accommodate the burgeoning population, which grew to 650,000 by the end of the century. Otherwise Persia owned no fortresses away from the borders with Turkey. The only element of security was provided by the feeble walls of the caravanserais, or way-stations.

Unfortunately Persia was still more subject than was Turkey to cycles of decline and revival – the product of the character of the ruler. Abbas died in 1629, and he was succeeded by a number of monarchs who lost ground heavily against the Turks.

In 1635 Sultan Murad took the field in person and began his career of re-conquest by taking Kars. He made further gains with the help of the wild mountaineers, who were used by the Turks to form a disorganised form of *Militärgrenze* against the Persians and Russians. Now that the way was clear, Murad marched in 1638 from Constantinople over the Anatolian mountains into the river plains, arriving after 196 days in front of Baghdad, the southern prop of the Persian Empire. The Turkish siegeworks rose 'like mountains amid clouds of dust' (Hammer, 1834–5, III, 182), and the artillery levelled the walls with the ground. The Turks then filled the ditches with boulders, palm-tree trunks and more than 300,000 sandbags, and subjected the ruins of the fortress to repeated assaults.

The Grand Vizier Tajjar was advancing sword in hand in the final, successful storm of 25 December when he was killed by a musket shot in the head. 'Oh Tajjar,' lamented Murad, 'you were worth more to me than a hundred fortresses like Baghdad!' (Hammer, 1834–5, III, 182). This admirable sentiment did not deter Murad from stipulating that

Persia had to make a formal cession of Baghdad in the peace settlement of 1639.

The increasingly decadent Sefavi dynasty died out at the end of the seventeenth century. It seems scarcely possible that one hundred years after the apparently irrevocable disasters of the 1630s Persia could have been capable of producing, in Nadir Shah, a man who was to become the terror of the whole of western Asia.

Turkish military engineering
The Turks prosecuted a remarkable and distinct style of military engineering, which endured with little change from the time of Suleiman the Lawgiver in the early sixteenth century to that of the mission of von Moltke three hundred years later.

Campaigning and logistics
The Turks were in the habit of making Constantinople the assembly-point for every year's campaigning (see p. 201); this added greatly to the difficulty of moving the Ottoman army to the scene of war. The wonder is that the Turks could find their way about at all, for few of their commanders could orientate themselves by a map until they were shown the position of Constantinople. They hauled a prodigious mass of material over these immense distances, for the soldiers were accustomed to enjoying tented camps, prompt and generous pay, and the support of a powerful artillery. As Montecucuccoli observed, 'their army is like a mobile fortress, which drags around with it everything that enables it to live and fight' (Silva, 1778, 24).

The Turks were slow to employ waggons on a large scale, and in Suleiman's time the equipment and supplies were carried on the backs of mules and camels. Camels, indeed, were cheaper to buy and feed than the wretched Turkish nags, and 22,000 of the savage creatures were used to transport the stocks of flour to the siege of Vienna in 1529. The camel, however, was of little use as a draught animal, and after the Turks introduced carts they had to have recourse to more powerful and expensive beasts like oxen and Wallachian horses.

The wheeled cannon carriage arrived in Turkey together with the Moorish and Jewish refugees from Spain, but the Ottoman version was so clumsy, with its wheels of barrel shape or of solid wood, that until at least the 1770s the Turks transported nearly all their ordnance on waggons:

They have no end of trouble when it comes to placing the barrels on the gun carriages and drawing them into the batteries – a period of delay which the enemy can put to good use (Tavannes, 1850, 283–4).

In view of these logistical problems, the Turks were usually content to reduce just one important fortress in each campaigning season. Beyond certain distances, the time which could be devoted to a siege decreased drastically with every score of miles which separated the army from Constantinople. If the commander was tempted to prolong his stay, he ran the risk of seeing his Tartar auxiliaries make off to their native steppes and his Janissaries break out in open mutiny. Thus the Turks were never more vulnerable than when they seemed to be most enterprising and dangerous, as before Vienna in 1529 and 1683.

The trench attack
The Turks conducted their sieges with shocking ruthlessness and energy. Gaspard de Tavannes explains how difficult it was to hold a fortress against an enemy of this kind:

Great numbers of men cover themselves with timbers and parapets, fill the ditches with earth, push forward earthen hills towards the town walls, and finally march to the assault with the least valuable troops in front. While fighting off these leading troops the defenders become weary with killing and their muskets are made unusable from excessive shooting – truly the Turks have learnt to extinguish fire with blood (Tavannes, 1850, 283–4).

On the mainland of Europe and Asia the Turks rarely bothered with the niceties of blockade and siege lines as they were carried on by the Christians. It was enough for the Tartars to infest the countryside around the chosen fortress and guard the rear of the army while it settled down to the siege.

In the sixteenth century the trench attack was very much the business and privilege of the Janissaries. Once the Sultan or Grand Vizier had made his reconnaissance and allotted the contingents to the various 'attacks', the Aga (chief) of the Janissaries led his men to the opening of the trenches with beating drums and flying colours. Sitting cross-legged, the Janissary proceeded to dig himself deeply and snugly into the ground. His trench was deeper and broader than its European counterpart, and in accordance with Suleiman's regulations it was furnished with two or three steps to enable him to fire his musket through the turf or sandbag embrasure of the parapet. He stayed night and day in the works, and when not on duty he dwelt in a tent-like circular shelter of branches and reeds, where he could enjoy at his ease the coffee and tobacco he purchased from roving cantinières. Food was brought to him regularly in great copper cauldrons.

The seventeenth century witnessed some departure from the strict letter of Suleiman's decrees. The original forty-day term of the Janissaries' duty in the trenches had proved quite adequate against the fortresses of the old Hungarian kingdom, but it fell very far short of the time needed to bring down places like Candia. The Ottomans therefore turned to the Christian provinces and hired large numbers of troops, who were granted privileges and plots of land by the Pashas in return for service as pioneers.

The Christian soldiers served the artillery in garrisons, they cleared the road for the army, and, according to Marsigli, 'during sieges they were employed in the trenches and other siege works. This earned them plenty of money, and attracted the jealousy of the Janissaries' (Marsigli, 1732, I, 86). Even the proud Spahis, or regular cavalrymen, were now called upon to make fascines and dig trenches – albeit with the help of their valets. The breakdown of specialisation became particularly noticeable after the siege of Candia, and by the 1680s the Turks were employing every kind of labour in their siegeworks, whether Janissaries, Spahis, irregular cavalry, Christian pioneers, slaves, artisans, soldier volunteers or forced or willing peasant workers.

At first sight nothing appeared more chaotic than the endless working and branching of the Turkish siegeworks. The trenches were certainly vulnerable to enfilade fire, and Marsigli claims that

the Turks have no idea how to avert this deficiency, for they lack experienced officers. The captains try to direct the works themselves, and they are fond of walking around with sticks in their hands in imitation of our engineers with their tracing fascines. However, they possess little experience in this kind of work, and they have laboured under a disadvantage ever since the officers who saw the siege of Candia have died off. Hence their approaches are almost always subject to enfilade. In addition they do not bother to level off the parapets of their siegeworks, and still less do they concern themselves about digging their trenches in a regular line (ibid., I, 140).

Nevertheless, the wanderings of the siegeworks grew out of a set plan. The formal attack began with the digging of the *Sigian-Jol*, an approach trench which was driven straight towards the fortress. From here the *Meteriz* (or parallels in Western parlance) were dug to right and left at frequent intervals. The batteries of cannon and mortars were sited behind the first one or two of these parallels, and the extremity of each trench curled to the rear in a *Joffek-Tabiesci*, or 'musket battery'. The danger of sorties grew as the successive parallels approached the fortress, and so the Turks prolonged the ends further and further to the rear until they met the 'musket batteries' of the parallels behind, giving the approaches a grid-iron pattern. By then the Turks would probably have delivered a good many assaults of their own. The parallels offered excellent jumping-off points for storms, and the Turkish troops and pioneers were adept at filling in ditches with causeways of fascines, sandbags or woolsacks.

The artillery attack

By the second half of the seventeenth century the Turks were falling behind the standards of Western Europe in the ways they used their artillery. They continued to site the guns behind the first parallels on natural or artificial hills, very much after the style

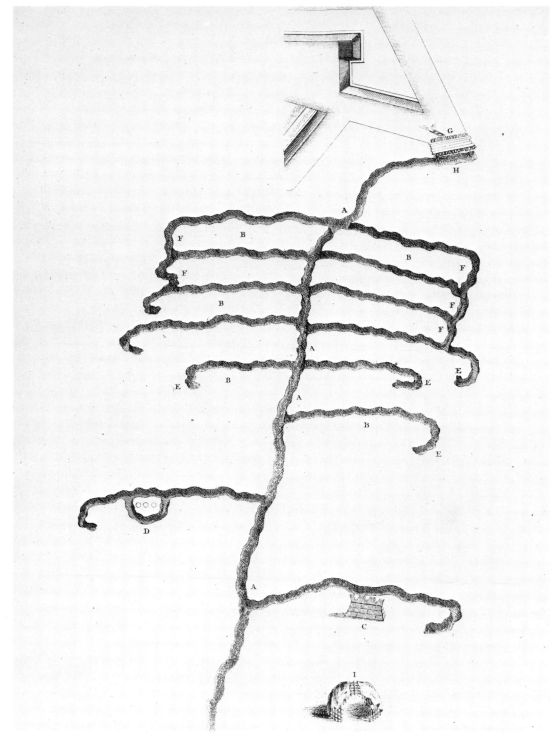

70 Turkish trench attack, with central approach trench and branching parallels

of the old European 'general batteries', and Marsigli notes that 'they seldom plant their batteries in the approaches ... on account of the difficulty of bringing the cannon across the maze of ditches and saps' (Marsigli, 1732, I, 140–1).

The Turkish siege guns kept up a continuous fire, which delighted the Turkish troops, but did little damage to the fortress apart from scouring the parapets. They had heavy guns, and plenty of them; and all the border fortresses were busy milling powder since saltpetre (normally the scarcest ingredient of gunpowder) was to be had in abundance from Egypt and by way of trade with the Christian countries. 'They have such a quantity of gunpowder,' wrote Montecuccoli, 'that they fire off more ammunition uselessly or capriciously than we do for essential purposes. . . . However, I must admit that their powder is excellent, as is evident from the noise of the discharge, and the velocity and range of the shot' (Montecucuccoli, 1735, II).

This is just about all that we can say in praise of the Turkish artillery. The renegade and native gunners were careless and ignorant, habitually overloading their badly-cast guns, and cheerfully firing a variety of shot from the same piece: if a cannon ball was obviously too small, it would be wrapped in sheepskin and fired off anyway. The heavy charges, solid wheels and massive carriages combined to wreck the planks of the gun platforms after a short period of firing, which militated against accuracy, as did the retention of the elevating wedge into the middle of the nineteenth century, long after it had been abandoned in the West in favour of screw elevation.

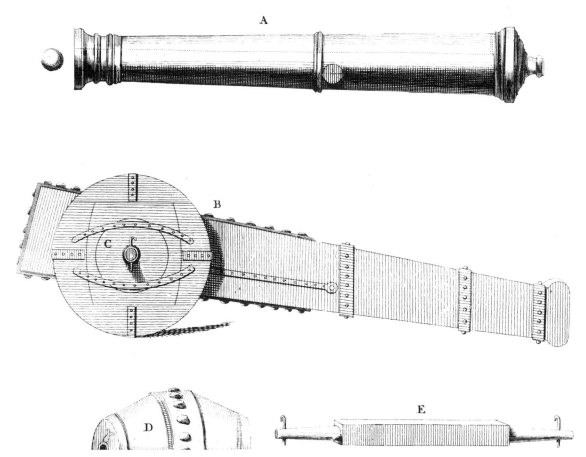

71 Turkish cannon and its massive carriage

The influence of the West was channelled through dog-eared textbooks, and by the agency of some able professional soldiers and a much larger number of fairly disreputable renegades. The age of the European 'great gonnes' was represented by the Hungarian and German founders of the middle of the fifteenth century who helped to cast bombards of the kind which reduced Constantinople in 1453. Tott saw some of these monster guns in the Dardanelles defences in 1770 and described them as being

all of brass, without trunnions or carriages, laid upon hollowed pieces of wood, with their breaches secured by large stones to prevent their recoil. A number of other pieces, lying in the sand, together with several mortars, seemed more like the ruins of a siege than preparations for a defence (Tott, 1786, II, 36).

One of these bombards, firing a massive stone ball, wreaked havoc on a British warship in 1807.

In the seventeenth century some modern cannon barrels were to be had by purchase from England, Sweden, Holland and France, in addition to the guns that were captured from the Austrians. However, the main influence felt in the domestic foundries was Italian, and in the early eighteenth century Marsigli saw a number of pieces which had been cast after the illustrations in Pietro Sardi's artillery manual.

Pasha Bonneval brought in some French ideas on the manufacture of artillery in the 1730s, and forty years later the French-educated Baron Tott made a train of field artillery by the very up-to-date technique of casting the barrels solid then boring them out. Tott made a present of Saint-Rémy's artillery treatise to Sultan Mustafa, who 'could only examine the plates, and these he had carried after him, when he went abroad, by one of his attendants' (ibid.). These few expert and dedicated men were no substitute for a proper school of native gunners, and all too often the Turks became the dupes of foot-loose charlatans. As Warnery remarked, 'in Turkey it is enough for you to be a European in order to be taken for an artillery expert' (Warnery, 1771, 93).

The Turks employed mortars in at least the same quantity as Western armies, usually in the form of great 'hanging' pieces of bronze. As always, the quality of the gunnery was appalling. Among the many stories of his life among the Turks, Baron Tott tells how a certain Pasha introduced him to a mosque-crier who had earned the reputation of being a skilled bombardier and engineer, even though one of his mortars had burst and killed seven people. Upon enquiry Tott discovered the muezzin did not know that he should have plugged the fuze-hole in the bomb by a fuze. 'This proves,' said the Pasha, 'that he wants but little to become an able technician' (Tott, 1786, II, 52).

The mine attack

The underground attack had always played a prominent part in Turkish sieges, and the Ottoman miners probably reached the peak of their efficiency in the half-century following the siege of Candia. Details of their methods were obtained by Marsigli from the Armenian masons who taught the art of mining at Constantinople. To his question as to how they began their operations, they replied that

in order to measure the distance to the rampart we intend to destroy, we get a skilful and enterprising miner to carry a stone and an attached string at night-time to the spot where we wish to open the gallery. He stays there, whether standing upright or lying on the ground, and throws the cord as far as the foot of the wall; he then cuts the string and pulls it back into the neighbouring entrenchment, where he measures it and thereby calculates the length of the mine gallery in feet (Marsigli, 1732, I, 37).

The gallery was kept on the correct line by the expedient of planting a peg on the surface above the entrance to the tunnel, and suspending therefrom a plumb line which was aligned with a candle placed at the working-face of the gallery.

The galleries were arch-shaped and only three or four feet high, which was very cramped by Western standards, but well-suited to the Turkish cross-legged attitude of working. The spoil was dumped on trays and drawn out by ropes. One of the masons told Marsigli that 'it was very awkward for them to load the mine in such a narrow gallery, but in compensation they could be pretty sure that the charge would work well, for they did not have such a large space to block up with the sandbags and woolsacks' (ibid., I, 37). The mine chambers were semi-circular in trace, and the powder was simply piled on a cloth which was spread out on the floor.

When the mine attack was begun in the actual ditch, the Turks sank a lodgment called 'the pigsty' (*Domus Damé*), and covered the entrance with beams and earth.

Fortification

It sometimes seemed as if the Turks were bent upon following their Tartar kinsmen, those people who were renowned among political philosophers for having dispensed with fortifications altogether. The once-powerful Byzantine fortresses of Adrianople, Philippopolis and Sofia were among the many places that the Turks converted into open towns by razing the walls. Marsigli explains that 'the Turks enjoyed a period of conquest and expanding imperial borders until the war of the 1680s, and they assumed that the various places they captured from time to time would be perfectly secure, from the simple fact that they were now in the Ottoman power. They never thought about providing for their defence' (ibid., I, 148). This comment does not apply to all the theatres of war, for as early as the sixteenth century the Turks had begun to build defensive systems along the borders with the Persians (see p. 207), and in the middle decades of the seventeenth century they constructed castles against the Venetians (see p. 197) and the Cossacks (see p. 207). These works had high masonry ramparts in the medieval or Byzantine style, and their construction was surrounded by age-old mumbo-jumbo: the architect himself had no authority over the works or the labourers until there arrived the Sultan's bag of red satin, which contained an inner wrapping of gold-embroidered handkerchiefs and an ebony folding ruler with silver hinges. Even then the work could not begin until the precise second of an hour appointed by an astrologer.

The borders with Austria were still studded with the ruinous strongholds of the old Hungarian kingdom. In 1573 the diarist Gerlach noted that even the most important of these places were in a decayed state, and more than a century later the Frenchman Blondel travelled on a diplomatic mission to Constantinople and was surprised to see that

Gran, Ofen and Belgrade were enclosed merely by simple walls, which were furnished with old-fashioned towers but lacked ditches and counter-scarps. I was still more astonished to find that Temesvár, which had withstood a great siege in times past, still possessed only an earthen rampart which was supported by an unflanked and partially decayed wattle revetment (Blondel, 1684, 7).

The needs of local defence in Turkish Hungary were met by the building of 'palankas', which were watch-towers, citadels or suburban enceintes of a distinctive wooden construction.

The smaller of these palankas were formed of a palisade perimeter and an external ditch. Larger palankas were impressive affairs, being made of a double stockade of stout tree trunks, with the interval filled with earth to form a walk-way. The stakes were held together against the push of the earth by heavy transverse timbers, the ends of which were pierced to receive large pins which pressed against the outer surfaces of the stockades. Circular towers were built at the corners of the palanka to mount a couple of cannon each. Szigeth, Temesvár and Kanizsa owned extensive works in palanka style, but most often the palankas were planted in open sites close to the villages and smaller towns.

The Austrian offensives at the end of the seventeenth century forced the Turks to mend their ways to some extent. Fortresses such as Belgrade suddenly sprouted retrenchments and bastioned works that were clearly designed by renegade Western architects, but it was still impossible for the native Turks to come to terms with European military engineering. They persisted in believing that their high, ruinous masonry walls offered excellent protection, and when Baron Tott tried to prove the contrary he was reduced to standing behind an earthen parapet of Western design and having a 36-pounder shot fired straight at him. The Turks enjoyed the performance, but they did not change their ways.

Kalai ou Fortexesle.

72   Turkish fortification in 'palanka' style

A European observer could still write in the 1820s:

With regard to the art of fortification among the Turks, little can be said in its praise. They have no idea of a regular system either of bastions or of lines, or outworks or covered ways, nor of conforming the height of the works to the nature of the ground in front. When we find anything of this kind in a Turkish fortress, we may be assured that it has been in the hands of some European power, by which it has been improved or originally constructed (Valentini, 1828, 53).

Turkish fieldworks were simple ditches dug three or four feet deep, with the earth thrown forward to form a parapet. An Austrian memorandum of 1787 noted that

the Janissaries plant their long swords on the summit of the parapet so as to have a rest upon which they can support and aim their muskets. As soon as one Janissary has fired, he makes way for another (Criste, 1904, Appendix VI, 276).

These trenches were very 'twentieth-century' in concept, and stood in striking contrast to the contemporary Western fieldworks, which had an elaborate trace of curtains and redans, and were built as high breastworks with *exterior* ditches.

The defence of Turkish fortresses

Turkish fortresses usually held infantry of all categories, but the core of the defence remained the Garrison Janissaries, a body which had been founded by Suleiman in order to hold vital fortresses like Belgrade, Cairo and Baghdad. The Garrison Janissaries already numbered 12,000 in 1519, and by the 1560s they reached a total of about 48,000. It was their particular responsibility to guard the keys of the fortresses, and they had regulations which determined how the gates were to be opened and shut.

In the course of time the Garrison Janissaries settled down to exercise civilian trades, and thus became completely identified with their fortress towns. Contemporaries could not agree as to whether it was a good idea to incorporate the Janissaries so closely with the townsfolk. According to Tott,

the permanence of the Turkish garrisons, by making each soldier an established citizen, furnishes him with too many interesting objects, which demand his care, for him to devote himself entirely to the defence of the citadel in which he is stationed (Tott, 1786, II, 37).

Count Kinsky, on the other hand, claimed that

when the Turk is fighting for his fortress he is also fighting for his fortune, for his goods and chattels, for his wife and children, and for his mosque. Although they have no idea of the art of defence, they put up a fierce resistance in their castles and fortresses, reposing their trust in their personal strength and bravery and in the number of their men (Kinsky, 1790, 46).

In any event the Turkish commandant had powerful motives for holding out a good deal longer than most European officers would have done in his place:

The moment he surrenders, his reign is at an end. From an absolute master, he becomes a slave, and is placed upon an equality with those over whose lives and properties he hitherto possessed unlimited power. If he retires by voluntary capitulation, he dare not flatter himself with finding indulgence or equitable judges. The silken cord, or kinschal, awaits him; for the Porte is accustomed to punish misfortune equally with incapacity (Valentini, 1828, 54–5).

The Sultan rarely stinted money to fill the magazines, and many Turkish fortresses were stocked up with a year's supply of coffee, raisins and figs as well as with simple basic foodstuffs and ammunition. Frugality remained one of the virtues of the Turkish soldier even amid this abundance. The Russian general Ushakov spoke in the early nineteenth century from bitter experience:

The economy of the Turks is quite astonishing. When necessary they can, like all Asiatics, subsist for twenty-four hours on the most meagre provisions – half a pound of bread, perhaps, or, when that is lacking, a handful of boiled rice or millet. And all of this without suffering any diminution in their strength. . . . The system of starving out fortresses by long blockades, however successful in Europe, will rarely produce the desired effect in Asia (Ushakov, 1838, II, 252).

Most Turkish fortresses owned a mass of artillery of the most diverse nationalities, ages and weights. The shot were piled up regardless of calibre, and the Turkish gunners picked out of the rusty heaps whatever missile took their fancy. They stuffed the cannon with as much powder as they would bear (and sometimes a little more), and the shot streaked from the muzzles with extraordinary velocity if no very great accuracy. Quite possibly the use of sub-calibre shot with ample wadding produced something of the effect of the modern armour-piercing discarding sabot. In 1828 a 12-pounder shot from the Turkish fortress of Braila was seen to drill clean through a nineteen-foot-thick Russian breastwork at six hundred paces.

Badly-protected magazines were scattered all over the fortress, to meet the heavy demands for ammunition, and in the excitement and haste the ground around the guns and between the batteries and the magazines became blackened with spilled gunpowder. A single spark or enemy bomb could produce fatal results. Conflagrations were also likely to break out in the wooden houses of the suburbs, which were packed against the inner towns like kindling. That is why the history of fortress warfare on the Eastern theatre is so often a tale of disastrous fires and exploding magazines in Turkish fortresses, or in fortresses which had been recently recovered by the Christians (Ofen 1686, the Acropolis 1687, Belgrade 1690, 1717 and 1789, Azov 1736, Ochakov 1737).

The fire from the Turkish wallpieces and beautifully-made muskets was probably more effective than that of the fortress artillery. Moltke wrote of the defence of Braila in 1828:

Every Turk, whether soldier or townsman, possesses a musket and provides his own ammunition. Since their houses afford them little protection anyway, all the males arrange themselves comfortably behind the parapet of the rampart and wait for suitable targets. This circumstance makes for a lively defence, particularly in the last stages of a siege (Moltke, 1845, 99).

Sorties were another Turkish speciality, and the troops were spurred on by a standing bounty on every severed head that was brought into the fortress. A Western besieger would be hard pressed if he had inexperienced or nervous troops, or failed to secure the flanks of his approaches.

Christian fortress warfare against the Turks

Like the Turks, the Western powers had to come to terms with the immense extent of the Eastern theatres of war. The Austrians usually had to traverse rather shorter distances than did the Russians, but this one advantage was offset by the difficulty which the Emperor used to experience in collecting his army in the first place. As Rycault put it,

though the Imperial forces united are of puissance sufficient to bid battle, and defiance to the numerous troops of the Ottoman power; yet in regard the union of that body depends on the assembly of Diets, treaties and long debates . . . the raising of such a formidable army becomes a matter always of time and difficulty (Rycaut, 1679–80, 75).

Another limitation on the Christian objectives was the extreme danger of undertaking a siege while an intact Turkish army was in the offing. An Austrian instruction explained in 1787 that

the Turkish cavalry commands the open field, which has the effect of restricting and hindering our movements, and interfering with the

forwarding of supplies. Indeed, we run the risk of being attacked or forced to give battle against our will, which may compel us to raise the siege. Whenever we wish to undertake a siege, we ought to finish with the fortress before the Turks take the field. The alternative is to wait until their armies have dispersed.

We encounter incredible difficulties in transporting a large artillery train through Turkish territory – both on account of the great distances we have to cover, and because of the soft ground, which produces bottomless roads as soon as the rain has fallen (Criste, 1904, Appendix VI, 281).

Montecuccoli had written much the same thing more than a century before, although he realistically gave a list of precautions which ought to be taken if the army happened to be caught in just such a position as has been described. He advised the commander to cover the siege by a strong circumvallation, and to make sure that he had enough supplies to carry on with the attack even if his communications were interrupted.

In some ways, however, it was easier to attack a Turkish stronghold than a Western fortress. It was well worth attempting a bombardment, as we have seen, and if you resorted to formal attack your siege batteries could easily silence the guns in the small flanks of the Turkish towers and bastions.

The defence of a Christian fortress demanded unceasing vigilance against surprise assault. Depth of defence was everything, for the only hope of resisting the repeated storms was to put up an obstinate resistance at every obstacle from covered way to interior retrenchment.

The Turks did not employ systematic counter-battery fire, and thus the retired bastioned flanks on the sixteenth-century Italian model continued to give a good account of themselves on the Eastern theatre long after they had become outmoded in Western warfare. A prepared system of counter-mines was another useful asset. Sorties, however, were liable to be wrecked on the deep and complicated Turkish siege works, and even if the Christians managed to penetrate some distance they were in danger of being assailed from the rear by Janissaries who emerged from undetected foxholes.

The usages of war

Ottoman narratives reveal the odd fact that Turks spoke and sometimes acted in much the same way as the early cinema's conception of the wicked sheikh of Araby. We hear great talk of 'pigsties' (i.e., Christian fortifications), and of consigning 'Infidels' to the 'perpetual fires of Hell'. Thus, when prisoners were taken during a siege they were nearly always executed unless they could give some pleasing information. The Turkish Master of Ceremonies writes of the scene after the capture of the small fortress of Hainburg in 1683 that 'the severed heads were brought to the Grand Vizier and rolled before him in the dust. The living prisoners who came before him were also beheaded' (*Kara Mustafa*, 1960, 25).

In recalling such incidents we should remember that German merchants used to send barrels of Turks' heads as curiosities to the Leipzig Fair, and that hundreds of these grisly objects were displayed by the Venetians in their trenches before Koron in 1685. Martin Luther was just one of many men of God who urged the utmost ferocity against the Turks.

In these circumstances it was a dangerous business to make the first overture for a truce. The Turks paid some respect to a white flag, but very little to a trumpeter, and it was prudent in a Christian to send his message by way of a Turkish prisoner. Once talks got under way, however, relations became reasonably polite. The capitulations were arranged in the same fashion as between Christian powers, though it was useful to know that the Turks set great store by gaining the honours of war and being allowed to retain their silken wares. A capitulation was seldom dishonoured by the Turks, and an untypical episode like the breach of faith at Famagusta in 1571 may be countered by citing the Grand Vizier's exquisite courtesy to the garrison of Candia in 1669.

As happened in the colonial wars in North America, most of the worst barbarities were perpetrated by the indisciplined auxiliaries of the two sides. As the Turkish garrison and people came out of the Transylvanian fortress of Lipova on 11 June 1688 they were mercilessly despoiled by the 'Austrian' soldiery, some of the defenders being slit open in the search for gold that might have been swallowed. A Turkish account explains that

the German officers tried to prevent these violent deeds, but they could not get anyone to obey their orders. As I saw myself, the generals on horseback even shot down several men who had robbed and killed a Moslem. The others took no notice and carried on with their plundering ('*Osman Aǧa*, 1962, 29).

Nine   Fortress Warfare beyond the Seas

Trading forts and strategic bases

In 1482, in their search for a secure base for their trade in gold and slaves, the captains of the Portuguese King John II set up the factory-fort of São Jorge da Mina, or Elmina, on the Gold Coast of West Africa. At that date the fort represented the most remote of all the *feitoras*, or factories, the defensible trading compounds which the Portuguese had adapted from the Arab commercial posts and the *fondachi* of the medieval Italian merchants. In the Portuguese version, trading and war often went together.

Over the next century and a half the principal maritime nations of Western Europe were to make their commercial presence, or at least their naval power, felt in every warm ocean of the world. Except in Central and South America, the object of the Europeans was not so much to occupy territory as to control the routes and the entrepôts of trade.

The thinly-spread presence of the Europeans could hardly have been supported without the help of their factory-forts, where they could refit and replenish their ships and stores and trade their goods. As the indispensable prop of the early colonial empires, the factory-fort is worth at least as close an examination as the vessels, the maps and the navigational techniques which enabled Europeans to reach those exotic shores in the first place.

African and Eastern waters

The colonial powers owed a great deal to the example of the first two viceroys of the Portuguese Indies: Francisco d'Almeida and Afonso d'Alboquerque. The Portuguese had been quick to exploit the new path to the spices of the East which was opened up after Dias rounded the Capes of Good Hope and Agulhas in 1487. Eleven years later Vasco da Gama reached the Malabar (south-western) coast of India in search of 'Christians and spices', and in the 1500s the Portuguese sent out armed expeditions which defeated the fleets of the Egyptian and Indian princes, and established fortified naval and commercial bases around the shores of the western Indian Ocean.

Distant fortress-building of this kind was something of a novelty, and d'Alboquerque sometimes had to plant these strongholds in the face of the opposition of his own captains, as happened at Ormuz in 1507 and Goa in 1510. Inevitably, the native rulers subjected the new forts to periodic attacks, for they rightly believed that the masonry walls signified that the Portuguese intended to stay on their shores for good. D'Alboquerque triumphed over all these hostile influences, and he could begin to issue licences to approved local shipping – another weapon of commercial mastery which was going to be copied by other powers.

The Portuguese ruled their establishments in the Indies and East Africa from the Malabar island of Goa. This place was already known as a busy shipping-centre and the focus of the Arab horse trade with India, and immediately after he took possession in 1510 d'Alboquerque worked night and day on the fortifications so as to protect his prize against the Sultan of Bijapur:

> Within the fortress he ordered them to lay the foundations of some very large store rooms, in order that in them he might collect every year large quantities of corn and rice, that from these might be victualled all the other fortresses and all the fleets of India, making preparations that there all the business of India should be carried out (Dalboquerque, 1875–84, II, 101–2).

Elsewhere on the coasts of India the Portuguese held Diu and Damão (on either side of the Gulf of Cambay), Mangalore, Cannanore, Cranganur, Cochin and Coulão (on the Malabar Coast), and Negapatam and São Tomé (around the corner on the Coromandel Coast). The posts of Manar Island, Colombo and Galle secured the western coast of Ceylon.

Malacca stood on the straits of the same name between Malaya and Sumatra, and was the foundation of Portugal's enterprises in the Far East. D'Alboquerque had come there in 1511 and built a

fort out of old tombstones in order to hold the place in 'subjection to our dominion' (ibid., III, 119). In the second decade of the century the Portuguese sailed from this port to China, and rounded Borneo and Celebes to reach the fabled Moluccas, or Spice Islands. A first factory on the clove island of Ternate was supplemented in the 1560s and 1570s by further posts on Amboina and Tidore.

By coming to the Moluccas the Portuguese impinged on the sphere of influence of the Spanish, who occupied Manila in 1571 and made it the capital of their Philippines. From there the Manila Galleon began its annual run to Mexico in perfect safety: heretical ships rarely penetrated these eastern waters, and the terminals were anyway strongly secured by the city enceinte at Manila and the fort of San Diego at Acapulco. In the long run, however, the wars against the fierce tribesmen of the interior made the occupation of the Philippines an expensive business for the Spanish. In the later 1630s the Jesuit engineer Melchor de Vera laid out a fortress at Zamboanga in order to hold the Moros of Mindinao in check, but this useful base had to be abandoned in

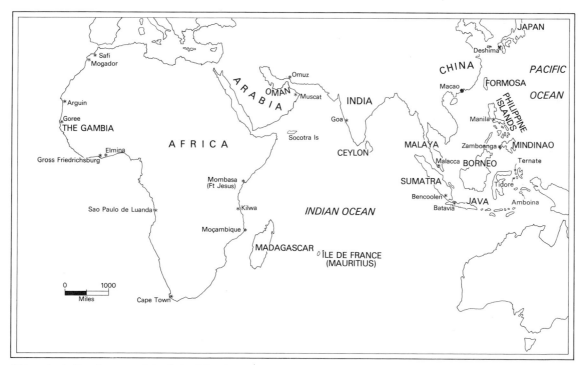

Africa, the Indian Ocean and the Spice Islands

1662 in the face of the danger from the Ming adventurer Koxinga (see p. 237).

True to the 'dog in the manger' aspect of their policy, the Portuguese had meanwhile been hard at work in the western half of the Indian Ocean, disrupting the trade of the Arabs by planting yet another series of fortified posts. Muscat and the island of Ormuz helped the Portuguese to seal off the Persian Gulf, and during its brief occupation Socotra island performed the same office for the mouth of the Red Sea.

The command of the ports of the 'Swahili Coast' of East Africa was however the decisive factor. Founded in 1507, the post on the narrow coral island of Moçambique became the main port of call between Portugal and the Indies, and the basis of commerce and strategy in East Africa. From 1558 the original works were replaced by a massive four-bastioned fortress built to the designs of Miguel d'Arruda.

Still in use to-day, the hulk of São Sebastião hovers in lonely fashion from its low white coral reef over the peacock sea. Within its walls were quarters for a thousand men, a gigantic cistern, a chapel; it was the most substantial Portuguese monument in the East (J. Duffy, 1959, 35).

A comparable gap along the west coast of Africa was filled in the 1560s, when the Portuguese planted the town and fort of São Paulo de Luanda, the foundation of the settlement of Angola.

During the sixteenth century the Portuguese colonial empire survived some very determined attacks from the resentful native powers. In 1558 Malacca braved the wrath of the Sultan of Aceh, who contrived to have cannon and four hundred gunners brought all the thousands of miles from Turkey. No less creditably the viceroy Luis de Ataide held Goa for two years of continuous blockade and siege between 1569 and 1571. Such was the superiority of Western forts and armament.

The decline of overseas Portugal proceeded from other causes. The support of the policy of far-flung bases and distant squadrons demanded too much from a population which in 1600 still numbered only one million and a quarter. As Sir Thomas Roe observed in 1613: 'Look at the Portuguese. In spite of all their fine settlements they are beggared by the maintenance of military forces; and even then their garrisons are only mediocre' (Hall, 1968, 247). Thus the entire 2,100-mile coastline of 'Portuguese' south-east Africa was held in 1600 by at the most four hundred white Portuguese. The vulnerability of the empire was exposed after the forcible union with Spain in 1580, which afforded the Portuguese little or no added protection and drew down the hostility of the Dutch, who were the most ambitious marine entrepreneurs of the time.

Amboina succumbed in 1605, as the first victim of the newly-founded Dutch East India Company, and the Portuguese presently lost all but the most strongly-fortified and deeply-rooted of their overseas possessions. The Dutch and their Javanese allies took Malacca by storm in January 1641, after an intermittent blockade which had begun in 1633. The Spanish-held fort of Quelang, a sugar entrepôt on Formosa, was taken by Van Diemen almost as an afterthought in 1642. By 1658 Ceylon and the lesser Portuguese posts in India had gone the same way. The vain attacks on Moçambique in 1604, 1607 and 1608 constituted the one notable Dutch setback.

Still in need of a port of call on the way to the Indies, 'Jan Company' established Cape Town in 1652 and so began the Dutch colonisation of South Africa. The French had already arrived in the same seas, but they had lost interest after they had made a vain attempt to plant a colony on Madagascar in 1642. The island was therefore left to come under the domination of the Merina tribe, which waged war against the other peoples from its long low fortified enclosures of laterite and cattle-dung.

In the eastern seas the Dutch replaced the Portuguese dominion by one of their own. Jan Pieterszoon Coen, a conscious empire-builder, occupied Batavia (Jakarta) on 30 May 1619, and built this small west Javan port into the centre of the Dutch fortified trading settlements throughout south-east Asia. Goods from the Indies were collected here during the year and sent to Holland under convoy every winter.

In the 1620s Batavia survived a serious onslaught by the Javan state of Mataram which, like the other native powers of the East Indies, knew how to employ muskets and cannon. Mataram remained an obstacle to Dutch expansion inland for the rest of the seventeenth century, but it destroyed itself in the succession wars of 1704–55 and left the way open for the Company to take over the whole island.

The English arrived comparatively late on the scene, and it was only by leave of the Moghuls that they founded a modest, almost cringing factory at Surat on the north-west coast of India in 1612. It took a violent provocation by the Portuguese to persuade the English Company to make an alliance with the Persians and go out to capture Ormuz in a joint siege in 1623. The English found the soldiers of Shah Abbas 'very ignorant of the right practice and proceeding in war', and the Persians clustered around the breach 'just as a swarm of bees upon a tree or bush that want a hive; or like a flock of sheep at a gap, where none is so hardy to enter, and the Portugals to put them out of that pain glean away four, five, six and sometimes more at a shot' (Monnox, 1930, 282). Ormuz was taken all the same.

Muscat, the last Portuguese foothold on the Persian Gulf, fell to the Imam of Oman in 1650. 'The Portuguese flanked them, from their forts on the mountains, with plenty of great and small shot; but the Arabs never looked back, nor minded the great numbers of their dead companions, but mounted the walls over the carcasses of their slain' (Hamilton, in Phillips, 1967, 46).

For the next half-century the Portuguese forts on the Swahili Coast were hemmed in on the sea side by the Omanis, who by now had learnt enough of European shipbuilding to become a formidable naval power, and on the land side by the ferocious Galla and Zimba tribes. Fort Jesus at Mombasa came under siege by the Omanis on 13 March 1696, and was taken by escalade on 13 December 1698, by when its garrison had been reduced to the governor, eight Portuguese, three Indians, three African women and a negro slave boy.

The Dutch ranged the South Atlantic as impudently as they did the Indian Ocean. They began to make inroads into the Portuguese colony of Brazil in 1630, and they held on there in the face of a patriotic rebellion until 1654. The need of slave labour for Brazil's plantations led the Dutch naturally on to capture Elmina in 1638, and this decisive breach in the Portuguese preserve of West Africa encouraged a rush into the region by the entrepreneurs of some of the most remote and chilly areas of Europe. The Swedes established their trading-fort of Carolusburg in 1655, but lost it nine years later to the English, who rebuilt the place in the 1670s as the headquarters of the Royal African Company. The Swedish move stirred the Danes into occupying the site of Christiansborg in 1661, and even the Duke of Kurland maintained a fort in the Gambia to provide slaves for his West Indian colony of Tortuga.

The Great Elector of Brandenburg was therefore only conforming to Baltic fashion when he staked out a claim of his own in 1682 and built the four-bastioned fort of Gross-Friedrichsburg. The Brandenburgers took possession of Arguin in 1685, but both this place and Gross-Friedrichsburg were ceded to the Dutch in 1718. The Prussians forgot their overseas ambitions until the later nineteenth century, when one of their military men could write:

The nation is once more showing a lively interest in the promising enterprises which the strong, purposeful statesmanship of our government is promoting in overseas territories. We are often reminded of the times when the flag of Brandenburg-Prussia fluttered over the ramparts of stately fortifications on the coast of West Africa (Anon., 1885, 99).

Central America and the West Indies
When the Spaniards conquered Central and South America they hardly ever engaged in fortress warfare, as the term would have been understood in Western Europe. The wretched, doomed Caribs put up no effective opposition when the Spanish planted the first of their West Indian settlements in the 1490s. At first sight we might have expected a more prolonged resistance from the Aztecs of Mexico or the Incas of the Peruvian Andes – expert stone-masons, whose huge, geometric constructions sometimes have a fortuitous resemblance to the bastioned fortifications of Europe. The Indians, however, did not actually live in the great temple enclosures. The houses of the city-dwellers were usually little more than adobe huts, and the bulk of

the population wandered from one temporary settlement to another in an endless search for new land to clear and cultivate.

Cortés' first entry into the Aztec capital of Tenochtitlán was unopposed, thanks largely to the awe in which Moctezuma stood of the pale, bearded strangers. The Aztecs finally rebelled and drove Cortés out, but the Spanish came on again in 1520, this time advancing down the canals on their *bergantines*, from which they battered the mud houses with their light cannon. The last resistance crumbled in 1521.

Pizarro, the conqueror of Peru, was fortunate to find the Incas in the throes of a civil war in 1533. The Indians made no attempt to occupy their fastness on the soaring crag of Sacsayhuamán, and the six hundred Spanish took the opportunity to occupy the open city of Cuzco which stretched below.

Following the example of their ancestors in the wars against the Moors, the first generation of Conquistadores consolidated their rule by establishing municipalities on the Castilian model. The towns were characteristically laid out on a grid-iron plan, as in the contemporary Italian textbooks on fortification, but defensive works were confined to the fortress-like churches, and the thick, loop-holed walls of the very earliest Spanish houses. The natives were being virtually annihilated by disease, and represented no threat to the Europeans.

It took alarming episodes like Sores's sack of Havana in 1555 to force the Spanish to look to the defence of their New World. In the 1560s Pedro Menéndez de Avilés, the governor of Cuba, worked out a strategy of armed convoys and fortified bases which was to endure for the next century and a half. Every year two fleets came out from Spain: the 'galleons' calling at Nombre de Dios on the Isthmus of Panama and at Cartagena in South America, while the *flota* made for Vera Cruz in New Spain (Mexico). The vessels spent the winter in the Caribbean, then joined up and took on supplies at the important naval base of Havana, on the north coast of Cuba. The homeward journey with their cargoes of gold, silver, dyestuffs and cocoa took them through the Florida Channel before the hurricane season arrived in high summer.

To support his convoys Menéndez built for-

tifications at Cartagena, Havana, and the harbour of San Juan on Puerto Rico, the easternmost of the major islands of the Spanish Indies. The Spanish government held true to the scheme long after Menéndez died in 1574. In the 1590s Antonelli was set to work on immense new fortifications at San Juan, as a windward station from where the Spanish could sweep at will down the chain of the Greater Antilles. The Moro Fort was built at about the same time to guard the entrance to Havana harbour, and in the 1640s the dockyards there constructed an entire battle squadron to defend the West Indies.

During the seventeenth century the Spanish lost the less tenable of their islands to expeditions of English, Dutch and French, and to freebooters of every nation and none. In the Lesser Antilles the 'English' island of Barbados was matched by the French settlements on Guadeloupe and Martinique. Off the shores of South America the Dutch captured Curaçao in 1634, and exploited to the full the island's potential for salt production and as a smuggling base. In 1655 an expedition from Cromwellian England was bold enough to take over the large but lightly-defended island of Jamaica 'in the very belly of all commerce' (Parry, 1966, 263). The French were playing for still higher stakes, and in 1697 they finally compelled the Spanish to recognise them as overlords of Saint-Domingue (Haiti), the western half of the island of Hispaniola.

The Spanish empire of the West Indies was now confined within more cramped but at the same time more defensible limits. Only very occasionally were the foundations of the old strategy shaken, as when Piet Heyn captured a *flota* in 1628 (and the Dutch used the proceeds to finance the conquest of Brazil), or in 1687 when the Frenchman de Pointis sacked Cartagena. Morgan's 'going respectable' was one sign that the old free-for-all was coming to an end, and in 1685 the English government sent out the first of its pirate-chasing squadrons. Towards the end of the seventeenth century the anarchy of the Caribbean was suppressed by international agreement, and the pirate and the smuggler, from being the spearheads of conquest, now became hunted outlaws.

(Forts in North America will be discussed in a further volume.)

The forts and their garrisons

Making a rather hazardous generalisation, we can say that the typical colonial fort was a rectangular, four-bastioned work which was built beside a harbour in order to protect trading, stores and shipping. There was seldom enough earth or room to spare for making outworks or a glacis, and the ramparts rose without a break from ground level to the summit of the masonry parapet.

The fort was weak by European standards, and indeed military considerations were not always paramount. In 1713, for instance, the Directors of the English East India Company could urge that it was inexpedient for Old Fort William at Calcutta to bear the appearance or even the name of a fortification, out of fear of offending the native rulers. Along the West African coast the forts of the rival trading companies were painted in dazzling washes, and were strung out prominently along the shoreline, touting for custom like so many gaily-painted stalls; triangular outer baileys were built on to many of these forts, less for additional defence than to provide pens for herding the slaves.

In time of siege the need to protect settlers and non-combatant natives could interfere seriously with the defence. In most cases the refugees simply crowded into the ditches or the courtyard of the fort, though in the West Indies the population preferred to take shelter in the 'deodands' (*dos d'ânes* = asses' backs), the fortified enclosures in the interior highlands, where goods and cattle could be collected in the same fashion as in the hill-forts of prehistoric Europe.

Circumstance and nationality could bring about many variations from our 'rectangular, four-bastioned fort'. The Portuguese were first upon the scene, and their works tell the full story of the evolution of fortification in the fifteenth and sixteenth centuries. The multi-storeyed keeps at Mogador, Safi, Calicut and Malacca were of decidedly medieval aspect, and only gradually did the Portuguese works come to reflect the Italian influence. The engineer Filippo Terzi was active in the Portuguese service in the 1570s, but the first major influx of Italian architects had to wait upon the Spanish annexation of 1580. Giovanni Batista Cairati of Milan was the most prominent of the newcomers, and in the thirteen years from 1583 until his death he served as *Arquitecto-mor* (Chief Architect) of the East Indies, working on Manar (Ceylon), Damão and Bassein (India), Malacca, Ormuz, Muscat and Mombasa.

The conquering Dutch could certainly build some uncommonly large and expensive fortifications – Fort Naarden at Negapatam was known with good reason as 'the castle with the golden walls'. On the whole, the Dutch nevertheless matched the extent of their fortifications very skilfully to their resources of manpower and money. Johann Saar explains that

whenever the Portuguese go to a foreign land, they mean to stay there for the rest of their days, never wishing to return to Portugal. But when a Dutchman comes to India he says to himself: 'When my six years are up, it's back to Holland!' For that reason he never bothers to build very much, whether in the country or the towns. Indeed, when the Dutch capture a fortress or town they usually cut off the landward-facing half of the place, while fortifying the seaward half very strongly, so that they may hold it with few men (Saars, 1672, 157).

As re-fortified by the Dutch in 1656, Colombo occupied only one-third of the space it had taken up under the Portuguese.

The workmanship and materials of colonial fortifications were subject to still more deviations than the design. In the West Indies there was ample labour on tap, whether it was made available through the imposition of the *corvée*, as in the French islands, or through the order of the Spanish governors, or by the vote of the English island assemblies. Fortress-building in Asia was commonly a more frustrating experience. In 1757 Captain Robert Barker resigned in exasperation at the difficulties he encountered at Old Fort William in Calcutta:

From want of regulation the coolies and people employed on the works have been found skulking in all holes and corners either sleeping, smoking or counting of cowries. Not above one-third of the people employed really work, so that the Company are at a terrible expense (Sandes, 1933–5, I, 104).

A great deal depended upon the prevailing style of

local building. In Bengal the native huts were of mud, and the few bricklayers were accustomed only to the small and flat Indian bricks and were ignorant of European methods of bonding.

For their Fort of San Marcos at St Augustine in Florida the Spanish made use of a stone of marine origin called *coquina*, which was easy to work, yet stood up well to weather, and, as an English besieger grumbled in 1702, absorbed cannon balls 'as though you would stick a knife into cheese' (Conly, 1966, 221). A well-behaved stone like this was very much an exception, and all the colonial powers at some time or other copied the early Portuguese practice of shipping masonry from the homeland to the building-site as ballast. Thus the West African fort of Gross-Friedrichsburg came to be built of the unlikely materials of stone and lime which had been carried all the way from Königsberg in East Prussia.

Fortress construction was usually financed from both central and local resources. The French and Dutch, followed by the English East India Company, levied taxes on the native peoples as some return for the security and opportunities for trade which they enjoyed. The Iberian powers were less immediately commercially-minded, but the Portuguese sometimes imposed a small customs surcharge for the upkeep of fortifications.

Gun carriages and iron barrels deteriorated rapidly in the tropical coastlands, and the ground around many forts was littered with unserviceable cannon which had been simply heaved over the ramparts. Home governments, and especially the English, were liable to meet calls for armament by emptying their arsenals of their most obsolete pieces. The Spanish and Portuguese were probably still worse off, for the production of artillery in the homelands came nowhere near the requirements, and the import of cannon from the Netherlands was disrupted by the Eighty Years War. In the first half of the seventeenth century the Portuguese sought to meet the demand by establishing a foundry for the Indies at Macao. The Dutch had a similar arsenal in their Japanese factory at Hirado, which turned out rather bad pieces with the help of local labour. The other Dutch colonial foundry, at Batavia, had to be moved inside the castle walls because it was 'too close to the view of all and sundry, and in particular

the natives and Javanese, from whom this art should certainly be kept secret' (Boxer, 1936, 27).

The colonial powers organised their garrisons in two contrasting manners (or three, if we include the miserable garrisons under the English Board of Ordnance).

By what we may term the 'North European System' the Dutch, English, French and the Baltic states were represented in Africa and the Indies by chartered companies, which maintained private forts and armed forces. A traveller who visited Fort St George at Madras in the early nineteenth century was struck by the dual military and commercial function of a place where 'you may contrast, at every step, the man of war with the man of traffic, the muster-roll with the ledger, the bayonet with the pen, the sentry-box with the desk and counter' (Anon., 1821, in Nilsson, 1968, 86).

The Dutch East India Company, the largest and probably the best-run of these organisations, made no secret of investing the chief authority in each fort with the *Opperkoopman*, or Senior Merchant. The officers of the Company's army were shunned by polite society, and they lived in ignominious seclusion, kippered in the tropical preservatives of tobacco and spirits. Engineering work often fell to the naval captains and gunners. The garrisons were made up of men shipped out from the Dutch ports by *Zielverkoopers* ('Soul-Sellers'), the touts who preyed upon desperate and ignorant drifters. Once arrived in the Indies, the soldiers subsisted well enough on rum, bread, cheese, eggs, vegetables, and occasional local delicacies like tiger.

In contrast the Portuguese and Spanish ran their colonies by state bureaucracy, with all authority emanating from the king and flowing through the viceroys. The monarch appointed his governors from a long list of waiting 'grantees', who regarded their 'fortress captaincies' as a return for service and a commodity which could be sold or bequeathed. The actual service was done by a 'captain', who naturally reimbursed himself as he saw fit. The system was a wretched one, and Captain João Ribeiro wrote in 1580 of his time in the East:

I do not doubt that amongst those who went out to govern those fortresses there were some who behaved kindly, but they could not set matters right; for the wrongs done by one bad man remain deeper impressed in the memory than the kindnesses done by a hundred good men (Boxer-Azevedo, 1960, 54).

The one reasonably effective check on the power of the captain within each fortress command was provided by the royal judge: the Spanish *oidor*, and the rather less formidable Portuguese *ouvidor*.

Unlike the Spaniards, the Portuguese maintained no royal troops in the colonial garrisons. Instead, the whole of the unmarried Portuguese laymen were designated *soldados*, and served on the ramparts without pay in time of emergency. Since nearly all the *soldados* had the expense of supporting unofficial native 'wives', these unfortunate bachelors had to live in wartime by begging or plunder.

The Spanish central bureaucracy engaged in mighty deliberations whenever there was talk of establishing a new fortress. Once, however, the decision was taken, the government exercised very little supervision over what works were carried out, at least until Prospero Verboom set up the Spanish engineering corps in 1711. A Spanish historian remarks that

as far as the Philippines are concerned, what we see up to that date are a disconnected series of fortifications which were built by the successive governors, each following his own notions. The impulse for the fortress-building was provided by the real or threatening danger of foreign attack, and it was inevitable that the works executed under those conditions did not correspond, indeed were incapable of corresponding, to any coherent plan of defence (Diaz-Spinola, 1959, 69).

Even at their least effective, the authorities in Madrid and Lisbon never entirely lost interest in what was going on in their colonies. This concern was not always evident in the dealings of the English Board of Ordnance, which was responsible for building and garrisoning the works in Newfoundland, Nova Scotia, Minorca, Gibraltar and all the plantations and colonies save India. The Board proceeded from the Tudor principle that fort and garrison must remain an indissoluble whole, with

the consequence that the English 'independent companies' and regiments might be stranded for decades on end in distant colonies without hope of relief or return. No official provision was made for barracks or quarters, and in 1739 the authorities in Bermuda could complain that they had received no stores of any kind since 1696. Piracy itself was not unknown among the starving and ragged garrisons of the English West Indies. If King Charles II was anxious to keep up a good garrison at Tangier, this was only because he saw the place as a nursery of the standing army which he could not tactfully maintain in good strength at home. Two regiments, the Queen's and the Royal Dragoons, were therefore hidden away from English eyes on the North African shore.

All told, it would have been difficult for the colonial powers to hold their forts without the support of native peoples who regarded the walls as their best protection against white predators and hostile tribes. At Wydah in West Africa the negroes continued to hoist the English and French flags over the mud forts, long after the garrisons had left, while at Gross-Friedrichsburg the 'Prussian' negro Jan Cuny refused to believe that the fort could have been ceded by treaty in 1718, and he put up a brave resistance until the great superiority of the besiegers forced him to disappear into the jungle. A Dutchman wrote after his countrymen had been repulsed from Macao in 1622 that

Many Portuguese slaves, Kaffirs and the like, having been made drunk, charged so fearlessly against our muskets, that it was a wonderful thing to see. . . . It was not done with any soldiers, for there were none in Macao, and only about three companies of 180 men in Malacca (Boxer, 1969, 302).

The Asiatic Powers

India

In 1526 Babur, a descendant of the Moghul (Mongol) house of Timur, irrupted from the northern mountains into the plains of India. He employed his field artillery with decisive effect against the Afghan Sultan of Delhi at the Battle of Panipat, and after this victory he was able to occupy the cities of Delhi and Agra without resistance. The history of India over the next two and a half centuries is largely that of the extension and ultimate retreat of the rule of Babur's successors over the sub-continent.

The greatest Moghul conquests were made in the reign of Emperor Akbar, who ruled from 1560 to 1605. His first achievement was to break through the great Rajput fortresses of northern central India. On 23 October 1567 he arrived before the stronghold of Chitor, which crowned a hill rising to four or five hundred feet above the plain. The place was held by 8,000 troops and 40,000 townspeople and peasants, and Akbar was forced to subject it to the whole of the considerable repertoire of Moghul siege techniques. He planted three batteries of cannon, and directed the casting of a 40-pounder mortar on top of the hill so as to save the labour of dragging it up from below. The work of the artillery was supplemented by sapping and mining, and a contemporary account reads that 'the *sābāt* (trench) which began from the Emperor's entrenchment was so wide, that ten horsemen could ride abreast along the bottom of it; and so deep that it hid a man seated on an elephant, holding a spear in his hand' (Irvine, 1903, 275).

All of this work brought the reduction of the fortress little nearer, and Akbar might have been forced to break off the siege if he had not been fortunate enough to kill the governor with a shot from his favourite matchlock *Sangram*, during a sortie on the night of 23–4 February. At dawn the Moghul army rushed into the demoralised fortress and cut down 30,000 of the garrison and population.

The reduction of Ranthambhor and Kalinjar completed this stage of Akbar's career. He went on to conquer Bengal in 1576, and Kashmir ten years later. Sind and Baluchistan succumbed between 1590 and 1595. Oddly enough, the Moghuls never actually encountered the Hindu kingdom of Vija-yanagar, the greatest Indian state of earlier times, which had already been broken by a league of Moslem sultanates in 1565.

The work of conquest was continued, on a more modest scale, by Akbar's gifted son Jahangar, who reduced Mewar, the last surviving Rajput fortress,

in 1614. Under the next-in-line, Shah Jehan, the Moghul prestige and culture were at their height. He was the first Moghul to recruit European gunners in any quantity, and when he captured Hooghly from the Portuguese in 1632 and the virgin fortress of Daulatabad in 1633 he demonstrated convincingly that his armies were well up to the varied work of formal sieges. Shah Jehan is now chiefly re-membered as the builder of the Taj Mahal, though his new fortress–cum–palace at Delhi was in its own way no less remarkable an achievement. The work began in 1639, and was completed in nine years at a cost of six million rupees, a sum which is largely accounted for by the cost of carting stone the 150 miles from Agra.

Shah Jehan's son Aurangzeb is accounted the last of the great Moghuls. Between 1685 and 1687 he destroyed two kingdoms of the Deccan (southern central India) by sieges which bear comparison with the great undertakings of Akbar a century before. The starving fortress of Bijapur opened its gates on 22 September 1686, after a year and a half of blockade and attack. The reduction of Golconda was another long and laborious business. Two Moghul mines blew back on the besiegers, and the flying stones killed 1,100 men before Aurangzeb's eyes. Further thousands were dying in his camp from famine, disease and flood. 'At night,' reads a chronicle, 'heaps of dead bodies used to accumulate. After some months, when the rains ceased, the white piles of skeletons looked from a distance like hillocks of snow' (Cambridge History, 1928–37, IV, 289). At last a soldier of the garrison was bribed to keep a postern gate open, and Golconda fell to a surprise assault on 2 October 1687.

Aurangzeb's last years were spent in long and profitless campaigns against the Marathas, the first of the series of confederations, sects and tribes which were to encompass the ruin of the Moghul Empire in the eighteenth century.

In all of these episodes we have been dealing with fortresses which did not differ in kind from the castles of medieval Europe. The sites were chosen with tactical skill on hill-tops or beside rivers, but as late as the middle of the eighteenth century the architects still built the strongholds as massive walls and closely-grouped towers in the ancient style. The crests of the ramparts were crenellated, and two or more rows of loopholes further down the walls betrayed the existence of interior galleries. There is little evidence that the architects ever intended to flank and command the ground beyond the fortification.

Outworks were almost unknown, except for barbicans such as those at Golconda and Bidar, and when engineers wished to endow a fortress with additional strength they merely built higher walls and more of them. The result was a step-like effect as in the triple-walled Fort of Agra, where a low outer rampart was backed by a higher intermediate enceinte which was in turn commanded by a soaring interior perimeter.

The Moghul invasion wrought no essential change in the style of military building. Still less influence was exercised by the hired European gunners of the seventeenth and eighteenth centuries, who gave their help only in purely mechanical tasks like hoisting cannon to the summits of lofty citadels. The workmanship of the fortresses remained superb throughout the period, and Babur himself, who affected to despise Indian architecture, had to admit that the native stonemasons were outstanding.

The massive works of the great cities and castles were reproduced, on a more modest scale, in the remote mountain-top forts which the minor princes built as places of refuge for their ammunition, treasure and persons. In the plains of the Ganges and Indus, however, the smaller fortified towns were built on artificial mounds, and depended for their protection upon ditches, pounds or marshes which were formed by digging out the earth.

As for siege techniques, the Moghuls were accustomed to going about things on a grand scale. Akbar and Aurangzeb made sure that their armies were strong enough to impose an effective investment, and once the fortress was tightly hemmed in they made a kind of circumvallation (*mūrchāl*) and worked forward by sap and mine. Thus far the routine came very close to the European practice of the time. Where the Moghuls and the other Indian princes fell short was in their inability to finish off the siege by making a breach. Their troops might be immobilised for months under a hail of stones, pottery grenades, and shots from wall-pieces.

Another circumstance which made for long sieges was the composition of the Moghul armies, which were congeries of noble contingents. The individual commanders were sometimes in treacherous correspondence with the garrison, and many proud nobles would rather have seen a siege fail than allow a rival to gain the credit for its success. If a fortress eventually did succumb, it was almost always through starvation, treason or accident.

A great deal obviously hung upon the loyalty of the governor. The Moghuls were careful to appoint and deal with the fortress governors direct from Delhi, out of fear that the gentlemen might combine with provincial rulers and make a bid for independence. The seventeenth-century Maratha leader Shivaji carried suspicion to an extreme; candidates for fortress appointments had to obtain a reference from a member of the royal household, and subject themselves to the beady stare of Shivaji himself; in addition he changed the governors at frequent intervals, and made sure that within each fortress the authority was minutely subdivided between a noble Maratha *havaldar* (governor), and Brahmin *sabnis* (treasurer and muster-master), and a Prabhu *karkhannis* (commissary).

The artillery did singularly little to abridge the sieges, for the armies took a strange pride in dragging along a great quantity of heavy, old and useless guns with them wherever they went. Most pieces of native manufacture were crude and defective, and the European trading companies were delighted to unload their old and honeycombed barrels upon the eager Indian buyers. The hired gunners from Europe were not always the most outstanding members of their profession. They served well enough under Shah Jehan, but grumbled mightily when Aurangzeb required them to load the cannon as well as point them.

It is misleading to pursue too close a comparison between Indian fortress warfare and the contemporary European methods. The circumstances were too different. Indian ways present many ingenious features of their own, and we must admire the clever ways in which the princes made use of the native flora and fauna.

Plains forts were sometimes embowered in thick brakes of bamboo, capable of turning a cannon ball, or set amid ten- or twenty-foot high walls of prickly pear, which were impervious to the fiercest flames. When there were no such obstacles in the way, elephants could be sent against the gates, as happened at Arcot in 1751:

The parties which attacked the gates drove before them several elephants who, with large plates of iron fixed to their foreheads, were intended to break them down: but the elephants, wounded by the musketry, soon turned and trampled on those who escorted them (Irvine, 1903, 177–8).

Many gates were studded with spikes as a protection against this form of attack.

The Marathas used to train monitor lizards or iguanas to scuttle up hillsides and walls with ropes around their middles and dig their claws into clefts in the rock, permitting the soldiers to haul themselves up after them. Sometimes, when a fortress refused to surrender, the Afghans would kill a dog and fling it in the direction of the walls – nobody knows precisely why.

Burma and Siam

In contrast to the pattern of native warfare in India, where European influence was minimal, the intervention of Western guns and technicians often proved decisive in the complicated quarrels of the Burmese, Thais, Indo-Chinese and Japanese.

Without the help of European adventurers the Burmese Toungoo dynasty and its successor, the line of Alaungpaya, could hardly have fought so long and so successfully against the united Thai (Siamese) kingdom of Ayut'ia. Thus Portuguese gunners and mercenaries helped the Toungoo kings Tabinshwehti (d. 1550) and Bayinnaung (d. 1579) to subdue their domestic enemies and launch several invasions of Siam, and it was largely through the awe-inspiring thunder of the Portuguese-served guns that the Burmese at last managed to take Ayut'ia in 1564. The Thais promptly rebelled and recovered Ayut'ia by treachery, but they lost it again in 1569 and did not retake the city until the 1580s, in the black period of Burmese history which followed the death of Bayinnaung.

Towards the end of the sixteenth century Burma was hemmed in on all sides. A dangerous Thai resurgence was headed by King Narasuen, who pushed the Burmese out of Lower Burma, and gained outlets on the Indian Ocean in 1593 by taking Tavoy and Tenasserim. To the west the coastal state of Arakan made friends with Portuguese soldiers and buccaneers, and in 1599 the Arakanese sent an expedition which captured Syriam, the port of Pegu on the Chindwin.

Narasuen died in 1605, which caused the pressure on the Burmese to slacken off, and in 1613 the Burmese retook Syriam from the European adventurer Philip de Brito. The Burmese planted de Brito on a stake, but they were intelligent enough to enrol most of his men in the royal guard as gunners and musketeers; and the following year they were able to wrest Moulmein and Tavoy from the Thais. Having earned their keep, the Portuguese mercenaries were allowed to settle in Burma, and for long afterwards their descendants formed a Christian community between the Chindwin and the Mu.

Now the Burmese went astray. Although they had regained their coastlands, they chose to establish their capital at Ava, which was an inland site and cut off from contact with the Western world. The Thais, in contrast, continued to accept just so much of the European presence as suited their purposes, a policy which was to stand them in a very good stead in later times.

Thus the appearance of Western gunners usually proved to be decisive. When, however, the Burmese and Thais were fighting without European help, their wars assumed a character and tempo of their own.

The larger cities were surrounded with a formidable belt of defence that comprised an earthen-backed masonry wall, a ditch and a massive outer stockade of teak. Within the city an especially strong compound housed the royal palace or seat of government – the same arrangement that we encounter in Indo-China and Japan. Out in the country the Burmese, Thais and Cambodians all made extensive use of palisaded camps.

The last word in choosing the site for a fortress or camp lay not with the architect but with the astrologers, who had the vital task of determining exactly how the locality lay in relation to the Axis of the Universe, which was the channel through which the defenders could tap divine power. Details of the processes involved are described in the Siamese *Treatise on the Art of War*, a work which dates largely from the sixteenth century, but which was republished as a textbook as late as 1825. It tells the commander to

post the elephants and cavalry in good positions to protect the main army. Let the porters cut wood and make camp with the help of the soldiers. Then the pandits and astrologers must make calculations. A gateway must be built, with a gong for marking the time. Then build the fortified camp with ditch and mound. Lay down spikes and

have an elevated area inside the camp. Outside and inside the camp bury talismans to avert misfortune and to protect against the enemy. . . . Stop persons coughing or groaning in their sleep (Quaritch Wales, 1952, 155–6).

An assault on a stockade was a straightforward affair, involving a rush by infantry bearing ladders, hooks, axes and ropes, and sometimes a push by elephants. On the subject of the siege of a city the *Treatise* speaks in terms which are at once ferocious and vague:

Someone should volunteer to lead the attack. The commander thereupon orders the city to be stormed. At dawn let the elephants, cavalry and

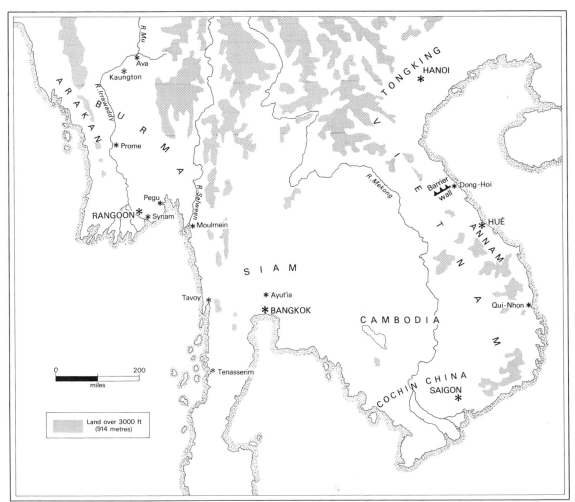

South-East Asia

foot flock forward to the assault. Some should put up scaffolds and scaling ladders, others quickly build fighting towers. Pull up the cannon and shoot continually, ruining all the city. Burn the city, let the flames rise brightly. Fire the cannon again until the enemy can fight no more and are destroyed. Then let the cannon, crossbows, horses and elephants, crowding together for mutual protection, force their way into the city.

Now seize the nobles and bring them up, also firmly tie up the soldiers and lead them away, battered and beaten (ibid., 183–4).

In most cases the siege commander simply directed his army to sit before the walls, hoping that some stratagem or treachery would admit him to the city. If nothing materialised, the arrival of the monsoon and the activity of the enemy guerrillas against his communications were usually enough to persuade him to retreat.

Indo-China

Cambodia, the Poland of south-east Asia, suffered heavily from falling within the spheres of influence of the rival powers of Siam and Annam (central Vietnam). The capital, Lovek, was taken by storm by the Thais in 1594, and the whole land was reduced to the status of a Siamese vassal from 1603 until the Cambodians won their liberty back in 1618. The Cambodians maintained their precarious independence through the seventeenth and eighteenth centuries only by ceding large tracts of land to Annam and Siam, and they kept up the size of the population through the equally dangerous expedient of admitting large numbers of Vietnamese settlers.

Annam was saved from this ignominious fate largely through the intelligence of the Nguyen dynasty. In 1620 war broke out between the Nguyens and the Trinh family, whose seat of power lay in Tongking (northern Vietnam). The Nguyen forces were small, but they were equipped with Portuguese arms, and they based their highly effective strategy on defending two walls which ran from the Central Highlands to the sea north of Hué.

Significantly enough, it was a Nguyen ruler, the early nineteenth-century emperor Gia-long, who

was going to represent the one south-east Asian commander who was totally proficient in Western military engineering.

The fall of the Chinese Mings

If the defensive had the upper hand in fortress warfare all over south-east Asia, in China this ascendancy came close to the absolute.

Chinese life, economy and government all revolved around the fortified town, or *ch'ĕng*, a word which denotes both 'city' and 'wall'. These fortress-towns were at their most imposing in the north, where the plains were dotted with their huge dun-coloured rectangular enclosures. The core of the ramparts was formed of packed clay, which was protected against weather and siege by exterior and interior revetments of bricks measuring two feet long, six inches wide and four-and-a-half inches thick.

The whole formed a mass some forty feet thick at the base, rising with a pronounced 'batter' as much as sixty feet to rampart walls built 'in such wise that three or four men abreast can walk upon them' (Boxer, 1953, 102). Towers were sited along the walls at intervals of fifty or sixty yards, and at the centre of each side of the fortress stood a wide, roofed-over gateway which served as a citadel and barracks. The interior defence was concentrated at a single pagoda-like tower where the four straight roads from the gateways met in the centre of the town. As was the case in India, the only outworks took the form of barbicans, which were sited in front of the gates of some of the larger cities.

The early Ming emperor Yung lo (d. 1425) moved the capital from Nanking to Peking, a mere forty miles south of the Great Wall, for he believed that it was important for the government to be close at hand to direct the defence of north-east China against the nomad tribes. Many of the walls of the northern towns date from the same period, but Peking was given the strongest defences of all. Its walls rose to ninety-nine feet, which was high enough to keep out the most nimble nomad, while avoiding devils who were known to fly around at an altitude of one hundred feet.

The ancient Wall itself constitutes the most

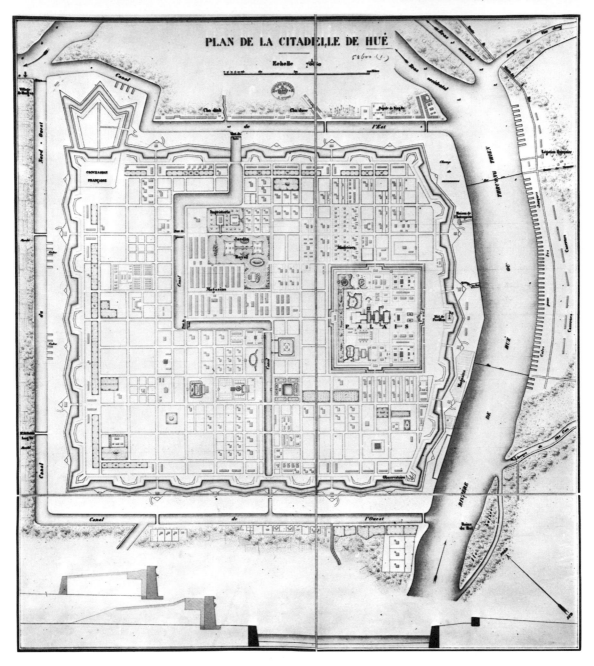

PLAN DE LA CITADELLE DE HUÉ

73   The bastioned 'Citadel' of Hué in Annam, built by French engineers for the Emperor Gia-long at the beginning of the nineteenth century. The Viet Cong seized the place in their Tet Offensive of 1968, and the Americans had to fight hard to get it back

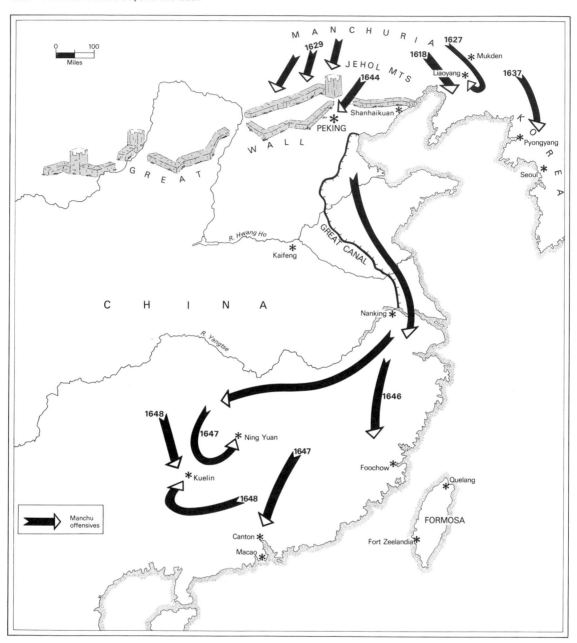

China under the Mings

enduringly successful and the largest work of defence in history – not even Vauban built defences which could be seen from the moon. It endowed whole regions with the same kind of security that was enjoyed by the walled cities, and Yung lo wisely rebuilt the eastern section, extending from the mountains near Wanchuan to the sea at the important fortress of Shanhaikuan. In front of this stretch of the Wall the barren mountains of Jehol provided a further barrier against Manchuria and barbarism. The nomads were therefore confronted with the same association of mountain range, wall and coastal fortress which checked the Trinhs in Annam in the seventeenth century.

The far perimeter of Manchuria was closed off by a continuous palisade, rather like the Russian Cherta, and the entire border was divided into *Wei*, or military districts, each of which was held by about 5,600 troops. In the interior provinces the *Wei* alternated with ordinary civil regions.

Gunpowder, which was the great destroyer of walls in other parts of the world, had been employed by the Chinese in warfare as early as the tenth century. Artillery proper appeared at about the same time as in Europe, and in 1356–7 the Chinese manufactured at least two cast-iron trunnioned cannon which were technically in advance of anything produced at that date in the West. However, the Chinese failed to carry the development of their artillery any further, perhaps because the mandarins feared that gun-founding was too dangerous an art to be allowed to become generally known.

Thus the artillery of the West came to China as a new and terrifying weapon. In 1517 the fleet of Fernão Peres caused a panic at Canton by what was intended to be a friendly salute, and for a long time afterwards the Chinese, in their instructively ambiguous fashion, used the same word (*Fo-lang-ki*) to signify both 'cannon' and 'foreigner'. Not until 1557 did the mandarins allow the Portuguese to trade from the rocky peninsula of Macao, in the Canton River estuary, and even then the Chinese were careful to seal off the foreign devils from the mainland by heavily-guarded fortifications.

The reintroduction of artillery in China was closely associated with the Jesuits, who had an important house at Macao. The fathers were skilled in the secular sciences, and in 1622 the Italian Jesuit Giacomo da Rho helped to defend Macao against the Dutch when he fired a shot which exploded a keg of powder in one of the siege batteries. The Chinese were duly impressed, and they granted the Portuguese permission to fortify Macao. As a further, almost gratuitous, proof of their mastery of gunnery, the Macao Jesuits proceeded to wreck the rival house of the Dominican monks by a devastating cannonade.

Other Jesuits travelled to the Ming court, where they won converts and influence. In 1642 the German Jesuit Johann Schall von Bell was invited by the Emperor to produce some mighty guns which were to be mounted on the walls of Peking against the Manchus. Schall responded magnificently, casting a score of 40-pounders. He had had to rely upon book-knowledge and the unwilling labour of Chinese eunuchs, but as a good Christian his most anxious moment had come when he learnt that the Chinese were about to make sacrifices to the God of Fire upon the gleaming new guns. He raced around the row of cannon, setting up improvised altars in front of each muzzle, then donned his cassock, stole and biretta and persuaded the Chinese to pray to the true God instead. The Emperor was delighted with the guns, and commissioned Schall to cast a whole train of field artillery.

The Chinese assumed that the Jesuits, being learned Europeans, must know all about fortifications as well. Schall made a wooden model to explain how Peking could be defended by a ring of ravelins, but an imperial architect frustrated the scheme by pronouncing that these strange triangular works would lie under the pernicious influence of the planet Mars.

The Jesuits and their Chinese converts proved to be of some help to the empire in its first, successful campaigns against the Manchus. These northern peoples were united and tamed in the early seventeenth century by the leader Nurhachu, who from 1619 was free to turn all his attention to the work of conquering China.

Nurhachu took the eastern Manchurian towns of Liaoyang and Mukden in 1621, but the Chinese managed to turn the tide with the help of the

Christian mathematician Ignatius Sun Yuan-hua, who familiarised the army with artillery and planned the counter-offensive. Nurhachu died of disease and discouragement in the calamitous year of 1626, when his troops were repulsed from Ning-yuan by the agency of a cook from Fukien, who proved to be a natural master of gunnery.

In 1629 and 1630 the new Manchu king T'ai-tsung achieved a measure of success when he by-passed Shanhaikuan and the other border fortresses and invaded China by way of the passes of the Jehol mountains. However, the Chinese emerged from the uncontained strongholds and cut the Manchu communications, compelling the invaders to retreat. The lesson was not lost upon T'ai-tsung, who brought Chinese officers into his service, and began to cast some cannon of his own. The new methods helped his armies to prosecute some successful campaigns in the 1630s in Korea, the Amur basin and eastern Manchuria, but the Manchus were still not up to the work of breaching the Chinese frontier by force.

Given the limited capacity of the Manchus, a tribe one generation removed from nomadic barbarism, it seems scarcely credible that in the course of the next few years they should have gone on to destroy the centuries-old Ming empire, with its new guns and near-impregnable fortresses.

Many processes contributed to this strange catastrophe. The handful of missionaries and gifted commanders could do little by themselves to raise the morale and efficiency of the effete soldier-scholars and mercenary rabble which made up the Ming armies. If any Westerner or general displayed the slightest signs of activity or enlightenment he was liable to attract the suspicion of the eunuchs and the hostile bureaucrats. We have already seen how the reactionaries wrecked Schall's plans to re-fortify Peking. More serious still was the victory of the anti-Christians over Sun Yuan-hua, whom they convicted on trumped-up charges after the temporary setbacks of 1629 and 1630. The pro-Western minister Hsu Kuang-chi managed to enlist the services of Gonsalvo Texeira and 400 Portuguese in 1637, but the officials were so jealous that they actually prevented the Europeans and their invaluable artillery from reaching the theatre of war.

The strategic equilibrium was finally upset by a peasant rebellion that had been raging in the central and northern provinces ever since 1626. The rebel leader Tzu-ch'eng was four times repelled from Kaifeng, which was the chief town of Honan, and the Ming authorities became so complacent that they saw no reason to withdraw troops from the war against the Manchus. This was one mistake too many. Tzu-ch'eng built up his army to an enormous size, and marched on Peking in two columns early in 1644. The authorities responded too late to the threat, and the rebels gained entrance to the city by treason on 25 April. The last Ming emperor thereupon committed suicide rather than let his sacred person fall into the hands of the peasants.

Now came another miscalculation. Hitherto the Ming general Wu San-kuei had been successfully holding the Wall and Shanhaikuan against the Manchus, but he was now so shocked by the almost casual loss of Peking and the emperor that he took the desperate gamble of inviting the Manchus across the Wall to help suppress the rebellion. Tzu-ch'eng was obliging enough to come out of Peking with 60,000 men to fight in the open field, and he was crushed by Wu San-kuei and the Manchus near Yungping. The victors entered Peking on 6 June, which was the second time within three months that the greatest fortress of China had gone under without a siege.

Once having gained their foothold in China proper, the Manchus cast off their Ming allies and set about conquering the land for themselves. As masters of Peking they were able to take the rest of the northern cities with little delay, for the *Wei* system of military organisation had encouraged the smaller towns to look to the example of the regional capitals.

Tactical considerations counted for so little that it was in the south, where the city walls were less imposing and less well-maintained, that the Manchus encountered by far the heaviest opposition. Indeed, Ming generals like the Christian Chu Shih-ssu probably benefited from the relaxation of centralised bureaucracy. In 1647 and 1648 he postponed the fall of the province of Kiangsi by putting up a spirited defence of the fortress of Kuei-lin, three times forcing the enemy to raise the siege by attacking with his infantry and artillery, and skilfully co-ordinating these sorties with the operations of the army of relief.

Treason among the Ming forces at last allowed the Manchus to gain some solid successes. They took Canton in 1650 after an eight-month siege, cutting down 100,000 of the citizens in the process, and they went on to capture the heroic stronghold of Kuei-lin. The Ming general Koxinga (anticipating the events of 1949) crossed to the island of Formosa in 1661 and carried on the struggle from there. This move incidentally involved him in hostilities with the Dutch, who commanded Formosa from their headquarters at Taiwan. Koxinga took Fort Zeelandia on 1 February 1662, and Formosa was held in the name of the Mings until the Manchus extinguished this last flame of resistance in 1683.

The conquerors held down the forty-fold greater population of China by distributing the eight 'banners' of the Manchu army as garrisons. The Manchus deliberately isolated themselves from the natives, and they were cut off for longer still from the outside world by their unrelenting hatred of the Western foreigners, men they had known only as the military counsellors of the fallen dynasty.

Japan

From anarchy to unity

The Japanese gained their first knowledge of European firearms from a Portuguese junk which was driven ashore in 1542 or 1543 on one of the small islands of the south-west. For two centuries now Japan had been a congeries of warring feudal states, whose daimyos (lords) were accustomed to a life of skirmishes, sieges and the snatching of castles. Folk like these were quick to learn the use of the new weapons.

At first the knowledge of matchlocks and mobile artillery was confined to the areas of Jesuit missionary activity in the south-west, but in the second half of the sixteenth century a succession of central daimyos achieved such a mastery of firearms that they were able to impose a new unity on Japan.

Oda Nobunaga (1534–82) was the first of this alarmingly competent line, 'the most able of captains to command an army, to attack places, to trace works of all kinds, and to select advantageous camps' (Murdoch-Yamagata, 1903–26, II, 181). He trained his matchlockmen to fire in volleys of one thousand at a time, a devastating technique which enabled him to beat the army of the Takeda lordship at Nagashino in 1575. Sieges, however, still proved to be lengthy affairs, and Nobunaga was long prevented from subjugating the central lordships by the opposition of the Monto princes, who held the five inter-connecting strongholds which made up the monastery of Osaka. After braving two vain sieges and a bloody assault Osaka finally capitulated in September 1580.

Nobunaga based his own power on the fortress-city of Kyoto. In the 1560s

all the princes and nobles of Japan came to help in the building operations; usually there were from fifteen to twenty-five thousand at work, all dressed in cloth breeches and short jackets made of skins. When he went around supervising the operations, he carried a sword in his hand or rested it on his shoulder, or else he carried a baton in his hand. He decided to build the castle of stone – something . . . quite unknown in Japan. As there was no stone available for the work, he ordered many stone idols to be pulled down, and the men tied ropes around the necks of these idols and dragged them to the site. . . . He set up a bell in the castle to summon and dismiss the men, and as soon as it was rung all the chief nobles and their retainers would begin working with spades and hoes in their hands. He always strode around girded about with a tiger skin on which to sit, and wore rough and coarse clothing. . . . Everybody, both men and women, who wanted to go and view the work passed in front of him; while on the site one day, he happened to see a soldier lifting up a woman's cloak slightly in order to get a glimpse of her face, and there and then the king struck off his head with his own hand (Cooper, 1965, 94).

In accordance with Japanese practice, the main fortress was screened by satellite strongholds: those of Fushimi, Zeze and Nijo.

Nobunaga was treacherously murdered in 1582, after he had extended his rule over thirty-two of the sixty-eight provinces of Japan. The work of reunification was continued by his vassal Hideyoshi, a wizened, swashbuckling dwarf. In 1583 he had the distinction of exploding what was probably the first gunpowder mine in Japanese history under the feudal castle of Kameyama. The demoralised garrison thereupon capitulated to the siege army of 4,000 men, which by Japanese standards was a very small force indeed. In the following years Hideyoshi subdued the islands of Shikoku and Kyushu, and in October 1590 he addressed himself with 150,000 men to besieging the last focus of resistance, the fortress of Odawara, south-west of Tokyo. Hideyoshi's methods were no longer a novelty, and it took a three-month blockade to break the resistance of the garrison.

Hideyoshi was a skilled diplomatist and administrator, and he extended his rule as much by winning over his rivals and entrusting them with responsibilities, as by breaking their power by sieges. At the same time he was careful to garrison all the castles for miles around Kyoto with his own men, and he formed the coastal city of Osaka into the mightiest fortress of sixteenth-century Japan. The work was accomplished in 1587 after four years' labour by a force of between 30,000 and 60,000 men. The massive double enceinte of hard stone rose to a height of 120 feet, one of the blocks being a granite monolith forty-seven feet long and nineteen feet high, which was provided by the Daimyo of Higo. The outer ditch measured thirty-six feet deep and no less than 240 feet wide, which helped to give the defences an exterior perimeter of almost nine miles. The artificial works were in turn surrounded by a complex of tidal creeks.

Having achieved unity at home, Hideyoshi could afford to devote some thought to restoring Japan's position in south-east Asia. The vast and apparently stable Chinese empire had grown in relative stature during Japan's centuries of anarchy, and in order to have a free hand against the potential enemy Hideyoshi decided to invade the nearby peninsula of Korea. The Japanese duly descended on Korea in the spring of 1592, and won a vital bridgehead by storming into Pusan. The Korean forces of easy-going nobles and serf-like peasants thereupon gave way in all directions, and allowed the invaders to occupy the principal town, Seoul, without offering resistance.

After this first run of disasters the ingenious Koreans managed to put up a very creditable performance at sea and around the fortresses – in other words in the kinds of war in which technical expertise counted the most.

Korean chroniclers leave no doubt that gunpowder appeared in their land at an early date:

At the end of 1392 a Chinese merchant . . . stayed in the home of a general in charge of weapons along the River Imjin near Songdo. The general told his servant to treat him kindly (the Koreans always got on well with the Chinese) and the merchant showed him how to mix saltpetre. This was the first time we had powder in Korea (Boots, 1934, 20).

In 1494 an official manual mentions the existence of cannon that were designed to throw stones and arrows, and by 1569 Korean gunnery was advanced enough to produce a large cannon called a 'flying, striking, earthquake heaven thunder', which hurled a fuzed explosive or incendiary missile for several hundred yards. The Koreans were backward only in the production of hand weapons, and the matchlock remained unknown to them until the Japanese envoy so unwisely presented them with a specimen in 1589. Many more weapons were captured from the Japanese in the war of 1592, and the Koreans were delighted to discover that you could strike a man down at a distance merely by 'pointing a dog's hind leg at him' (ibid.).

The design of Korean fortifications was distinctive, not to say bizarre. The walls rarely rose more than twenty feet high, and the hundreds of merlons along the crest formed so many miniature citadels, each between six and ten feet long, pierced by three loopholes, and roofed over to the rear. Every stone block of the revetment was dressed on the inner side into a pyramid, which served to fix the masonry into the rampart's core of earth and loose stones. However, the workmanship and materials of the wall were liable to vary a great deal from one section to the other, for the construction was carried on by separate gangs, each with its own way of working. In time of siege the soul of defence was the town prefect, who took up station in the upper storey of the main gate and beat encouraging noises on a great drum. An historian comments that

since the Koreans were geometrically and psychologically always on the defence in warfare, the wall naturally came to be their most respected and efficient weapon. . . . By this mental attitude and the actual physical protection of her walled retreats, Korea was able to maintain for so long her individuality as a nation and to turn her enemies' assaults into empty victories by holding them for months without their gates until the shortage of supplies and weakened spirit made their 'victorious' return home the better part of valour (ibid., 36–7).

These cunning enemies soon made the Japanese regret that they had ever invaded Korea. The Koreans were victorious at sea, thanks largely to an iron-plated 'tortoise-boat' of their invention, and on land the guerrillas were so active that the Japanese had to maintain heavy garrisons in a series of forts along the communications between Seoul and Pyongyang. The Korean levies under General Pak Jin actually went over to the offensive, and used a 'flying, striking, earthquake heaven thunder' to throw a large bomb into the town of Kyongju. The fizzing missile attracted a crowd of Japanese, and repaid their curiosity by blowing a score of them to bits. The rest of the garrison abandoned the town in terror.

Thus the Koreans prolonged their resistance until, early in 1593, the Chinese poured over the Yalu to their help. Pyongyang fell to a Chinese escalade in February, and the Japanese retreated to a series of fortified camps on the south coast (much as the United Nations forces were to do in the face of the North Korean invasion of 1950). The enforced concentration of their troops in the south at least enabled the Japanese to gain their last notable success of the war, when they annihilated the 60,000 or 70,000 Korean defenders of the long-isolated fortress of Chinju. The siege was crude, even by Japanese standards: almost one hundred assaults were repulsed, and the Japanese made their breach only by advancing a 'sow' to the corner of a wall and prising the stones loose by crowbars.

The Japanese held their coastal camps against intermittent attack until they concluded peace with the Chinese in 1598. The last of the expeditionary force was withdrawn from Korea not long afterwards.

Hideyoshi died in 1597, and his followers started to fight each other in their haste to take over the guardianship of his young son Hideyori. The struggle was won by one of Hideyoshi's 'reconciled' enemies, Tokugawa Ieyasu, who obtained artillery, muskets and gunners from the Dutch ship *Liefde*, and beat his rivals at the Battle of Sekigahara on 21 October 1600. The victory had a double importance. It enabled Ieyasu to set himself up in 1603 as the first of the Tokugawa shoguns, or hereditary prime ministers, who owned far more power than that distant and semi-divine figure, the emperor. Second, it opened Japan to penetration by the Dutch, whose single-minded pursuit of money proved more acceptable to the Tokugawa authorities than the proselytising tendencies of the Portuguese and Spanish. In 1609 the Dutch were allowed to set up a factory at Hirado. The English followed them there in 1613, and both the Protestant nations sold and presented large quantities of artillery and ammunition to the shogunate.

In 1614 and 1615 Ieyasu employed one demi-cannon and four culverins of English manufacture in his attack on Osaka, which was the last refuge of Hideyori and his 90,000 supporters. Hideyori had many guns of his own, pointing through embrasures in the walls and towers, and he mounted two of the mightiest cannon in Japan – *Taro* and *Jiro* – on the tower in front of the Sakura Gate. Fire-projecting mangonels were placed along the ramparts, at intervals of one hundred yards.

The 180,000-man strong siege army completed the investment of Osaka on 29 December 1614. The defenders kept up a lively fire of musketry from the start, and on 3 January 1615 they repelled an assault with very heavy casualties. Ieyasu accordingly gave orders that 'no imprudent attack should be made and whenever such was attempted and failed he manifested the strongest displeasure' (Murdoch-Yamagata, 1903–26, II, 553).

On 15 January Ieyasu got his best gunners to fire against the tower housing the apartments of

Hideyori's formidable mother. One of the shots killed two maids of honour and smashed a quantity of china. The lady's morale was shaken still further by reports that enemy miners were at work, and on 21 January Hideyori made peace with Ieyasu.

Ieyasu made the very large assumption that the deal entitled him to demolish the fortifications, and he contrived to raze the outer rampart and fill in both ditches before Hideyori took umbrage and reopened hostilities in May. The garrison made some hurried repairs and re-dug sections of the inner ditch, but the fortress was no longer equal to withstanding a serious siege. The number of defenders was down to 54,000, even though many Christian converts had thrown in their lot with Hideyori's party. A missionary wrote: 'Six great banners bore as devices, together with the Holy Cross, the images of the Saviour and of St James – the patron of Spain – while some of them even had as a legend "The Great Protector of Spain"' (ibid., II, 543).

Rather than hold Osaka under such disadvantages the garrison sallied forth to do battle, and was heavily defeated south of the city on 3 June. Ieyasu immediately stormed into Osaka, and on the following day Hideyori and the last of his followers committed *seppuku* in the inner castle. Thus, in characteristic Asian fashion, the possession of the most powerful fortress of Japan was determined by a victory in the field. It was the same story when Babur occupied Delhi in 1526, and the Manchus entered into possession of Peking in 1644.

After the reduction of Osaka, according to the chronicler Pagès (ibid., II, 552), Ieyasu, in order to 'disconcert the lords and render them impotent . . . issued orders that all fortresses should be razed, with the exception of a single residence for each of the princes. Four hundred citadels disappeared in a few days.' Ieyasu further shackled the samurai class by issuing a code of laws, which were to be re-affirmed on the accession of each shogun. Article Six reads: 'Even when castles are repaired the matter must be reported to the authorities. Much more must all new construction be stopped. . . . High walls and deep ditches are the cause of great upheavals when they belong to others' (Sadler, 1937, 373).

Ieyasu and his sons had meanwhile been hard at work consolidating the Tokugawa rule by dedicated fortress-building on their own account. Yedo (Tokyo) was determined as the capital in 1603. The core of the fortress city was formed by the five-mile pentagonal circumference of the inner ditch of the Imperial Palace, and no less than 300,000 labourers and 5,000 stone-carrying vessels were requisitioned for the work. The expense to the state was minimal, for the terrified daimyos had to provide the men, materials and transport at their own cost. As always in Japan, the building was carried out under the close personal supervision of the rulers, and Ieyasu's son Hitetade had tea-pavilions set up on the site so that he could refresh himself on his rounds.

A Spanish official was conducted around the completed Palace at Yedo in 1609, and observed that

the first and primary wall is made up of huge square blocks of hewn stone, without mortar or any other mixture but simply set in the wall. The wall itself is very broad and has openings through which to fire artillery, of which they have some but not a great deal. Below this wall there is a moat through which flows a river, and the biggest drawbridge I have ever seen. The gates are very strong, and when they opened them for me, I saw two ranks of soldiers armed with arquebuses and muskets; as far as I could judge, they numbered more than one thousand men. . . . We walked along about three hundred paces to the second gate, where I saw another kind of rampart made of earthworks. Here was grouped a company of four hundred soldiers bearing pikes and lances. They took me to a third gate, which is set in another wall built of boulders a dozen feet in height, and there are, as it were, loop-holes at intervals along this wall for the use of arquebuses and muskets (Cooper, 1965, 141).

Gifu and about thirty other small fortresses were planted as satellites in a radius of between ten and sixty miles from Yedo. Further to the east, the rebuilt fortress of Shizuoka and the magnificent castle of Nagoya helped to command the east-west routes across the narrow neck of Honshu between the bays of Wakasa and Owari.

The discipline and turn-out of Ieyasu's garrisons were excellent. In 1613 John Saris witnessed the triennial change of the garrison at Fushimi:

CHINA

R. Yalu

Pyongyang *

R. Imjin

* Seoul

KOREA

Kyongju *

Pusan
Chinju *   *

SEA OF JAPAN

* Kanazawa

Wakasa
Bay

HONSHU

Sendai *

Fukushima *

YEDO *

L. Biwa

KYOTO *

Himeji *
Kobe *

Gifu
*

Odawara
*
Shizuoka
*Nagoya

* Fushimi
* OSAKA   * Kameyama

Owari Bay

Wakayama *

Odawara

Hirado *   * Fukuoka

Kumamoto
Deshima Is.   *
Nagasaki * * Hara

KYUSHU

Kagoshima *

0   100

Miles

Tanegashima Is.

Japan and Korea

Such good order was taken for the passing and providing for, of these three thousand soldiers, that no man either travelling or inhabiting upon the way where they lodged, was in any way injured by them, but cheerfully entertained them as other guests, because they paid for what they took, as all other men did (ibid., 144).

Ieyasu died in 1616, but the Tokugawa shogunate remained true to his principles for the two and a half centuries of its existence. The Christians were subjected to increasing suspicion and persecution, which caused Catholic refugees of all classes to crowd together in the western wastes of Arima and Amakusa. In 1637 a rebellion broke out under the leadership of the Christian priest and samurai, the seventeen-year-old Masuda Shiro. The enterprise was hopeless, and on 10 January 1637 20,000 fighting men and 17,000 women and children retreated to the ruinous castle of Hara on a high and windswept peninsula twenty miles south of Shimabara.

The ramparts of Hara were adorned with wooden crosses and scores of flags bearing the same sign in red, and on 3 February the garrison beat off the first of the assaults with blasts of musketry and cries of *Jesus! Maria! St Jago!* On 14 February a further storm was thrown back with 5,000 casualties. The Dutch now came under severe pressure to co-operate with the Tokugawas, and they did not shrink from dispatching the warship *De Rijp* against Hara and sending a 12-pounder and other cannon overland from Hirado. Happy to relate, the performance of the Dutch gunners was abysmal, and one of the land-based cannon burst at the muzzle, 'whereby the assistant gunner Gylak was struck in the belly, and thrown over the eastern bamboo palisade and on to the ground outside the battery, so that he died' (Boxer, 1936, 28–9). The Dutch sailed ingloriously away.

By the middle of March the shogunate had concentrated 106,000 men against Hara, and the lack of food and powder began to tell on the defenders. On the night of 11–12 April an unauthorised assault by the Hizen clan developed into a full-scale storm, when the besiegers saw that the Christians were defenceless. All save 106 of the garrison and refugees lost their lives in a last, hopeless fight with stones, sticks and rice-bowls – their sole remaining weapons.

The siege of Hara must be counted one of the decisive actions of Japanese history, for it provoked the shogunate to turn away from the Christian West. The Tokugawas declared the ports closed to Europeans, the Dutch alone being allowed to maintain a factory on Deshima Island off Nagasaki, thanks to their unholy conduct at Hara. For a short time, even, it appeared that the Japanese were looking to the heretics to help them to keep abreast of military advances in the West. There was a passing fashion for English and Dutch engravings and maps, and the Hosokawa family is known to have possessed a magnificent print of the siege of s'Hertogenbosch of 1629. The surveyor and cartographer Hojo Ujinaga went so far as to write a treatise on Dutch siege methods, after he had received a few months' instruction in 1650 from the gunner Juriaan Schaedel.

In 1639 the Dutch agreed to a request from the authorities to lay on a demonstration of mortar shooting, and on 21 June two of the weapons were aimed against a group of houses at Yedo. One of the mortars burst, and neither scored any direct hits, but the Japanese were undeniably impressed with the spectacle when a bomb landed in a paddy-field and 'burst with such violence that all the mud, slime and filth were hurled so high into the air, that all who saw it were astonished' (ibid., 31). The Dutch proceeded to cast seven mortars for the Japanese in the following year, but the Tokugawas regarded the presents as little more than noisy toys.

During the following centuries of isolation there were just a few scholars and officials who kept up a tenuous contact with European ways. They received some encouragement from the unusually outward-looking shogun Yoshimune, who in 1721 lifted the ban on the translation of Western books, and encouraged his officers to learn as much from the Dutch as possible. In the next generation the samurai Hayashi Dhikei (1738–93) made the acquaintance of the Dutch at Deshima, and tried to draw the attention of his countrymen to the danger of Russia's eastward expansion in two works: the political and strategic essay *Sanyoku Tsuran*

(*Exhaustive View of Three Countries*) of 1786, and the *Kaikoku Heidan* (*Talks on the Military Affairs of the Sea-Country*), a treatise on coastal defence which he published in 1791. Other authors of the time brought out translations of European military texts.

Tokugawa officialdom remained unmoved by all the learned activity, and in 1808 the English frigate *Phaeton* cruised impudently through Nagasaki harbour in search of Dutch shipping. There followed a spate of sappuku among the officers in command of the coastal batteries, and the scholars Motogi and Otsuki Gentaku took advantage of the brief revival of military awareness in order to translate a number of Dutch works on coastal defence and fortification. The Tokugawas, however,

were incapable of appreciating the significance of the *Phaeton* episode, and the shogunate survived in stagnation until Commodore Perry's 'Black Ships' appeared in Yedo Bay in 1853.

Japanese military engineering

In 1599 the Jesuit visitor-general Valegnani could speak of a 'universal erection of new castles and the demolition of many old ones', a process which was 'occasioned by nothing else than that under Hideyoshi a new method of warfare was devised which calls for new and much more strongly-fortified castles' (quoted in Murdoch and Yamagata, 1903, II, 315).

74 Japanese tower, at Odawara, with granite base and timber superstructure

Valegnani did not exaggerate the impact of the re-introduction of gunpowder to Japan. At the beginning of the sixteenth century the Japanese castles had numbered about one thousand, insignificant shelters of wood and thatch which crouched inside crude perimeters of palisade and ditch. In the last quarter of the century these were replaced by two hundred strongholds of radically new design, all probably deriving their inspiration from the Castle of Azuchi, which Nobunaga founded beside Lake Biwa in 1576. The Azuchi castle was the first structure to combine fortress, palace and barracks in one complex of buildings. The architecture was designed as much to impress by its taste and splendour, as to deter by its strength. The social implications were far-reaching, because the provision of accommodation did much to hasten the development of the distinctive samurai class, divorced from lesser folk who lived outside the walls.

The main strength of the new fortresses resided in their granite walls. These ranged in height from twenty feet (the usual scale) to an occasional 130 feet. In section, the wall was made up of an outer layer of massive, unmortared granite blocks, a thick intermediate layer of stones and gravel, and a core of earth. This form of construction allowed the rain

75 Himeji (White Heron) Castle

and melting snow to drain away freely. The 'batter' (slope) of the wall was calculated at thirty-five degrees in the case of dressed masonry, and at twenty or thirty degrees for rough stones. Geometric formulae were used to achieve a graceful concave batter at the corners, a procedure which one architect is known to have concealed by setting up bamboo screens around the building site. Everywhere we detect the Japanese reverence for stone. This substance was considered eternal, and the Japanese gave it a name that was synonymous with strength and firmness.

The Japanese preserved a sense of artistic proportion by setting light, almost fanciful superstructures upon or inside the masonry walls. The thin, high sides of these works were built of timber frameworks and mud filling. Some little protection against fire was provided by multiple coats of white plaster, and a steeply-pitched roof of durable black tiles. The effect of lightness was enhanced by figures of leaping dolphins which terminated the curved eaves. The kingposts of the whole upper framework simply rested on granite blocks, and this discontinuity of foundation and walls enabled the entire structure to bounce about in an earthquake without coming to serious damage.

The gunports and the stone-throwing ports were usually closed by shutters. The other windows of the towers were guarded by heavy vertical bars, and allowed a little light to enter interiors that were fragrant with beautifully-carpentered cedar woodwork, charcoal warmers, and the oils that were burning in paper lanterns. The missionaries Almeida and Frois could not say too much in favour of the workmanship, beauty and cleanliness of the new castles they visited.

On flat sites most of the Japanese fortresses were arranged as a *haro-jiro*, that is a complex formed of an inner keep, or *honmaru*, with second and third enceintes known respectively as *ninomaru* and *sannomaru*. We have seen how a Spanish official walked through three perimeters of this kind at Yedo in 1609.

In some smaller hilltop fortresses or castles, like the famous White Heron Castle at Himeji (1609), the main interior building took the form of a tall, multi-storeyed and multi-roofed keep, which was connected by twisting corridors with smaller satellite towers. A stronghold built on this plan was called a *hirayama-jiro*.

It was in such towers that the commanders assembled their treasures and families in the event of siege:

When they can no longer hold out, they kill their women and children to prevent their falling into the hands of the enemy. Then, after setting fire to the tower with gunpowder and other materials so that not even their bones or anything else may survive, they cut their bellies (Cooper, 1965, 131).

Except in the great city-fortresses, the outer defence relied less on depth than on complexity. Barbicans were built on the oblong *masugata* plan, which brought the visitor over a timber bridge and through one side of the walled enclosure, then made him turn to the right through the main entrance. Once inside, the stranger had to find his way to the interior through a maze-like complex of baileys and corridors.

For various reasons the mortality rate among the architects was high. They were sometimes put to death after they had completed their work, so as to preserve the secret of all the traps and passages. Perfectionism also took its toll. Genkei Sakurai, the rebuilder of the White Heron Castle, was told by his wife that the keep was leaning a little to one side, whereupon he climbed to the top and jumped to his death.

The design of the new fortresses owed little or nothing to contemporary European models. Like the earthworks of the nineteenth-century Maoris of New Zealand, they were the response of an intelligent and adaptable people to the problems posed by the advent of new weapons.

In the late sixteenth century and in the seventeenth century the Japanese castle-town, or *jokamachi* formed the administrative centre of its district, and greatly helped Hideyoshi and the Tokugawas in their work of unity. The most prominent of these places was represented by Yedo, followed by Nagoya, Sendai, Fukushima, Kumamoto, Wakayama, Shuzuoka, Kagoshima, Fukuoka, Kanazawa and about one hundred others. Such fortresses, however, never dominated society as completely as did their counterparts in China. The populations remained static, due to restrictions of commerce and industry, and the main urban growth took place in open cities, or in expanded suburban villages such as those around Osaka.

A formal siege on the European pattern remained unknown in Japanese warfare. Instead, the attack on a fortress followed an almost unvarying sequence of assault (nearly always repulsed), investment and negotiation. Commanders sometimes enlivened the proceedings by bringing up a siege tower, as at Nagashino in 1570 or Niroyama in 1590, but their main task was to keep their forces amused during the long blockades. In the course of the wearisome investment of Odawara in 1590 Hideyoshi

attempted no assault, but passed the time in giving feasts. Dancing-girls, musicians and actors were brought into the various camps, and merry-making was the order of the day. It was indeed more like a

gigantic picnic party than a great host intent on slaughter . . . though at times there might be silence in the city, soon it would be broken by the strains of a flute or the twang of strings, or the click of *go*, or chessmen, or the sudden shouting of drunken dancers (Murdoch and Yamagata, II, (1903), II, 256, and Sadler (1937), 158).

Artillery rarely played a prominent part in the attack. Ieyasu borrowed English guns for the siege of Osaka in 1614–15, but, as we have noticed, he did little with them beyond smashing a service of crockery.

Yet, even in those times, a Dutchman was ready to question whether it was a good idea to have introduced modern artillery to 'this proud and haughty nation' (Boxer, 1936, 38). Fortunately for the rest of Asia the Japan of the shogunate was withdrawing so rapidly into itself that for more than two centuries the state lost all interest in the sciences of the West.

Ten The Fortress and Humankind

Fortress warfare in the early modern age established or reinforced a number of trends which have powerfully influenced human affairs over the centuries, making it impossible for us to fix a neat termination in 1660 or any other particular date. In this concluding chapter we shall touch lightly on the ways in which fortification has affected strategy, town life and the world of the imagination.

The stronghold as a force for change

'Fortresses', 'frontiers' and 'sieges' are emotive words, which conjure up visions of epic defences, beleaguered heroes and the propping up of crumbling borderlands. We have witnessed the endurance of garrisons which seemed to hold the sky suspended above some sore-beset outpost of empire, and we have come across small states like Bavaria and Piedmont-Savoy, which elevated the retreat into a fortress system into one of the fundamental principles of statecraft.

All the same, the weight of evidence indicates that the influence of fortification in history has not been primarily a preservative one. The cost of the new ordnance and fortification certainly promoted the rise of the nation state, and hastened the decline of feudal lords and such city-states as could not organise themselves to meet the new challenge. Then again, some of the mightiest conquerors – Gustavus Adolphus, Louis XIV, Frederick of Prussia and Napoleon – would have been powerless to put their aggressive schemes into effect without the help of their fortified depôts and way-stations. These great captains regarded fortification as a versatile weapon of war, and not as a reason to lapse into pious neutrality and abdicate common sense. The trading-forts and 'factories' of the colonial powers and the log-built outposts of the Muscovites make up a further category of offensive fortification, which offered defensible bridgeheads for the first phase of Western expansion beyond the confines of Europe.

Walls and ditches were quite incapable of helping governments which, after a decade or more of peace, allowed a coolness to grow between themselves and their peoples, and entrusted their strongholds to feeble governors. Thus the mere passive strength of fortification did little to assist the French on their northern frontier in 1636, the Venetians in the Morea in 1714 and 1715, the Austrians in Silesia in 1740, the Dutch in 1672, the 1740s and 1787, or the Prussians in 1806.

When the authorities had cause to fear a revolt, they would have done well to raze every fortification in the disaffected area, build up their field forces, and try to reconcile the malcontents. Nothing could have been more misguided than the conduct of the Spanish in the Netherlands or the English in their American colonies, when they left their troops and cannon scattered among a number of isolated strongpoints which succumbed to ruffian bands in the first exciting months of revolt. The ground was never entirely made up again. The nineteenth-century revolutions provide many further instances of the ways in which fortification could work against the interests of established government.

Fortifications likewise precipitated social changes of great variety. If the pride of the samurai was inflated by their new quarters in Azuchi Castle and its imitators, then the increasing importance of siege warfare in contemporary Muscovy worked in the opposite direction, by depriving the mounted Russian nobility of much of its usefulness to the state.

The profession of military engineer

At the tactical level a fortress was simply an arrangement of fire-swept obstacles, a prepared battlefield on which the advantages were piled up on the side of the defender. Thus it was far more useful to have some good engineers, who were the men who had mastered the trade of fighting on this ground, than to know the secret of some 'infallible' system of attack or defence.

We have seen how the new fortification of the sixteenth century originated among small circles of officers and architects in central and northern Italy, from where individuals went out to spread the gospel through Europe. The word met with an enthusiastic reception in Holland, where further groups of specialists showed how the Italian innovations could best be adapted to the terrain of Northern Europe. After hearing the experts out, the field commanders were agreeably surprised to find that military engineering was not so mysterious after all, with the result that from the late sixteenth century until about the middle of the seventeenth century the foremost practitioners of fortress warfare proved to be soldier-engineers, men like Parma, Spinola, Maurice and Frederick Henry of Nassau, Turenne and Montecuccoli.

By the 1650s military engineering appeared to be near the limit of its progress: the Italians were dispersed, the Dutch were for the most part complacent and uninventive, and the marvellous old commanders were approaching their end or already dead. The unity and sense of purpose which had informed military engineering in earlier times was shown to be vulnerable and precarious, for it had depended too much upon personal energy, whether manifest among 'families' of Italian or Dutch experts, or in individual commanders. For this reason the trio of great late seventeenth-century engineers, Vauban, Coehoorn and Dahlberg, were at pains to *institutionalise* fortress warfare by setting up self-regenerating corps of expert practitioners.

The eighteenth century was a period of consolidation. More and more rulers were persuaded to found engineering corps of their own, and even to organise bodies of specially-trained engineer troops – something which Vauban and Dahlberg had been unable to achieve in their lifetimes. Sweden, being politically advanced, or rather anarchic, actually gave birth to the first of the politician engineers, in the person of Augustin Ehrensvärd. The one great prince who set himself against everything that had been achieved since Vauban's time was Frederick of Prussia, who was the foremost soldier of his age, yet was unaccountably loath to treat his engineers as human beings, let alone as members of an honourable corps.

By the Napoleonic period, then, the evolution of the profession of military engineer was almost complete. The last stage, the achievement of full parity of status with the officers of the field arms, was reached very rapidly indeed in the American service, but not quite so quickly elsewhere. In 1870, after a successful campaign in Abyssinia, Sir Robert Napier was made commander-in-chief in India, which provoked the *Spectator* magazine (2 May 1870) into uttering the comment: 'He is the first engineer, indeed the first scientifically-trained officer, ever appointed to independent command, and his success is considered at the Horse Guards almost a calamity. Imagine a man who has studied mathematics, and is unconnected with any great family, being acknowledged in the British Army as a great General! We shall have commands distributed according to capacity next, and then where will the British Constitution be?'

The 'colonial' and Asiatic peoples failed for a variety of reasons to make any significant contribution to the general development of fortress warfare. In North America, Asiatic Russia and Ireland, the indigenous population lacked any industrial base which might have helped them to build up the artillery and engineering arms. The Indian princes, it is true, were enthusiastic gunfounders, but neither they nor their European advisers managed to develop their engineering techniques to the point where they could gain a convincing superiority over the peculiarly massive fortifications of the sub-continent.

In Burma, Siam and Indo-China there were comparatively flimsy fortifications which succumbed with startling speed to the attentions of European-style artillery: unfortunately the southeast Asians were entirely dependent for their knowledge of Western ways upon the fleeting and sporadic visitations of more or less disreputable people, like roving adventurers and stranded mariners. The 'Vietnamese' of the generation of Gia-long stand out as the one exception: not only were they helped by respectable French officers, but they took the trouble to train themselves in the techniques of Western fortress-building.

The first effects of European-type firearms in China and Japan was catalytic, and yet all progress in military technology had come to a halt in the middle of the seventeenth century. The reason was that the Christian missionaries had managed to identify themselves with the doomed regimes of the Mings and the house of Hideyoshi. The victorious invaders and usurpers, the Manchus and the Tokugawas, learnt enough of muskets and cannon to ensure their success, but once established in power they were interested only in isolating their empires from all outside contamination.

In taking cosmic overviews of this kind, it is easy to forget that the demands on the moral resources of the military engineer were peculiar and extreme. Until the second half of the nineteenth century nearly all field battles were over and done with in a single day, and the survivors did not have to fight again for weeks or months to come. Conditions in fortress warfare, on the other hand, were much more 'modern', for the combatants stood in peril for weeks on end, and the normal conditions compounded the horrors of the execution cell and the charnel house in a way that was otherwise unknown until World War I.

Together with the constant technical demands, these circumstances called for 'a calm mind wholly bent upon its business' (Maigret, 1727, 334), and 'a quite extraordinary courage in order to be able to endure the blows of the enemy without having any means of hitting back, other than the eventual damage which the siege works may inflict' (De Guignard, 1725, II, 235). There was a great deal to chill the blood, but not much to send it racing through the veins, which was why great captains like Charles XII, Frederick the Great and Rommel suddenly lost their powers of decision when they were faced with a fortified obstacle.

The laws of war

Siege warfare was waged within the framework of a number of restraints and rules which were derived from civil and canon law and the code of medieval chivalry. The sixteenth- and seventeenth-century jurists Vitoria, Gentili, Suárez and Grotius (see bibliography) had the laudable ambition of raising these generally-accepted rules to the status of a body of international law, but when, in their arguments, they invoked some of the more barbaric passages of biblical and classical history, they probably retarded rather than promoted the amelioration of the asperities of war: what sticks in the mind is the ferocity of the quoted passages, and not the explainings-away and the well-intentioned casuistry. Grotius, indeed, was sometimes willing to let the message stand in all its original rigour. The entirely different mood of the eighteenth century, secular, rational and humane, was represented by the Swiss jurist Emerich de Vattel (1714–67), who based his *Droit des Gens* nominally on natural law, but in fact entirely on what he had learnt of accepted custom. He therefore tells us more of what actually happened in sieges than did his scholarly and intense predecessors.

The besieger began his operations in hopeful fashion, by inviting the defenders to give themselves up. Nobody but a poltroon or lunatic would ever avail himself of the kind invitation, and thus the besiegers had to proceed to the formal opening of the attack, which was signified by 'breaking ground' for the trenches or firing the first cannon shot. The code of tacitly-recognised laws continued to make its influence felt throughout the siege, and Vattel talks of 'several customs which are highly commendable, and frequently carried to the extreme of politeness. Sometimes refreshments are sent to the governor of a besieged town; and it is usual to avoid firing on the king's or the general's quarters' (Vattel, 1773, III, chapter 8).

After a few weeks, one side or the other declared its willingness to reopen talks. The belligerents respected the flag of truce the first time it appeared, but they were under no obligation to admit the deputation to their lines, or to hold their fire if the enemy came out again after a first refusal.

The capitulation was a formal legal document, which was drawn up under the ancient *lex deditionis*. If, however, the defenders refused to capitulate upon terms they were eventually faced with the alternatives of withstanding a general storm, or surrendering 'at discretion'. In the latter case they stripped themselves of all legal and moral protection, and in theory laid themselves open to the kind of cold-blooded execution which Alva visited upon the garrison of Haarlem in 1573. The more barbaric interpretations of surrender 'at discretion' went out of fashion by the eighteenth century, and were replaced by the general practice of detaining prisoners in good conditions until they were exchanged by cartel or through the signing of a peace treaty. The Austrian and Russian empires, in their battles and sieges in World War I, were the last pair of combatants to hold to these fine old traditions.

Even in the eighteenth century there were some people who, by their trade, were considered to have deprived themselves of any claim to consideration or mercy. At the siege of Yorktown in 1781 George Washington warned Sergeant Joseph Martin and the other sappers that if they were taken prisoner, they were not on any account to reveal what kind of troops they were. 'We were obliged to him for this kind advice', wrote Martin, 'but we considered ourselves as standing in no great need of it. For we knew as well as he did that sappers and miners were allowed no quarter, at least were entitled to none, by the rules of warfare' (Scheer-Rankin, 1959, 556).

Life in a besieged town

We have seen how fortress warfare wore a decidedly twentieth-century aspect in the demands it made on the engineers. These old sieges also have a modern relevance because they plunged settled populations into more immediate danger than did any other kind of warfare until the advent of aerial bombing. There grew up whole generations of town-dwellers who, like the Prince de Ligne, had witnessed several sieges in their childhood.

Most people in a theatre of war considered themselves lucky to have walls and a garrison as protection against marauding bands, but once a siege army arrived in the offing, all comfort and security came to an end. The governor was liable to regard villas, sheds and gardens as obstructions to his field of fire, and he might destroy them wholesale. Gaspard de Tavannes spoke with harsh military logic: 'Suburbs are fatal to fortresses. No well-advised governor, if he has the time, will ever leave houses, hedges or ditches unlevelled, for he knows that these features offer useful cover to the besiegers at the beginning of the attack' (Tavannes, 1850, 285).

Reviewing the military and commercial storehouses, the governor could well conclude that there was not enough food to nourish all the civilian population for any length of time. In this event the citizens who had not had the money or providence to lay in stocks of their own food now ran the risk of being designated 'useless mouths' and expelled from the fortress. At Siena, on 25 February 1555, 4,400 of these creatures were turned out by the governor Montluc. The Frenchman had to admit that 'of all the pitiful and afflicting sights I have seen, I truly believe that I have never witnessed, nor will ever again witness, anything quite so frightful. . . . These poor folk made their way towards the enemy, who merely chased them back to us. . . . But we remained firm, and the agony lasted for eight days. The refugees had only grass to eat, and more than half of them died, for the enemy helped to kill them off and very few managed to escape' (Monluc, 1571, II, 124).

The civilised French, in the civilised eighteenth century, deliberately chased refugee townspeople back into the fortifications at Freiburg in 1713 and 1744, and at Tournai in 1745. When the governor of the citadel of Tournai complained of the inhumanity, the Marshal de Saxe coolly replied: 'It is quite natural, monsieur, that we should profit by every advantage when we are forced to go to great efforts to reduce a fortress' (Augoyat, 1860–4, I, 351).

It is difficult to escape the conclusion that the 'rules of war' afforded more protection to the belligerents than to the civilians who were caught up in their quarrel.

The townspeople took a greater or lesser part in the defence according to local custom and the passions of the time. Thus the weak central government of old Muscovy relied heavily on the energy of its citizens to supply the lack of any effective system of national defence (Laskovskii, 1858–65, I, 207). Spain was another nation on the fringe of Europe where a tradition of popular resistance retained all its native vigour. At the defence of San Matheo against the French in 1649 'the undaunted women . . . like valiant Amazons, not only put their hands to such labours as their small strength was capable of, but also many of them, armed *cap-à-pé*, stood on the walls firing at the enemy so incessantly, that most of them lost one of their breasts, valuing, it seems, the honour of their sovereign above their own lives, and the defence of their country beyond the suckling of their offspring'.

In more civilised areas of Europe, the spirit of popular participation was preserved in con-fraternities of archers, sharpshooters and gunners, and by a general obligation of service upon able-bodied men. At Metz in 1552 and Turin in 1706 grand dignitaries like Duke Francis of Guise and Lieutenant-General Wirich Daun displayed a mastery of the common touch, and persuaded the citizens to play a vital part in the defence.

Whether they helped the garrison or not, all citizens were in peril of losing life and property if the town came under bombardment. Artillery was capable of inflicting frightful damage on a town. The effect of the notorious French cannonade of Brussels in 1695 is portrayed by Pierre Dorselaer:

We all believed . . . that we were quite able to withstand assault or even a formal siege, but a bombardment was something else again. Everyone was in a panic. Nobody knew where to hide his papers or treasures, and most of the people who were able to move betook themselves to the upper part of the town, which was the remotest area from the enemy.

On 13 August the French opened fire with a battery

76   Starvation in a besieged town

of eighteen heavy cannon and twenty-five mortars.

The first seconds were terrible. Everyone ran about shrieking. Women and children fled in all directions. . . . Great fires broke out simultaneously at several points, and none of the men knew where to obtain orders or where they should go to lend help.

The next day Pierre and Jean Dorselaer made their way towards the Grande Place:

The streets were a dreadful sight. As we approached the centre of the city we encountered more and more difficulty in making our way across the stones and assorted wreckage strewn across the ground. Whole blocks of houses had been destroyed, and our feet were burnt as we climbed over their still-smoking ruins (Dorselaer, 1908, 30–8).

The popular German literature of the Seven Years War confirms the impression that townsfolk were more alarmed by the possibility of bombardment than the certainty of regular siege. Poetasters like Cruez, Cronegk, Lichtwer, Ramler, Triller and Zacharias knew how to produce a gratifying shudder in their readers by introducing the mortar bomb as a symbol of destruction. (Very often the bomb is compared with a star or meteor, as it traces its fiery path through the night sky. The imagery is taken up by Adjutant Kalugin in Tolstoy's *Sevastopol*.)

The authorities gave the matter a great deal of consideration. The jurists Vitoria and Suárez conceded that the death of innocent persons was sometimes an unavoidable accompaniment to the attack on a town. Vattel was forced to agree, with specific reference to bombardment, 'but it is only in cases of the last extremity, and with reluctance, that good princes exert a right of so rigorous a nature' (Vattel, 1773, III, chapter 9).

Among the soldiers, Coehoorn was an opponent of the cannonade of towns; and the French, under the influence of Vauban, were generally unwilling to resort to bombardment, despite later lapses from grace at Brussels in 1695 and Bergen-op-Zoom in 1747. The English, Germans and Russians laboured under no such inhibitions, for they were almost incapable of making a formal artistic siege. The Spanish doctrine on bombardment seems to have been a compromise between the French and the Teutonic. According to De la Mina,

once the fortresses cease to offer suitable targets for the mortars, such as magazines, barracks, cisterns, etc., it is legitimate to aim the bombs at the remaining buildings – the cathedral, the convents and the great houses – so that the howls of the clergy, monks and nobles (and, following their example, the people) will reach the ears of the governor and urge him to capitulate (De la Mina, 1898, I, 38).

During the 1680s and 1690s there was a passing vogue for bombardment from the sea. French, English and Dutch all threw themselves into the business with great enthusiasm, arguing that they were meting out just punishment for insults or piracies. However, the results were rarely commensurate with the cost.

Sometimes the ordeal of the siege ended when the besiegers gave up the fight and marched away. More commonly, the fortress fell to the enemy and the townspeople had to live under whatever terms the governor had agreed with the enemy. (It was not until about the middle of the seventeenth century that the capture of a town by a full belligerent usually implied a complete replacement of sovereignty. It took another century for the conqueror's legal system to be imposed as well. See Lameire, 1902–11.)

There was little consistency in the treatment of subject townspeople. In the 1700s, in the former Swedish provinces of the southern Baltic shore, the Russians acted in a truly twentieth-century manner, deporting the populations of Dorpat and other towns to the interior. By the time of the Seven Years War, however, the Russian regular forces (as opposed to the Cossacks) had become perfect gentlemen. The French, too, were making a generally favourable impression in the little towns they seized in central Germany. Michaelis testifies that 'I went through a good many unpleasant episodes in the Seven Years War, but I must admit that I had some very pleasant times as well. Generally speaking the French were the best enemies you could imagine. They behaved towards

us with the greatest politeness and even affability'
(Schwarze, 1936, 37).

Townspeople always preferred a peaceful occupation, however harsh the conditions, to the horrors
attendant upon the capture of their city by storm.
Theologians and jurists were forced to bow to the
regrettable fact to which de Saxe referred when he
was in the siege works at Eger in 1742, namely that
'the thing which keeps all soldiers so cheerful and
makes them work with superhuman energy is the
promise I made to them that they could plunder the
town, if they took it by storm' (Augoyat, 1860–4, II,
225).

The unholy business of plunder had a custom and
routine of its own. La Noue heard that the general
opinion was 'that the sack of a town should last only
three days. You should certainly observe this limit if
you intend to keep the town afterwards. The time is
allocated as follows: one whole day to plunder the
town, another day to carry away the booty, and the
third to restore the army to order. But in all such
affairs the commanders allow a greater or lesser time
according to their own intentions and the difficulty
they know they will experience in getting the troops
to obey orders. The troops will return to obedience
much sooner in small and poor towns than in large
and wealthy cities' (La Noue, 1850, 602). Vitoria
protested that it was 'undoubtedly unjust to the
extreme to deliver up a city, especially a Christian
city, to be sacked, without the greatest necessity and
weightiest reason' (Vitoria, 1532, chapter 52, lxviii),
but Grotius showed himself to be more interested in
the rules which governed the dividing of plunder
than with the right to take the booty in the first place.

Grotius is predictably ferocious in what he has to
say on the subject of massacre. 'How wide the
allowance of doing harm to enemies extends, may be
understood from this: that the slaughter of infants
and women is allowed to have impunity, as
comprehended in that right of war. I will not here
adduce the slaying of the women and the little ones
of Heshbon (Deut. ii, 34), and what they did to the
Canaanites and their allies, for these are the doings
of God, who had a more absolute right over men
than men have over brutes. But a passage which
approaches more nearly to a testimony of the
common usage of nations is that of the Psalms,

cxxxvii, 9, "Happy shall he be that taketh and
dasheth thy little ones against the stones"'
(Grotius, 1625, III, chapter 4). Not many people
would have been prepared to go quite as far as that.
Vitoria (1532, chapter 45) recoils from the harsh
message of the Old Testament, and concludes that it
is not justifiable to cut down any person who had
fought in good faith, even if his sovereign happens to
be in the wrong. Two centuries later Santa Cruz and
Vattel set themselves firmly against any maltreat-
ment of the innocent townspeople.

The decisive arguments against massacre and
unrestricted plunder were nevertheless military
ones. A ravaging army was liable to lose all
discipline, and might need weeks to be restored to
fighting order. Besides, the sack of a town would
probably destroy stores and accommodation, and
would certainly deprive the victor of that other
valuable commodity, the goodwill of the townspeople.

Whatever the outcome of the siege, more civilians
and soldiers were likely to die of pestilence than the
work of sword, musket and cannon. In the course of
any long siege the town and the trenches became
populated with hungry, dirty and weak human
beings, decaying corpses, and flourishing generations of rats, lice and fleas. Sometimes the
consequent epidemics became so deadly as to throw
out all the calculations of generals and engineers. In
1552 the Imperialists were forced to abandon their
attack on Metz largely because of the ravages of
scurvy, dysentery and typhus in their camp. After
Wrangel took Frederiksodde in 1657 'the dead
bodies, having been thrown by heaps into holes, and
but ill-covered, broke out again, insomuch, that the
streets ran with gore and matter, which issued from
those disinterred carcasses' (Manley, 1670, 55). The
infection compelled the Swedes to leave the place the
next year.

The circumstances of a siege, with thousands of
men concentrating to defend or attack a stronghold,
and dispersing afterwards in all directions, were
ideally suited to the spreading of disease over an
entire continent. Naples was a notorious reservoir of
all kinds of horrid infection. It was here that syphilis
– the New World's revenge on the Old – first
established itself in virulent form. The pox struck

down thousands of townspeople and soldiers after the French captured the place in 1495, and the demobilised troops and camp-followers spread the infection throughout Europe. Thirty-five years later half of Lautrec's army succumbed to typhus before the same city, which gave rise to another continent-wide epidemic. The disease became endemic in eastern Europe, from where the survivors of the Turkish wars periodically re-infected the rest of the continent. During the English Civil War Dr Edward Greaves was observant enough to establish the relationship between the *Morbus Castrensis* which had ravaged the Imperial army in Hungary in 1566, and the disease which was carrying away the Royalist garrison at Oxford, 'it being seldom or never known that an army where there is so much filth and nastiness of diet, worse lodging, unshifted apparell, etc., should continue long without contagious diseases' (Varley, 1932, 96).

Bubonic plague was another classic 'siege' or 'camp' disease. In 1710 the plague-ridden garrison of Revel capitulated on good terms to the Russians, and carried the disease back with them to Scandinavia, with devastating results. In Sweden alone thirty thousand people died of the epidemic between August 1710 and February 1711.

In some of the Mediterranean ports, quarantine (literally 'forty days' isolation') was established as a defensive system against disease as early as the second half of the fourteenth century. The Austrian Empire came to serve as Europe's main buffer against the plague-ridden East, and in the eighteenth century the military governors of the border provinces were careful to maintain a network of informers in the Turkish dominions. As soon as warning of plague arrived, the border was placed under military guard, and travellers were detained in pest houses until the incubation period was over.

Garrison and townsfolk

For all but a tiny fraction of its existence a fortress contained military and civilian communities which remained untouched by the march of grand events. The histories and memoirs tell us a great deal about the relationship between governor and townspeople during the excitement of sieges, but we catch only the briefest glimpses of the day-to-day life of a fortress in time of peace.

The surviving evidence is mostly concerned with the many causes of friction which set soldiers and townspeople at odds. In frontier zones the traveller and the citizen were faced with the inconvenience of having to pass the gates before the doors were shut at sunset. Even in daytime it was risky to stride too briskly past the guards, for you ran the danger of being interrogated as a suspected spy.

The area of the fortifications and the glacis was a military zone in which the townspeople were allowed only on sufferance. Vauban regarded Philippeville as a model town of how a fortress should be maintained: 'The covered ways are as uniform and clean as a wooden table top. Both cattle and people are forbidden to walk on the covered ways, or on any of the parapets of the ramparts of the outworks' (D'Aiglun, 1910, II, 83).

Since the townspeople were normally denied territorial rights, the officers of the garrison could fight among themselves for the rights to cut the trees on the ramparts, catch the fish in the ditches and inundations, and mow the grass of the parapets and glacis.

These annoyances were as nothing compared with the monstrous imposition of billeting, by which the garrison lived on the townspeople. In France the householders of the garrison towns were under an obligation to lodge whatever soldiers were deposited on them, to do their cooking, and to provide them with fuel, bedding, knives, plates, pepper, salt and vinegar. In 1646 the citizens of Perpignan suggested that it would be a good thing to put up all the soldiers in specially-built houses near the fortress gates. Michel Le Tellier found the proposal 'reasonable and advantageous' (André, 1906, 363), but it was not until 1719, when the barrack system was generally established, that the French townspeople were relieved of their onerous obligations.

Some governments placed their towns under virtual military occupation. Such was notoriously the case in the Prussia of Frederick the Great. It was hardly surprising that the people of most of the Prussian fortress-towns looked on with complete indifference when the French attacked the garrisons in 1806.

Misunderstandings and quarrels were inevitable when town and garrison were separated by nationality and religion, as in the Dutch Barrier Fortresses in the Austrian Netherlands. In 1735 the municipality of Namur lodged a complaint to the effect that 'the garrison seems to go out of its way to display its delinquent soldiers and prostitutes on the wooden horse in the centre of the main square at the very instant when religious processions are due to pass by. This actually happened on the last feast of Corpus Christi' (Hubert, 1901–3, 45–6). The Dutch replied in their turn that the citizens were touchy, foul-mouthed and violent.

However, garrisons preferred to do their service in a fortress-town than to be marooned in some God-forsaken battery or fort, where all the desolation of a purely military establishment reigned supreme. Strindberg, one of the gloomy Scandinavian dramatists of the turn of the century, was careful to stipulate that his story of married misery, *The Dance of Death*, should be set in 'the interior of a circular fort of grey stone. In the background two large gates with glass doors, showing a sea-coast with batteries and the sea.' Conditions like these broke the spirit of a whole generation of American officers before the Civil War. Robert E. Lee wrote in 1833 from Fort Monroe: 'Know, my friend, that it is a situation full of pains, and one from which I shall modestly retire on the first fitting opportunity. . . . My opinion on these matters has been formed, from the little experience I have had of a garrison life in time of peace, where I have seen minds for use and ornament, degenerate into sluggishness and inactivity, requiring the stimulus of brandy or cards to rouse them to action' (Freeman, 1934–5, I, 122).

The fortress and the imagination
Of all the various kinds of building the fortress is one of the most compelling, pressing in as it does on human beings by its great physical mass and the number of images it suggests. These may be categorised variously as the dramatic, the spooky, the sexual and the quasi-religious.

Ever since the days of Homer storytellers have appreciated that a siege affords them a naturally strong narrative line, together with the opportunity to explore the motives and characters of the combatants at greater length than is possible when the subject is a brisk affair like a battle in the open field. The treatment of the theme has ranged from the preposterousness of Marlowe's *Jew of Malta* (*c.* 1590) to the pomposity of the Restoration 'heroic play' (D'Avenant's *Siege of Rhodes*, 1661, Orrery's *Tragedy of Mustafa*, 1668) and the splendidly-flowing *Siege of Corinth* (set in 1715) by Lord Byron, which relies for its effect on sonorous rhythm and a judicious sprinkling of technical terms.

Byron's siege of Corinth reaches a suitably dramatic climax when the Turks storm in and massacre the garrison. A siege which provides a merciful contrast was the Spanish attack on Breda in 1625, which ended in a peaceful composition and the embrace of Spinola and the tough old governor Justin of Nassau. This one episode inspired artistic enterprises as diverse as the famous canvas by Velázquez, Lope de Vega's ode in honour of Marquis Spinola (see p. 101), Calderón's play *La Redención de Breda*, and Richard Strauss's little opera *Friedenstag*.

It did not take dramatists long to discover that a fortress setting offered them a dungeon for incarcerating heroes (like Florestan in Beethoven's *Fidelio*), a courtyard or hall for crowd-scenes, banquets and dances, and precipitous steps and rampart walks from which people could fall to their deaths (witness the fate of de Piracquo at Alicante in Middleton's *The Changeling* (1622), and the leap from the Castle of Sant'Angelo which puts a welcome end to Tosca and the whole of Puccini's opera).

In 1750 Horace Walpole announced his ambition 'to build a little Gothic Castle at Strawberry Hill'. When the physical structure was mostly complete he proceeded to write a novel, *The Castle of Otranto* (1764), which permitted him to fill the place in his imagination with clanking pieces of armour, skeletal hermits, and 'a deep and hollow groan' which sounded through the castle from the battlements. The first foreign imitation, von Gerstenberg's *Ugolino*, appeared only five years later, for the Continentals had lingering memories of the *Torre de fame*, or *Burgverliess*, the sinister towers of medieval times which swallowed souls without trace. In

77   Maidenly virtue under attack

Walpole's own country all the horrific, dramatic and picturesque aspects of the Gothick Castle were explored over the next century by such devotees of the genre as Mrs Radcliffe, Matthew Lewis, Walter Scott, Robert Southey, and Bram Stoker who accompanies us to the abode of Count Dracula, 'a vast, ruined castle, from whose tall black windows came no ray of light, and whose broken battlements showed a jagged line against the moonlit sky' (1897). Edgar Allan Poe brought the Gothick horrors to the United States.

All of this helped to give fortresses a bad name. The Austrian and Tsarist governments did not improve the reputation when they confined the more excitable of their political agitators in otherwise very praiseworthy strongholds like the Spielberg at Brünn and the Peter-Paul Fortress at St Petersburg.

We encounter a subtler approach in Kafka, whose *Castle* (1926) was a rambling, unmilitary, unthreatening place, which housed a closed and impenetrable bureaucracy. Nearly three centuries before Kafka's time, the same isolated and slightly unreal nature of life inside a stronghold was represented by Calderón in *Life is a Dream*, where two travellers, marooned in a Polish fortress, speculate on whether they can be sure of their own existence, let alone that of the mysterious prisoner Prince Segismundo.

There are a number of siege histories which are specific in their comparison of a beleaguered, virgin fortress with a maiden who is fighting in defence of her virtue. The original inspiration came from the Castle of Love of the medieval troubadours, but the Elizabethan and Jacobean poets and dramatists, being lusty folk and well-versed in military affairs, exploited the simile in more earthy terms. Thus Arthur Broke describes the victorious siege of his 'Julieit'

And now the virgin's fort hath warlike Romeus got,
In which as yet no breach was made by Force of cannon shot.

According to Beaumont and Fletcher there was another girl, much less obliging, who fortified her maidenhead so strongly that Spinola himself would have been 'just a ditcher to her' (*The Woman's Prize*). Shakespeare's Helena, in *All's Well that Ends Well*, is only following accepted convention when she exclaims, 'Bless our poor virginity from underminers and blowers up!' (Act 1, Scene 1). Similar metaphors became current in French literature after the Wars of the Fronde.

All this, of course, is probably some kind of roundabout invitation. It has been translated into modern terms by the girls of the Hamburg Reeperbahn, who display themselves in windows with barbed wire wound about their boots.

More serious-minded people, and sometimes entire embattled communities, have derived comfort from associating themselves with the notion of a fortress under siege. The ancient message of Psalm 18 was echoed in Luther's *Ein feste Burg ist unser Gott*, and the epic defences of Masada and Londonderry have held something more than historical interest for the young nation of Israel and the Protestants of Northern Ireland. The imagery is remarkably persistent. The Republic of South Africa has adopted the bastioned pentagon as insignia for its aircraft, while the workers of the Asahi Chemical Company of Japan proclaim every day that their company is 'a living fortress to be guarded against calamity'.

The fortress as architecture

Functionalism may be defined as the strange doctrine which proclaims that if a building happens to be well-designed for a particular purpose, some divine dispensation will make sure that the result will look right, as well as do its job. You are almost convinced that there is something in the idea, when you look at some colonial or Mediterranean fortress, which is built of dazzling white stone and pleases the eye with the advancing and receding planes of its walls. An Italian art historian throws himself into raptures over the fortress of Civitavecchia, where the finishing touches were applied by Michelangelo himself: 'The towers and the polygonal keep advance on the shore like the metal-shod rams of ancient vessels. The surrounding cordon, which separates the cylindrical parts of the towers from the conical, appears almost to compress the fortress like a tight rope of steel. The surfaces are almost luminous, so polished are they, so shining and well-turned, while the cornice which surrounds the whole mass possesses the fine-drawn delicacy of a silken ribbon' (Venturi, 1938–9, I, 531).

Unfortunately, a place like this is very much an exception. The generality of fortresses prove to be non-architectural assemblages of grassy mounds, ditches, and low-lying walls, at once vast and unimpressive. At Florence the dull walls of the Fortezza da Basso look disconcertingly like an embankment of the nearby railway. To find a striking visual impression we must go to the fortress plans, where the lines of rampart, ditch and outwork describe rhythmical zig-zags across the paper, foreshadowing the work of the twentieth-century Vorticists and artists like Eugenio Carmi or Delima Madeiros.

The deadening weight of artillery fortification crushes the life out of ornamental eclecticism as effectively as from functionalism. In the middle of the nineteenth century, when the restoration of Cologne Cathedral was in train, King Frederick William IV of Prussia was inspired to have the new fortifications of Königsberg decked out with turrets, battlements, portrait-medallions and rosettes, all executed in red sandstone. The result was merely incongruous. Vauban showed better taste when he built his fortress gates in an austere style which looks forward a century to the neo-classicism of Ledoux. The tall, gaudy gates at Lille are the work not of Vauban, but of his assistant Simon Vollant.

It is not easy to determine exactly when and where the professions of military and civil architect parted company. In Italy, as we have seen, the division was complete in the second half of the sixteenth century (see p. 41).

Outside Italy the split does not appear to have been so absolute. If fortification became rather too technical for primarily civilian architects to tackle with confidence, there were still some non-Italian military engineers who continued to make forays outside their speciality. Vauban ran up some sober but very competent churches at Neuf-Brisach, Mont-Dauphin and Givet. His ideas on architecture were presented to the next generation by the highly-influential Belidor, who collected such of the master's teachings as were preserved among engineers and masons, and was at pains to prevent the younger officers from falling into the grips of a narrow professionalism:

All too many folk are ready to set themselves up as

experts because they can trace a front of fortifications on paper, and all too many imagine that everything which does not directly concern fortification belongs to the province of the civilian architects. There are even engineers who believe that they debase themselves when they apply themselves to architecture, as if it were more glorious to build a barrack block than a portico (Belidor, 1729, V, 2).

It is plain that Belidor was already fighting something of a losing battle in France. In Germany, however, the tradition of the old-time soldier-architect was actually at its apogee. A touch of Italian lightness was brought to the Austrian High Baroque by Johann Lucas von Hildebrandt (1663–1745), who had been schooled in all the branches of architecture in Rome, and accompanied Prince Eugene as military engineer on the Piedmontese campaigns of 1695 and 1696.

In the 1720s and 1730s Hildebrandt was engaged with the Franconian engineer-gunner Johann Balthasar Neumann (1687–1753) in the planning and execution of the episcopal *Residenz* at Würzburg. Neumann, however, was solely responsible for the design of the stairway hall, which is one of the largest and most impressive enclosed spaces in secular architecture. The military engineer Johann Jacob Küchel (1703–69) was a pupil of Neumann, and his colleague in the service of the Schönborn bishops. In the 1740s they collaborated to build the pilgrimage church of Vierzehnheiligen. Neumann worked out the ground plan of intersecting ovals, while Küchel contributed the free-standing *Gnadenaltar*, that swirling body of porphyry columns, rococo confectionery and gesticulating saints. It seems as if Küchel and his friend were rejoicing in the opportunity to break loose from everything that was grim, purposeful and earth-bound in their trade of military engineering.

The fortress-town as habitat

The influence of the engineer was not confined to the fortifications, or to individual buildings inside the town. In fact the whole urban area represented a subtle compromise between the two concepts of the city as a place for people to live in and a place for soldiers to defend.

In some places the two purposes went in tandem. The Danish and Swedish monarchs of the sixteenth and seventeenth centuries regarded their new fortresses as centres of communications and trading, as well as military strongpoints. Similarly the Venetians and the Spanish did everything they could to attract people and commerce to the splendid but under-inhabited fortresses at Palmanova and Charleroi. Concerning Charleroi a royal patent of 1688 reads: 'The town being empty, we have resolved to fill it with a large number of inhabitants. Not only will we present them with the sites for their buildings and houses, but we will defray the cost of all the house walls and facades which are built inside the enceinte. The populace will be exempt from all taxes and levies' (Lavedan, 1959, 249). The Russians did not bother with such incentives when they wished to populate their new settlements in Siberia: they simply deported military families and civilian communities *en masse*.

In the case of long-established and flourishing cities, the authorities were faced with the very different problem of how to bring the galloping suburbs under some kind of control. At Paris the government issued threatening pronouncements about further building in 1627, 1633, 1638, 1724, 1728 and 1765. All were ignored. Louis XIII boldly built a new enceinte between 1633 and 1636, and saw it almost immediately swallowed up by a new mushroom growth of civilian building. In these circumstances it was almost impossible to provide the suburbs with an effective defence against serious attack. A remedy adopted in the eighteenth century was to contain the vast urban areas by miles of lightly-built 'excise walls', which gave the authorities the means of levying tolls on passing traffic, and halting deserters and other suspicious people.

The masonry-built Vienna *Lienienwälle* dated from 1724, and followed the trace of the earthworks which were thrown up twenty years earlier against roving bands of Hungarian cavalry. Its perimeter is represented today by the line of the *Gürtel*. The Berlin customs wall was founded by Frederick William I in 1737, and was intended from the beginning to second the work of the police and the excise officials. The most famous surviving relic of this perimeter is Langhans' Brandenburger Tor of 1784, which, for all the grandiose bellicosity of its design, was never intended to ward off an enemy. The *Mur des Fermiers Généraux* at Paris was built between 1785 and 1787 along the line of the present outer boulevards. It was over fourteen miles long, and was inset with the forty-seven gates which are famed in history and fiction for the rigorous searches of traffic which were instituted at the time of the Terror.

The excise walls were flimsy affairs compared with the massive enceintes which protected the hearts of cities and towns against formal siege by heavy artillery. These girdles of masonry and earth were immensely deep, Vauban's fortifications at Neuf-Brisach measuring no less than seven hundred feet from the 'tail' of the glacis to the townward-facing talus. Consequently the new fortifications proved to be far more difficult to extend or adapt than were the comparatively thin town walls of medieval times. Strasbourg, which had undergone four extensions between 1200 and 1450, was contained within essentially the same perimeter of artillery fortifications between 1580 and 1870, even though the population had risen three-fold in the same period.

Within the severely-circumscribed compass of the fortress-towns the people had to build upwards in order to find space to live and work. Whole generations of Continental town-dwellers grew up in flats, jammed together in a proximity that was startling to visitors from eighteenth-century England, where the almost unlimited urban space enabled the gentry and merchants to take up their residence in town houses which were disposed around tree-shaded squares. Lady Wortley Montagu (1887, I, 112–13) discovered that the Inner City of Vienna 'did not at all answer to my ideas of it, being much less than I expected to find it. . . . The town being so much too little for the number of people that desire to live in it, the builders seem to have projected to repair that misfortune by clapping one town on top of the other, most of the houses being of five, and some of six storeys. You may easily imagine that the streets being so narrow, the lower rooms are extremely dark; and, what is an incon-

veniency much more intolerable, in my opinion, there is no house that has so few as five or six families in it. The apartments of the greatest ladies, and even of the ministers of state, are divided but by a partition from that of a tailor or shoemaker' (1716).

Lewis Mumford, the historian of urban life, has drawn a dark picture of the plight of the poorer people of the Continental fortress-cities, who had lost the open spaces they had enjoyed in the Middle Ages, and were now separated from the open country by the deep, sterile band of the new artillery fortifications (Mumford, 1966, 413). This representation is altogether too gloomy. The fortress-towns had a taut, crowded vitality of their own, and even the poorest citizen enjoyed the convenience of having markets, churches and places of work within walking distance of his home. The country was a long way away, to be sure, but in compensation the park-like rampart walks and glacis were close at hand on all sides. In 1963 an Austrian town-planner looked back with envy on the disposition of the fortified city of the Baroque period: 'Around the city centre are grouped the units of satellite towns, separated from the centre by the broad green area of the glacis. Other "green belts" separate the satellite towns from each other. Here we see a functionally clearly organised yet lively, nature-connected urban organism' (Gruen, 1965, 37).

Then there is the aesthetic aspect. The Prince de Ligne, a fairly sure guide on matters of taste, said of the Inner City of Vienna that 'the very compactness of the kernel of the city lends it a startling and agreeable air, through the movement of its immense population. If Vienna were joined to the suburbs it would become a large but totally insignificant city' (De Ligne, 1795, X, 231). In de Ligne's time the closely-packed spires and roofs of the European fortress-towns rose dramatically from within their girdle of dun-coloured ramparts, and presented the traveller with a striking and immediately comprehensible impression of the character of the place. This precious sense of arriving at a town has been diminished by almost every urban development of the nineteenth and twentieth centuries: the demolition of the ramparts, the extension of the suburbs and industries, and the building of the railways, motorways and airports by which men

78   Vienna in the later seventeenth century. View across the Danube Canal to the Biberbastei, at the north-eastern angle of the enceinte. The Dominikanerbastei is at the top of the engraving, and the bastion known later as the Rotenturmbastei at the right

Opposite

79 *above*   The first of a series of photographs taken in about 1858, shortly before the demolition of the fortifications. We are looking down the south-eastern side of the enceinte from the tall Franz Josef fortified barracks, built on the site of the Biberbastei and Dominikanerbastei. The bastion to the front is sometimes known as the Braunbastei, and the building with columns is the Coburg Palace, sometime quarters of the governor of Vienna

80 *below*   The corresponding view westwards, looking up the Danube Canal, towards the Rotenturmtor and the Rotenturmbastei

nowadays slide from one urban complex to another, carrying with them little or no awareness of having left their home town.

The military architect has the distinction of being numbered among the first people who were prepared to consider every element of a town in relation to the whole organism; in other words, he was a conscious urbanist. The eighteenth-century Anglo-German engineer John Müller states that 'towns were formerly built anyhow, according to the builder's fancy, without the least regard to regularity of beauty: but nowadays, when a place is fortified, which is not occupied by any houses or other buildings, great care is taken to make every part within as regular as possible' (Müller, 1755, 208–9). What motivated the engineer was not so much the

ideal of symmetry for its own sake, as the need to arrange the town so as to provide easy access to the ramparts for the guns and men, and to enable the garrison to command the streets from a few central points.

From that highly-respected ancient, Vitruvius, and from contemporary writers like Francesco di Giorgio Martini and Girolamo Maggi, the Italian engineers of the sixteenth century derived two methods of laying out a town on regular lines: the radial scheme and the gridiron plan.

The radial-concentric (spider's web) scheme of street planning was carried out on a fairly modest scale in the 1540s and 1550s in a number of fortress-towns along the Ardennes border of France and the Spanish Netherlands (the French town of

81, 82 Side and frontal views of the Kärntnertor, on the southern side of Vienna. The site is now one of the busiest traffic junctions of Vienna, just by the Opera House, and it is difficult to imagine that such high walls and such a narrow gate ever stood on this spot (Courtesy of the Historical Museum of the City of Vienna)

Villefranche-sur-Meuse 1545, and the Spanish towns of Mariembourg 1546, Hesdin 1554 and Philippeville 1555), and in a much more ambitious style at the Venetian fortress of Palmanova in 1593. The Dutch followed suit at Coevorden in 1597. The radial plan was simple in concept, and attractive to the eye, but suffered from the one great disadvantage of dividing the town into segment-shaped blocks which became more and more narrow as they approached the city centre. The greatest practicable number of radial spokes was found to be eleven, a quantity which was achieved in 1666 at Charleroi, the last important essay in the style.

The prosaic but practical gridiron plan provided strong competition for the radial scheme from the very beginning. As early as 1545 Girolamo Marini chose to build the showpiece fortress-town of Vitry-le-François as a series of rectangular blocks. The still more famous fortress of Valletta was laid out on the same lines in 1566. Bernardo Morando brought the gridiron to Zamosc in Poland in 1578, while the Dutch adopted the pattern with enthusiasm, and applied it in their homeland, in the fortresses they designed in Sweden and Denmark, and in the arrangement of the crocodile-haunted creeks at Batavia. The English architects, who were far from being the most advanced in their profession, laid out the new Ulster towns of Derry and Coleraine on gridiron schemes in the early 1600s. Turin was rebuilt on strict gridiron plans in the seventeenth and eighteenth centuries, and so was Lisbon after the earthquake of 1755. The inhuman practice of

designating blocks by letters or numbers probably began at Mannheim in 1699. The Western fashion did not escape the notice of the princely mathematician and astronomer Jai Singh, who had his city of Jaipur built on the most exact gridiron principles in 1728. (L. M. Tverskoi makes an unconvincing attempt to establish Russian precedence in town-planning by drawing attention to such allegedly advanced exercises in urbanism as the 'gridiron' at Tiumen in Siberia (1586) or the 'radial' expansion of Moscow and Putivl. The wandering, irregular patterns of these places reveal no evidence of deliberate design, and there is no sign of any continuity with the layouts which were adopted under Western influence at Elisavetgrad in 1754, Sevastopol and Ekaterinoslav in 1784, or Ekaterinodar and Odessa in 1794.)

Where Vauban had a free hand in setting out a town he invariably employed the gridiron plan (Hüningen, Sarrelouis and Longwy 1679, Mont-Louis 1681, Mont-Dauphin 1692–93 and Neuf-Brisach 1698), and was careful to make the main square spacious enough to accommodate the entire garrison at morning parade. Belidor, who went into the question in some detail, held that a fortress of eleven or twelve bastions required a central square with sides between 180 and 190 yards long. The main streets were to be twelve yards wide, which would accommodate three carts abreast together with the pedestrians. Where the main streets approached the gates they were to be enlarged into small squares, which would act as a safeguard against the surprise of the guards from the townward side, and afford parking space for the vehicles queuing to leave the fortress.

So it was that military engineering preserved the traditions of Renaissance urbanism until they were taken up again by the civil architects in the Baroque period. At Erlangen, Mannheim, Karlshafen and Ludwigslust the princely palaces form the same kind of focus for the streets that was provided by the citadel at Coevorden a century earlier. William Penn, the most peaceful of souls, adopted the gridiron scheme for his open city of Philadelphia, founded in 1682. Similar plans were carried out at Baltimore in 1729 and Savannah in 1733, and became the norm for new settlements in North America.

By the second half of the nineteenth century the old, continuous town enceintes were giving way to a new fortification based on detached forts which stood miles out into the country. Many fortress-towns, famous as such throughout the centuries, became almost indistinguishable from the run of ordinary, unheroic open places. In France bulwark gave way to 'boulevard', which is essentially the same word, while in the Germanic lands the city fathers replaced the fortified perimeters by monumental *Ringstrassen*, which were bordered by an array of governmental buildings, parks, railway stations and slab-like hotels and apartment blocks. The fortifications of the Inner City of Vienna were demolished in 1858 and the following years; the Line Wall disappeared in 1893, and the *Gürtel*, which replaced it, provided a convenient means of communication between the three railway stations that were disposed around the perimeter: the Franz-Josef Bahnhof, the Westbahnhof and the Südbahnhof. The Berlin excise wall went in 1867, and gave way to the Ringbahn.

'Ghost fortresses' make an uncanny appearance in the plans of many towns where the fortifications have disappeared centuries ago. The primitive radial plan of the Dutch town of New Amsterdam still determines the street pattern of the lower part of Manhattan Island: present-day Beaver Street is the descendant of one of the radiating spokes, while Wall Street represents the line of the stockade which was raised in 1633 against the English and all the savages of North America.

At Vienna the area of the historic and blood-drenched Burg Ravelin is now covered with cafés and rosebeds. Other towns, less ambitious, were content to let almost the whole circuit of the fortifications enter a dignified retirement as public gardens. The war-weary Andrew Marvell at last had an answer to his question:

Shall we never more
That sweet militia restore
When gardens only had their towers,
And all the garrisons were flowers;
When roses only arms might bear,
And men did rosy garlands wear?

(A Garden. Written after the Civil Wars)

Bibliography

Note References to *Nouvelle Collection des mémoires pour souir à l'histoire de France*, ed. Michaud and Poujoulat, Paris, 1850 are abbreviated as *Nouvelle Collection*.

Adelung, F. V. (1846), *Kritisch-Literärische Übersicht der Reisenden in Russland*, 2 vols, St Petersburg.

d'Aiglun, Rochas (1910), *Vauban, sa famille et ses écrits*, 2 vols, Paris.

Alex, W. (1968), *Japanese Architecture*, London.

Allent, A. (1805), *Histoire du corps impériale du génie*, first and only vol. Paris. Despite the title, Allent traces the history of French engineering from the earliest days of the royal corps.

Almirante, J. (1876), *Bibliografía Militar de España*, Madrid. Especially on the first Spanish textbooks.

Almirante, J. (1923), *Bosquejo de la Historia Militar de España*, 4 vols, Madrid.

Alva, Duke of (1952), *Epistolario del III Duque de Alba*, 3 vols, Madrid.

Anderson, R. C. (1952), *Naval Wars in the Levant*, Liverpool.

Anderson, W. (1970), *Castles of Europe*, London. Excellent.

d'Andilly (1850), *Mémoires de Messire Robert Arnauld d'Andilly*, in *Nouvelle Collection*, 2nd series IX, Paris.

Andrada (1930), *Commentaries of Ruy Freyre de Andrada*, trans. and ed. C. R. Boxer, London.

André, L. (1906), *Michel le Tellier et l'organisation de l'armée monarchique*, Paris.

Anon (1885), 'Brandenburg-Preussen auf der Westküste von Afrika 1681–1721', in *Kreigsgeschichtliche Einzelschriften*, VI, Berlin.

Anon (1823), *A Brief Journall of the Siege against Lathom*, printed London.

Anon (1867), *The Garrisons of Shropshire during the Civil War, 1642–48*, Shrewsbury.

Anon (1630), *Histoire des deux dernières sièges de La Rochelle*, Paris.

Anon (1631), *Le Siège de Breda*, Antwerp.

Anon (1821), *A Visit to Madras*, London, quoted in S. Nilsson (1968), *European Architecture in India 1750–1850*, London.

(Aparaci y Garcia, J.) (1846), 'Resumen Historico del Arma de Ingenieros', in *Memorial de Ingenieros*, I, Madrid.

Aparici y Garcia, J. (1851), 'Trata de la Biographias de los Ingenieros que Existieron en España en el Siglo XVI', in *Memorial de Ingenieros*, VI, Madrid.

Arnauld (1850), *Mémoires de l'Abbé Arnauld* (son of d'Andilly), in *Nouvelle Collection*, 2nd series, IX, Paris.

Augoyat, M. (1860–4), *Aperçu historique sur les fortifications, les ingénieurs et le corps du génie de France*, 2nd edn, 3 vols, Paris. Probably the most important single work on the history of military engineering.

d'Aumale (1850), *Mémoirs-Journaux de Francois de Lorraine, Duc d'Aumale et de Guise*, in *Nouvelle Collection*, 1st series, VI, Paris.

d'Aumale, Duc (1886–96), *Histoire des Princes de Condé*, vols III–IV, Paris.

d'Avenel, G. (1884–95), *Richelieu et la Monarchie absolue*, 2nd edn, 4 vols, Paris.

Axelson, E. (1940), *South-East Africa 1488–1530*, London.

Axelson, E. (1960), *Portuguese in South-East Africa 1600–1700*, Johannesburg.

Balbi di Coreggio, Francisco (1568), *The Siege of Malta 1565*, trans. E. Bradford, London, 1965.

Baldock, T. S. (1899), *Cromwell as a Soldier*, London.

Barado, F. (1895), *Sitio de Amberes en 1584–1585*, Madrid.

Barker, T. M. (1975), *The Military Intellectual and Battle:*

Raimondo Montecuccoli and the Thirty Years War, Albany.

Barry, Gerrat (1627), *The Siege of Breda*, Louvain. Barry was one of the many Irish soldiers in Spinola's army.

Barry, Gerrat (1634), Discourse of Military Discipline, Brussels.

Barry, J. (1959), 'The Military History of Youghal', in *The Irish Sword. The Journal of the Military History Society of Ireland*, IV, no. 15, Dublin.

Bassompierre (1850), *Mémoires du Maréchal de Bassompierre*, in *Nouvelle Collection*, 2nd series VI, Paris. An intelligent commentary on the wars of Louis XIII.

Baudart, G. (1616), *Les Guerres de Nassau*, 2 vols, Amsterdam. An informative account with many lively illustrations.

Bayley, A. R. (1910), *The Great Civil War in Dorset 1642–1660*, Taunton.

Belidor, B. F. (1729), *La Science des ingénieurs*, Paris.

Du Bellay, G. and M. (1850), *Mémoires* (1569), in *Nouvelle Collection*, 1st series V, Paris. The French writers of this period are more than usually intelligent, chatty and informative. Many of the best accounts have been brought together in the useful volumes of the *Nouvelle Collection*.

Belleroche, E. (1892), *The Siege of Ostend or the New Troy*, London.

Belli, Pierino (1936), *A Treatise on Military Matters and Warfare* (1563), 2 vols, Oxford. Belli was an auditor in Charles V's armies.

Benevolo, L. (1978), *The Architecture of the Renaissance*, 2 vols, London.

Bentivoglio, Cardinal, (1678), *The History of the Wars of Flanders*, trans. Henry Earl of Monmouth, 2nd edn, London.

Birch, J. H. (1938), *Denmark in History*, London.

Blaes, J. B. (ed.) (1859–61), *Mémoires anonymes sur les troubles des Pays-Bas 1565–1580*, 3 vols, Brussels.

Blondel (1684), *Nouvelle Manière de Fortifier les Places*, The Hague.

Blondel (1685), *L'art de jetter les bombes*, The Hague.

Bonaparte, Louis-Napoléon (1851), *Etudes sur le passé et l'avenir de l'artillerie*, vol. II, Paris. Traces the history of fortress warfare up to 1648.

Bonin, U. v. (1877–8), *Geschichte des Ingenieurkorps und der Pioniere in Preussen*, 2 parts, Berlin.

Bonneval (1738), *Mémoires du Comte de Bonneval*, 2nd edn. 3 vols, The Hague.

Boots, J. L. (1934), 'Korean Weapons and Armour', in *Transactions of the Korea Branch of the Royal Asiatic Society*, XXIII, part 2, Seoul.

Boxer, C. R. (1936), *Jan Compagnie in Japan, 1600–1817*,

The Hague. New edn (1968), London.

Boxer, C. R. (1951), *The Christian Century in Japan 1549–1650*, London.

Boxer, C. R. (ed.) (1953), *South China in the 16th Century* (Hakluyt Society) London.

Boxer, C. R. (1965), *The Dutch Seaborne Empire*, London.

Boxer, C. R. (1969), *The Portuguese Seaborne Empire*, London.

Boxer, C. R., and Azevedo, A. de (1960), *Fort Jesus and the Portuguese in Mombasa 1593–1729*, London.

Boyd, A (1962), *Chinese Architecture and Town-Planning 1500 B.C.–A.D. 1911*, London.

Boynton, L. (1967), *The Elizabethan Militia*, London.

Boyvin, J. (1638), *Le Siège de la ville de Dôle*, Antwerp. A vivid eyewitness account of the defence of the town in 1636.

Bradford, E. (1961), *The Great Siege* (Malta 1565), London.

Branthôme (1858–78), *Oeuvres complètes de Pierre de Bourdeilles, Abbé at Seigneur de Branthôme*, ed. L. Lacour. The relevant vols, are I–VII, Paris.

Braudel, F. (1949), *La Méditerranée et le monde méditerranéen à l'époque de Philippe II*, Paris. The standard work on Mediterranean history.

Brienne (1850), *Mémoires du Comte de Brienne*, in *Nouvelle Collection*, 3rd series, III, Paris. Especially on the campaigns against the Huguenots in the 1620s.

Brockman, E. (1969), *The Two Sieges of Rhodes*, London.

Brouwer, J. (1933), *Kronieken van Spaansche Soldaten uit het Begin van den Tachtigjarigen Oorlog*, Zutphen.

Brown, D. M. (1948), 'The Impact of Fire-Arms on Japanese Warfare 1543–8', in *The Far Eastern Quarterly*, VII, New York.

Broxap, E. (1905), 'The Sieges of Hull during the Great Civil War', in *English Historical Review*, July.

Broxap, E. (1910), *The Great Civil War in Lancashire (1642–1651)*, Manchester.

de Bruijn, C. A. and Reinders, H. R. (1967), *Nederlandse Vestingen*, Bussum.

Bryan, D. (1959), 'Ballyshannon Fort, Co. Kildare 1642–1650', in *The Irish Sword*, IV, no. 15, Dublin.

Buchan, J. (1934), *Oliver Cromwell*, London.

Buisseret, D. (1964), 'L'Organisation défensive des frontières au temps de Henri IV', in *Revue historique de l'armée*, XX, Paris.

Buisseret, D. (1968), *Sully*, London.

Buonaparte, J. (1836), 'Le Sac de Rom', in *Choix de chroniques et mémoires sur l'histoire de France*, ed. J. A. Buchon, Paris.

Burne, A. H. and Young, P. (1959), *The Great Civil War*.

A Military History of the First Civil War 1642–1646, London.

Bury, J. B. (1977), *Francisco de Holanda's Evidence on Fortification in Italy, 1538–40*, paper delivered to the Fortress Study Group, Canterbury.

Butler, G. and Maccoby, S. (1928), *The Development of International Law*, London.

Caball, J. (1956), 'The Siege of Tralee 1642', in *The Irish Sword*, II, no. 9. Dublin.

Camblin, G. (1951), *The Town in Ulster*, Belfast. Especially on the Jacobean 'new towns'.

The Cambridge History of India (1928–37), III–IV, Cambridge.

Campion (1857), *Mémoires de Henri de Campion*, Paris. On the wars of the 1630s and 1640s.

Carlsson, W. (1912), *Gustav II Adolf och Stralsund 1628–Juli 1630*, Uppsala.

Carnero, A. (1625), *Historia de las Guerras Civiles que ha Avido en los Estados de Flandes*, Brussels.

Caron, F. and Schouten, J. (1935), *A True Description of the Mighty Kingdoms of Japan and Siam*, Eng. trans. of 1663, ed. C. R. Boxer, London.

da Carpi, Alghisi (1570, 1584), *Della Fortificazione*, Venice.

Castelnau (1850), *Mémoires de Michel de Castelnau*, in *Nouvelle Collection*, 1st series IX, Paris. A Catholic officer's view of the troubles between 1559 and 1569.

Cataneo, Pietro (1554), *I Quattro Primi Libri d'Architettura*, Venice.

Cellarius, Andreas (1645), *Architectura Militaris*, Amsterdam.

Charles, J.-L., 'Le Sac des Villes dans les Pays-Bas au XVIe Siecle Étude Critique des Règles de la Guerre', in *Revue Internationale d'Histoire Militaire*, no. 24, Brussels.

de la Chastre (1850), *Mémoire du voyage de M. le Duc de Guise en Italie, son retour, la Prinse de Callais et de Thionville 1556 et 1557*, in *Nouvelle Collection*, 1st series VIII, Paris.

Cipolla, C. M. (1965), *Guns and Sails in the Early Phase of European Expansion 1400–1700*, London.

Clarendon, Edward, Earl of (1826), *The History of the Rebellion and Civil Wars in England*, 8 vols, Oxford.

Clarke, J. A. (1966), *Huguenot Warrior. The Life and Times of Henri de Rohan, 1579–1638*, The Hague.

Clausse, G. (1900–2), *Les San Gallo*, 3 vols, Paris.

Clayburn, P. M. (1965), 'Japanese Castles', in *History Today*, January.

Clinch, C. (1915), *English Coast Defences from Roman Times to the Early Years of the 19th Century*, London.

Coate, M. (1933), *Cornwall in the Great Civil War and Interregnum 1642–1660*, Oxford, and Truro 1963.

Cobham, C. D. (1895), edited and translated accounts of the sieges of Nicosia and Famagusta by Giacomo Diedo, Paolo Paruta and Angelo Calepio, in *Excerpta Cypria*, Nicosia.

Cobham, C. D. (ed.) (1899), R. Midgley's trans. of A. Graziani's *De Bello Cyprio* (1624), as *The Sieges of Nicosia and Famagusta*, London.

Cockle, M. J. (1901), *A Catalogue of Books Relating to the Military History of India*, Simla.

Cockle, M. J. (1957), *A Bibliography of Military Works up to 1642*, new edn, London.

van Coehoorn, Stichting Menno (1956–present), annual *Jarboek*, and *Atlas van Historische Vestings-Werken in Nederland*, The Hague.

Collado, Luis (1592), *Prática Manual de Artilléria*, Milan.

Colligny (1850), *Discours de Gaspar de Colligny*, in *Nouvelle Collection*, 1st series, VIII, Paris.

Coloma, C. (1853), *Las Guerras de los Estados-Bajos, 1568–1599*, in *Historiadores de Sucesos Particulares*, II, Madrid, which is vol. XXVIII of *Biblioteca de Autores Españoles*, ed. M. Rivadeneyra.

Conly, R. L. (1966), 'St Augustine', in *National Geographic*, CXXIX, no. 2, Washington, February.

Cooper, Duff (1949), *Sergeant Shakespeare*, London.

Cooper, M. (ed.) (1965), *They Came to Japan. An Anthology of European Reports on Japan, 1543–1640*, London.

Corbet, J. (no date), *An Historical Relation of the Military Government of Gloucester*, Tewkesbury. By one of the Parliamentarian defenders.

Criste, O. (1904), *Kriege under Kaiser Josef II*, Vienna.

de la Croix, H. (1960), 'Military Architecture and the Radial City Plan in Sixteenth-Century Italy', in *The Art Bulletin*, XLII, no. 4, New York.

de la Croix, H. (1963), 'The Literature on Fortification in Renaissance Italy', in *Technology and Culture*, Cleveland. A valuable bibliography.

de la Croix, H. (1972), *Military Considerations in Town Planning: Fortification*, New York.

Cruikshank, C. G. (1966), *Elizabeth's Army*, 2nd edn, Oxford.

Cruickshank, C. G. (1969), *Army Royal. Henry VIII's Invasion of France 1513*, Oxford.

Cyrus, A. (1947), *Vaxholms Fästning*, Vaxholm.

Dagbok (1912), *Erik Dahlberghs Dagbok, (1625–1699)*, ed. H. Lundström, Stockholm.

Dalboquerque (1875–84), *The Commentaries of the Great Afonso Dalboquerque*, trans. and ed. W. de Gray Birch (Hakluyt Society), 4 vols, London.

Danvers, F. C. (1894), *The Portuguese in India*, 2 vols, London.

Davies, J. (1612), *A Discovery of the True Causes why Ireland was never Entirely Subdued*, London.

Davila, H. C. (1758), *Historia delle Guerre Civili di Francia*, Venice 1630, trans. E. Farneworth, *The History of the Civil Wars of France*, 2 vols, London.

Delaborde, H. (1888), *L'Expédition de Charles VIII en Italie*, Paris.

Diffie, B. W. and Winius, D. (1978), *Foundations of the Portuguese Empire 1415–1580*, Oxford.

Dmochowski, Z. (1956), *The Architecture of Poland*, London.

Dolleczek, A. (1887), *Geschichte der Österreichischen Artillerie*, Vienna. Informative and entertaining. Covers more ground than the title suggests.

Dore, R. N. (1966), *The Civil Wars in Cheshire*, Chester.

van Dorselaer, P. (1908), *Souvenirs d'une famille Bruxelloise. Le bombardement de 1695*, ed. E. Lagrange, Brussels.

Drexler, A. (1955), *The Architecture of Japan*, New York.

Droysen, G. (1869–70), *Gustaf Adolf*, 2 vols, Leipzig.

Duffy, C. (1975), *Fire and Stone. The Science of Fortress Warfare 1660–1860*, Newton Abbot.

Duffy, J. (1959), *Portuguese Africa*, Cambridge, Mass.

Dunbar, J. G. (1966), *The Historic Architecture of Scotland*, London.

Dunne, G. H. (1962), *Generation of Giants. The Story of the Jesuits in China in the Last Decades of the Ming Dynasty*, London.

Duparcq, E. de la Barre (1864), *L'Art militaire pendant les guerres de réligion*, Paris.

Duyck (1862–6), *Journal van Anthonis Duyck . . . (1591–1602)*, 3 parts, The Hague. By the advocate-fiscal of Maurice's Council of State.

Eimer, G. (1961), *Die Stadtplanung im Schwedischen Ostseereich*, Stockholm. With a valuable bibliography on urbanism on pp. 147–8.

Ekama, C. (1872), *Beleg en Verdediging van Haarlem in 1572 en 1573*, The Hague.

Elliott, J. H. (1963), *The Revolt of the Catalans*, Cambridge.

Ellison, G. (no date), *The Sieges of Taunton*.

Environment, Dept. of (1975), *History of the King's Works 1485–1660*, London.

Ericsson, E. (1935), *Olof Hansson Örnehufvud och Svenska Fortifikations-väsendet*, Uppsala.

van der Essen, L. (1933–7), *Alexandre Farnese, Prince de Parma, Gouverneur Général des Pays-Bas 1545–1592*, 5 vols, Brussels. The main secondary source on the Spanish side of the campaigns of the 1580s and 1590s.

van der Essen, L. (1944), *Le Cardinal-Infant et la politique Européene de L'Espagne 1609–1641*, Brussels.

Estrada, P. E. (1682), *Las Guerras de Flandes*, Sp. trans, 3 vols, Cologne.

Estrées (1850), *Mémoires du Maréchal d'Estrées*, in *Nouvelle Collection*, 2nd series, VI, Paris.

Fabre, Sieur de (1629), *Les Practiques de Sieur Fabre sur l'Ordre et Reigle de Fortifier, Attaquer et Défendre les Places*, Paris.

Falls, C. (1950), *Elizabeth's Irish Wars*, London.

Falls, C. (1955), *Mountjoy. Elizabethan General*, London.

Fernández-Santamaria, J. A. (1977), *The State, War and Peace. Spanish Political Thought in the Renaissance 1516–1559*, Cambridge.

Firth, C. H. (1921), *Cromwell's Army*, 3rd edn, London.

Fitzgerald, C. P. (1901), *China, A Short Cultural History*, 3rd edn, London.

Fleurange, Robert de la Mark, Seigneur de (1850), *Histoire des Choses Mémorables*, in *Nouvelle Collection*, 1st series, V, Paris. Written by the *Grand Sanglier des Ardennes* while in Spanish captivity at Sluis.

Fontenay-Mareuil, (1850), *Mémoires de Messire François Duval, Marquis de Fontenay-Mareuil*, in *Nouvelle Collection*, 2nd series, V, Paris. On the wars of Henry IV.

Fortescue, J. W. (1910–30), *A History of the British Army*, 13 vols, London.

Forti, L. C. (1975), *Le Fortificazioni di Genova*, new edn, Genoa. This beautifully illustrated work is of wide interest.

Fortress Study Group Newsletter, Liverpool, 1976, etc. The best source of information on recent publications and discoveries.

Foster, W. (1906), *The English Factories in India*, Oxford.

Fourquevaux, Raymond de Beccarie de Pavie, Sieur de (1548), *Instructions sur le faict de la guerre*, ed. C. Dickinson, London, 1954.

Freeman, D. S. (1934–5), *R. E. Lee*, 4 vols, New York.

Freitag, Adam (1630), *Architectura Militaris Nova et Aucta oder Neue Vermehrte Fortification*, Leyden, and many later edns. (Freitag was a Polish-born German, and served under Prince Frederick Henry at the sieges of s'Hertogenbosch.)

Fruin, F. (1927), *The Siege and Relief of Leyden in 1574*, The Hague and Oxford.

Fuensaldaña, El Conde de (1880–8), *Relación de lo Sucedido en Flandes desde 1648 hasta 1653*, in *Colección de Documentos Ineditos*, LXXV, Madrid.

Fujioka, M. (1970), *Japanese Castles*, Osaka.

Furtenbach, B. (1956), *Eda Skansar. Värmlands Gransforsvar genom Tiderna*, Karlstad.

Gachard, M. (1940–60), *Correspondance de Philip II sur les affaires des Pays-Bas*, 5 vols, Brussels, 1848–79, Part 2, ed. J. Lefèvre, Brussels.

Garbutt, M. (1907), 'Military Works in Old Japan', in *Transactions and Proceedings of the Japan Society of London*, VIII, London.

Generalstaben (Swedish General Staff) (1936–8), *Sveriges Krig 1611–1632*, 5 vols and 2 supplementary vols, Stockholm.

General Staff, Malta Command (1920), *History of the Fortifications of Malta*, Malta.

Genet, A. (1847–8), 'Relation du siège de la Rochelle par le Duc d'Anjou, en 1573', in *Le Spectateur militaire*.

Gentili, Alberico (1598), *De Jure Belli Libri Tres*.

Geyl, P. (1961), *The Netherlands in the Seventeenth Century*, part I, new edn, London.

Geyl, P. (1962), *The Revolt of the Netherlands 1555–1609*, 2nd edn, London.

Gill, B. (1964), *Les Ingénieurs de la Renaissance*, Paris.

Gindely, A. (1885), *Geschichte des Dreissigjährigen Krieges*, 3 parts, Prague and Leipzig. A good history with some striking contemporary illustrations.

Glückstadt-Rode, F. C. (1940), *Kriegsgeschichte der Festung Glückstadt und der Niederelbe*, 2 vols, Glückstadt.

Gode, P. K. (1939), 'Use of Guns and Gunpowder in India from A.D. 1400 onwards', in *New Indian Antiquary*, II, no. 3, Bombay June.

Godwin, G. N. (1904), *The Civil War in Hampshire (1642–45) and the Story of Basing House*, new edn, Southampton and London.

Goethals (1841), *Notice historique sur la vie et les ouvrages de S Stevin de Bruges*, Brussels.

Grammont (1850), *Mémoires du Maréchal de Grammont*, in *Nouvelle Collection*, 3rd series, VII, Paris.

von Grimmelshausen, H. J. C. (1911), *Der Abenteurliche Simplicissimus* (1669), trans. ATSG, London.

Grotius, H. (*c.* 1604), *De Jure Praedae*.

Grotius, H. (1853), *De Jure Belli ac Pacis* (1625), ed. W. Whewell, 3 vols, Cambridge.

Grotius, H. (1657), *Annales et Historiae de Rebus Belgicis*, Amsterdam. Eng. trans. T. Manley, London, 1665.

Gruen, V. (1965), *The Heart of our Cities*, London.

Guerlac, H. (1944), 'The Impact of Science on War', in *Makers of Modern Strategy*, (ed.) E. M. Earle, Princeton.

Guicciardini, F. (1929), *Storia d'Italia* (1562). Many edns and translations. New Italian edn by C. Panigada in the series *Scrittori d'Italia*, 5 vols, Bari.

Guignard, Chevalier de (1725), *L'Ecole de Mars*, 2 vols, Paris.

Guilmartin, J. F. (1974), *Gunpowder and Galleys. Changing Technology and Mediterranean Warfare at Sea in the Sixteenth Century*, Cambridge. A work of major importance for the military history of the early modern period.

Guise (1850), *Mémoires du Duc de Guise* (i.e. Henri de Guise), in *Nouvelle Collection*, 3rd series, VII, Paris.

Gutkind, E. A. (1964–7), *International History of City Development*, 3 vols, London.

Haestens, H. (1615), *La Nouvelle Troye*, Leyden.

Hale, J. R. (1957), 'International Relations in the West: Diplomacy and War', in *New Cambridge Modern History*, I, Cambridge. By the foremost authority on Renaissance warfare.

Hale, J. R. (1958), 'Armies, Navies, and the Art of War', in *New Cambridge Modern History*, II, Cambridge.

Hale, J. R. (1961), *The Art of War and Renaissance Engineering*, Washington.

Hale, J. R. (1965), 'The Development of the Bastion', in *Europe in the Late Middle Ages*, ed. J. R. Hale, J. Highfield, B. Smalley, London.

Hale, J. R. (1968), 'Francesco Tensini and the Fortification of Vicenza', in *Studi Veneziana*, X, Venice.

Hale, J. R. (1970), 'The End of Florentine Liberty – the Fortezza da Basso', in *Florentine Studies*, London.

Hale, J. R. (1977), *Renaissance Fortification. Art or Engineering?*, London.

Hall, A. R. (1952), *Ballistics in the Seventeenth Century*, Cambridge.

Hall, D. G. (1968), *A History of South-East Asia*, 3rd edn, London.

Hall, J. (ed.) (1889), T. Malbon, 'Memorials of the Civil War in Cheshire', and E. Burghall, 'Providence Improved', in *The Record Society for the Publication of Original Documents Relating to Lancashire and Cheshire*, XIX, London.

Hamilton, H. (1920), *The Irish Rebellion of 1641*, London.

von Hammer, J. (1834–5), *Geschichte des Osmanischen Reiches*, 2nd edn, vols II and III, Pest.

Hayes-McCoy, G. A. (1957), 'The Defence of the Moyry Pass 1600', in *The Irish Sword*, III, no. 10, Dublin.

Hayes-McCoy, G. A. (1969), *Irish Battles*, London. Especially the treatment of strategic geography.

van Hemelrijk, H. (1950), *De Vlaamse Krijgsbouwkunde*, Tielt.

Henrard, P. (1890), *Histoire du siège d'Ostende (1601–1604)*, Brussels and Leipzig.

Herbst, S. and Zachwatowicz, J. (1936), *Twierdza Zamosc. La Place Forte de Zamosc*, Warsaw. With a French summary.

Hexham, H. (1633), *A Journal of the Taking in of Venlo*, Delft.

Hexham, H. (1642–3), *The First Part of the Principles of the Art Military, Practised in the Warres of the United Netherlands*, 3 parts, Delft and Rotterdam. Captain Henry Hexham was a veteran of the Dutch service, and became quartermaster to Goring in the Civil War.

Hogg, F. O. (1963), *English Artillery 1326–1716*, Woolwich.

Hogg, I. V. (1975), *Fortress. A History of Military Defence*, London. Especially on fortress armament.

Hondius, Hendrik (1634), *Onderrichtinge van de Generale Regeln der Fortificatie*, The Hague. Useful for the many examples drawn from sieges of the time.

Hook, J. (1976), *New Fortifications, Old Finances, and the Collapse of the Siennese State*, paper delivered to the Fortress Study Group, Southampton.

Hough, R. (1964), *Dreadnought*, London.

Hubert, E. (1901–3), 'Les Garnisons de la barrière dans les Pays-Bas Autrichiens (1715–1782)', in *Mémoires . . . de l'académie royale*, LIX, Brussels.

Hughes, J. Quentin (1956), *The Building of Malta*, London.

Hughes, J. Quentin (1969), *Fortress Architecture and Military History in Malta*, London.

Hughes, J. Quentin (1974), *Military Architecture*, London. The best general survey.

Hugo, S. J. H. (1626), *Obsidio Bredana*, Antwerp. Trans. C. H. G. as *The Siege of Breda*, London 1627. A popular and widely-reprinted history. Spinola's siegeworks are described in great detail.

Hutchinson (1885), *Memoirs of Colonel Hutchinson*, ed. C. H. Firth, 2 vols, London.

von Imhof, G. (1871), *Albrecht Dürer in seiner Bedeutung für die Moderne Befestigungskunst*, Nördlingen.

Irvine, W. (1903), *The Army of the Indian Moghuls*, London.

Israel, J. I. (1977), 'A Conflict of Empires: Spain and the Netherlands 1618–1648', in *Past and Present*, LXXVI, London.

Jähns, M. (1889–91), *Geschichte der Kriegswissenschaften vornehmlich in Deutschland*, 3 parts, Munich and Leipzig. A critical bibliography of vast dimensions. Max Jähns has the useful habit of quoting long passages from the remoter authors on fortification.

James (1962), *The Memoirs of James II. His Campaigns as Duke of York 1652–1660*, ed. A. L. Sells, London. More lively and perceptive than you would expect from James's record as king.

Jany, C. (1967), *Geschichte der Preussischen Armee*, new edn, 4 vols, Osnabrück.

Jones, F. M. (1954), 'The Destination of Don Juan del Aguila in 1601', in *The Irish Sword*, II, no. 5, Dublin.

Jones, F. M. (1954), 'The Plan of the Golden Fort at Smerwick, 1580', in *The Irish Sword*, II, no. 5, Dublin.

Jones, F. M. (1955), 'An Indictment of Don Juan del Aguila', in *The Irish Sword*, II, no. 7, Dublin.

Jorgensen, P. A. (1956), *Shakespeare's Military World*, Berkeley. A very comprehensive treatment of Elizabethan military affairs.

Kara Mustafa vor Wien (1960), trans. and ed. R. F. Kreutel, Graz. One of the very few Turkish accounts to have been translated into a Western language.

Keen, M. H. (1965), *The Laws of War in the Later Middle Ages*, London.

Kenyon, J. R. (1976), 'Early Artillery Fortification in England and Wales', in *Fortress Study Group Newsletter*, 1, Liverpool.

Kingston, A. (1897), *East Anglia and the Great Civil War*, London.

Kinsky, Count (1790), *Ueber Türkenkrieg*, Wiener Neustadt.

Knolles, R. (1888), *The Generall Historie of the Turkes*, London.

Kostochkin, V. V. (1969), *Krepostnoe Zodchestvo drevnei Rosi*, Moscow.

Laber, H. O. (1932), 'Die Schweden in Augsburg 1632–1635', in *Münchener Historische Abhandlungen*, 2nd series I, Munich.

Lach, D. F. (1965), *Asia in the Making of Europe*, I, books 1 and 2, Chicago.

Lallemand, M. and Boinette, A. (1884), *Jean Errard de Bar-le-Duc*, Paris and Bar-le-Duc.

Lameire, I. (1902–11), *Théorie et Pratique de la Conquête dans l'Ancien Droit*, 5 vols, Paris.

Langenskiöld, E. (1938), *Michele Sanmicheli the Architect of Verona*, Uppsala. A first-class biography.

Langenskiöld, E. (1943), 'Bastionssystemets Upprinelse och Tidigare Utveckling', in *Antikvariska Studier*, I, Stockholm.

Langsam, C. G. (1951), *Martial Books and Tudor Verse*, New York.

Laskovskii, F. (1858–65), *Materiali dlya Istorii Inzhenernogo Iskusstva v Rossii*, 3 vols, St Petersburg. An authoritative history of Russian military engineering. Untouched by the rabid nationalism which distorts most Soviet writing on the history of military technology.

Lattimore, O. (1962), *Studies on Frontier History* (China), London. Inscrutable.

Lavallée, T. (1864), *Les Frontières de France*, Paris.

Lavedan, P. (1959), *Histoire de l'Urbanisme*, Paris.

Lawrence, A. W. (1963), *Trade Castles and Forts of West Africa*, London. Probably the most useful single study of colonial fortification.

Lebey, A. (1904), *Le Connétable de Bourbon 1490–1527*, Paris.

Lechuga, Cristobal de (1611), *Discorso de la Artillería*, Milan.

Lenet (1850), *Mémoires de Pierre Lenet*, in *Nouvelle Collection*, 3rd series, II, Paris.

de Lestoile, Pierre (1850), *Registre-Journal de Henri III 1574–1589*, and *Registre-Journal de Henri IV et de Louis XIII*, both in *Nouvelle Collection*, 2nd series, I, Paris.

Leycester (1844), *The Correspondence of Robert Dudley, Earl of Leycester, during his Government of the Low Countries in the Years 1585 and 1586*, ed. J. Bruce, Camden Society, London.

Ligne, Prince de (1795), 'Mémoire sur Vienne', in *Mélanges*, 30 vols, Dresden.

Lisk, J. (1967), *The Struggle for Supremacy in the Baltic 1600–1725*, London.

Lloyd, H. A. (1973), *The Rouen Campaign 1590–1592*, Oxford.

Loeber, R. (1977) 'Biographical Dictionary of Engineers in Ireland 1600–1730', in *The Irish Sword*, XIII, no. 50, Dublin. An excellent piece of scholarship.

Lonchay, H., Cuvelier, J., Lefèvre, J. (1923–30), *Correspondance da la Cour d'Espagne sur les Affaires du Pays-Bas au XVIIIe Siècle*, 3 vols, Paris.

Lorenzen, V. (1937), *Christian IVs Byanlaeg*, Copenhagen.

Lorenzen, V. (1947–58), *Vore Byer*, 5 vols, Copenhagen. Histories of Danish towns.

Ludlow (1890), *The Memoirs of Edmund Ludlow*, ed. C. H. Firth, 2 vols, Oxford.

de Luna y Mora (1880–8), *Relación de la Campaña del Ano de 1635 por el Capitan Don Diego de Luna y Mora*, in *Colección de Documentos Ineditos*, LXXV, Madrid.

McCornish, W. A. (1969), 'The Survival of the Irish Castle in the Age of Cannon', in *The Irish Sword*, IX, no. 34, Dublin.

Macchiavelli, N. (1519), *Arte della Guerra* (1519 or 1520). Book VII is on fortification. New edn by F. Flora and C. Cordiè in *Macchiavelli, Tutti le Opere*, 3 vols, Milan 1949–58.

MacIvor, I. (1965), 'The Elizabethan Fortifications of Berwick-upon-Tweed' in the *Antiquawaries Journal*, XLV, part 1, Oxford.

McNeil, W. H. (1964), *Europe's Steppe Frontier, 1500–1800*, Chicago and London.

Maggi, Girolamo and Castriotto, Fusto (1564). *Della Fortificazione*, Venice.

Maggiorotti, L. A. (1933–9), *L'Opera del Genio Italiano all'Estero. Gli Architetti Militari*, 3 vols, Rome. A survey of the activity of sixteenth-century Italian engineers in southern and eastern Europe and the Spanish colonies.

Maigret, P. (1727), *Traité de la Sûreté et Conservation des Etats par le Moyen de Fortresses*, Paris, Eng. trans *A Treatise*.

de Mailles, J. (1927), *Histoire du Seigneur de Bayart*, new edn, Paris.

Mallet, A. M. (1673), *Travaux de Mars*, 3 vols, Paris.

Mallett, M. (1974), *Mercenaries and their Masters*, London.

Malthus, J. (1629), *A Treatise of Artificial Fireworks*, London. Fr. Trans. *Pratique de la guerre, contenant l'usage de l'artillerie, bombes et mortiers*, Paris, 1646.

Mangan, H. (1951–2), 'Del Aguila's Defence of Kinsale, 1601–2', in *The Irish Sword*, I, no. 3, Dublin.

Mangan, H. (1956), 'A Vindication of Don-Juan del Aguila', in *The Irish Sword*, II, no. 9, Dublin.

Manley, Sir Roger (1670), *The History of the Late Warres in Denmark . . . in the Years 1657, 1658, 1659, 1660*, London.

Mann, G. (1976), *Wallenstein*, London.

de'Marchi, Francesco (1599), *Della Architettura*, Brescia.

de Marillac, Guillaume, *Vie du Connétable Charles de Bourbon*, in *Choix de Chroniques* op. cit. Marillac was Bourbon's secretary.

Markham, C. A. (1870), *A Life of the Great Lord Fairfax*, London.

Marolois, Samuel (1614), *Oeuvres mathematiques traictant de géometrie perspective, architecture et fortification*, The Hague, and *Fortification ou architecture militaire tant offensive que deffensive*, The Hague, 1615.

di Marsigli, Conte (1732), *Stato Militare dell'Imperio Ottomanno (L'État Militaire de l'Empire Ottoman)*, The Hague and Amsterdam. Italian and French texts in one volume. An account of Turkish military affairs from both the Turkish and Western viewpoints.

Mayers, W. F. (1871), 'On the Introduction and Use of Gunpowder and Firearms among the Chinese', in *Journal of the North China Branch of the Royal Asiatic Society*, new series, VI, Shanghai.

Medina Barba, Diego Gonzales de (1599), *Examen de Fortificación*, Madrid.

Mehrotra, K. (1934), *Horace Walpole and the English Novel. A Study of the Influence of 'The Castle of Otranto' 1764–1820*, Oxford.

de Mendoza, B., *Comentarios de lo Sucedido en las Guerras de los Paises-Bajos, 1567–1577*, in Rivadeneyra, (1853), XXVIII.

Merualt, P. (1648), *Histoire du dernier siège de la Rochelle*, Rouen. An eyewitness account by the son of the chief gunner of the garrison.

de Meteren, E. (1618), *Histoire des Pays-Bas*, The Hague.

Michael, F. (1942), *The Origin of Manchu Rule in China. Frontier and Bureaucracy as Interacting Forces in the Chinese Empire*, Baltimore. One of the very few accessible studies on this interesting period.

Michaelov, O. (1621), *Code of Military and Artillery Practice and Other Affairs Relating to the Art of War*.

Mina, De la (1898), *Memorias Militares*, 2 vols, Madrid.

Moltke, Baron v. (1845), *Der Russisch-Türkische Feldzug in der Europäische Türkei 1828 und 1829*, Berlin.

Monnox (1930), *History at Large of the Taking of Ormuz Castle*, in *Andrada*, ed. Boxer, 282.

Monro (1637), *Monro his Expedition with the Worthy Scots Regiment*, London.

Montagu, Lady Wortley (1887), *Letters and Works*, 2 vols, London.

Montecucuccoli, R. (1735), *Mémoires*, 2 vols, Strasbourg.

Montglat (1850), *Mémoires de Monglat*, in *Nouvelle Collection*, 3rd series, V, Paris. A full and impartial account of the campaigns against the Spanish in the 1630s, 1640s and 1650s.

Montluc (1571), *Commentaires de Blaise de Monluc*, ed. P. Courteautt, 3 vols, Paris, 1911–25. Possibly the best of the French memoirs.

de Montpleinchamp, Bruslé (1693), *l'Histoire de l'Archiduc Albert*, Cologne. By the chaplain to the Elector of Bavaria, the governor-general of the Netherlands at the time of the siege of Ostend.

Ed. Moody, T. W., Martin, F. X., Byrne, F. J. (1976), *A New History of Ireland*, III, Oxford.

Moos, S. (1974), *Turm und Bollwerk. Beiträge zu einer Politischen Ikonographie der Italienischen Renaissancearchitektur*, Zürich.

Morgan, W., ed. Caldecott-Baird (1976), *The Expedition in Holland 1572–1574*, London.

Morris, R. H. (1924), *The Siege of Chester 1643–1646*, Chester.

Mulcahy, M. (1959), 'Elizabeth Fort, Cork', in *The Irish Sword*, IV, no. 15, Dublin.

Müller, J. (1755), *Practical Fortification*, London.

Mumford, L. (1966), *The City in History*, London.

Munthe, L. (1902–52), continued by E. Ericsson, G. Grabe and P. H. Enger, *Kungl. Fortifikationens Historia*, 6 parts, Stockholm. The later parts were published as appendices to the *Tidskrift i Fortifikation* – 4(ii) in 1932–42, and 5(i) in 1951–52.

Murdoch, J. and Yamagata, I. (1903–26), *A History of Japan*, vols II and III, Kobe. Outdated but useful.

Nef, J. (1950), *War and Human Progress*, London.

Nordenskiöld, E. (1942), 'Fortifications in Ancient Europe and Peru', in *Ethnos*, VII, no. 1, Lund. Very unconvincing.

de la Noue (1850), *Mémoires du Sieur François de la Noue*, in *Nouvelle Collection*, 1st series, IX, Paris. A Protestant's account of the years 1562–70. There are some interesting comments on the rôle of fortresses in the French religious wars.

Oberleitner, K. (1860), 'Österreichs Finanzen und Kriegswesen unter Ferdinand I', in *Archiv für Kunde Österreichischer Geschichts-Quellen*, XXII, Vienna.

Öhlander (1904), *Det Egentliga Sveriges Forsvar mot Danmark-Norge ... 1657–1660*, Uppsala.

Oman, C. (1937), *A History of the Art of War in the Sixteenth Century*, London.

O'Neil, B. H. (1945), 'Stefan von Haschenperg, an Engineer to King Henry VIII and his Work', in *Archaeologia*, XCI (2nd series XLI), Oxford.

O'Neil, B. H. (1960), *Castles and Cannon. A History of Early Artillery Fortifications in England*, Oxford. Published posthumously from Bryan O'Neil's lectures.

d'Orléans (1850), *Mémoires de Gaston, Duc d'Orléans*, in *Nouvelle Collection*, 2nd series, IX, Paris.

Orrery, Roger Boyle, Earl of (1677), *A Treatise on the Art of War*, London.

'Osman (1962), '*Der Gefangene der Giauren*'. *Die Abenteurlichen Schicksale des Dolmetschers 'Osman Aĝa aus Temeschwar*, trans. and ed. K. Kreutel and O. Spies, Graz.

Palma-Cayet, P. V. (1850), *Chronologie Novenaire ... 1589 ... 1598*, in *Nouvelle Collection*, 1st series, XII, Paris.

Palmer, J. (1822), *History of the Siege of Manchester ... 1642 ... To which is Added the Complaint of Lieutenant-Colonel John Rosworm*, Manchester. Rosworm was a German engineer hired by the Mancunians.

Pankov, D. V. (ed.) (1952), *Iz Istorii Voenno-Inzhenernogo Iskusstva*, Moscow. A collection of articles on Russian military engineering.

Papini, P. (1946), *Francesco di Giorgio Architetto*, 3 vols, Florence.

Parker, G. (1972), *The Army of Flanders and the Spanish Road 1567–1659*, Cambridge.

Parker, G. (1977), *The Dutch Revolt*, London.

Parry, J. H. (1949), *Europe and a Wider World*, London.

Parry, J. H. (1963), *The Age of Reconnaissance*, London.

Parry, J. H. (1966), *The Spanish Seaborne Empire*, London.

Parry, V. J. and Yapp, M. E. (eds) (1975), *War, Technology and Society in the Middle East*, Oxford.

Partington, J. (1960), *A History of Greek Fire and Gunpowder*, Cambridge.

Paulsson, T. (1958), *Scandinavian Architecture*, London.

Penny, F. (1900), *Fort St George, Madras*, London.

Pepper, S. (1973), 'The Meaning of the Renaissance Fortress', in *Architectural Association Quarterly*, V, no. 2, London.

Pepper, S. (1976), 'Planning versus Fortification – Sangallo's Project for the Defence of Rome', in *Architectural Review*, no. 949, London.

Pernot, J. F. (1978), 'Un Aspect peu connu de l'Oeuvre d'Antoine De Ville, Ingénieur du Roí (1596?–1656?), in *Revue Historique des Armées*, 1978, no. 1, Paris.

Peters, C. H. (1909), *De Nederl Stedenbouw, de Stad als Veste, Woon-en Handelsplats*, Leiden.

Le Petit, J. F. (1601), *La Grande Chronique Ancienne et Moderne de Hollande*, 2 vols, Dordrecht.

Petrie, C. (1964), 'Ireland in Spanish and French Strategy, 1558–1815', in *The Irish Sword*, VI, no. 24, Dublin.

Phillips, W. (1967), *Oman. A History*, London.

Pieri, P. (1952), *I Rinascimento e la Crisi Militare Italiana*, Turin.

du Plessis (1850), *Mémoires du Maréchal du Plessis*, in *Nouvelle Collection*, 3rd series, VII, Paris. On the marshal's part in the Franco-Spanish campaigns of the 1640s and 1650s.

de Pointis (1850), *Mémoires du Sieur de Pointis*, in *Nouvelle Collection*, 2nd series, VI, Paris. A vivid account of the wars of Louis XIII.

Poirson, M. A. (1856), *Histoire du règne de Henri IV*, 2 vols, Paris.

Polišenský, J. V. (1971), *The Thirty Years War*, London.

Polišenský, J. V. (1978), *War and Society in Europe 1618–1648*, Cambridge.

Porter, W., and others (1889–1958), *History of the Corps of Royal Engineers*, 9 vols, London and Chatham.

Powell, R. J. (1932), 'Blake's Reduction of Jersey', in *The Mariner's Mirror*, London.

Poyntz (1908), *The Relation of Sydnam Poyntz 1624–1636*, ed. A. T. Goodrick, (Camden Society), London.

Prace Naukowe Instytutu Historii Architektury (ed.) (1975), *Bastejowe Fortyfikacje w Polsce*, Breslau. With summaries in Russian and a kind of English. Like most modern Polish studies, it is compelled on political grounds to give blanket coverage to both Polish and former German territories – which had in fact very different traditions of fortification.

van Prinsterer, G. Groen (ed.) (1838–47) (1857–9), *Archives et correspondance inédites de la Maison d'Orange-Nassau*, for the Eighty Years War see 1st series V–VIII, Leyden, and 2nd series I–IV, Utrecht.

Promis, C. (1862), 'Vita di Girolamo Maggi d'Anghiari', in *Miscellanea di Storia Italiana*, I, Turin. This was followed by a series of further articles in the same journal: 'La Vita di Francesco Paciotto da Urbino', IV (1863a); 'Gli Ingegneri e gli Scrittori Militari Bolognese del XV e XVI Secolo', IV (1863b); 'Gli Ingegneri che Operarono o Scrissero in Piemonte dal 1300 al 1650', XII (1871); and 'Biografie di Ingegneri Militari Italiani dal Secolo XIV alla Meta del XVIII', XIV (1874).

de Puységur (1690), *Les Mémoires de Messire Jacques de Chastenet, Chevalier Seigneur de Puységur*, 2 vols, Paris. This edn contains the *Instructions Militaires* which are omitted in the edn by P. Tamizey de Larroque, entitled *Les Guerres du Règne de Louis XIII et de la Minorité de Louis XIV*, 2 vols, Paris, 1883.

Quaritch Wales, H. G. (1952), *Ancient South-East Asian Warfare*, London.

de Rabutin (1850), *Commentaires des Dernières Guerres en la Gaule Belgique par Francois de Rabutin*, in *Nouvelle Collection*, 1st series VII, Paris. On the years 1551–58.

Railo, E. (1927), *The Haunted Castle. A Study of the Elements of English Romanticism*, London.

Ramelli, A. C. (1964), *Dalle Caverne ai Rifugi Blindati. Trenta Secoli di Architettura Militare*, Milan.

Rauchensteiner, M. (1972), 'Vom Limes zum "Ostwall"', in *Militärhistorische Schriftenreihe*, XXI, Vienna.

Rawlinson, H. G. (1920), *British Beginnings in Western India 1579–1657*, Oxford.

Rayeur, I. A. (1894), *La Trouée des Ardennes*, Charleville.

Razin, E. A. (1957), *Voennoe Iskusstvo Feodal'nogo Perioda Voiny*, vol. II of *Istorya Voennogo Iskusstva*, Moscow. Much useful material.

Razin, E. A. (1963), *Voennoe Iskusstvo Manufakturnogo Perioda Voiny XVI–XVII vv*, vol. III of *Istorya*, Moscow.

Redlich, F. (1956), *De Praeda Militari: Looting and Booty 1500–1815*, Wiesbaden.

Reps, J. W. (1965), *The Making of Urban America*, Princeton.

Richelieu (1850), *Mémoires du Cardinal de Richelieu sur le Règne de Louis XIII*, in *Nouvelle Collection*, 2nd series, VII–IX, Paris.

de Riocour, Du Bois (1841), *Histoire de la Ville et des deux Sièges de La Mothe* (the sieges of 1634 and 1635), Neufchateau. A remarkable eyewitness account.

Roberts, M. (1953–8), *Gustavus Adolphus. A History of Sweden 1611–1632*, 2 vols, London. Indispensable.

Roberts, M. (1967), *Essays in Swedish History*, London.

Roberts, M. (1968), *The Early Vasas. A History of Sweden 1523–1611*, Cambridge.

Rocchi, E. (1894), *Le Origini della Fortificazione Moderna*, Rome.

Rocchi, E. (1908), *Le Fonte Storiche dell' Architettura Militare*, Rome.

Rocolle, Col. (1973), *2000 Ans de Fortification Française*, Limoges.

de Rohan (1850), *Mémoires du Duc de Rohan sur la Guerre de la Valtelline*, in *Nouvelle Collection*, 2nd series, V. Paris.

Rojas, Cristobal de (1598), *Teorica y Prática de Fortificación*, Madrid.

Rosenau, H. (1959), *The Ideal City*, London.

Ross, W. G. (1887), 'Military Engineering during the Great Civil War 1642-9', in *Professional Papers of the Corps of Royal Engineers. Occasional Papers*, XIII, Chatham. A very important study.

Roth, C. (1925), *The Last Florentine Republic, 1527-30*, London.

Routh, E. M. (1912), *Tangier 1661-1684*, London.

Rüsensteen (1654), *Versterckte Vesting*, in Amsterdam, Eng. trans. *The Strengthening of Strong-Holds*, London, 1668.

Rycaut, P. (1679-80), *History of the Turkish Empire from the Year 1623 to the Year 1677*, London. Well-informed. Rycaut was English consul at Smyrna.

Saars (1662), *Johann Jacob Saars Ost Indianische Fünfzehnjährige Kriegsdienst* (1662), new edn, The Hague, 1930. Life in Dutch East Indian garrisons.

Sadler, A. L. (1937), *The Maker of Modern Japan. The Life of Tokugawa Ieyasu*, London.

de Salignac (1850), *Le Siège de Metz par l'Empereur Charles V en l'an 1552, par Bertrand de Salignac*, in *Nouvelle Collection*, 1st series, VIII, Paris.

de Saluces, A. (1817-18), *Histoire Militaire du Piémont*, 5 vols, Turin.

Salvi, G. (1970), 'Michelangelo Architetto Militare', in *Quadrante*, 5th year, 1 March.

Sanabre, J. (1956), *La Acción de Francia en Cataluña en la Pugna por la Hegemonia de Europa (1640-1659)*, Barcelona.

Sandes, E. W. (1933-5), *The Military Engineer in India*, 2 vols, Chatham.

Sansom, G. (1964), *A History of Japan*, III, London.

Sardi, Pietro (1639), *Architettura Militare*, Venice.

Savel'ev, A. (1874), 'Zametka o Znachenii Nashikh Starinnykh Ukreplenii', in *Inzhenernyi Zhurnal*, no. 2, St Petersburg.

Scamozzi, Vincenzo (1615), *L'Idea della Architettura Universale*, Venice.

Scheer, G. F. and Rankin, H. F. (1959), *Rebels and Redcoats*, New York.

Schiavo, A. (1949), *Michelangelo Architetto*, Rome.

Schmidtchen, V. (1978), *Bombarden, Befestigungen, Büchsenmeister*, Düsseldorf. Good on early siege artillery.

Schnitter, H. (1973), 'Militärische und politisch-soziale Probleme des Kampfes um befestigte Küstenstädte im Ostseeraum während des 17. und 18. Jahrhunderts', delivered to International Colloquy on Military History, Stockholm.

Schuster, O. and Francke, F. (1885), *Geschichte der Sächsischen Armee*, 3 vols, Leipzig. There are details of the Saxon fortress system in the appendices to vol. III.

Schwarze, K. (1936), *Der Siebenjährige Krieg in der Zeitgenossischen Deutschen Literatur*, Berlin.

Semenzato, C. (1960), 'Michele Sanmicheli Architetto Militare', in *Michele Sanmicheli. Studi Raccolti*, Verona.

Sen, Surendranath (1928), *Military System of the Marathas*, Calcutta.

Sepulveda, C. Ayres de Magalhaes (1902-8), *Historia Organica e Politica do Exercito Portuguez*, 4 vols, Lisbon.

Severini, G. (1970), *Architetture Militari di Giuliano da Sangallo*, Pisa.

Seydel, F. S. (1818-24), *Nachrichten über Vaterländische Festungen und Festungskriege*, 4 vols, Leipzig and Züllichau. On Prussian engineering and fortresses.

Shelby, L. R. (1967), *John Rogers. Tudor Military Engineer*, Oxford. Describes the first employment of the bastion by English engineers.

Silke, J. J. (1970), *Kinsale. The Spanish Intervention in Ireland at the End of the Elizabethan Wars*, Liverpool.

da Silva, Marquis (1778), *Considérations sur la Guerre de 1769 entre les Russes et les Turcs*, new edn, Turin.

Simms, J. G. (1955), 'The Blackwater Forts', in *The Irish Sword*, II, no. 7, Dublin.

Simms, J. G. (1957), 'Hugh Dubh O'Neill's Defence of Limerick 1650-1651', in *The Irish Sword*, III, no. 11, Dublin.

Simms, J. G. (1960), 'Cromwell's Siege of Waterford, 1649', in *The Irish Sword*, IV, no. 6, Dublin.

Skork (1829), *Das Volk und Reich der Osmanen, in besonderer Darstellung ihrer Kriegsverfassung und ihres Kriegswesens*, Pirna.

Skovgaard, J. (1973), *A King's Architecture. Christian IV and his Buildings*, London.

de la Solaye, L. (1670), *Mémoires ou Rélation Militaire . . . de la Déffens de la Ville de Candie depuis l'Année 1645*, Paris.

Spanheim (1634), *Le Soldat Suédois*, no place of publication.

Spence, J. (1969), *The China Helpers: Western Advisers in*

China 1620–1960, London.

Spencer, Edmund (1630), *A View of the State of Ireland* (1596), Dublin.

Diaz-Spinola, M. L. (1959), *Arquitectura Espanola en Filipinas (1565–1800)*, Seville.

Sprigge, J. (1647), *Anglia Rediviva. England's Recovery*, London. Reprinted Oxford, 1857 and Gainesville, 1960.

Stafford, T. (1633), *Pacata Hibernia*, London.

Stagg, F. H. (1956), *East Norway and its Frontier*, London.

Staudinger, K. (1901), *Geschichte des Bayerischen Heeres*, vol. I, Munich.

Steckzén, B. (1939), *Johan Banér*, Stockholm.

Stevin, Simon (1594), *Stercken-Bouwing*, Leyden, 2nd edn Amsterdam, 1624 (a work strongly influenced by Italian ideas) also *Castrametatio*, Rotterdam, 1617, and Leyden, 1633 (on field fortification), and *Nieuwe Maniere vom Sterctebau door Spilschluysen*, Rotterdam, 1617 (on the application of hydraulic works to fortification).

Sticca, G. (1912), *Gli Scrittori Militari Italiani*, Turin.

Storry, R. (1961), *A History of Modern Japan*, 2nd edn, London.

Suárez, Francisco (1621), *De Triplici Virtute Theologica*.

Suárez (1944), *Selections from Three Works of Francisco Suárez S.J.*, ed. J. E. Scott, 2 vols, Oxford.

de Sully, Maximilien de Béthune, Duc (1850), *Mémoires des Sages et Royale Oeconomies d'Estat de Henry le Grand*, in *Nouvelle Collection*, 2nd series, II, Paris.

Tadama, R. W. (1856), *Geschiedenis der Stad Zutphen*, Arnhem and Zutphen.

Taegio, F. (1525), *Le Siège de Pavie*, undated trans. by Morillon of the original ed. of 1525.

Tapia, Santans y (1644), *Tratado de Fortificacion Militar de Estos Tempos*, Brussels.

Tartaglia, Niccolo (1546, 1554, 1556), *Quesiti et Inventioni diverse*, several parts, Venice.

Tavannes (1850), *Mémoires de Très-Noble et Très-Illustre Gaspard de Saulx, Seigneur de Tavannes*, in *Nouvelle Collection*, 1st series, VIII, Paris. Many interesting asides on the warfare of the period.

Taylor, F. L. (1921), *The Art of War in Italy 1494–1529*, Cambridge.

Tenenti, A. (1962), *Cristoforo da Canal. La Marine Vénitienne avant Lepanto*, Paris.

Ten Raa, F. and others (1911), *Het Staatsche Leger 1568–1795* (still in progress), The Hague and Breda.

Terlinden, Vicomte (1965), 'Le Siège de Louvain en 1635', in *Revue Internationale d'Histoire Militaire*, no. 24, Brussels.

Terry, C. S. (1899), *The Life and Campaigns of Alexander Leslie. First Earl of Leven*, London.

Teuber, C. O. (1895), *Die Österreichische Armee von 1700 bis 1867*, 2 vols, Vienna.

Thomas-Stanford, C. (1910), *Sussex in the Great Civil War and the Interregnum, 1642–1660*, London.

Thompson, I. A. (1976), *War and Government in Habsburg Spain 1560–1620*, London.

Thompson, J. W. (1909), *The Wars of Religion in France 1559–1576*, New York, new edn, 1958.

Tiersch, Major (1911), 'Führung und Persöhnlichkeit im Festungskriege', in *Beiheft zum Militär-Wochenblatt*, IV, Berlin.

Tingsten, L. (1932), *Fältmarskalkarna Johan Banér och Lennart Torstensson såsom Härförare*, Stockholm.

Tohall, R. (1958), 'Charlemont Fort, Co. Armagh', in *The Irish Sword*, II, no. 12, Dublin.

de Tott (1786), *Memoirs of Baron de Tott*, Eng. trans., 2nd edn, 2 vols, London. Amusingly written recollections of an Hungarian renegade.

Tough, D. L. (1928), *The Last Years of a Frontier. A History of the Borders during the Reign of Elizabeth*, Oxford.

Toy, S. (1957), *The Strongholds of India*, London.

Toy, S. (1965), *The Fortified Cities of India*, London.

Trantner, N. (1965), *The Fortified House of Scotland*, III, London.

Trenchard, C. (1924), *The Siege of Bridgwater*, Bridgwater.

Truttmann, P. (1975), *Fortification, architecture et urbanisme aux XVIIe et XVIIIe Siècles*, Thionville.

Tucker, N. (1958), *North Wales in the Civil War*, Denbigh.

Turenne (1782), *Collection des lettres et mémoires du Maréchal de Turenne*, ed. de Grimoard, 2 vols, Paris.

Turnbull, S. R. (1977), *The Samurai. A Military History*, London.

Tverskoi, L. M. (1953), *Russkoe Gradostroitél'stvo do Kontsa XVII Veka*, Leningrad and Moscow.

Ufano, Diego (1613), *Tratado de Artilleria*, Brussels.

Ushakov, General (1838), *Geschichte der Feldzüge in der Asiatischen Türkei, während der Jahre 1828 und 1829*, Germ. trans., 2 parts, Leipzig.

v. Valentini, Major-General (1828), *Military Reflections on Turkey*, Eng. trans., London.

Varley, F. J. (1932), *The Siege of Oxford*, Oxford.

Vasari, G. (1550), *Le Vite de' Più Excellenti Architetti, Pittori, e Scultori Italiani*. In many edns and translations, including the new edn by C. Ragghianti, 4 vols,

Florence, 1942–50.

Vassal-Reig, C. (1934), *La Guerre en Roussillon sous Louis XIII (1635–1639)*, Paris.

Vassal-Reig, C. (1939), *La Prise de Perpignan*, Paris.

Vath, A. (1933), *Johann Adam Schall von Bell S.J.*, Cologne.

de Vattel, E. (1773), *Droit de Gens*, trans. *The Law of Nations*, London, 1834.

Vauban (1704), *Traité des Sièges*, Paris edn 1829.

Vazquez, A. (1879–80), *Los Sucesos in Flandes y Francia*, in *Colección de Documentos Ineditos para la Historia de España*, LXXII–LXXV, Madrid.

Venturi, A. (1938–9) *Architettura del Cinquecento*, 2 parts Milan, vol. XI of *Storia dell' Arte Italiana*.

Verdugo (1610), *Comentario del Coronel Francisco Verdugo de la Guerra de Frisia*, Brussels, 1899.

Vere (1672), *The Commentaries of Sir Francis Vere*, London. Vere commanded English contingents in the campaigns of the 1590s and in the defence of Ostend.

Vernadsky, G. (1969), *The Tsardom of Moscow*, V, New Haven and London.

Vieilleville (1850), *Mémoires de la Vie de François de Scepeaux, Sire de Vieilleville*, in *Nouvelle Collection*, 1st series, IX, Paris. On the years 1527–71.

Vignère (1615), *L'Art militaire de Onosender*, Paris.

Vigon, J. (1947), *Historia de la Artilleria Española*, 3 vols, Madrid.

Villa, A. Rodríguez (1904), *Ambrósio Spínola. Primer Marqués de los Balbases*, Madrid.

Villars (1850), *Mémoires du Sieur Francois de Boyvin, Chevalier, Baron du Villars (1610)*, in *Nouvelle Collection*, 1st series, X, Paris.

Ville, Chevalier de (1629), *Fortifications*, Amsterdam.

Villemain, P. (1958), *Journal des assiégés de La Rochelle 1627–1628*, Paris.

Vincart, J. A. (1880–8), *Relación de la Campaña de 1643*, and *Relación de la Campaña del Ano de 1650*, in *Colección de Documentos Ineditos*, LXXV, Madrid.

Viollet-le-Duc, E. (1860), *An Essay on the military Architecture of the Middle Ages*, Oxford and London. Useful on the transitional period.

de Vitoria, F. (1532), *De Indis et de Jure Belli Relectiones*, trans. and ed. J. B. Scott as *The Spanish Origin of International Law. Francisco de Vitoria and his Law of Nations*, Oxford, 1934.

Voyce, A. (1955), *The Moscow Kremlin*, London.

Warburton, E. (1849), *Memoirs of Prince Rupert and the Cavaliers*, 3 vols, London.

Ward, R. (1639), *Animadversions of Warre*, London.

Warnery, Major-General (1771), *Remarques sur le Militaire des Turcs et des Russes*, Breslau.

Watson, F. (1938), *Wallenstein. Soldier under Saturn*, London.

Webb, H. J. (1965), *Elizabethan Military Science. The Books and the Practice*, Madison and London.

Wedgwood, C. V. (1938), *The Thirty Years War*, London.

Wenham, P. (1970), *The Great and Close Siege of York 1644*, Kineton.

Wernham, R. B. (1961), 'Elizabethan War Aims and Strategy', in *Essays Presented to Sir John Neale*, ed. S. T. Bindoff, London.

Wijn, J. W. (1942), *Het Beleg van Haarlem*, Amsterdam.

Williams, R. (1618), *The Actions of the Low Countries*, Ithaca, New York, 1964.

Willis-Bund, J. W. (1905), *The Civil War in Worcestershire, 1642–1646; and the Scotch Invasion of 1651*, Birmingham and London.

Wood, A. C. (1937), *Nottinghamshire in the Civil War*, Oxford.

Wrangel, E. (1901), *De Betrekkingen tussen Zweden en de Nederlanden op het Gebied van Letteren en Wetenschap*, Leyden.

Young, P. and Emberton, W. (1978), *Sieges of the Great Civil War*, London.

Young, P. and Holmes, R. (1974), *The English Civil War*, London.

Young, P. and others (1964), *Newark-on-Trent. The Civil War Siegeworks* (Royal Commission on Historical Monuments), London. With a useful discussion of siege techniques.

Zarebska, T. (1973), 'Théories militaires et habitation collective', in *Anfänge des Sozialen Wohnbaus*, Niederteufen.

Zinkeisen, J. W. (1854–7), *Geschichte des Osmanischen Reiches in Europa*, parts II–IV, Gotha. The most reliable of the monster histories of Turkey.

Zinsser, H. (1935), *Rats, Lice and History*, London.

General Index

Subject Index

Weapons and techniques, defensive

Weapons and techniques, offensive